ALSO BY LiSA LiLLiEN

Hungry Girl:
Recipes and Survival Strategies for
Guilt-Free Eating in the Real World

Hungry Girl 200 Under 200:
200 Recipes Under 200 Calories

Hungry Girl 1-2-3:
The Easiest, Most Delicious,
Guilt-Free Recipes on the Planet

Hungry Girl Happy Hour:
75 Recipes for Amazingly Fantastic
Guilt-Free Cocktails & Party Foods

Hungry Girl:
The Official Survival Guides:
Tips & Tricks for Guilt-Free Eating
(audio book)

Hungry Girl Chew the Right Thing:
Supreme Makeovers for 50 Foods You Crave
(recipe cards)

Hungry Girl

300 UNDER 300

300 BREAKFAST, LUNCH & DINNER DISHES Under 300 Calories

LISA LILLIEN

St. Martin's Griffin

New York

HUNGRY GIRL 300 UNDER 300: 300 BREAKFAST, LUNCH & DINNER DISHES UNDER 300 CALORIES. Copyright © 2011 by Hungry Girl, Inc. All rights reserved. Printed in the United States of America. For information, address St. Martin's Press, 175 Fifth Avenue, New York, N.Y. 10010.

www.stmartins.com

Cover design and book design by Elizabeth Hodson

Illustrations by Jack Pullan

Food styling and photography by General Mills Photography Studios

      Photographer: Val Bourassa

      Food Stylist: Carol Grones

      Art Director: Janet Skalicky

      Prop Stylist: Rhonda Watkins

ISBN 978-0-312-67681-0

First Edition: April 2011

10 9 8 7 6 5 4 3 2 1

This book is dedicated to the
Hungry Girl staff, an incredibly
devoted, talented, and amazing
group of people whose appetite for
helping to create the best content
in the universe never wanes.
You are so appreciated.

CONTENTS

Acknowledgments   **xv**

Introduction   **2**
TOP ATE Things to Know About *300 Under 300*
Recommended Products
How to HG-ify Your Kitchen!

BREAKFAST

Ch 1: Egg Mugs   12
Pizza! Pizza! Egg Mug
BTA (Bacon, Tomato, Avocado) Egg Mug
Buffalo Chicken Egg Mug
California Love Mug
Crunchy Beefy Taco Egg Mug
It's All Greek to Me Egg Mug
Chicken Fajita Scramble Mug
Egg Mugs 101
Denver Omelette in a Mug
Veggie Eggs-plosion Mug
All-American Egg Mug
Bean 'n Cheesy Soft Taco in an Egg Mug
Eggs Bene-chick Mug
Say Cheese! Egg Mug
The HG Special Egg Mug
Lasagna-Like Egg Mug

Ch 2: Breakfast Bowls   30
Banana Split Growing Oatmeal
Apple Pie Oatmeal Bonanza
Large & In Charge Neapolitan Oatmeal
Major Mocha Cappuccino Oatmeal
Very Veggie-Eggy Explosion
Pumpkin Pie Oatmeal Parfait
Sweet and Savory Breakfast Bread Pudding Bowl
S'mores Oatmeal
PB & Chocolate Oatmeal Blitz
Cinn-a-nilla Apple Oatmeal Parfait
Hot Dog & Scramble
Turkey Club B. Bowl
Super-Sized Berry-nana Oatmeal Parfait
Breakfast Rice Pudding
PB&J Oatmeal Heaven
HG and the Growing Oatmeal . . . Tips & Tricks!
HG Hash Scramble

Ch 3: Breakfast Plates   56
Sausage, Egg 'n Cheese ChickGriddle
Rockin' Red Velvet Pancakes
Nice to See Ya! Quesadilla
Hola Breakfast Tostada
Cheesy Bean Breakfast Quesadilla
Creamy Crab Cakes Benedict
Crazy-Good Carrot-Cake Pancakes
Buenos Días Breakfast Fajitas
Salt-Slashing Swaps for Recipe Ingredients

Breakfast Scramble Pizza
Strawberry Short Stack
Gimme S'more Pancakes
The Morning Waffle Dip
Breakfast Pizza Mexicali
Erin-Go-Breakfast Boxty
Hot Stack Morning Sliders

Ch 4: No-Cook B-fasts   84

Breakfast Sundae Supreme
Double-O-Strawberry Quickie Kiwi Smoothie
PB&J Yogurt Parfait
Smokey Salmon Lettuce Wraps
Tropical AM Smoothie
Tropical Wonder B-fast Bowl
Hawaiian B-fast Stacks

Ch 5: Crowd Pleasers   94

Fluffy-Good Zucchini Nut Muffins
HG's Big Breakfast Casserole
Crazy-Delicious Cheesy Cherry Danish
Egg Cups a la Hungry
Breakfast Bruschetta
Chocolate-Chippy Cheese Danish
Quiche Me Bacon Tarts
Ham & Cheese Egg Strata Bake
Corn MegaMuffins
Coffee Cake Scones
Banana Split Bread

Early-Riser Pigs in a Blanket
Ratatouille Frittata
Egga-Pinwheels
*Dough the Right Thing . . . Tips for Working with
    Refrigerated Dough*

LUNCH & DINNER

Ch 6: BIG Salads   126

In-N-Outrageous Animal-Style Salad
Thanksgiving in a Salad Bowl
Mexi-licious Shrimp & Corn Fandango Salad
Island Time Salad
Asian BBQ Shrimp Salad
Classic Cheesesteak Salad
Hot & Cold 10-Veggie Explosion
BBQ Grilled Veggie Salad
Nacho-ed Up Mexi-Chop
Feta 'n Fuji Chicken Salad
Lean 'n Green Fruity Tuna Bowl
Deconstructed Falafel Salad
Classic Club Salad
Classic Warm Asian Chicken Salad

Ch 7: Return of the Foil Packs 150

Too-EZ Fish Taco Supreme
Rockin' Chicken Ratatouille
Dreamy Butternut Chicken Foil Pack
No-Nonsense Nacho Lettuce Cups
Sweet Potato Apple Pack
Steamy Creamy Squash Packet
Woohoo! Bayou Fish Pack
Winner Winner Onion Chicken Dinner
Meat Prep 101
Hot Tuna Stuffed Tomatoes
Colossal Asian Veggie 'n Chicken Pack

Ch 8: Comfort Foods 172

Cheeseburger Mashed Potato Parfaits
Chicken Pot Pockets
Cheesy Pigs in Bacon Blankies
Turkey Tetrazzini Bake
Plate-Lickin'-Good Chicken 'n Waffles
Funkadelic Chili Mac
Buffalo Chicken Wing Macaroni & Cheese
Lasagna Cupcakes
iHungry Spaghetti Tacos
Hungry Chick Shepherd's Pie
Faux-Fried Green Tomatoes
Super-Duper Spaghetti Pie Part Deux
Floosh's Stuffed Cabbage
Beef Strogataki

Ch 9: International Favorites 202

Nacho-rific Stuffed Chicken
Surprise, It's Pumpkin! Enchiladas
Grilled Go Fish! Soft Tacos
SW BBQ Chicken Quesadilla
Better Off Shred: HG's EZ Guide to Shredded Chicken
Cheesy Chicken Enchiladas
'Bella Asada Fajitas
Shrimpylicious Egg Rolls
Egg-cellent Foo Young
Sweet & Sour Chicken 1-2-3
Chicky Pad Thai
WOWOWOW! Kung Pao
Super-Delicious Shrimp Scampi with Fettuccine
Faux-Fried & Fabulous Calamari
Takes-the-Cake Ziti Bake
EZ Cheesy Lasagna for Two
Veggie-rific Noodle-Free Lasagna
Three-Cheese Chicken Cannelloni
Pepperoni-Poppin' Veggie Calzones
Falafel Pita Pockets with Dill-icious Yogurt Dip
Pow! Sock! Bam! Jambalaya
Grind Luck: The 411 on Fiber One Crushing . . .

Ch 10: All Things Pizza 244

Loaded 'n Oated Spinach & Mushroom
    Girlfredo Pizza
Pepperoni Pizza Pinwheels
Pizza Puffs

Supremely Stuffed Pizza-fied Eggplant
Just Veggin' Pizza
BLT Pizza
Pizza-fied Grilled Cheese
Grilled Greek Pizza Minis
Pizza-bellas
Purple Pizza Eaters
Cheesy Pizza Quesadilla
Pizza Burgers a la HG
The Great Greek Pizza
Crispy Cheeseburger Pizza

Ch 11: Sandwiches   272

Monte Cristo Sandwich
Spicy Mexican Sandwich
A+ Avocado Burger
Grilly Girl Cheesy Turkey & Bacon 'Wich
So-Good Grilled Veggie Panini
Flat-Top Patty Melt
BLTA Club
Thanksgiving Turkey Sandwich
Ring-My-Bella Mushroom Sandwich
Flat Bun 411 and Alternatives
Grilled Fuji-n-Chick 'Wich
Perfect Portabella Club
Faux-Fried Mozzarella-n-Basil
          Eggplant Sandwiches
The Skinny Elvis
Open-Faced Chicken Salad Melt
Grilled Cheese 'n Veggie Sandwich

Ch 12: Crock-Pot Fun   298

Very VERY Veggie Stew
Crock-Pot Coq Au Vin
Crock-Pot Cinna-Apples 'n Oats
Crock-Pot Fake-Baked Beans
'Cue the Pulled Pork
Cheeseburger Mac Attack
Sweet 'n Red Hot Apple Mash
Chicken and Sausage Gumbo
Outside-In Turkey Tamale Pie
Very Veggie Bisque
Ten-Alarm Southwestern Corn Chowder
All the Rage Bolognese
Chicken Chili Surprise

Ch 13: Stir-Frys & Skillet Meals 320

HG's Caribbean Shrimp Surprise
Skillet-Seared Scallops Fra Diavolo
The Club Skillet
Cheesy Burger Skillet
Sweet Apple & Chicken Stir-Fry
Tempting Teriyaki Trifecta
Breakfast for Dinner Skillet
Rockin' Creamy Broc 'n Chicken
Cheesy Bacon Noodle Skillet

Ch 14: Fast-Food/Drive-Thru Makeovers   **338**

Spicy Chicken Crunchtastic Supreme
Chicken Fajita Burrito
Amazing Ate-Layer Open-Faced Taco
Twice-as-Nice *Guapo* Taco
Flat-tastic Ranchy Bacon Wrap
Snack-tastic Burger Wrap
Big Bad Breakfast Burrito
Neat-O Chili-Frito Burrito
Totally Stacked Steak-Style HG Burger
Crispity Crunchity Drumsticks
Loaded Bacon-Wrapped Hot Dogs

STARTERS, SOUPS & SIDES

Ch 15: Starters   **360**

Crabby Patties
Grilly-Good Eggplant Bites
Rockin' Roasted Corn Guac 'n Chips
Sassy Wonton Tacos
Mexi-licious Pot Stickers
So-Good Spinach Bites
Cheesy Chicken Egg Rolls
Ab-Fab Artichoke Crab Dip

Hot Dog–Hot Potato Hotcakes
Mini Nacho Dippers
Sweet Coconut Crunch Shrimp
Sassy 'n Steamy Artichoke
United We Chew! Red, White & Blue Nachos
Baked Clam Halfsies
Southwest Stuffed Tomatoes
The Crab Rangoonies
Crispy-licious Faux-Fried Frenzy
Gooey-Good Queso Dip 'n Chips

Ch 16: Soups   **394**

The Whole Enchilada Chicken Soup
I'll Take Manhattan Clam Chowder
Fully Loaded Baked Potato Soup
Big Apple Butternut Squash Soup
Creamy Carrot Soup
WOWOWOW! Wonton Soup
Zazzled-Up Zuppa
Mmm-mmm Minestrone
No-Buns-About-It Chili Dog Chili

Ch 17: Sides   **410**

Loaded Miracle Mashies
Creamy Dreamy Macaroni Salad
Insanely Irresistible Corn Pudding
Cold Dog Slaw
Ranch-tastic Butternut Fries with Bacon

Sweet 'n Squashed Biscuits
For the Love of Sweet Garlic Butternut Fries
German-ish Potato-ish Salad
Vegged-Out Potato Salad
Bean There, Yum That Salad
Crazy-Delicious Caribbean Black Bean
    Broccoli Slaw
*Squash It! Hungry Girl's Guide to Mastering
    the Butternut Squash*

TRIOS

Ch 18: Chicken Trios   434

Balsamic BBQ Chick Skillet
Basil-icious Chicken
Tomato-Infused Chicken Rollup
Crispy Nacho Chicken
Fruity BBQ Chicken for Two
Sweet 'n Spicy Chicken Lettuce Cups
Bacon-Wrapped BBQ Chicken
Chicken a la Pot Pie
World's Easiest Chicken Empanadas
EZ Pineapple Chicken
Naked Chicken Parm
Super-Speedy Chinese Stir-Fry
Easy BBQ Chicken Nachos

Ch 19: Tortilla Trios   450

Fruity Quesadilla
Speedy Beany-rito
Easiest Thin-Crust Pizza Ever
Lean 'n Green Shrimp-chilada
EZ Cheesy Tostada
Amazin' Onion Quesadilla
Raw Apple Rollup
Garlic Shrimp Tostada

Ch 20: Tuna Trios   460

Broc 'n Ginger Tuna Bowl
Looney Tuna-Stuffed Pepper
Hawaiian Tuna Salad
Cheesy Tuna Muffin 'Wich
Sun-Dried Tomato Tuna Salad
Salsa to the Tuna Salad!
Tuna Mushroom Cups
Salsa-fied Tuna Stacks
Fancy-Pants Fast Tuna 'n Beans
Best-Ever Tuna Slaw

Ch 21: Ground Meat Trios   472

Sloppy Joe Stir-Fry Slaw
Gravy-Good Beef Casserole
Crunchy Turkey Tacos

OMG! Burgers (Onion Mushroom Goodness Burgers)
Vegged-Up Ground Beef
Broccoli Beef Stir-Fry
Mexi-Bolognese
Simply Sweet Meatballs
BBQuick Saucy Turkey
Veggie-rific Meatloaf
Bacon Cheeseburger Patty

Ch 22: Meatless Burger Patty Trios   486
Bacon Bleu Burger
Fruitiyaki Patty
Burgs in a Blanket
Sweet Spinach Stir-Fry
Curry in a Hurry Trio
Grinder Lettuce Cups
Three-Step Pizza Burger
Cheesy Noodles 'n Burgs!
Fast-Food Hamburger Scramble
Bunless Mediterranean Burger
Burger-ific Mushroom Melt

Ch 23: Hot Dogs, Hot Trios   500
"Wrap the Dog" Foil Pack
Pigs on a Stick in a Bacon-Wrapped Blanket
Yo! Chili Dog Wrap
Hot Dog Stroganoff

Pigs on a Mattress
Hot Doggy Home Fries
Hot Diggity Dog Casserole
Fresh 'n Fruity Skewer Dogs
Hot Dog Stir-Fry
Sloppy Beans 'n Franks
HOT, HOT, HOT Dog!

Ch 24: Noodle Trios   514
Sweetness, Spice & 3-Things Nice Noodles
EZ Chili Mac
Creamy Chicken & Noodles
Not-Quite-Homemade Chicken Noodle Soup
Cheesy Squashataki
Where in the World Is Tofu Shirataki?
"*Yo Quiero* Taco Bowl" Noodles
Tuna Noodle Casse-Bowl
EZ Mock Vodka Pasta
BBQ Spaghetti
Thai Peanut Noodle Trio
Quick 'n Spicy Fettuccine Hungry Buff-redo
Quickie-yaki Stir-Fry

Index   531

ACKNOWLEDGMENTS

I wish I could say this book was a cinch to create, but that would be a HUGE lie. That being said, the following people need to be acknowledged for their tireless efforts to not only put together this book, but to also help keep Hungry Girl at the forefront of guilt-free eating.

To the HG Editorial & Production Staff . . .

Jamie Goldberg—You continue to shock and amaze me with your eagerness to grow and take on new challenges. Your unlimited time, energy, and effort have helped catapult Hungry Girl to new levels. Simply put, YOU ROCK.

Alison Kreuch—You are WAY more than HG's ridiculously successful Director of Marketing and Advertising. You are an incredible human, a good friend, and an all-around fun person to be around. Thank you.

Lynn Bettencourt—We were all sad to see you move across the U.S. but are thrilled that you're still VERY much a part of the HG world. Thanks for your efforts on this book and all things HG.

Lisa Friedman—Thanks for continuing to give 110 percent and doing it with a smile!

Dana DeRuyck—You're awesome in so many ways . . . and a lot of fun to have around. Thank you for going above and beyond, and for ALL you do in HG Land.

Callie Pegadiotes—Great to have you and your super-creative taste buds on the team; so glad you went to that book signing two years ago. Lucky us!

Melissa Klotz—You're the newest HGer. And your love for over-caloried, full-fat cookies is excused . . . but only because you're our graphic designer. Thank you.

And to the HG part-timers—**Michelle Ferrand**, we love having you around, you kitchen dynamo! **Jenny Harmon**, HG fan/Nano winner turned intern extraordinaire. **Amanda Pisani**, the proofreading MACHINE that never runs out of batteries. THANK YOU ALL!

Special thanks to **Elizabeth Hodson**—the very FIRST HG employee, who is no longer our full-time designer but is the official Hungry Girl book designer and will be (if I can help it!) until the end of time. This book looks PHENOMENAL. You continue to outdo yourself. Thank you!

More, More, More . . .

John Vaccaro—You're truly the BEST. And I'm lucky to have you in my life, both personally and professionally. Now move to Los Angeles already.

Neeti Madan—You're more than the world's best agent. You are my official NYC sushi partner. And I'm not sure which is more important . . . Thank you!!!!

Matthew Shear and Jennifer Enderlin—The best publishing team in the business. Hands down. I love you guys and hope the feeling is mutual because you're stuck with me for a long time . . .

John Karle—Thank you for being such a completely lovable publicist and continuing to promote each HG book as if it were the first.

Anne Marie Tallberg—You marketing goddess, you! Thanks for keeping the creative and fun ideas flowing freely.

John Murphy—I still love you. Muah!

Running Out of Room . . .

HUGE THANKS also to my lovable legal and management-type peeps—**Tom Fineman**, **Jeff Becker**, and **Bill Stankey**.

More thanks to **Jack Pullan**, **David Witt**, **Nanci Dixon** and the super-talented **General Mills photography crew**, **Eileen Opatut**, **Ronnie Weinstock**, **Kevin Lezak**, **Val Pensky**, and **Jackie Mgido**.

And Of Course . . .

Thanks also to my fantastic mom and dad, **Florence and Maurice Lillien**, for creating me and supporting me in all of my endeavors. To my hungry sister **Meri Lillien**, to **Jay Lillien**, and to the entire **Lillien and Schneider families**. To **Jackson** and **Cupcake**—xoxoxo. You keep me sane, you furry beasts, you.

To my million-plus friends, **the Hungry Girl subscribers**—thank you for your loyalty and for being there since the beginning.

And to my husband, **Daniel Schneider**—Psssst . . . I LOVE YOU!!!!!!!

TOP ATE THINGS TO KNOW ABOUT 300 UNDER 300

1. What Is Hungry Girl?

Hungry Girl is a free daily email subscription service about guilt-free eating. The emails (which are read by over a million people a day) feature news, food finds, recipes, and real-world survival strategies. Hungry Girl was started by me, Lisa Lillien. I'm not a doctor or nutrition professional; I'm just hungry! Back in 2004, I decided I wanted to share my love and knowledge of guilt-free eating with the world, so Hungry Girl was born. To sign up for the daily emails or to see what you've missed since the beginning, go to Hungry-Girl.com.

2. The HG "Recipe Lab" Scoop . . .

When it comes to creating HG recipes, the goal is to make them taste delicious—but also to keep them low in fat and calories. We often aim for high fiber counts and a fair amount of protein as well, since those are filling. Even though these recipes focus on keeping calorie and fat counts down, nutritional info is also provided for sodium, carbs, sugars, etc., so you can look at a recipe and decide if it works for you. You can, of course, make substitutions for products and ingredients, but the taste and nutritional info will vary accordingly—so consider yourself "heads-upped."

3. The Significance of 300 Calories . . .

Eating several small meals and snacks throughout the day is great because it keeps you feeling satisfied, gets your metabolism going, and prevents you from ever becoming SUPER-HUNGRY. If you don't eat often enough and find yourself super-hungry, you're more likely to overeat or make questionable food choices. The under-300-calorie limit is not meant to suggest that your meals should contain less than 300 calories. It's just so you can have more options for what you can eat throughout the day. This book is PACKED with recipes for main dishes, starters, and sides that are delicious, SO easy to make, and completely guilt-free. Pair 'em up with each other (and with those in the other HG cookbooks) to make fantastic full-on meals! Speaking of which . . .

4. Meals, Meals & MORE Meals!

Plain and simple, this book is JAM-PACKED with recipes for MEALS. Big, small, hot, cool, breakfasts, lunches, dinners . . . They're all here! Yes, there are appetizers and sides as well, but those fall into the world of mealtime dishes as far as I'm concerned; so feel free to mix & match away! Over the years, I've been receiving more and more requests for mealtime recipes, so I decided it was time to make a book chock-full of them. THIS is that book. There are 300 recipes here, and I would say that at least 297 of them are INCREDIBLE. (Now you're *dying* to know which three aren't quite as fantastic, aren't you?)

5. What Else Is Inside and Why . . .

So you already know the book has lots of meals. (I have said it repeatedly, so if you don't know, you haven't been paying attention!) There are huuuge sections for each meal type and more: BREAKFAST, LUNCH & DINNER, and STARTERS, SOUPS & SIDES. You'll find some wildly popular, frequently requested HG favorites. There's an entire chapter of HG's now famous EGG MUGS, recipes featuring egg scrambles made in a mug. (No mess and they couldn't be easier to make!) There are tons of HG's GROWING OATMEAL BOWLS—another concept that people have been going nuts over! We've got entire chapters of CROCK-POT recipes and FOIL-PACK creations—two more types of recipes people LOVE. There's even a whole chapter filled with recipes for everything PIZZA. In short, recipes in this book ROCK. Oh, and one more thing: There's a future-classic concept launching in this book. Introducing . . .

6. Hungry Girl TRIOS!

What's a Trio, you ask? Come on . . . if you think for a few seconds it'll come to you. A Hungry Girl Trio is a recipe with only THREE ingredients. (Get it?! TRIO!) They're crazy-easy to make and they taste fantastic. There are more than 75 Trios in the book, conveniently categorized by main ingredient: chicken, hot dogs, noodles, and MORE. We are obsessed with Trios here at the HG HQ, and soon you will be too. I am sure of it! I'm so excited about the Trios in this book I could scream. AAAAAAAAAAAAAHHHHHHHHHHHHHHHHHHH!!!! (OK, I did just actually scream. Sorry.)

7. Nutritionals: How We Do It . . .

We carefully calculate the stats for each recipe by doing extensive research—using extremely reliable nutritional databases and countless product labels. When recipes call for generic ingredients (like tortillas or burger patties), we calculate averages based on a wide variety of national brands. Also taken into account are the small amounts of calories and fat in many so-called no-calorie and fat-free ingredients. We work extremely hard to determine the most accurate nutritional information possible for our recipes—not only because we care about you, but because we make and eat these too!

8. Photos and *PointsPlus*™ Values: What's the Story?

As you can see, the photos in this book are beautiful. But not every single recipe in this book is lucky enough to have a photo here. For photos of all 300 recipes, and the Weight Watchers *PointsPlus*™ values* for them as well, go to hungry-girl.com/books. Yay!!!

*The PointsPlus™ values for these products and/or recipes were calculated by Hungry Girl and are not an endorsement or approval of the product, recipe, or its manufacturer or developer by Weight Watchers International, Inc., the owner of the PointsPlus™ registered trademark.

RECOMMENDED PRODUCTS

There are many products that fit the bill, but these are some HG favorites . . .

Pantry

No-calorie sweetener packets
Splenda
Truvia

25-calorie packets hot cocoa mix
Swiss Miss Diet
Nestlé Fat Free

Low-fat baked tortilla chips
Guiltless Gourmet
Baked! Tostitos Scoops

Breadbox

Light bread
Sara Lee Delightful
Nature's Own Light

100-calorie flat sandwich buns
Arnold Select/Oroweat Sandwich Thins
Pepperidge Farm Deli Flats
EarthGrains Thin Buns
Nature's Own Sandwich Rounds

Medium-large high-fiber flour tortillas with about 110 calories each
La Tortilla Factory Smart & Delicious Low
    Carb High Fiber or 100 Calorie
Mission Carb Balance
Tumaro's Healthy or Low in Carbs
Flatout Light Wraps

Fridge

Fat-free liquid egg substitute
Egg Beaters Original
Better'n Eggs

**Light whipped butter
or light buttery spread**
Brummel & Brown
Land O' Lakes Whipped Light Butter

Light vanilla soymilk
8th Continent Light
Silk Light

Fat-free yogurt
Yoplait Light
Fiber One

Fat-free Greek yogurt
Fage Total 0%
Chobani 0%

Sugar-free pancake syrup
Log Cabin Sugar Free
Mrs. Butterworth's Sugar Free

**Hot dogs with about 40 calories
and 1g fat or less**
Hebrew National 97% Fat Free Beef Franks
Hoffy Extra Lean Beef Franks

Precooked real crumbled bacon
Oscar Mayer
Hormel

Turkey pepperoni
Hormel

Light/low-fat salad dressing
Newman's Own Lighten Up!
Litehouse (low-fat varieties)

Sprayable dressing
Wish-Bone Salad Spritzers
Ken's Steakhouse Lite Accents

Freezer

Meatless hamburger-style patties with about 100 calories each
Boca Original Vegan Meatless Burgers
Amy's Bistro Burgers
Morningstar Farms Grillers Vegan

Ground-beef-style soy crumbles
Boca Meatless Ground Crumbles
Morningstar Farms Meal Starters
   Grillers Recipe Crumbles

Meatless or turkey sausage patties with about 80 calories each
Morningstar Farms Original Sausage Patties
Jimmy Dean Turkey Sausage Patties

Low-fat waffles
Kashi GoLean or Heart to Heart
Eggo Nutri-Grain Low Fat Whole Wheat
Van's Lite Totally Natural

HOW TO HG-iFY YOUR KITCHEN!

Looking to stock up on basic kitchen equipment, HG-style? Here's what you need . . .

Stovetop cookware: a basic skillet, a wok or large skillet, and small and large nonstick pots

Baking needs: a large baking sheet (or two!), an 8-inch by 8-inch pan, a 9-inch by 13-inch pan, and a 12-cup muffin pan

Microwave-safe essentials: LARGE mugs, small and large bowls, and plates

Measuring must-haves: spoons, cups, and a kitchen scale

Countertop tools: a crock pot/slow cooker, a good blender, a Magic Bullet or other small food processor (optional), a meat mallet, a strainer, and kitchen shears (optional, but helpful!)

BREAKFAST

Bored chewin' the same
old, same old in the AM?
This section will perk
you right up . . .

CHAPTER 1: EGG MUGS

Egg Mugs are now famous . . . and with good reason. You get a protein-packed, low-calorie HOT breakfast—and you don't even need to mess up the kitchen or clean any pots or pans. SCORE!

small bowl, large microwave-safe mug, nonstick spray

PREP:
5 minutes

COOK:
5 minutes

PIZZA! PIZZA! EGG MUG

Now, thanks to this recipe, you can embrace those crazy morning pizza cravings . . .

PER SERVING (entire recipe): 134 calories, 3.25g fat, 746mg sodium, 5g carbs, 0.5g fiber, 3g sugars, 17.5g protein

Ingredients

2 tablespoons canned crushed tomatoes
⅛ teaspoon Italian seasoning
½ cup fat-free liquid egg substitute
1 wedge The Laughing Cow Light Creamy Swiss cheese
6 slices turkey pepperoni, chopped
½ teaspoon reduced-fat Parmesan-style grated topping

Directions

In a small bowl, combine crushed tomatoes with Italian seasoning. Mix well and set aside.

Spray a large microwave-safe mug with nonstick spray. Add egg substitute and cheese wedge, breaking the cheese wedge into pieces as you add it. Microwave for 1 minute.

Gently stir. Microwave for another 30 seconds.

Add seasoned tomatoes and pepperoni to the mug. Mix well. Microwave for 30 seconds, or until scramble is just set.

Lightly stir. Sprinkle with grated topping. Allow to cool slightly, and then ENJOY!

MAKES 1 SERVING

Tomato Tip! ✳

Use leftover crushed tomatoes in a BUNCH of ways—just look 'em up in the index to see all the crushed-tomatoes-required dishes we've got!

BTA (BACON, TOMATO, AVOCADO) EGG MUG

This protein-packed mug o' hot breakfastness is AMAZING!

PER SERVING (entire recipe): 175 calories, 7.25g fat, 813mg sodium, 8.5g carbs, 3g fiber, 3.5g sugars, 19.5g protein

Ingredients

½ cup fat-free liquid egg substitute
2 tablespoons precooked real crumbled bacon
⅓ cup chopped tomatoes, patted to remove excess moisture
1 ounce diced avocado (about ¼ of an avocado)
2 tablespoons salsa
Optional: salt and black pepper

Directions

Spray a large microwave-safe mug with nonstick spray. Add egg substitute and microwave for 1 minute.

Gently stir. Add bacon and tomatoes. Microwave for 1 minute, or until scramble is just set.

If you like, season to taste with salt and pepper. Top with avocado and salsa. Now dig in!

MAKES 1 SERVING

large microwave-safe mug, nonstick spray

PREP:
5 minutes

COOK:
5 minutes

For more recipes, plus food finds, tips 'n tricks, and MORE, sign up for FREE daily emails at hungry-girl.com!

YOU'LL NEED:

large microwave-safe mug, nonstick spray

PREP:

5 minutes

COOK:

5 minutes

HG Alternative!

Don't like blue cheese dressing? Swap it out for light ranch.

BUFFALO CHICKEN EGG MUG

> If you love chicken wings, you'll FREAK over this creative bar-food-inspired breakfast.

PER SERVING (entire recipe): 180 calories, 2.25g fat, 801mg sodium, 6g carbs, og fiber, 2g sugars, 33g protein

Ingredients

¾ cup fat-free liquid egg substitute
1 teaspoon dried minced onion
2 ounces cooked and chopped skinless lean chicken breast
½ tablespoon Frank's RedHot Original Cayenne Pepper Sauce
1 teaspoon light blue cheese dressing
½ teaspoon reduced-fat Parmesan-style grated topping

Directions

Spray a large microwave-safe mug with nonstick spray. Add egg substitute and onion and microwave for 1½ minutes.

Gently stir in chicken. Microwave for 1 minute, or until scramble is just set.

Allow to cool slightly. Top with hot sauce, blue cheese dressing, and Parm-style topping. Grab a spoon and eat up!

MAKES 1 SERVING

CALIFORNIA LOVE MUG

This morning mug is unique and fabulous. Much like yourself . . . only, um, you're not creamy and infused with avocado.

YOU'LL NEED:
large microwave-safe
mug, nonstick spray

PREP:
5 minutes

COOK:
5 minutes

PER SERVING (entire recipe): 140 calories, 4.5g fat, 456mg sodium, 7g carbs, 2g fiber, 3g sugars, 16g protein

Ingredients

½ cup chopped spinach
½ cup sliced mushrooms
½ cup fat-free liquid egg substitute
2 tablespoons diced tomatoes
1 wedge The Laughing Cow Light Creamy Swiss cheese
2 tablespoons diced avocado

Are you an egg-mug newbie?

Visit page 21 for a fun little intro!

Directions

Spray a large microwave-safe mug with nonstick spray. Add spinach and mushrooms. Microwave for 1 to 2 minutes, until veggies have softened.

Blot any excess moisture from the veggies. Add egg substitute, tomatoes, and cheese wedge, breaking the cheese wedge into pieces as you add it. Mix well, and then microwave for 1 minute.

Gently stir, and then microwave for 1 more minute, or until scramble is just set.

Lightly stir and allow to cool slightly. Top with avocado and enjoy!

MAKES 1 SERVING

YOU'LL NEED:

large microwave-safe
mug, nonstick spray

PREP:

5 minutes

COOK:

5 minutes

📷 **For a pic
of this recipe,
see the first
photo insert.
Yay!**

CRUNCHY BEEFY
TACO EGG MUG

Is it CRAZY to try to stuff a taco into an egg mug? Uhhh . . .
NO WAY. It's BRILLIANT!

PER SERVING (entire recipe): 168 calories, 0.75g fat,
749mg sodium, 12.5g carbs, 1.75g fiber, 3g sugars, 26.5g protein

Ingredients

¼ cup frozen ground-beef-style soy crumbles
¼ teaspoon taco seasoning mix
¾ cup fat-free liquid egg substitute
1 tablespoon fat-free shredded cheddar cheese
4 low-fat baked tortilla chips, roughly crushed
1 tablespoon salsa
1 tablespoon fat-free sour cream

Directions

Spray a large microwave-safe mug with nonstick spray.
Add frozen crumbles and microwave for 45 seconds, or
until thawed.

Add taco seasoning and mix well. Add egg substitute, stir,
and microwave for 1½ minutes.

Gently stir and then sprinkle with cheese. Microwave for
1 minute, or until scramble is just set. Top with tortilla chips,
salsa, and sour cream!

MAKES 1 SERVING

IT'S ALL GREEK TO ME EGG MUG

Never been to Greece? Don't know how to pronounce *spanakopita*? Worry not—you'll STILL love this feta-infused egg mug!

PER SERVING (entire recipe): 117 calories, 2g fat, 459mg sodium, 8g carbs, 1g fiber, 3g sugars, 16g protein

Ingredients

½ cup chopped spinach
¼ cup chopped red onion
½ cup fat-free liquid egg substitute
2 tablespoons diced tomatoes
2 tablespoons crumbled reduced-fat feta cheese
½ tablespoon chopped fresh basil

Directions

Spray a large microwave-safe mug with nonstick spray. Add spinach and onion, and microwave for 1 to 2 minutes, until softened.

Blot any excess liquid from veggies. Add egg substitute and mix well. Microwave for 1 minute.

Stir gently. Add all other ingredients and lightly stir. Microwave for 1 minute, or until scramble is just set.

Gently stir, and then allow to cool slightly. Dig in!

MAKES 1 SERVING

YOU'LL NEED:
large microwave-safe mug, nonstick spray

PREP:
5 minutes

COOK:
5 minutes

Leftover feta alert!

Have extra? Flip to the index, locate the cheese listing, and make something else that contains fabulous feta. Woohoo!

For a pic of this recipe, see the first photo insert. Yay!

large microwave-safe
mug, nonstick spray

PREP:

5 minutes

COOK:

5 minutes

For full-color
photos of all the recipes
in this book, check out
hungry-girl.com/books.
Woohoo!

CHiCKEN FAJiTA SCRAMBLE MUG

Peppers? CHECK! Onions? CHECK! Chicken? YUP! All your favorite fajita flavors in one li'l eggy mug.

PER SERVING (entire recipe): 163 calories, 0.75g fat, 583mg sodium, 12g carbs, 1.25g fiber, 5.5g sugars, 26g protein

Ingredients

¼ cup chopped red bell pepper
¼ cup chopped onion
1 ounce cooked and chopped skinless lean chicken breast
1 teaspoon fajita seasoning mix
½ cup fat-free liquid egg substitute
2 tablespoons shredded fat-free cheddar cheese
1 tablespoon fat-free sour cream

Directions

Spray a large microwave-safe mug with nonstick spray. Add veggies, chicken, and fajita seasoning. Stir well to distribute seasoning. Microwave for 1 to 2 minutes, until veggies have softened.

Add egg substitute and mix well. Microwave for 1 minute.

Add cheese and gently stir. Microwave for 1 minute, or until scramble is just set.

Allow to cool slightly. Top with sour cream and enjoy!

MAKES 1 SERVING

Egg Mugs 101

* Use a LARGE mug (the bigger the better)! The egg mix expands when it's nuked, so you'll need that extra room. No oversized mugs around? Just use a microwave-friendly bowl.

* Egg-mug recipes are super low in calories. (There's only so much you can fit in a mug!) So feel free to pair one with a piece of fruit, stuff it into a high-fiber pita or wrap it up in a fiber-packed tortilla, eat two at a time . . . Whatever!

* Soak your mug right after you're done eating! Otherwise, it could be REALLY hard to scrub off the remaining egg bits.

large microwave-safe
mug, nonstick spray

PREP:

5 minutes

COOK:

5 minutes

For the Weight Watchers
PointsPlus™ values of
all the recipes in this
book, check out
hungry-girl.com/books.
Yay!

DENVER OMELETTE IN A MUG

You don't need to go to a diner for this one, people. Here's a new HG classic!

PER SERVING (entire recipe): 122 calories, 0.75g fat, 702mg sodium, 6g carbs, 0.5g fiber, 2.5g sugars, 21.5g protein

Ingredients

¼ cup chopped green bell pepper
2 tablespoons chopped onion
½ cup fat-free liquid egg substitute
1 ounce (about 2 slices) 97% to 98% fat-free ham, chopped
2 tablespoons shredded fat-free cheddar cheese

Directions

Spray a large microwave-safe mug with nonstick spray. Add veggies and microwave for 1 to 2 minutes, until softened.

Blot any excess liquid from veggies. Add egg substitute, mix well, and microwave for 1 minute.

Add ham and cheese and lightly stir. Microwave for 1 minute, or until scramble is just set.

Let cool slightly, and then eat up!

MAKES 1 SERVING

VEGGIE EGGS-PLOSION MUG

So many veggies in one mug . . . YAY!!!

YOU'LL NEED:
large microwave-safe mug, nonstick spray

PREP:
5 minutes

COOK:
5 minutes

PER SERVING (entire recipe): 130 calories, 1.75g fat, 445mg sodium, 10g carbs, 2g fiber, 5.5g sugars, 16.5g protein

Ingredients

½ cup sliced mushrooms
¼ cup thinly sliced onion
¼ cup chopped asparagus
¼ cup diced tomatoes
½ cup fat-free liquid egg substitute
1 wedge The Laughing Cow Light Creamy Swiss cheese
Optional: black pepper, garlic powder

Directions

Spray a large microwave-safe mug with nonstick spray. Add all veggies and microwave for 2 minutes, or until veggies have softened.

Thoroughly blot excess moisture from the veggies. Add egg substitute and mix well. Microwave for 1 minute.

Add the cheese wedge, breaking it into pieces as you add it. Gently stir, and then microwave for 1 minute, or until scramble is just set.

Allow to cool slightly. If you like, season to taste with black pepper and garlic powder. Enjoy!

MAKES 1 SERVING

YOU'LL NEED:
large microwave-safe mug, nonstick spray

PREP:
5 minutes

COOK:
5 minutes

ALL-AMERICAN EGG MUG

Everyone's favorite b-fast stuff, crammed into one taste-tastic morning mug!

PER SERVING (entire recipe): 173 calories, 4g fat, 730mg sodium, 7.5g carbs, <0.5g fiber, 2g sugars, 22g protein

Ingredients

1 frozen meatless or turkey sausage patty with about 80 calories
1 tablespoon sugar-free pancake syrup
½ cup fat-free liquid egg substitute
1 slice fat-free American cheese

Directions

Spray a large microwave-safe mug with nonstick spray. Add sausage patty and microwave for 45 seconds, or until warm.

Use a fork to crumble the patty into pieces inside the mug. Add syrup and toss to coat. Add egg substitute, mix well, and microwave for 1 minute.

Gently stir and microwave for 1 more minute, or until scramble is just set.

Tear cheese into pieces and add to the mug. Microwave for 15 seconds, or until cheese has melted.

Lightly stir, let cool slightly, and then eat up!

MAKES 1 SERVING

BEAN 'N CHEESY SOFT TACO IN AN EGG MUG

Love Mexi-licious meals? This one's a keeper!

YOU'LL NEED:
small bowl, large microwave-safe mug, nonstick spray

PREP:
5 minutes

COOK:
5 minutes

PER SERVING (entire recipe): 190 calories, 0.25g fat, 835mg sodium, 20g carbs, 4g fiber, 2.5g sugars, 25g protein

Ingredients

¼ cup fat-free refried beans
¼ teaspoon taco seasoning mix
¾ cup fat-free liquid egg substitute
Half a 6-inch corn tortilla, torn into bite-sized pieces
1 tablespoon shredded fat-free cheddar cheese
1 tablespoon salsa

Directions

In a small bowl, mix beans with taco seasoning. Set aside.

Spray a large microwave-safe mug with nonstick spray. Add egg substitute and microwave for 1 minute.

Gently stir. Microwave for 30 seconds, or until scramble is almost set.

Gently stir in seasoned beans and tortilla pieces. Sprinkle with cheese. Microwave for 20 seconds, or until scramble is just set. Top with salsa and dig in!

MAKES 1 SERVING

Never nuked a scramble?

Page 21 has helpful hints!

YOU'LL NEED:

large microwave-safe mug, nonstick spray, small microwave-safe bowl

PREP:

5 minutes

COOK:

5 minutes

HG Sodium Tip!

Shave about 140mg of sodium off the stats by using reduced-sodium ham.

EGGS BENE-CHICK MUG

A truly decadent breakfast classic, prepared guilt-free . . . and in a mug. YES!!!

PER SERVING (entire recipe): 153 calories, 1.75g fat, 831mg sodium, 15.5g carbs, 3g fiber, 2.5g sugars, 20g protein

Ingredients

½ cup fat-free liquid egg substitute
1 ounce (about 2 slices) 97% to 98% fat-free ham, roughly chopped
½ light English muffin, lightly toasted
2 teaspoons fat-free mayonnaise
1 teaspoon Dijon mustard
1 drop lemon juice

Directions

Spray a large microwave-safe mug with nonstick spray. Add egg substitute and microwave for 1 minute.

Gently stir and add ham. Break muffin half into bite-sized pieces and add to the mug. Gently stir. Microwave for 1 additional minute, until just set. Set aside.

In a small microwave-safe bowl, combine mayo, mustard, and lemon juice; mix well. Microwave until warm, about 15 seconds. Pour over your egg mug, give it a little stir, and dig in!

MAKES 1 SERVING

SAY CHEESE! EGG MUG

Simple. Cheesy. A-MAZING.

YOU'LL NEED:
large microwave-safe
mug, nonstick spray

PREP:
5 minutes

COOK:
5 minutes

PER SERVING (entire recipe): 172 calories, 5.5g fat, 645mg sodium, 6g carbs, <0.5g fiber, 3g sugars, 22g protein

Ingredients

½ cup fat-free liquid egg substitute
1 teaspoon dried minced onion
Dash garlic powder, or more to taste
Dash black pepper, or more to taste
1 piece The Laughing Cow Mini Babybel Light cheese, chopped
1 tablespoon light or low-fat ricotta cheese
1 wedge The Laughing Cow Light cheese (any flavor)
½ teaspoon reduced-fat Parmesan-style grated topping

Directions

Spray a large microwave-safe mug with nonstick spray. Add egg substitute and microwave for 1 minute.

Add all remaining ingredients *except* Parm-style topping, breaking the cheese wedge into pieces as you add it. Lightly stir and microwave for 1 minute, or until scramble is just set.

Give it another stir and top with Parm-style topping. Dig in!

MAKES 1 SERVING

YOU'LL NEED:

large microwave-safe
mug, nonstick spray

PREP:

5 minutes

COOK:

5 minutes

THE HG SPECIAL EGG MUG

creamy cheese. Awesome onion flavor. TURKEY. Mmmmmmmmmm . . . If HG says it's special, you know it's worth trying!

PER SERVING (entire recipe): 125 calories, 2.25g fat, 772mg sodium, 3.5g carbs, 0g fiber, 2g sugars, 19.5g protein

Ingredients

½ cup fat-free liquid egg substitute
1 ounce (about 2 slices) 98% fat-free turkey breast slices, roughly chopped
1 wedge The Laughing Cow Light French Onion cheese
Optional: dried minced onion

Directions

Spray a large microwave-safe mug with nonstick spray. Add egg substitute and microwave for 1 minute.

Gently stir. Add turkey and cheese, breaking the cheese wedge into pieces as you add it. Microwave for 1 minute, or until scramble is just set.

If you like, add a little dried minced onion. Give it a light stir, and then dig in!

MAKES 1 SERVING

HG Sodium Tip!

Save about 250mg of sodium by using cooked and sliced skinless lean turkey breast as opposed to packaged slices.

LASAGNA-LiKE EGG MUG

It's a little like lasagna and a LOT like a delicious breakfast. Mamma mia!

YOU'LL NEED:
blender or food processor (optional), small bowl, large microwave-safe mug, nonstick spray

PREP:
5 minutes

COOK:
5 minutes

PER SERVING (entire recipe): 187 calories, 4.5g fat, 635mg sodium, 8g carbs, 1.75g fiber, 3.5g sugars, 27g protein

Ingredients

1 stick light string cheese
2 tablespoons canned crushed tomatoes
⅛ teaspoon Italian seasoning
½ cup fat-free liquid egg substitute
¼ cup frozen ground-beef-style soy crumbles
2 tablespoons light or low-fat ricotta cheese

Directions

Break string cheese into thirds and place in a blender or food processor—blend at high speed until cheese takes on a shredded or grated consistency. (Or just tear string cheese into pieces and roughly chop.) Set aside.

In a small bowl, season crushed tomatoes with Italian seasoning. Set aside.

Spray a large microwave-safe mug with nonstick spray. Add egg substitute and soy crumbles and stir well. Microwave for 1 minute.

Gently stir and microwave for 1 minute, or until scramble is almost set.

Fluff with a fork and then very gently stir in ricotta cheese, shredded/grated string cheese, and seasoned tomatoes.

Microwave for 15 seconds, or until hot. *Buon appetito!*

MAKES 1 SERVING

***

Got leftover crushed tomatoes?

We've got more recipes to use 'em in! Just look up tomatoes in the index.

29

CHAPTER 2: BREAKFAST BOWLS

If it's a large bowl of items to chew you crave in the AM, you're gonna LOVE these . . .

YOU'LL NEED:
nonstick pot, bowl

PREP:
5 minutes

COOK:
20 minutes

BANANA SPLIT GROWING OATMEAL

Is it an ice cream dessert or breakfast?! Umm... it's breakfast. But it's got BANANA POWER!!!

PER SERVING (entire recipe): 285 calories, 7.5g fat, 338mg sodium, 51.5g carbs, 6.5g fiber, 12g sugars, 7g protein

Ingredients

½ cup old-fashioned oats
Dash salt
1 cup Unsweetened Vanilla Almond Breeze
1 tablespoon sugar-free strawberry preserves
½ banana, thinly sliced
2 tablespoons Fat Free Reddi-wip
1 teaspoon mini semi-sweet chocolate chips

Directions

Combine oats and salt in a nonstick pot on the stove. Add Almond Breeze and 1 cup water. Bring to a boil, and then reduce to a simmer.

Cook for 12 to 15 minutes, stirring frequently, until very thick and creamy.

Transfer to a bowl and allow to slightly cool and thicken.

Stir in preserves, and then top with banana, Reddi-wip, and chocolate chips. Eat up!

MAKES 1 SERVING

APPLE PiE OATMEAL BONANZA

> Sweet-n-tart apples, vanilla, cinnamon . . . This huge bowl of oats will make you happy. Promise!!!

PER SERVING (entire recipe): 258 calories, 6g fat, 364mg sodium, 44.5g carbs, 7g fiber, 8.5g sugars, 6g protein

Ingredients

½ cup old-fashioned oats
½ cup chopped apple
1 tablespoon sugar-free pancake syrup
1 teaspoon fat-free non-dairy powdered creamer
½ teaspoon cinnamon, or more to taste
½ teaspoon vanilla extract
Dash salt
2 no-calorie sweetener packets
1 cup Unsweetened Vanilla Almond Breeze

Directions

Combine all ingredients in a nonstick pot on the stove. Add 1 cup water and mix well. Bring to a boil, and then reduce to a simmer.

Cook for 12 to 15 minutes, stirring frequently, until very thick and creamy.

Transfer to a bowl, allow to slightly cool and thicken, and then dig in!

MAKES 1 SERVING

YOU'LL NEED:
nonstick pot, bowl

PREP:
5 minutes

COOK:
20 minutes

For more recipes, plus food finds, tips 'n tricks, and MORE, sign up for FREE daily emails at hungry-girl.com!

YOU'LL NEED:

nonstick pot, bowl

PREP:

5 minutes

COOK:

15 minutes

CHILL:

2 hours

LARGE & IN CHARGE NEAPOLITAN OATMEAL

Who else puts strawberries and chocolate chips in chilled oatmeal? Ummmm . . . NO ONE! This is one ROCKIN' O-meal bowl.

PER SERVING (entire recipe): 275 calories, 9g fat, 339mg sodium, 42.5g carbs, 7g fiber, 10g sugars, 7g protein

Oatmeal tip alert!

Just turn to page 53. Trust me.

Ingredients

½ cup old-fashioned oats
1 teaspoon sugar-free French vanilla powdered creamer
2 no-calorie sweetener packets
Dash salt
1 cup Unsweetened Vanilla Almond Breeze
¼ teaspoon vanilla extract
½ cup sliced strawberries
½ tablespoon mini semi-sweet chocolate chips

Directions

Combine oats, creamer, sweetener, and salt in a nonstick pot on the stove. Add Almond Breeze, vanilla extract, and 1 cup water. Bring to a boil, and then reduce to a simmer.

Cook for about 12 minutes, stirring often, until thick and creamy.

Transfer to a bowl and allow to cool slightly. Cover and refrigerate until chilled, about 2 hours.

Stir oatmeal thoroughly until uniform in texture. Evenly top with berries and chocolate chips. Eat up!

MAKES 1 SERVING

MAJOR MOCHA CAPPUCCINO OATMEAL

Think this one sounds a little "different"? You're right. But it tastes INCREDIBLE.

YOU'LL NEED:
nonstick pot, bowl

PREP:
5 minutes

COOK:
20 minutes

PER SERVING (entire recipe): 242 calories, 6.75g fat, 490mg sodium, 37g carbs, 6g fiber, 6g sugars, 7.5g protein

Ingredients

½ cup old-fashioned oats
One 25-calorie packet hot cocoa mix
1 teaspoon sugar-free French vanilla powdered creamer
¾ teaspoon instant coffee granules
1 no-calorie sweetener packet
Dash salt
1 cup Unsweetened Vanilla Almond Breeze
¼ cup Fat Free Reddi-wip

Directions

Combine oats, cocoa mix, powdered creamer, coffee granules, sweetener, and salt in a nonstick pot on the stove.

Add Almond Breeze and 1 cup water and mix thoroughly.

Bring to a boil, and then reduce to a simmer.

Cook for 12 to 15 minutes, stirring often, until very thick and creamy.

Transfer to a bowl and allow to slightly cool and thicken. Top with Reddi-wip and enjoy!

MAKES 1 SERVING

YOU'LL NEED:

skillet, nonstick spray,
bowl

PREP:

5 minutes

COOK:

10 minutes

VERY VEGGIE-EGGY EXPLOSION

This breakfast skillet has it ALL ... and tastes even better with a little ketchup. Mmmmm!

PER SERVING (entire recipe): 184 calories, 1.75g fat, 584mg sodium, 16g carbs, 2.5g fiber, 4.5g sugars, 22.5g protein

Ingredients

½ cup frozen potatoes O'Brien
½ cup spinach
½ cup chopped mushrooms
¾ cup fat-free liquid egg substitute
¼ cup chopped tomato
1 wedge The Laughing Cow Light Creamy Swiss cheese
Optional: salt, black pepper, Italian seasoning, ketchup, salsa

Directions

Bring a skillet sprayed with nonstick spray to medium-high heat on the stove. Add potatoes, spinach, and mushrooms. Stirring occasionally, cook until potatoes have thawed, spinach has wilted, and mushrooms have softened, about 3 minutes. Transfer contents of the skillet to a bowl and set aside.

Remove skillet from heat, re-spray, and return to medium-high heat. Add egg substitute, tomato, and cheese, breaking the cheese wedge into pieces as you add it. Scramble until egg substitute is fully cooked, about 3 minutes.

Add egg scramble to the bowl and stir to mix. If you like, season to taste with salt, pepper, and Italian seasoning and top with ketchup or salsa. Enjoy!

MAKES 1 SERVING

YOU'LL NEED:

small nonstick pot,
bowl, tall glass

PREP:

5 minutes

COOK:

15 minutes

CHILL:

1½ hours

PUMPKIN PiE OATMEAL PARFAiT

The invention of oatmeal parfaits was a stroke of genius. This pumpkin pie version will leave you speechless . . .

PER SERVING (entire recipe): 292 calories, 7.25g fat, 542mg sodium, 51g carbs, 7g fiber, 7.5g sugars, 7g protein

Ingredients

Oatmeal
⅓ cup old-fashioned oats
¾ cup Unsweetened Vanilla Almond Breeze
⅓ cup canned pure pumpkin
2 no-calorie sweetener packets
¼ teaspoon cinnamon
¼ teaspoon pumpkin pie spice
¼ teaspoon vanilla extract
Dash salt

Parfait
One 60-calorie sugar-free vanilla pudding snack
1 sheet (4 crackers) low-fat honey graham crackers, roughly crushed
Optional topping: Fat Free Reddi-wip

Directions

Combine all ingredients for oatmeal in a small nonstick pot on the stove. Add ¾ cup water and mix well. Bring to a boil, and then reduce to a simmer.

Cook for about 9 minutes, stirring often, until somewhat thick and creamy. (It will thicken more upon chilling.) Allow to cool slightly. Transfer to a bowl, cover, and refrigerate until chilled, at least 1½ hours.

Stir oatmeal thoroughly until uniform in texture. Spoon half of the oatmeal into a tall glass, and top with half of the pudding snack and half of the crushed graham crackers. Repeat with remaining oatmeal, pudding, and crushed graham crackers.

Top with Reddi-wip, if you like, and dig in!

MAKES 1 SERVING

Prevent crimes against canned pumpkin . . .

by not letting it go to waste! Use the rest to make Crazy-Good Carrot-Cake Pancakes (page 68) or the Surprise, It's Pumpkin! Enchiladas (page 206).

YOU'LL NEED:

skillet (optional),
nonstick spray,
microwave-safe bowl,
small bowl

PREP:

5 minutes

COOK:

10 minutes

SWEET AND SAVORY BREAKFAST BREAD PUDDING BOWL

Breakfast meat and bread and egg and syrup . . . cooked to perfection. Clap for it!!!

PER SERVING (entire recipe): 263 calories, 4.75g fat, 760mg sodium, 33.5g carbs, 6g fiber, 4.5g sugars, 23g protein

Ingredients

1 frozen meatless or turkey sausage patty with
   about 80 calories
2 slices light bread, lightly toasted
½ cup fat-free liquid egg substitute
⅛ teaspoon vanilla extract
½ teaspoon cinnamon, or more for topping
¼ cup sugar-free pancake syrup, divided
½ teaspoon powdered sugar

Directions

Prepare patty on the stove in a skillet sprayed with nonstick spray or in a microwave-safe bowl in the microwave. (Refer to package instructions for exact temperature and time.) Once cool enough to handle, crumble or chop and set aside.

Spray a microwave-safe bowl with nonstick spray. Tear toasted bread into bite-sized pieces and place in the bowl. Add crumbled sausage and set aside.

In a small bowl, combine egg substitute, vanilla extract, cinnamon, and 2 tablespoons pancake syrup. Mix well. Pour mixture over the bread pieces and crumbled sausage. If needed, gently stir to ensure bread is thoroughly soaked.

Microwave for 2 minutes and 15 seconds, or until bread pudding is set. (It will puff up once set.)

Top with remaining 2 tablespoons syrup, powdered sugar and, if you like, an extra sprinkle of cinnamon. Enjoy!

MAKES 1 SERVING

YOU'LL NEED:

nonstick pot, bowl

PREP:

5 minutes

COOK:

20 minutes

📷 For a pic of this recipe, see the first photo insert. Yay!

S'MORES OATMEAL

What do you do if you love chocolate, graham crackers, and marshmallow? MAKE S'MORES OATMEAL. Doy!

PER SERVING (entire recipe): 299 calories, 9g fat, 512mg sodium, 47.5g carbs, 6.5g fiber, 13g sugars, 8.5g protein

Ingredients

½ cup old-fashioned oats
One 25-calorie packet hot cocoa mix
Dash salt
1 cup Unsweetened Vanilla Almond Breeze
2 teaspoons mini semi-sweet chocolate chips, divided
2 tablespoons mini marshmallows
¼ sheet (1 cracker) low-fat honey graham crackers, crushed

Directions

Combine oats, cocoa mix, and salt in a nonstick pot on the stove. Add Almond Breeze and 1 cup water. Bring to a boil, and then reduce to a simmer.

Cook for 12 to 15 minutes, stirring occasionally, until very thick and creamy.

Remove pot from heat. Add 1 teaspoon chocolate chips and stir until melted.

Transfer to a bowl and top with marshmallows, crushed graham cracker, and remaining 1 teaspoon chocolate chips. Enjoy!

MAKES 1 SERVING

PB & CHOCOLATE OATMEAL BLiTZ

Craving peanut butter cups? Who needs 'em? Get your PB & C fix with this dazzling b-fast bowl!

YOU'LL NEED:
nonstick pot, bowl

PREP:
5 minutes

COOK:
20 minutes

PER SERVING (entire recipe): 295 calories, 10.5g fat, 515mg sodium, 41g carbs, 6g fiber, 9g sugars, 11g protein

Ingredients

½ cup old-fashioned oats
One 25-calorie packet hot cocoa mix
Dash salt
1 cup Unsweetened Vanilla Almond Breeze
1 tablespoon peanut butter baking chips, roughly chopped

Directions

Combine oats, cocoa mix, and salt in a nonstick pot on the stove. Add Almond Breeze and 1 cup water. Bring to a boil, and then reduce to a simmer.

Cook for 12 to 15 minutes, stirring frequently, until very thick and creamy.

Remove pot from heat. Add chips and stir until melted.

Transfer to a bowl, allow to slightly cool and thicken, and eat!

MAKES 1 SERVING

CiNN-A-NiLLA APPLE OATMEAL PARFAIT

Gigantic and a must-swallow for apple pie fans across the globe.

PER SERVING (entire recipe): 240 calories, 4.5g fat, 355mg sodium, 42.5g carbs, 5.75g fiber, 18g sugars, 8g protein

Ingredients

Oatmeal
⅓ cup old-fashioned oats
¾ cup Unsweetened Vanilla Almond Breeze
1 no-calorie sweetener packet
½ teaspoon cinnamon
⅛ teaspoon vanilla extract
Dash salt

Parfait
½ cup fat-free vanilla yogurt
¼ teaspoon cinnamon, divided
½ cup chopped apple

Directions

Combine all ingredients for oatmeal in a small nonstick pot on the stove. Add ¾ cup water and mix well. Bring to a boil, and then reduce to a simmer. Cook for about 9 minutes, stirring often, until somewhat thick and creamy. (It will thicken more upon chilling.) Allow to cool slightly. Transfer to a bowl, cover, and refrigerate until chilled, at least 1½ hours.

In a small bowl, mix yogurt with ⅛ teaspoon cinnamon. In a separate small bowl, sprinkle chopped apple with remaining ⅛ teaspoon cinnamon and toss to coat. Set aside.

Stir oatmeal thoroughly until uniform in texture. Spoon half of the oatmeal into a tall glass, and top with half of the yogurt and half of the chopped apple. Repeat with remaining oatmeal, yogurt, and chopped apple.

Serve and enjoy!

MAKES 1 SERVING

Attention, oatmeal eaters!

Turn to page 53 for tips 'n tricks you need to read.

YOU'LL NEED:

small bowl, whisk,
skillet, nonstick spray

PREP:

5 minutes

COOK:

10 minutes

HOT DOG & SCRAMBLE

There's a reason why hot dogs are so popular. They're delicious! So why not embrace this way to eat 'em for breakfast???

PER SERVING (entire recipe): 141 calories, 1g fat, 962mg sodium, 14g carbs, 0.75g fiber, 7g sugars, 18.5g protein

Ingredients

½ cup fat-free liquid egg substitute
½ tablespoon ketchup, or more for topping
½ tablespoon yellow mustard, or more for topping
½ tablespoon dill relish
1 hot dog with about 40 calories and 1g fat or less, chopped
⅓ cup chopped onion

Directions

In a small bowl, combine egg substitute, ketchup, mustard, and relish. Whisk for 1 minute, or until mostly uniform. Set aside.

Bring a skillet sprayed with nonstick spray to medium-high heat on the stove. Add chopped hot dog and onion and cook until browned, about 5 minutes.

Add egg mixture to the skillet and scramble until fully cooked, about 4 minutes. Plate your scramble and drizzle with additional ketchup and/or mustard, if you like. Enjoy!

MAKES 1 SERVING

TURKEY CLUB B. BOWL

Now you can have that turkey club flavor right in your kitchen . . . and you don't even need to wait 'til lunchtime. Woo and hoo!

YOU'LL NEED:
skillet, nonstick spray, bowl

PREP:
5 minutes

COOK:
5 minutes

📷 For a pic of this recipe, see the first photo insert. Yay!

PER SERVING (entire recipe): 276 calories, 4g fat, 862mg sodium, 15g carbs, 3g fiber, 4.5g sugars, 42g protein

Ingredients

1 slice light bread
¾ cup fat-free liquid egg substitute
2 ounces cooked and chopped skinless lean turkey breast
1 tablespoon precooked real crumbled bacon
1 wedge The Laughing Cow Light Creamy Swiss cheese
¼ cup chopped tomato

Directions

Toast bread and tear into bite-sized pieces. Set aside.

Bring a skillet sprayed with nonstick spray to medium-high heat on the stove. Add egg substitute and scramble until halfway cooked, about 1½ minutes.

Add turkey, bacon, and cheese, breaking the cheese wedge into pieces as you add it. Continue to scramble until egg substitute is mostly cooked, about 1 minute.

Add tomato and continue to scramble until fully cooked, about 30 seconds.

Gently stir in bread pieces. Transfer to a bowl and dig in!

MAKES 1 SERVING

YOU'LL NEED:

small nonstick pot, bowl, glass

PREP:

5 minutes

COOK:

15 minutes

CHILL:

1½ hours

📷 **For a pic of this recipe, see the first photo insert. Yay!**

SUPER-SIZED BERRY-NANA OATMEAL PARFAIT

Layering fruit, yogurt, and oatmeal is just plain delicious (and brilliant)!

PER SERVING (entire recipe): 285 calories, 4.5g fat, 359mg sodium, 54g carbs, 6.5g fiber, 21.5g sugars, 9g protein

Ingredients

Oatmeal
⅓ cup old-fashioned oats
¾ cup Unsweetened Vanilla Almond Breeze
1 no-calorie sweetener packet
⅛ teaspoon cinnamon
⅛ teaspoon vanilla extract
Dash salt

Parfait
½ cup fat-free vanilla yogurt
½ cup sliced strawberries
½ banana, sliced

Directions

Combine all ingredients for oatmeal in a small nonstick pot on the stove. Add ¾ cup water and mix well. Bring to a boil, and then reduce to a simmer. Cook for about 9 minutes, stirring often, until somewhat thick and creamy. (It will thicken more upon chilling.)

Allow to cool slightly. Transfer to a bowl, cover, and refrigerate until chilled, at least 1½ hours.

Stir oatmeal thoroughly until uniform in texture. Spoon half of the oatmeal into a glass, and top with ¼ cup yogurt, ¼ cup sliced strawberries, and ¼ sliced banana. Repeat with remaining oatmeal, yogurt, strawberries, and banana.

Serve and enjoy!

MAKES 1 SERVING

YOU'LL NEED:

medium-large
nonstick pot,
small bowl

PREP:

5 minutes

COOK:

25 minutes

✳ For more recipes,
plus food finds,
tips 'n tricks, and MORE,
sign up for FREE daily
emails at
hungry-girl.com!

BREAKFAST RICE PUDDING

Thick, creamy, and sweet—just the way you dreamed it would be.
Except with WAY fewer calories . . .

PER SERVING (½ of recipe, about 1 cup): 290 calories, 4g fat,
244mg sodium, 55g carbs, 4g fiber, 9g sugars, 12g protein

Ingredients

1½ cups cooked brown rice

2½ cups light vanilla soymilk, divided

2 tablespoons plus 2 teaspoons Splenda No Calorie
   Sweetener (granulated)

1 teaspoon cornstarch

Dash salt

2 tablespoons fat-free liquid egg substitute

½ teaspoon light whipped butter or light buttery
   spread, room temperature

½ teaspoon vanilla extract

1 teaspoon cinnamon, divided

½ tablespoon brown sugar (not packed)

Directions

In a medium-large nonstick pot, combine rice, 2 cups soymilk,
Splenda, cornstarch, and salt. Bring to a low boil, stirring
occasionally.

Once boiling, reduce heat to medium high. Continue to cook for
10 to 15 minutes, stirring frequently, until thick and creamy.

Meanwhile, in a small bowl, combine egg substitute, butter, vanilla
extract, ¾ teaspoon cinnamon, and remaining ½ cup soymilk.
Mix well.

Once the mixture in the pot is thick and creamy, add egg mixture and stir well.

Cook for 5 minutes, stirring frequently, until mixture returns to a thick and creamy consistency.

Sprinkle with brown sugar and mix well. Top each serving with a dash of the remaining cinnamon and enjoy—hot, cold, or anywhere in between!

MAKES 2 SERVINGS

HG Natural Sweetener Alternative!

Try a no-calorie granulated stevia product that measures cup-for-cup like sugar. Just replace the Splenda in this recipe with an equal amount of it. EZ!

YOU'LL NEED:
nonstick pot, bowl, small microwave-safe bowl

PREP:
5 minutes

COOK:
20 minutes

📷 **For a pic of this recipe, see the first photo insert. Yay!**

PB&J OATMEAL HEAVEN

Yo! Skip the peanut butter & jelly sandwiches. Indulge in this ginormous bowl of oatmeal instead.

PER SERVING (entire recipe): 285 calories, 10.25g fat, 417mg sodium, 42g carbs, 6.75g fiber, 5g sugars, 9g protein

Ingredients

Oatmeal
½ cup old-fashioned oats
⅓ cup chopped strawberries
2 teaspoons sugar-free strawberry preserves
1 no-calorie sweetener packet
Dash salt
1 cup Unsweetened Vanilla Almond Breeze

Topping
2 teaspoons Unsweetened Vanilla Almond Breeze
2 teaspoons reduced-fat peanut butter, room temperature
Optional garnish: additional chopped strawberries

Directions

Combine all ingredients for oatmeal in a nonstick pot on the stove. Add 1 cup water and mix well. Bring to a boil, and then reduce to a simmer. Stirring often, cook until very thick and creamy, 12 to 15 minutes. Transfer to a bowl and set aside.

In a small microwave-safe bowl, combine ingredients for topping. Microwave until warm, about 10 seconds. Stir until blended.

Drizzle topping over the oatmeal. If you like, garnish with additional chopped strawberries.

Allow to slightly cool and thicken. Enjoy!

MAKES 1 SERVING

HG and the Growing Oatmeal . . . Tips & Tricks!

* HG oatmeal recipes generally call for twice the amounts of liquid and cooking time as standard recipes for old-fashioned oats. Why? Because slow-simmering them with extra liquid yields ginormous serving sizes! Don't be thrown by the amount of liquid. Your oatmeal will thicken as it cooks. It'll thicken even more once you remove it from the heat. This is especially true for chilled oatmeal recipes.

* Old-fashioned oats are a must for these recipes. Why? Because instant oats won't work here. Don't question it, just grab a canister of the kind Mom used to make and enjoy!

* When cooking your oatmeal, stir it often. Gently run your spoon or spatula along the bottom and sides of the pan. This way your bowl of deliciousness will have a perfectly even and creamy consistency.

* Helpful HG hint: For chilled oatmeal recipes, make the oatmeal base (the first part of the recipe's directions) and refrigerate it overnight—then just assemble the parfait or add the toppings the next morning!

* These recipes call for Unsweetened Vanilla Almond Breeze, made by Blue Diamond, a delicious milk swap with only 40 calories per cup. It's generally found with the shelf-stable boxed milk substitutes at supermarkets. (It can also be ordered online, and it's available in refrigerated form at select markets.) You can use light vanilla soymilk in its place, just know that the calorie counts will vary accordingly. And if you do use a sweetened milk swap, you may want to nix the sweetener in the recipe and then sweeten it, as needed, at the end.

YOU'LL NEED:

skillet with a lid,
nonstick spray, bowl

PREP:

10 minutes

COOK:

15 minutes

HG HASH SCRAMBLE

This breakfast should become one of your go-to morning meals. It's AWESOME!

PER SERVING (entire recipe): 285 calories, 3g fat, 1,032mg sodium, 33.5g carbs, 5g fiber, 11g sugars, 31g protein

Extra Canadian bacon on hand?

Try the Hot Stack Morning Sliders (page 82) or the Hawaiian B-fast Stacks (page 92)!

Ingredients

2 ounces (about 3 slices) Canadian bacon, chopped
¾ cup frozen shredded hash browns
1 cup chopped bell pepper
½ cup chopped onion
½ cup fat-free liquid egg substitute
2 tablespoons shredded fat-free cheddar cheese
Optional topping: ketchup

Directions

Bring a skillet sprayed with nonstick spray to medium-high heat on the stove. Add Canadian bacon and hash browns and, stirring occasionally, cook until warm, about 2 minutes.

Add pepper and onion to the skillet. Stirring often, cook until veggies have softened and hash browns have begun to brown and crisp, about 4 minutes. Transfer contents of the skillet to a bowl and set aside.

Remove skillet from heat, re-spray, and bring to medium heat. Add egg substitute and scramble until just cooked, about 3 minutes. Return hash mixture to the skillet and toss to mix.

Reduce heat to low and sprinkle cheese over the contents of the skillet. Cover and cook until cheese has melted, about 2 minutes.

Transfer everything to the bowl and, if you like, top with ketchup. Yum!

MAKES 1 SERVING

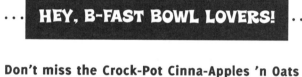

HEY, B-FAST BOWL LOVERS!

Don't miss the Crock-Pot Cinna-Apples 'n Oats recipe on page 304.

CHAPTER 3: BREAKFAST PLATES

Do big plates of food in the AM make you smile? Flash those pearly whites, kiddo . . .

YOU'LL NEED:

1 to 2 microwave-
safe bowls, skillet,
nonstick spray

PREP:

5 minutes

COOK:

20 minutes

For full-color
photos of all the recipes
in this book, check out
hungry-girl.com/books.
Woohoo!

SAUSAGE, EGG 'N CHEESE CHICKGRIDDLE

The fast-food version of this incredible morning treat is
embarrassingly high in calories & fat. Why do it?!

PER SERVING (entire recipe): 205 calories, 6g fat,
774mg sodium, 18g carbs, 1.5g fiber, 1.5g sugars, 17.5g protein

Ingredients

1 teaspoon light whipped butter or light buttery spread
2½ tablespoons sugar-free pancake syrup
1½ tablespoons whole-wheat flour
¼ teaspoon baking powder
1 frozen meatless or turkey sausage patty with
about 80 calories
1 slice fat-free American cheese
¼ cup fat-free liquid egg substitute
Optional dip: additional sugar-free pancake syrup

Directions

To make the pancake batter, place butter in a microwave-safe
bowl and nuke for 10 seconds, or until melted. Add syrup, flour,
and baking powder, and mix thoroughly.

Bring a skillet sprayed with nonstick spray to medium heat on
the stove. Add batter to form two small pancakes. Cook until
golden brown, 3 to 4 minutes per side, flipping carefully. Plate
and set aside.

Prepare patty in a skillet sprayed with nonstick spray or in
a microwave-safe bowl in the microwave. (Refer to package
instructions for exact temperature and time.)

Top one pancake with the sausage patty, followed by the cheese slice. Set aside.

Remove skillet from heat, re-spray, and return to medium heat. Add egg substitute and allow it to spread out evenly—do not scramble. Once mostly cooked through, flip and allow it to finish cooking. Gently fold it in half once, and then in half again. Place over the cheese-topped sausage patty, and finish it all off with the remaining pancake. If you like, dunk your ChickGriddle in some syrup. Yum time!

MAKES 1 SERVING

small microwave-safe
bowl, tall glass, bowl,
skillet, nonstick spray

PREP:

5 minutes

COOK:

10 minutes

📷 **For a pic
of this recipe,
see the first
photo insert.
Yay!**

ROCKIN' RED VELVET PANCAKES

Guilt-free red velvet pancakes, people! You're welcome . . .

PER SERVING (entire recipe, 2 pancakes with glaze): 273 calories,
3g fat, 717mg sodium, 46g carbs, 7.5g fiber, 9g sugars, 17.5g protein

Ingredients

Icing
2 tablespoons Cool Whip Free, thawed
1 tablespoon fat-free cream cheese, room temperature
1 no-calorie sweetener packet

Pancakes
One 25-calorie packet hot cocoa mix
1 tablespoon unsweetened cocoa powder
1 teaspoon mini semi-sweet chocolate chips, divided
⅓ cup whole-wheat flour
½ teaspoon baking powder
2 no-calorie sweetener packets
Dash salt
¼ cup fat-free liquid egg substitute
1 tablespoon light vanilla soymilk
3 drops red food coloring

Directions

In a small microwave-safe bowl, combine all icing ingredients and
mix until smooth. Set aside.

In a tall glass, combine cocoa mix, cocoa powder, and ½
teaspoon chocolate chips. Add ¼ cup very hot water and stir until
ingredients have dissolved. Set aside.

In a bowl, combine flour, baking powder, sweetener, and salt. Add cocoa mixture, egg substitute, and soymilk. Mix thoroughly. Add food coloring and mix well. Stir in remaining ½ teaspoon chocolate chips.

Bring a skillet sprayed with nonstick spray to medium-high heat on the stove. Add half the batter to form one large pancake. Cook until batter begins to bubble and is solid enough to flip, 2 to 3 minutes.

Gently flip and cook until both sides are lightly browned and inside is cooked through, 1 to 2 minutes. Plate your pancake and set aside.

Remove skillet from heat, re-spray, and return to medium-high heat. Repeat with remaining batter to make a second pancake.

Microwave icing until warm, about 20 seconds. Spread over your pancakes and eat up!

MAKES 1 SERVING

skillet, nonstick spray,
microwave-safe plate
(optional), bowl

PREP:
10 minutes

COOK:
20 minutes

✳ For full-color
photos of all the recipes
in this book, check out
hungry-girl.com/books.
Woohoo!

NICE TO SEE YA! QUESADILLA

It truly is nice to see this Mexican-inspired creation staring at you in the morning. Every time. No lie . . .

PER SERVING (entire recipe): 285 calories, 6g fat, 1,205mg sodium, 34.5g carbs, 15g fiber, 6.5g sugars, 34g protein

Ingredients

1 slice center-cut bacon or turkey bacon
½ cup thinly sliced bell pepper
¼ cup sliced onion
½ cup fat-free liquid egg substitute
2 tablespoons canned black beans, drained and rinsed
1 tablespoon fat-free sour cream
1 tablespoon salsa verde
1 La Tortilla Factory Smart & Delicious Low Carb High
    Fiber Large Tortilla
¼ cup shredded fat-free cheddar cheese
Optional: chopped fresh cilantro, salsa, additional
    fat-free sour cream

Directions

Prepare bacon in a skillet sprayed with nonstick spray or on a microwave-safe plate in the microwave. (Refer to package instructions for exact temperature and time.) Once cool enough to handle, roughly chop and set aside.

Bring a skillet sprayed with nonstick spray to medium-high heat on the stove. Add pepper and onion and, stirring occasionally, cook until slightly softened, about 3 minutes.

Add egg substitute and scramble until fully cooked, about 3 minutes. Transfer contents of the skillet to a bowl.

Add bacon, beans, sour cream, and salsa verde to the bowl. If you like, add cilantro as well. Lightly mix and set aside.

Remove skillet from heat. If needed, clean and dry. Re-spray skillet with nonstick spray, and bring to medium-high heat on the stove. Place tortilla flat in the skillet and sprinkle evenly with cheese. Spoon egg mixture over one half of the tortilla, fold the other half over the mixture to form the quesadilla, and then press down with a spatula to seal. Cook until both sides are crispy, about 2 minutes per side. (Flip very carefully.)

Plate your quesadilla and cut it into triangles. If you like, top with salsa and additional sour cream. Enjoy!

MAKES 1 SERVING

HG Alternative!

If you can't get your hands on the 80-calorie La Tortilla Factory tortilla called for in the recipe, just seek out the lowest-calorie medium-large flour tortilla you can find and adjust the calorie count accordingly. No problem!

YOU'LL NEED:

baking sheet,
nonstick spray,
large skillet

PREP:

5 minutes

COOK:

20 minutes

For the Weight Watchers
PointsPlus™ values of
all the recipes in this
book, check out
hungry-girl.com/books.
Yay!

HOLA BREAKFAST TOSTADA

A tostada isn't a typical breakfast item ... but this one's got bacon, egg, and cheese. It gets TWO YUMS UP!!!

PER SERVING (entire recipe): 234 calories, 3.5g fat, 889mg sodium, 28.5g carbs, 7g fiber, 4g sugars, 25.5g protein

Ingredients

1 medium-large high-fiber flour tortilla with about 110 calories
¼ cup diced red and green bell peppers
2 tablespoons diced onion
½ cup fat-free liquid egg substitute
1 tablespoon precooked real crumbled bacon
2 tablespoons shredded fat-free cheddar cheese
Optional: hot sauce
Optional toppings: fat-free sour cream, salsa, ketchup

Directions

Preheat oven to 375 degrees.

Place tortilla on a baking sheet sprayed with nonstick spray. Bake in the oven until slightly crispy, about 5 minutes per side. Transfer to a plate and set aside.

Bring a large skillet sprayed with nonstick spray to medium-high heat on the stove. Add peppers and onion and, stirring occasionally, cook until slightly softened, about 3 minutes.

Add egg substitute and bacon to the skillet. If you like, add a few dashes of hot sauce. Scramble until egg substitute is fully cooked, about 3 minutes.

Top the baked tortilla with scrambled egg mixture and sprinkle with cheese. If you like, add optional toppings. Enjoy!

MAKES 1 SERVING

CHEESY BEAN BREAKFAST QUESADILLA

Beans and chilies and corn tortillas . . . AHHHHH! How can this be under 300 calories?!? Who cares? It ROCKS!

PER SERVING (entire recipe): 255 calories, 3g fat, 829mg sodium, 35g carbs, 5.25g fiber, 6.5g sugars, 18.5g protein

Ingredients

½ cup fat-free liquid egg substitute
Two 6-inch corn tortillas
1 wedge The Laughing Cow Light Creamy Swiss cheese
2 tablespoons fat-free refried beans
¼ cup canned diced tomatoes with green chilies, drained
2 tablespoons chopped onion
Optional topping: fat-free sour cream

Directions

Bring a skillet sprayed with nonstick spray to medium-high heat on the stove. Add egg substitute and scramble until fully cooked, about 3 minutes. Transfer to a plate and set aside.

Lay tortillas flat on a clean dry surface. Spread cheese on one tortilla and beans on the other. Set aside.

Remove skillet from heat. If needed, clean and dry. Re-spray skillet and return to medium-high heat. Place the cheese-covered tortilla in the skillet, cheese side up. Top with egg scramble, tomatoes with chilies, and onion. Place the other tortilla on top, bean side down. Cook until lightly browned and crispy, about 2 minutes per side, flipping carefully.

Once cool enough to handle, slice into wedges and if you like, top with sour cream. Enjoy!

MAKES 1 SERVING

Chances are . . .

you're gonna have leftover refried beans. So flip to page 346 and make a Twice-as-Nice *Guapo* Taco!

bowls, blender or
food processor,
whisk, baking sheet,
nonstick spray, skillet

PREP:
10 minutes

COOK:
15 minutes

📷 **For a pic of this recipe, see the first photo insert. Yay!**

CREAMY CRAB CAKES BENEDICT

A fun new spin on a classic breakfast. You won't believe how incredible it tastes and that it's so low in calories & fat. YAY!!!

PER SERVING (¼th of recipe, 1 crab cake benedict): 149 calories, 3.25g fat, 912mg sodium, 12.5g carbs, 1.5g fiber, 3.5g sugars, 17g protein

Ingredients

Sauce
¼ cup fat-free mayonnaise

1 tablespoon Hellmann's/Best Foods Dijonnaise

1 tablespoon light whipped butter or light buttery
　　spread, room temperature

1 tablespoon lemon yogurt or 1 tablespoon plain
　　yogurt with a drop of lemon juice

Crab Cakes
2½ slices light white bread, lightly toasted

Two 6-ounce cans lump crabmeat, drained
　　(about 1 cup drained crabmeat)

2 tablespoons finely diced onion

1 teaspoon chopped garlic

Dash each salt and black pepper, or more to taste

One wedge The Laughing Cow Light Creamy Swiss cheese

1 tablespoon fat-free mayonnaise

½ tablespoon Hellmann's/Best Foods Dijonnaise

½ teaspoon lemon juice

½ teaspoon light whipped butter or light buttery
　　spread, room temperature

1 cup plus 3 tablespoons fat-free liquid egg
　　substitute, divided

Optional: hot sauce

Directions

Preheat oven to 450 degrees.

Combine all sauce ingredients in a bowl and mix well. Set aside.

Tear lightly toasted bread into pieces and place in a blender or food processor. Pulse until reduced to crumbs, and then transfer to a second bowl.

Add crabmeat, onion, garlic, salt, and pepper to the bowl of crumbs. Gently mix and set aside.

Break cheese wedge into pieces and place in a small bowl. Add mayo, Dijonnaise, lemon juice, butter, and 3 tablespoons egg substitute. If you like, add a few drops of hot sauce. Whisk until smooth.

Pour the cheese-egg mixture over the crabmeat mixture, and gently mix.

Spray a baking sheet with nonstick spray. Take one-fourth of the crab cake mixture and gently form it into a ball. Place it on the sheet and flatten it into a cake about ½-inch thick. Repeat with remaining crab mixture so that you have four crab cakes.

Bake in the oven until crab cakes are slightly firm and cooked through, about 14 minutes.

Meanwhile, bring a skillet sprayed with nonstick spray to medium heat on the stove. Add remaining 1 cup egg substitute and scramble until fully cooked, about 4 minutes.

Plate crab cakes and evenly top with scrambled egg substitute. Give sauce a stir and evenly spoon over the scrambled egg substitute.

Dig in!

MAKES 4 SERVINGS

YOU'LL NEED:

2 microwave-safe
bowls, large bowl,
skillet, nonstick spray

PREP:

10 minutes

COOK:

10 minutes

CRAZY-GOOD CARROT-CAKE PANCAKES

Classic carrot cake flavor in HG-friendly pancakes?! How can it be? Don't ask questions; just enjoy . . .

PER SERVING (entire recipe, 2 pancakes with glaze): 290 calories, 1.5g fat, 510mg sodium, 54g carbs, 8g fiber, 15g sugars, 16g protein

Ingredients

Take that leftover crushed pineapple . . .

and make a Tropical AM Smoothie (page 90). DO IT!

Pancakes
¼ cup shredded carrots, chopped
¼ cup fat-free liquid egg substitute
2 tablespoons canned pure pumpkin
2 tablespoons crushed pineapple packed in juice, drained
2 tablespoons light vanilla soymilk
½ teaspoon vanilla extract
1 tablespoon raisins
⅓ cup whole-wheat flour
¼ teaspoon baking powder
1 no-calorie sweetener packet
¾ teaspoon cinnamon
½ teaspoon pumpkin pie spice
Dash salt

Glaze
½ teaspoon powdered sugar
1 no-calorie sweetener packet
⅛ teaspoon vanilla extract
1 tablespoon light vanilla soymilk
1 tablespoon fat-free cream cheese, room temperature

Directions

Place carrots in a microwave-safe bowl with 1 tablespoon water. Cover and microwave for 1 minute, or until softened. Once cool enough to handle, add egg substitute, pumpkin, pineapple, soymilk, vanilla extract, raisins, and 2 tablespoons water. Mix well and set aside.

In a large bowl, combine all remaining pancake ingredients. Stir well. Add carrot-egg mixture and mix thoroughly.

Bring a skillet sprayed with nonstick spray to medium-high heat on the stove. Add half of the batter to the skillet to form one large pancake. Cook for 2 to 3 minutes, until pancake begins to bubble and is solid enough to flip. Gently flip and cook for an additional 1 to 2 minutes, until both sides are lightly browned and inside is cooked through. Plate your pancake.

Remove skillet from heat, re-spray, and return to medium-high heat. Repeat with remaining batter to make a second pancake.

To make the glaze, combine powdered sugar, sweetener, vanilla extract, and soymilk in a microwave-safe bowl. Mix thoroughly. Add cream cheese and microwave for 30 seconds. Stir until smooth. Spread over your pancakes and eat up!

MAKES 1 SERVING

Sure, breakfast is covered . . .

but use leftover pumpkin to make Surprise, It's Pumpkin! Enchiladas (page 206) for dinner and a Pumpkin Pie Oatmeal Parfait (page 38) for dessert!

YOU'LL NEED:

skillet, nonstick
spray, large plate,
microwave-safe plate

PREP:

5 minutes

COOK:

10 minutes

📷 **For a pic
of this recipe,
see the first
photo insert.
Yay!**

BUENOS DÍAS BREAKFAST FAJITAS

> You can never have too many Mexican morning meals. These are loaded with classic fajita flavor and, um, sausage 'n eggs!

PER SERVING (entire recipe, 2 fajitas): 285 calories, 5.5g fat, 742mg sodium, 32.5g carbs, 5g fiber, 5.5g sugars, 22.5g protein

Ingredients

⅓ cup sliced onion
⅓ cup sliced bell pepper
⅓ cup fat-free liquid egg substitute
1 frozen meatless or turkey sausage patty with about 80 calories
Two 6-inch corn tortillas
2 tablespoons shredded fat-free cheddar cheese
2 tablespoons salsa

Directions

Bring a skillet sprayed with nonstick spray to medium heat on the stove. Add onion and pepper and, stirring occasionally, cook until softened, about 5 minutes. Transfer to a large plate and set aside.

Remove skillet from heat, re-spray, and return to medium heat. Add egg substitute and scramble until fully cooked, about 2 minutes. Place on the plate, next to the veggies, and set aside.

Prepare patty in a skillet sprayed with nonstick spray or on a microwave-safe plate in the microwave. (Refer to package instructions for exact temperature and time.) Once cool enough to handle, slice into strips, and place on the plate beside the egg scramble and veggies.

Place tortillas on a microwave-safe plate, and warm slightly in the microwave, about 30 seconds. Assemble fajitas by evenly distributing veggies, scrambled eggs, and sausage strips between the two tortillas. Evenly top each with shredded cheese and salsa. Roll or fold 'em up and eat!

MAKES 1 SERVING

Salt-Slashing Swaps for Recipe Ingredients

Broth: Using no-salt-added broth instead of regular will save 400mg of sodium per cup.

Salsa: Swap premade versions for chopped tomatoes, onions & herbs and save 700mg of sodium per ½ cup.

Deli Meat: Bake/roast your own chicken and/or turkey, slice it thin, use in place of deli slices, and save 250mg of sodium per ounce.

Canned Beans: Rinsing them (as called for in these recipes) saves you about 20 percent of the sodium amount listed on the can. Seek out no-salt-added beans and save another 500mg per cup.

Canned Tuna: Opting for low-sodium tuna saves 300mg of sodium per ½ cup used.

YOU'LL NEED:

skillet, nonstick spray, microwave-safe plate (optional), baking sheet, blender or food processor (optional)

PREP:

5 minutes

COOK:

35 minutes

For more recipes, plus food finds, tips 'n tricks, and MORE, sign up for FREE daily emails at hungry-girl.com!

BREAKFAST SCRAMBLE PiZZA

Yup, pizza for breakfast. And if you want it later in the day too, check out the All Things Pizza chapter on page 244!

PER SERVING (entire recipe): 270 calories, 7.25g fat, 933mg sodium, 32.5g carbs, 7.5g fiber, 6g sugars, 23.5g protein

Ingredients

1 slice center-cut bacon or turkey bacon
⅓ cup fat-free liquid egg substitute
1 medium-large high-fiber flour tortilla with about 110 calories
1 stick light string cheese
¼ cup canned crushed tomatoes
Dash Italian seasoning, or more to taste
2 tablespoons finely chopped onion
2 tablespoons finely chopped red bell pepper
Optional: reduced-fat Parmesan-style grated topping

Directions

Preheat oven to 350 degrees.

Prepare bacon on the stove in a skillet sprayed with nonstick spray or on a microwave-safe plate in the microwave. (Refer to package instructions for exact temperature and time.) Once cool enough to handle, crumble or chop and set aside.

Bring a skillet sprayed with nonstick spray to medium heat on the stove. Add egg substitute and scramble until fully cooked, about 2 minutes. Remove from heat and set aside.

Place tortilla on a baking sheet sprayed with nonstick spray. Bake in the oven for 5 minutes per side, or until slightly crispy. Remove from oven, but do not turn oven off.

Meanwhile, break string cheese into thirds and place in a blender or food processor—blend at high speed until cheese takes on a shredded or grated consistency. (Or just tear string cheese into pieces and roughly chop.) Set aside.

Spread crushed tomatoes over the tortilla, leaving a ½-inch border around the edge. Sprinkle with a dash or more of Italian seasoning. Evenly distribute scrambled eggs over the tomatoes and top with shredded/grated string cheese, onion, pepper, and bacon.

Bake in the oven for 8 to 10 minutes, until pizza is hot and cheese has melted. If you like, top with some Parm-style grated topping. Slice it into quarters and eat up!!!

MAKES 1 SERVING

YOU'LL NEED:

2 bowls,
microwave-safe bowl,
skillet, nonstick spray

PREP:

10 minutes

COOK:

15 minutes

For full-color photos of all the recipes in this book, check out hungry-girl.com/books. Woohoo!

STRAWBERRY SHORT STACK

Pink pancakes?! CUUUTE! And guess what . . . They TASTE even better than they LOOK!

PER SERVING (entire recipe, 2 pancakes with filling): 289 calories, 1.75g fat, 471mg sodium, 60.5g carbs, 7.5g fiber, 7g sugars, 14g protein

Ingredients

⅓ cup whole-wheat flour

2 tablespoons old-fashioned oats

½ teaspoon baking powder

1 no-calorie sweetener packet

Dash salt

¼ cup fat-free liquid egg substitute

1 tablespoon light vanilla soymilk

2 tablespoons sugar-free strawberry preserves

½ cup sliced strawberries

¼ cup Cool Whip Free, thawed

Optional toppings: Fat Free Reddi-wip, sugar-free pancake syrup

Directions

To make the batter, combine flour, oats, baking powder, sweetener, and salt in a bowl. Add egg substitute, soymilk, and 2 tablespoons water. Mix well and set aside.

Place preserves in a microwave-safe bowl and nuke for 20 seconds, until softened and warm. Stir into pancake batter until thoroughly integrated.

Bring a skillet sprayed with nonstick spray to medium-high heat on the stove. Add half the batter to form a large pancake. Cook for 2 to 3 minutes, until pancake begins to bubble and is solid enough to flip. Gently flip and cook for an additional 1 to 2 minutes, until both sides are lightly browned and inside is cooked through. Plate your pancake and set aside.

Remove skillet from heat, re-spray, and return to medium-high heat. Repeat with remaining batter to make a second pancake, and then set that aside as well.

While pancakes cool slightly, combine strawberries with Cool Whip in a bowl and lightly stir. Spoon this mixture evenly over one pancake, and then place the second pancake lightly on top.

If you like, add a squirt of Reddi-wip and a drizzle of pancake syrup. Woohoo!

MAKES 1 SERVING

YOU'LL NEED:

bowl, skillet,
nonstick spray

PREP:

5 minutes

COOK:

10 minutes

GIMME S'MORE PANCAKES

can you tell we're s'mores-obsessed at the HG HQ? FYI, there's nothing wrong with that . . .

PER SERVING (entire recipe, 2 pancakes with topping): 281 calories, 3.25g fat, 523mg sodium, 52g carbs, 5.5g fiber, 14.5g sugars, 13g protein

Ingredients

⅓ cup whole-wheat flour

½ teaspoon baking powder

1 no-calorie sweetener packet

Dash salt

¼ cup fat-free liquid egg substitute

1 tablespoon light vanilla soymilk

½ tablespoon mini semi-sweet chocolate chips

10 mini marshmallows, halved

½ tablespoon Hershey's Lite chocolate syrup

2 tablespoons Fat Free Reddi-wip

½ sheet (2 crackers) low-fat honey graham crackers, crushed

Directions

To make the batter, combine flour, baking powder, sweetener, and salt in a bowl. Add egg substitute, soymilk, and 2 tablespoons water. Mix thoroughly. Stir in chocolate chips. Stir in halved marshmallows, adding them slowly and individually so they don't stick to each other.

Bring a skillet sprayed with nonstick spray to medium-high heat on the stove. Add half the batter to form a large pancake. Cook for 2 to 3 minutes, until pancake begins to bubble and is solid enough to flip. Gently flip and cook for an additional 1 to 2 minutes, until both sides are lightly browned and inside is cooked through. Plate your pancake and set aside.

Remove skillet from heat, re-spray, and return to medium-high heat. Repeat with remaining batter to make a second pancake. Stack your pancakes and top them with chocolate syrup, Reddi-wip, and crushed graham crackers. Enjoy!!!

MAKES 1 SERVING

YOU'LL NEED:

skillet or
microwave-safe
plate, nonstick spray,
microwave-safe bowl

PREP:

5 minutes

COOK:

10 minutes

THE MORNING WAFFLE DiP

A traditional b-fast sandwich on waffle "bread"?! For under 300 calories? AHHHHHHHHHHHH!!!

PER SERVING (entire recipe): 299 calories, 5g fat, 1,075mg sodium, 43.5g carbs, 3g fiber, 5g sugars, 23.5g protein

Ingredients

1 slice center-cut bacon or turkey bacon
½ cup fat-free liquid egg substitute
2 frozen low-fat waffles
1 slice fat-free American cheese
¼ cup sugar-free pancake syrup

Directions

Prepare bacon in a skillet sprayed with nonstick spray or on a microwave-safe plate in the microwave. (Refer to package instructions for exact temperature and time.) Set aside.

To make the egg patty, spray a microwave-safe bowl with nonstick spray. Add egg substitute and microwave for 1 minute. Gently stir, and then microwave for 1 additional minute. Set aside.

Toast waffles, and then place them side-by-side on a plate. Transfer egg patty from the bowl onto one of the waffles.

Break bacon in half and place over the egg patty. Top with cheese, and finish it off with the other waffle.

Cut your sandwich in half and serve with syrup for dipping. Dig in, you!

MAKES 1 SERVING

BREAKFAST PIZZA MEXICALI

As seen in the very first episode of the HG television show, here's an AM Mexican pizza that'll blow your mind!!! (Pssst . . . An entire chapter of pizza goodness starts on page 244.)

PER SERVING (entire recipe): 225 calories, 10g fat, 1,075mg sodium, 10g carbs, 2.5g fiber, 4g sugars, 24g protein

Ingredients

1 ounce soy chorizo
½ cup fat-free liquid egg substitute
¼ cup salsa
¼ cup shredded reduced-fat Mexican-blend cheese

Directions

Bring a small skillet sprayed with nonstick spray to medium heat on the stove. Add soy chorizo and cook until browned, about 3 minutes, using a spatula to break it into pieces. Remove chorizo from the skillet and set aside.

Remove skillet from heat, re-spray, and bring to low heat on the stove. Pour in egg substitute but do not scramble. Cover and cook for 3 minutes, or until egg "crust" starts to form.

Carefully flip your egg. Cover and cook for another minute.

Evenly top your egg crust with salsa, cheese, and cooked chorizo. Cover again and cook over low heat for 2 minutes, or until cheese has melted. Enjoy!

MAKES 1 SERVING

YOU'LL NEED: small skillet with a lid, nonstick spray

PREP: 5 minutes

COOK: 10 minutes

ERiN-GO-BREAKFAST BOXTY

What's a boxty? A delicious Irish potato pancake, that's what! This is a guilt-free version of the international favorite with a breakfast-y spin. Please try it . . . PLEASE!!!

PER SERVING (¼th of recipe, 2 loaded pancakes): 233 calories, 2.5g fat, 840mg sodium, 20.5g carbs, 4.5g fiber, 4.5g sugars, 31.5g protein

Ingredients

1 large head cauliflower

4 ounces (about half a medium) russet potato, peeled

2½ cups fat-free liquid egg substitute, divided

½ cup light plain soymilk

¼ cup whole-wheat flour

¼ teaspoon dried parsley

⅛ teaspoon black pepper, or more to taste

1 cup shredded fat-free cheddar cheese

¼ cup precooked real crumbled bacon

Optional toppings: salt, salsa, fat-free sour cream, chopped scallions

Directions

Remove leaves and the tough end from the cauliflower head, and break cauliflower down into large chunks. Using the coarse-grating side of a box grater, carefully grate the stems into shreds over a large microwave-safe bowl, reserving the florets. Grate potato into the bowl, and toss to combine the shreds.

Lay the potato and cauliflower shreds on a layer of paper towels. Cover with another layer of paper towels, and press down firmly to remove all excess moisture. Repeat until shreds are as dry as possible. Set aside.

Chop 2 cups' worth of reserved cauliflower florets, and place in the now-empty microwave-safe bowl with 2 tablespoons water. (Save remaining cauliflower for another recipe or for snacking.) Cover and microwave for 6 minutes. Once cool enough to handle, drain any excess water.

Add ½ cup egg substitute and the soymilk to the bowl. Using a potato masher, mash thoroughly. Add flour, parsley, and pepper, and mix thoroughly. Add the potato and cauliflower shreds and stir well.

Bring a large skillet sprayed with butter-flavored nonstick spray to medium-high heat on the stove. Working in batches, spoon batter into the skillet to form eight pancakes, each about 4 inches in diameter. Cook until lightly browned, about 5 minutes per side.

While still in the skillet, top each pancake with 2 tablespoons cheese. Cover and continue to cook until cheese has melted, about 1 minute. Plate and set aside.

Remove skillet from heat, re-spray, and bring to medium heat. Add remaining 2 cups egg substitute and scramble until fully cooked, about 4 minutes.

Evenly distribute scrambled egg substitute and crumbled bacon among the pancakes. If you like, top with additional pepper, salt, salsa, sour cream, and scallions.

ENJOY! (You deserve it!)

MAKES 4 SERVINGS

YOU'LL NEED:
medium skillet,
nonstick spray, plate

PREP:
5 minutes

COOK:
10 minutes

HOT STACK
MORNING SLIDERS

cute mini sandwiches worth waking up for!

PER SERVING (entire recipe, 3 sliders): 254 calories, 3.5g fat,
1,260mg sodium, 26g carbs, 4.75g fiber, 5g sugars, 31.5g protein

Ingredients

One 100-calorie flat sandwich bun
1 slice fat-free American cheese
½ cup fat-free liquid egg substitute
3 slices (about 2 ounces) Canadian bacon

Directions

Slice bun into three wedges. (Picture a clock. Cut at 12, 4, and 8.)
Separate the top and bottom pieces and set aside. Cut cheese into
thirds in the same way and set aside.

Bring a medium skillet sprayed with nonstick spray to medium
heat on the stove. Add egg substitute and tilt skillet so the egg
substitute coats the bottom, creating an egg pancake. Without
stirring, cook until solid enough to flip, about 2 minutes. Carefully
flip and cook until firm, about 1 minute. Remove and, once cool
enough to handle, slice into three large wedges. Transfer to a
plate and set aside.

Remove skillet from heat. If needed, clean and dry. Re-spray skillet with nonstick spray, and return to medium heat. Lay Canadian bacon slices flat in the skillet, and cook until lightly browned on the bottom, about 1 minute.

Flip slices and, while still in the skillet, carefully place an egg wedge over each, folding it to fit (doesn't have to be perfect!). Top each egg layer with a piece of cheese. Cover and continue to cook for about a minute, until cheese has melted. Using a spatula, slide each stack onto a bottom piece of the bun. Finish each off with a top piece, and eat ASAP!

MAKES 1 SERVING

What do you do with leftover Canadian bacon?

Throw together the HG Hash Scramble (page 54) or Hawaiian B-fast Stacks (page 92). That's what!

CHAPTER 4:
NO-COOK
B-FASTS

Feeling lazy? *No problemo* . . . These
no-heat-required morning meals
are AWESOME!

BREAKFAST SUNDAE SUPREME

The idea of eating a sundae for breakfast is just fun . . . There's no way around it.

PER SERVING (entire recipe): 215 calories, 3.5g fat, 311mg sodium, 40.5g carbs, 6.5g fiber, 22g sugars, 11g protein

Ingredients

¼ cup fat-free cottage cheese
¼ cup fat-free strawberry yogurt
1 no-calorie sweetener packet
1 drop vanilla extract
½ cup sliced banana
¼ cup sliced strawberries
2 tablespoons Fiber One Original bran cereal
½ tablespoon thinly sliced dry-roasted almonds
1 teaspoon mini semi-sweet chocolate chips
Optional garnish: mint sprig

Directions

In a bowl, combine cottage cheese, yogurt, sweetener, and vanilla extract. Mix well.

Top with fruit, cereal, almonds, and chocolate chips. If you like, garnish with mint. Dig in!

MAKES 1 SERVING

DOUBLE-O-STRAWBERRY QUICKIE KIWI SMOOTHIE

A fast and DELICIOUS fruity fix . . .

YOU'LL NEED:
blender, tall glass

PREP:
5 minutes

PER SERVING (entire recipe): 167 calories, 0.5g fat, 59mg sodium, 38g carbs, 5g fiber, 25.5g sugars, 4.5g protein

Ingredients

1 cup frozen unsweetened strawberries, partly thawed
1 kiwi, peeled
½ cup fat-free strawberry yogurt
1 cup crushed ice *or* 5 to 8 ice cubes

Directions

Place all ingredients in a blender, and blend at high speed until smooth.

Pour into a tall glass and sip away . . . maybe even with a schmancy straw!

MAKES 1 SERVING

PB&J YOGURT PARFAIT

If peanut butter, jelly, and layered food items are your thing, prepare to FREAK.

For the Weight Watchers *PointsPlus*™ values of all the recipes in this book, check out hungry-girl.com/books. Yay!

PER SERVING (entire recipe): 203 calories, 2.25g fat, 190mg sodium, 37.5g carbs, 3g fiber, 26g sugars, 8g protein

Ingredients

One 6-ounce container (¾ cup) fat-free strawberry yogurt
½ cup chopped strawberries
¼ cup low-fat peanut butter cereal, lightly crushed
1 teaspoon peanut butter baking chips, crushed

Directions

Spoon half of the yogurt into a parfait glass (or any glass).

Top with half of the strawberries, followed by half of the crushed cereal. Sprinkle half of the crushed chips over the layer of crushed cereal.

Continue layering with remaining yogurt, strawberries, crushed cereal, and crushed chips.

Dig in!

MAKES 1 SERVING

SMOKEY SALMON LETTUCE WRAPS

These wraps are so good, you'll want to serve them to everyone you know. (Well, almost everyone. Definitely the people you like a lot!)

📷 **For a pic of this recipe, see the first photo insert. Yay!**

PER SERVING (entire recipe, 3 wraps): 145 calories, 6g fat, 905mg sodium, 10.5g carbs, 2.75g fiber, 3.5g sugars, 15.5g protein

Ingredients

- 3 medium-large leaves romaine lettuce
- 1 tablespoon fat-free cream cheese
- ¼ teaspoon salt-free lemon pepper seasoning
- 2 ounces smoked salmon
- ½ teaspoon dried minced onion
- 1 small seedless cucumber, thinly sliced
- 2 tablespoons sun-dried tomatoes packed in oil, drained and sliced

Directions

Lay lettuce leaves on a plate and evenly spread the inside of each with cream cheese. Sprinkle with lemon pepper seasoning and top with smoked salmon.

Sprinkle salmon with minced onion. Equally distribute cucumber slices among the lettuce leaves. Evenly top with sun-dried tomatoes.

Wrap 'em up and devour!

MAKES 1 SERVING

blender, tall glass

5 minutes

TROPICAL AM SMOOTHIE

You don't have to be on vacation to sip this satisfying island-inspired blended beverage . . .

PER SERVING (entire recipe): 185 calories, <0.5g fat, 99mg sodium, 40g carbs, 2.25g fiber, 30g sugars, 6.5g protein

Ingredients

One 6-ounce container (¾ cup) fat-free peach yogurt
¼ cup crushed pineapple packed in juice (not drained)
½ banana, sliced and frozen
½ teaspoon lime juice
1 cup crushed ice *or* 5 to 8 ice cubes

Directions

Place all ingredients in a blender, and blend at high speed until smooth. Pour into a tall glass and sip away!

MAKES 1 SERVING

Got extra crushed pineapple?

Use it to make Crazy-Good Carrot-Cake Pancakes (page 68) . . . or just eat it plain. Your call.

TROPICAL WONDER B-FAST BOWL

This island-y bowl of cottage cheese and fruit will transport your taste buds to some sort of tropical paradise. Try it and see for yourself!

YOU'LL NEED:
bowl

PREP:
5 minutes

PER SERVING (entire recipe): 230 calories, 5g fat, 579mg sodium, 29g carbs, 4.5g fiber, 19g sugars, 18g protein

Ingredients

⅔ cup fat-free cottage cheese
1 no-calorie sweetener packet
1 to 2 drops coconut extract
Dash cinnamon, or more to taste
1 kiwi, peeled and sliced
½ cup sliced strawberries
½ tablespoon shredded sweetened coconut
½ tablespoon chopped dry-roasted pecans
Optional: sugar-free pancake syrup

Directions

In a bowl, combine cottage cheese, sweetener, 1 drop coconut extract, and cinnamon. Stir well and, if you like, add another drop of coconut extract and additional cinnamon, to taste.

Top with fruit, shredded coconut, and pecans. If you like, add a drizzle of syrup. Yum time!

MAKES 1 SERVING

HG Tip!

This tastes fantastic warmed in the microwave for 30 seconds or so!

📷 For a pic of this recipe, see the first photo insert. Yay!

HAWAiiAN B-FAST STACKS

This open-faced breakfast sandwich is so delicious and unique, you'll want to share it with EVERYONE (even some people you don't like all that much)!

PER SERVING (entire recipe, 2 stacks): 249 calories, 3g fat, 912mg sodium, 43.5g carbs, 7g fiber, 17g sugars, 16.5g protein

Ingredients

- 1 light English muffin
- 1 tablespoon fat-free cream cheese
- 1 teaspoon Hellmann's/Best Foods Dijonnaise
- 2 slices (about 1½ ounces) Canadian bacon
- 2 pineapple rings packed in juice, drained
- 2 tablespoons fruity tomato-based salsa

Directions

Split English muffin into halves and plate with the inside facing upward. Spread evenly with cream cheese followed by Dijonnaise.

Top each muffin half with one slice of Canadian bacon followed by one pineapple ring. Finish each off with a tablespoon of salsa and enjoy!

MAKES 1 SERVING

CHAPTER 5: CROWD PLEASERS

Whipping up breakfast or brunch for a crowd? These recipes will make EVERYONE happy . . . even the pickiest of humans. And the best part? No one would ever suspect these have totally low calorie counts. Yes!!!

YOU'LL NEED:

large bowl, medium
bowl, 12-cup muffin
pan, baking liners
(optional), nonstick
spray

PREP:

20 minutes

COOK:

25 minutes

FLUFFY-GOOD ZUCCHINI NUT MUFFINS

Forget the muffins . . . YOU'D have to be a nut to not enjoy these!

PER SERVING (⅑th of recipe, 1 muffin): 147 calories, 3.5g fat, 246mg sodium, 25g carbs, 2.5g fiber, 7g sugars, 4.5g protein

Ingredients

1 cup whole-wheat flour

½ cup all-purpose flour

⅔ cup Splenda No Calorie Sweetener (granulated)

⅓ cup brown sugar (not packed)

1½ teaspoons baking powder

1 teaspoon cinnamon

½ teaspoon ground nutmeg

½ teaspoon salt

1½ cups shredded zucchini (about 1 large zucchini)

½ cup fat-free liquid egg substitute

½ cup no-sugar-added applesauce

3 tablespoons light whipped butter or light buttery spread, room temperature

1 teaspoon vanilla extract

3 tablespoons crushed walnuts, divided

Directions

Preheat oven to 350 degrees.

In a large bowl, combine both types of flour, Splenda, brown sugar, baking powder, cinnamon, nutmeg, and salt. Set aside.

In a medium bowl, mix together the zucchini, egg substitute, applesauce, butter, and vanilla extract. Slowly add this mixture to the first bowl, and stir until thoroughly blended. Mix half the crushed walnuts (1½ tablespoons) into the batter.

Line 9 cups of a 12-cup muffin pan with baking liners and/or spray with nonstick spray. Evenly distribute batter among the 9 cups. Top each cup with a sprinkling of the remaining 1½ tablespoons crushed walnuts.

Bake in the oven for 20 to 25 minutes, until a toothpick poked into the center of a muffin comes out clean. Let cool and then enjoy!

MAKES 9 SERVINGS

HG Sweet Alternative!

Fan of plain sugar? Replace the Splenda in this recipe with an equal amount of granulated sugar, and each muffin will have 196 calories, 38g of carbs, and 22g of sugars. Yay!

YOU'LL NEED:

8-inch by 8-inch glass baking pan, nonstick spray, large bowl, whisk, microwave-safe bowl

PREP:

15 minutes

COOK:

55 minutes

For the Weight Watchers *PointsPlus*™ values of all the recipes in this book, check out hungry-girl.com/books. Yay!

HG'S BiG BREAKFAST CASSEROLE

Ooooh! A puffy AM casserole packed with eggs and onions and mushrooms and cheese and sausage-y goodness . . . AHHHHH!

PER SERVING (¼ of casserole): 176 calories, 1.25g fat, 852mg sodium, 10g carbs, 2g fiber, 4g sugars, 28g protein

Ingredients

3 cups fat-free liquid egg substitute
½ cup light plain soymilk
1 cup frozen sausage-style (or ground-beef-style) soy crumbles
1 tablespoon dry onion dip/soup mix
1 cup sliced mushrooms
½ cup thinly sliced onion
½ cup thinly sliced green bell pepper
¼ cup sliced tomato
½ cup shredded fat-free cheddar cheese
Optional: salt, black pepper

Directions

Preheat oven to 350 degrees.

Spray an 8-inch by 8-inch glass baking pan with nonstick spray. Set aside.

In a large bowl, combine egg substitute with soymilk and whisk for about 1 minute. Stir in soy crumbles and onion dip/soup mix. Set aside.

Put mushrooms, onion, and pepper in a microwave-safe bowl. Add 2 tablespoons water, cover, and microwave until veggies have softened, about 3 minutes.

Once cool enough to handle, drain any excess water from the microwave-safe bowl. Evenly place vegetables in the bottom of the baking pan. Pour the egg mixture over the veggies.

Bake in the oven for about 25 minutes. Carefully remove pan from the oven. Evenly place tomato over the egg and sprinkle with cheese.

Return to the oven and bake until firm, about 25 minutes.

Let cool slightly, slice into quarters, and serve it up! If you like, season to taste with salt and black pepper!

MAKES 4 SERVINGS

small microwave-safe
bowl, medium bowl,
large baking sheet,
nonstick spray,
rolling pin (optional)

HG Sweet Alternative!

Swap out the Splenda in this recipe for the same amount of granulated sugar, and each serving will have 147 calories, 22.5g of carbs, and 9g of sugars. Not bad!

📷 **For a pic of this recipe, see the first photo insert. Yay!**

CRAZY-DELICIOUS CHEESY CHERRY DANISH

This is one of those recipes that's actually TOO GOOD to not try. Warning: You may cry actual tears when you taste it . . .

PER SERVING (1/8th of recipe, 1 slice): 135 calories, 4.75g fat, 312mg sodium, 19.5g carbs, 0.5g fiber, 6g sugars, 4g protein

Ingredients

Icing
1½ teaspoons Splenda No Calorie Sweetener (granulated)
1 teaspoon powdered sugar
1 teaspoon cornstarch
1 drop vanilla extract
1 tablespoon Jet-Puffed Marshmallow Creme
1 tablespoon Cool Whip Free, thawed

Danish
Half an 8-ounce tub fat-free cream cheese, room temperature
¼ cup old-fashioned oats
2 tablespoons Splenda No Calorie Sweetener (granulated)
1 tablespoon light vanilla soymilk
¼ teaspoon almond extract
1 cup frozen unsweetened dark sweet cherries, thawed
1 package Pillsbury Crescent Recipe Creations Seamless Dough Sheet

Directions

Preheat oven to 350 degrees.

To make the icing, combine Splenda, powdered sugar, and cornstarch in a small microwave-safe bowl. Add vanilla extract and 1½ teaspoons cold water, and mix until ingredients have dissolved.

Add Marshmallow Creme and microwave for 5 seconds, or until creme is soft enough to fold into mixture. Stir until smooth. Add Cool Whip and stir again, until evenly combined. Refrigerate icing until you're ready to ice the Danish.

In a medium bowl, combine cream cheese, oats, Splenda, soymilk, and almond extract, and stir until thoroughly mixed. Fold in cherries and set aside. This is your filling.

Spray a large baking sheet with nonstick spray. Roll out dough on the sheet into a large rectangle of even thickness. Arrange baking sheet in front of you so that the short sides are on the left and right and the long sides are on the top and bottom. Spoon cherry filling lengthwise across the middle third of the dough, leaving 1-inch borders on the left and right of the filling.

Starting from the top, make vertical cuts—about 1 inch apart—along the top section of the dough, stopping about ½ inch above the filling. Repeat with the bottom section of the dough, cutting upward toward the filling. This will create 1-inch-wide strips of dough on both the top and bottom of the filling.

Alternate folding the 1-inch strips from the top and the bottom over the filling, covering filling completely and creating a criss-crossed, "braided" appearance. After all the strips have been folded, fold the left and right sides of the dough in toward the filling, so filling cannot escape, and pat firmly to seal.

Bake in the oven for 15 to 20 minutes, until pastry is crispy and golden brown. Allow to cool completely.

Just before serving, drizzle entire Danish with icing. Cut into 8 slices and indulge! (P.S. Refrigerate leftovers.)

MAKES 8 SERVINGS

YOU'LL NEED:

12-cup muffin pan, rolling pin (optional), nonstick spray, large skillet

PREP:

10 minutes

COOK:

25 minutes

EGG CUPS A LA HUNGRY

These packed-with-yum pastry cups are so good! Make 'em the next time you have people over for breakfast or brunch, and watch heads explode! You know, from the deliciousness . . .

PER SERVING (1/12th of recipe, 1 egg cup): 118 calories, 4.75g fat, 370mg sodium, 9g carbs, <0.5g fiber, 2g sugars, 7.5g protein

Ingredients

1 package Pillsbury Crescent Recipe Creations Seamless Dough Sheet

4 frozen meatless or turkey sausage patties with about 80 calories each

2 cups fat-free liquid egg substitute

4 wedges The Laughing Cow Light Creamy Swiss cheese

Directions

Preheat oven to 375 degrees.

Spray a 12-cup muffin pan with nonstick spray and set aside.

Roll out dough into a large rectangle of even thickness. Cut into 12 equally sized squares. Place a square of dough into each cup of the muffin pan, pressing it into the bottom and up along the sides.

Bake in the oven until golden brown, 8 to 10 minutes. Once cool enough to handle, remove from the pan and set aside.

Meanwhile, bring a large skillet sprayed with nonstick spray to medium heat on the stove. Add sausage patties and cook until hot and cooked through, about 4 minutes per side. Once cool enough to handle, crumble or chop and set aside.

If needed, clean and dry skillet. Re-spray skillet and bring to medium-high heat on the stove. Add egg substitute and scramble until mostly cooked, about 3 minutes.

Add sausage and cheese to the skillet, breaking cheese wedges into pieces as you add them. Continue to scramble until egg substitute is fully cooked and cheese has melted, about 1 minute.

Evenly distribute the scrambled egg mixture among the cooked dough cups. Let cool slightly and then dig in!

MAKES 12 SERVINGS

YOU'LL NEED:

sharp serrated knife,
2 large baking sheets,
small microwave-safe
bowl, pastry brush,
large skillet, nonstick
spray

PREP:

5 minutes

COOK:

15 minutes

For a pic
of this recipe,
see the first
photo insert.
Yay!

BREAKFAST BRUSCHETTA

Egg bruschetta? Yup! Who says that's weird? Kooks, that's who. This recipe takes the Italian favorite to a whole new level.

PER SERVING (⅛th of recipe, 4 pieces): 132 calories, 2.75g fat, 335mg sodium, 17g carbs, 0.5g fiber, 1.5g sugars, 9g protein

Ingredients

One to two 2-inch-wide French baguettes
    (about 8 ounces total)
¼ cup light whipped butter or light buttery spread
1 teaspoon garlic powder
2 cups fat-free liquid egg substitute
2 plum tomatoes, chopped
½ cup chopped fresh basil
Optional: salt, black pepper

Directions

Preheat oven to 450 degrees.

Using a sharp serrated knife, carefully cut baguettes into 32 half-inch-thick slices. (Discard the ends or reserve for another use.) Spray two large baking sheets with nonstick spray and evenly place bread on the sheets. Set aside.

Place butter in a small microwave-safe bowl, and microwave until melted, about 15 seconds.

Using a pastry brush, brush each slice of bread with melted butter and sprinkle with garlic powder.

Bake in the oven until warm and crispy, about 8 minutes.

Meanwhile, bring a large skillet sprayed with nonstick spray to medium-high heat on the stove. Add egg substitute and scramble until mostly cooked, about 3 minutes.

Add tomatoes and basil to the skillet and continue to scramble until fully cooked, about 1 minute.

Evenly distribute scrambled egg mixture among the baked bread slices. If you like, season with salt and pepper. Enjoy!

MAKES 8 SERVINGS

YOU'LL NEED:

small microwave-safe bowl, medium bowl, large baking sheet, nonstick spray, rolling pin (optional)

PREP:

20 minutes

COOK:

20 minutes

* For more recipes, plus food finds, tips 'n tricks, and MORE, sign up for FREE daily emails at hungry-girl.com!

CHOCOLATE-CHiPPY CHEESE DANiSH

This sweet morning pastry doubles as a decadent dessert. It's sooooo awesome and chocolatey!!!

PER SERVING (1/8th of recipe, 1 slice): 141 calories, 6g fat, 313mg sodium, 18.5g carbs, 0.5g fiber, 6g sugars, 4g protein

Ingredients

Icing
1½ teaspoons Splenda No Calorie Sweetener (granulated)
1 teaspoon powdered sugar
1 teaspoon cornstarch
1 drop vanilla extract
1 tablespoon Jet-Puffed Marshmallow Creme
1 tablespoon Cool Whip Free, thawed

Danish
Half an 8-ounce tub fat-free cream cheese, room temperature
2 tablespoons Splenda No Calorie Sweetener (granulated)
1 tablespoon light vanilla soymilk
½ teaspoon vanilla extract
¼ teaspoon cinnamon
¼ cup old-fashioned oats
2 tablespoons mini semi-sweet chocolate chips
1 package Pillsbury Crescent Recipe Creations
    Seamless Dough Sheet

Directions

Preheat oven to 350 degrees.

To make the icing, combine Splenda, powdered sugar, and cornstarch in a small microwave-safe bowl. Add vanilla extract and 1½ teaspoons cold water, and mix until ingredients have dissolved.

Add Marshmallow Creme and microwave for 5 seconds, or until creme is soft enough to combine with mixture. Stir until smooth. Add Cool Whip and stir again, until evenly combined. Refrigerate until you're ready to ice the Danish.

In a medium bowl, combine cream cheese, Splenda, soymilk, vanilla extract, and cinnamon, and stir until thoroughly mixed. Fold in oats and chocolate chips, and set aside. This is your filling.

Spray a large baking sheet with nonstick spray. Roll out dough on the sheet into a large rectangle of even thickness. Arrange baking sheet so that the short sides are on the left and right and the long sides are on the top and bottom. Spoon filling lengthwise across the middle third of the dough, leaving 1-inch borders on the left and right of the filling.

Starting from the top, make vertical cuts—about 1 inch apart—along the top section of the dough, stopping about ½ inch above the filling. Repeat with the bottom section of the dough, cutting upward toward the filling. This will create 1-inch-wide strips of dough on both the top and bottom of the filling.

Alternate folding the 1-inch strips from the top and the bottom sections over the filling, covering it completely and creating a criss-crossed or "braided" appearance. After all the strips have been folded, fold the left and right sides of the dough in toward the filling, so filling cannot escape, and press firmly to seal.

Bake in the oven for 15 to 20 minutes, until pastry is crispy and light golden brown. Allow to cool completely.

Just before serving, drizzle entire Danish with icing. Cut into 8 slices and indulge! (P.S. Refrigerate leftovers.)

MAKES 8 SERVINGS

HG Sweet Alternative!

Trade the Splenda in this recipe for an equal amount of granulated sugar, and each serving will have 153 calories, 21.5g of carbs, and 9g of sugars. Still a bargain!

QUICHE ME BACON TARTS

Are they quiches or are they tarts? Ahhhh, who cares? As long as they have bacon (and, um, THEY DO) . . .

PER SERVING (⅛ᵗʰ of recipe, 2 tarts): 162 calories, 7.5g fat, 501mg sodium, 17g carbs, <0.5g fiber, 3.5g sugars, 6.5g protein

Ingredients

3 slices center-cut bacon or turkey bacon

2 wedges The Laughing Cow Light Creamy Swiss cheese

⅔ cup fat-free liquid egg substitute

2 tablespoons diced onion

2 tablespoons diced green bell pepper

1 package Pillsbury Crescent Recipe Creations Seamless Dough Sheet

Directions

Preheat oven to 375 degrees.

Bring a skillet sprayed with nonstick spray to medium heat on the stove. Add bacon and cook until crispy, about 4 minutes per side. Set aside.

Put cheese wedges in a medium-large microwave-safe bowl, and microwave until warm, about 20 seconds. Stir until smooth. Add egg substitute, mix well, and set aside.

Remove skillet from heat, re-spray, and return to medium heat on the stove. Add onion and pepper and, stirring occasionally, cook until softened, about 2 minutes. Pat veggies dry, if needed, and transfer to the bowl with the egg substitute.

Crumble or chop bacon into bite-sized pieces and add to the bowl. Mix well and set aside.

Spray a 12-cup muffin pan with nonstick spray and set aside.

Roll out dough into a large rectangle of even thickness. Cut into 12 equally sized squares. Place a square of dough into each cup of the muffin pan, pressing it into the bottom and up along the sides.

Evenly distribute egg mixture among the dough cups. Bake in the oven until dough is lightly browned and egg mixture is fully cooked, about 14 minutes.

Allow to cool slightly, and then serve and enjoy!

MAKES 6 SERVINGS

Need a little dough help?

Go to page 123 for the lowdown on working with the stuff . . .

YOU'LL NEED:

skillet, nonstick spray, 2 bowls, whisk, 8-inch by 8-inch baking pan

PREP:

10 minutes

CHILL:

30 minutes

COOK:

65 minutes

For the Weight Watchers *PointsPlus*™ values of all the recipes in this book, check out hungry-girl.com/books. Yay!

HAM & CHEESE EGG STRATA BAKE

This recipe is unique yet has all the traditional and beloved breakfast flavors. A brunch-time favorite in HG land!

PER SERVING (⅛th of recipe): 164 calories, 1.5g fat, 781mg sodium, 15.5g carbs, 3.5g fiber, 2g sugars, 23g protein

Ingredients

2 cups sliced mushrooms

1 cup chopped green bell pepper

3 cups fat-free liquid egg substitute

1 tablespoon Hellmann's/Best Foods Dijonnaise

½ cup light plain soymilk

¼ teaspoon salt

⅛ teaspoon black pepper

3 light English muffins

3 ounces cooked lean ham, chopped

½ cup shredded fat-free cheddar cheese, divided

Directions

Bring a skillet sprayed with nonstick spray to medium-high heat on the stove. Add mushrooms and bell pepper and, stirring occasionally, cook until softened, about 5 minutes.

Transfer cooked veggies to a bowl lined with paper towels to absorb excess moisture. Pat thoroughly with additional paper towels, if needed. Set aside.

In a separate bowl, whisk together egg substitute, Dijonnaise, soymilk, salt, and black pepper. Add veggies and stir. Set aside.

Lightly toast English muffins and tear into bite-sized pieces. Evenly place half of the muffin pieces in an 8-inch by 8-inch baking pan sprayed with nonstick spray. Evenly top with half of the ham and ¼ cup cheese, followed by remaining muffin pieces and remaining ham.

Pour egg mixture evenly over the contents of the baking pan. Sprinkle with remaining ¼ cup cheese.

Cover and refrigerate for 30 minutes. Meanwhile, preheat oven to 325 degrees.

Bake in the oven until firm, about 1 hour.

Let stand for 15 minutes. Then serve and enjoy!

MAKES 6 SERVINGS

large bowl, medium
bowl, whisk, 12-cup
muffin pan, baking
liners (optional),
nonstick spray

PREP:

10 minutes

COOK:

20 minutes

CORN MEGAMUFFINS

These are just like traditional corn muffins . . . only they have
around HALF the calories. You'd never know it though—they're
sweet, moist, and packed with creamy corn goodness!

PER SERVING (⅑th of recipe, 1 muffin): 158 calories, 0.5g fat,
358mg sodium, 32g carbs, 1.5g fiber, 9g sugars, 6g protein

Ingredients

1 cup all-purpose flour

¾ cup yellow cornmeal

¼ cup Splenda No Calorie Sweetener (granulated)

¼ cup granulated sugar

1 tablespoon baking powder

¼ teaspoon salt

1½ cups canned cream-style corn

¾ cup fat-free liquid egg substitute

¾ cup fat-free plain Greek yogurt

Directions

Preheat oven to 375 degrees.

Combine flour, cornmeal, Splenda, sugar, baking powder, and
salt in a large bowl. Mix well and set aside. In a separate
medium bowl, mix together corn, egg substitute, and yogurt.
Whisk thoroughly. Add contents of the medium bowl to the
large one, and stir until completely mixed.

Line 9 cups of a 12-cup muffin pan with baking liners and/or
spray with nonstick spray. Evenly distribute batter among the
9 cups—cups will be VERY full. (We don't call 'em MegaMuffins
for nothin'!)

Bake in the oven for 15 to 20 minutes, until a toothpick inserted into the center of a muffin comes out clean. Allow to cool and then enjoy!

MAKES 9 SERVINGS

HG Sweet Alternative!

Swap the Splenda in this recipe for the same amount of granulated sugar, and each muffin will have 174 calories, 36g of carbs, and 14g of sugars. Swell!

YOU'LL NEED:

baking sheet,
nonstick spray,
blender or food
processor, medium
bowl, large bowl

PREP:

10 minutes

COOK:

15 minutes

COFFEE CAKE SCONES

These lightened-up treats are sweet, cinnamon-y, and amazing in the morning with your favorite coffee. Hooray for guilt-free scones!!!

PER SERVING (¼th of recipe, 1 scone): 153 calories, 4g fat, 242mg sodium, 28.5g carbs, 6g fiber, 4g sugars, 4g protein

Ingredients

Topping

½ cup Fiber One Original bran cereal

2 tablespoons fat-free liquid egg substitute

1 tablespoon brown sugar (not packed)

1 tablespoon light whipped butter or light buttery spread, room temperature

¾ teaspoon cinnamon

¼ teaspoon vanilla extract

Dash ground nutmeg

Scones

⅔ cup old-fashioned oats

⅓ cup Bisquick Heart Smart Baking Mix

⅓ cup light vanilla soymilk

1 tablespoon brown sugar (not packed)

2 teaspoons light whipped butter or light buttery spread, room temperature

2 teaspoons cinnamon

½ teaspoon baking powder

Directions

Preheat oven to 400 degrees.

Spray a baking sheet with nonstick spray and set aside.

In a blender or food processor, grind cereal to a breadcrumb-like consistency. Transfer crumbs to a medium bowl, and add all other topping ingredients. Stir until completely mixed. Set aside.

Combine all scone ingredients in a large bowl. Mix well. Evenly form and place four mounds of batter on the baking sheet. Bake in the oven until mostly firm, about 8 minutes.

Remove sheet from the oven. Using your fingers to help form the crumbs, evenly top each scone with the topping mixture, lightly pressing the crumbs into the scones. Return sheet to the oven, and bake until firm and cooked through, about 4 minutes.

Allow to cool slightly. Then enjoy!

MAKES 4 SERVINGS

large loaf pan (about 9 inches by 5 inches), nonstick spray, 2 large bowls, small microwave-safe bowl

PREP:

20 minutes

COOK:

50 minutes

📷 **For a pic of this recipe, see the first photo insert. Yay!**

BANANA SPLiT BREAD

Yup, a banana split oatmeal is hanging out on page 32, and here's a banana split bread. Who loves you?!?!

PER SERVING (⅛th of recipe, 1 thick slice): 169 calories, 1.5g fat, 267mg sodium, 35.5g carbs, 3.75g fiber, 13g sugars, 5g protein

Ingredients

1¼ cups whole-wheat flour
¼ cup all-purpose flour
½ cup Splenda No Calorie Sweetener (granulated)
2 teaspoons baking powder
½ teaspoon salt
1½ cups mashed ripe bananas (about 4 bananas)
½ cup fat-free liquid egg substitute
½ cup no-sugar-added applesauce
1 teaspoon vanilla extract
2 tablespoons mini semi-sweet chocolate chips
¼ cup low-sugar (or sugar-free) strawberry preserves
Optional topping: Fat Free Reddi-wip

Directions

Preheat oven to 350 degrees.

Spray a large loaf pan with nonstick spray and set aside.

In a large bowl, combine both types of flour, Splenda, baking powder, and salt. Mix well and set aside.

In another large bowl, combine mashed bananas, egg substitute, applesauce, and vanilla extract. Add this mixture to the bowl with the dry ingredients, and stir until just blended.

Gently mix chocolate chips into the bread batter. Spoon half of the batter into the loaf pan and set aside.

Place preserves in a microwave-safe bowl and microwave until warm and softened, about 20 seconds. Stir until smooth.

Drizzle preserves over the batter in the pan. Evenly top with remaining batter.

Bake in the oven for 50 minutes, or until a knife inserted into the center comes out clean.

Allow to cool. Remove from pan and cut into 8 slices. Serve and, if you like, top with Reddi-wip!

MAKES 8 SERVINGS

HG Natural Sweetener Alternative!

Replace the Splenda with an equal amount of a no-calorie granulated stevia product that measures cup-for-cup like sugar.

YOU'LL NEED:

large baking sheet,
nonstick spray,
rolling pin (optional)

PREP:

20 minutes

COOK:

15 minutes

EARLY-RISER PIGS IN A BLANKET

Sweet 'n sausage-y, these flaky li'l guys are all wrapped up and ready for some serious chewing action.

PER SERVING (⅛th of recipe, 2 pigs in a blanket with 2 tablespoons syrup): 185 calories, 7.75g fat, 590mg sodium, 21.5g carbs, 2g fiber, 3.5g sugars, 10.5g protein

Ingredients

- 1 package Pillsbury Reduced Fat Crescent rolls refrigerated dough
- 16 meatless sausage-style breakfast links with about 40 calories each, thawed if frozen
- 32 sprays zero-calorie butter spray
- ½ teaspoon cinnamon, more or less to taste
- 2 teaspoons powdered sugar
- 1 cup sugar-free pancake syrup

Directions

Preheat oven to 375 degrees.

Spray a large baking sheet with nonstick spray and set aside.

Slightly stretch or roll out one of the triangle-shaped portions of dough, forming a larger triangle. Cut it into 2 long narrow triangles. Beginning at the base of each triangle, roll a breakfast link up in the dough until the point of each triangle wraps around the center. Place both mini pigs on the baking sheet, about 1 inch apart.

Repeat 7 times with remaining ingredients, so that you have 16 evenly spaced pigs in a blanket on the sheet. Spray the tops with butter spray, about 2 sprays per blanketed pig. Immediately sprinkle with cinnamon.

Bake in the oven for 12 to 14 minutes, until dough appears slightly browned and crispy.

Sprinkle with powdered sugar, and then let cool slightly. Dip your piggies in syrup (or drizzle them with the stuff) and enjoy!

MAKES 8 SERVINGS

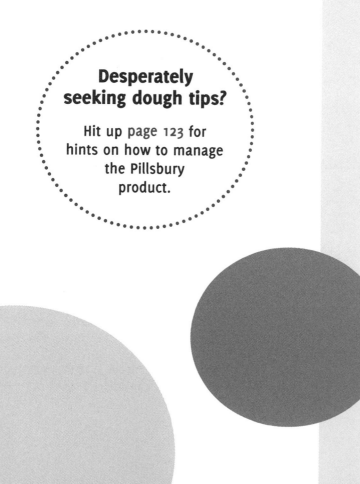

Desperately seeking dough tips?

Hit up page 123 for hints on how to manage the Pillsbury product.

YOU'LL NEED:

bowl, large
oven-safe skillet,
nonstick spray,
aluminum foil
(optional),
microwave-safe bowl

PREP:

15 minutes

COOK:

20 minutes

📷 **For a pic of this recipe, see the first photo insert. Yay!**

RATATOUILLE FRITTATA

Yup, it's a great breakfast. But this eggplant-packed egg recipe is so satisfying and delicious, people love to gobble it up any time of day!

PER SERVING (¼ of frittata): 140 calories, 4g fat, 508mg sodium, 11g carbs, 2.5g fiber, 5.5g sugars, 14g protein

Ingredients

1½ cups fat-free liquid egg substitute
2 tablespoons finely chopped fresh basil
½ teaspoon chopped garlic
⅛ teaspoon salt, or more to taste
1 cup cubed eggplant
½ cup chopped red bell pepper
½ cup sliced and halved zucchini
½ cup canned fire-roasted diced tomatoes, drained
½ cup roughly chopped onion
1 teaspoon olive oil
½ cup shredded part-skim mozzarella cheese
¾ cup canned crushed tomatoes
Dash Italian seasoning, or more to taste
Dash crushed red pepper, or more to taste
Dash black pepper, or more to taste

Directions

Preheat broiler.

In a bowl, combine egg substitute, basil, garlic, and salt. Stir thoroughly and set aside.

Bring a large oven-safe skillet sprayed with nonstick spray to medium heat on the stove. (If you're not sure if the handle of your pan is oven-safe, wrap the handle with aluminum foil before heating.) Add eggplant, bell pepper, zucchini, diced tomatoes, and onion, and drizzle with oil. Stirring occasionally, cook until softened, about 8 minutes.

Add egg mixture to the skillet, tilting the skillet back and forth to ensure egg mixture is evenly distributed. If needed, run a spatula along the sides of the pan to help egg flow underneath the veggies. Sprinkle cheese over the top and cook for 2 minutes.

Place skillet under the broiler and broil for about 4 minutes, until egg mixture has puffed up and set. Set aside to cool slightly.

Meanwhile, in a microwave-safe bowl, combine crushed tomatoes, Italian seasoning, crushed red pepper, and black pepper. If you like, season to taste with additional spices. Mix thoroughly and warm in the microwave, about 1 minute. Stir well and set aside.

Slice frittata into quarters and top or serve with seasoned crushed tomatoes. Enjoy!

MAKES 4 SERVINGS

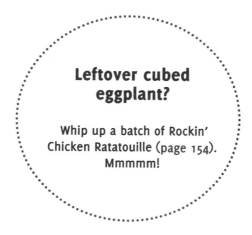

Leftover cubed eggplant?

Whip up a batch of Rockin' Chicken Ratatouille (page 154). Mmmmm!

YOU'LL NEED:
skillet, nonstick spray,
baking sheet, rolling
pin (optional), sharp
serrated knife

PREP:

20 minutes

COOK:

20 minutes

*For full-color
photos of all the recipes
in this book, check out
hungry-girl.com/books.
Woohoo!

EGGA-PINWHEELS

Weeeee! These are beautiful AND delicious. They also travel well—so whip
up a batch, bring 'em to a friend's house, and reheat for instant YUM.

PER SERVING (⅛th of recipe, 1 pinwheel): 134 calories, 5g fat,
555mg sodium, 13.5g carbs, <1g fiber, 3g sugars, 8.5g protein

Ingredients

1 cup fat-free liquid egg substitute
1 package Pillsbury Crescent Recipe Creations
    Seamless Dough Sheet
4 ounces (about 16 slices) shaved/thinly sliced lean deli ham
3 slices fat-free American cheese, broken into pieces

Directions

Preheat oven to 350 degrees.

Bring a skillet sprayed with nonstick spray to medium heat on
the stove. Add egg substitute and scramble until fully cooked,
about 3 minutes. Remove from heat and set aside. Prepare a
baking sheet by spraying it with nonstick spray, and set that
aside as well.

Roll out dough into a large rectangle of even thickness, with
the shorter sides on the right and left.

Evenly distribute ham over the dough, leaving a 2-inch border
of exposed dough along the right side only. Evenly top ham with
scrambled eggs and cheese pieces.

Starting with the left side, roll up dough tightly into a log, and
seal by pinching together the right edge and the roll itself.

Using a sharp serrated knife, slice the log into 8 pinwheels, and lay them flat on the baking sheet, evenly spaced.

Bake for 15 minutes, or until golden brown. Allow to cool slightly, and then chew!

MAKES 8 SERVINGS

Dough the Right Thing . . .

Tips for Working with Refrigerated Dough

* Make sure your workspace is clean and dry before you lay out the dough. If cutting's involved, pick an appropriate surface.

* If the dough is sticky and hard to unroll, rub a bit of flour on your hands or rolling pin.

* The sheet may be thicker in some places than others. Use a rolling pin or your hands to smooth the dough to an even thickness.

* If you spot a tear in the dough, pinch the torn edges together, and use a rolling pin to smooth it out.

* When cutting uncooked dough, a pizza cutter is a GREAT tool.

* Little-known fact: Pillsbury Crescent Recipe Creations Seamless Dough Sheet and Reduced Fat Crescent roll dough are essentially the exact same thing! (One's perforated, and they list different serving sizes, but other than that . . .) So if you need one and can only find the other, just seal up the perforations by hand *or* slice it into eight triangles as needed!

LUNCH & DINNER

Majorly satisfying no-guilt
dishes for afternoon and
evening meals are right here,
right now. Your food-related
dreams are about to
come true . . .

CHAPTER 6: BIG SALADS

There's simply no way around it. Big. Salads. Rock. And these are 47 percent better than any others out there. It's true. Why doubt it? Let the preppin' & chewin' begin . . .

YOU'LL NEED:

large plate or bowl,
skillet, nonstick spray,
small bowl

PREP:

5 minutes

COOK:

15 minutes

IN-N-OUTRAGEOUS ANiMAL-STYLE SALAD

This salad is a no-guilt take on an LA burger favorite ... It is a MUST-TRY!

PER SERVING (entire recipe): 270 calories, 4.25g fat, 1,032mg sodium, 39.5g carbs, 11.75g fiber, 17.5g sugars, 21g protein

Ingredients

4 cups chopped romaine lettuce
1 large tomato, chopped
2 tablespoons roughly chopped dill pickle
½ cup chopped onion
1 frozen meatless hamburger-style patty with about 100 calories
1 teaspoon yellow mustard
2 tablespoons shredded fat-free cheddar cheese
2 tablespoons fat-free Thousand Island dressing

Directions

Place lettuce on a large plate or in a large bowl and top with chopped tomato and pickle. Set aside.

Bring a skillet sprayed with nonstick spray to high heat on the stove. Add onion and cook until slightly browned and softened, about 3 minutes. Transfer to the large plate/bowl and set aside.

Remove skillet from heat, re-spray, and bring to medium heat. Add patty and cook for about 4 minutes per side, until cooked through.

Once cool enough to handle, crumble or chop patty and place in a small bowl. Add mustard and toss to coat.

Transfer the mustard-y burger bites to the salad. Evenly top salad with cheese and dressing. Now EAT!

MAKES 1 SERVING

THANKSGIVING IN A SALAD BOWL

Every day can feel like Thanksgiving with this super-delicious salad! (Sorry, turkeys!)

YOU'LL NEED:
large plate or bowl, small bowl, whisk

PREP:
10 minutes

PER SERVING (entire recipe): 296 calories, 7g fat, 497mg sodium, 28.5g carbs, 5g fiber, 19g sugars, 32g protein

Ingredients

Salad
2 cups chopped romaine lettuce
2 cups chopped spinach
3 ounces cooked and chopped skinless lean turkey breast
2 tablespoons dried sweetened cranberries, chopped
2 tablespoons crumbled fat-free feta cheese
1 tablespoon chopped pecans

Dressing
1 tablespoon canned whole cranberry sauce
½ tablespoon balsamic vinegar
½ teaspoon honey mustard
Dash each salt and black pepper

Directions

On a large plate or in a large bowl, combine all salad ingredients. Mix well and set aside.

In a small bowl, combine dressing ingredients and whisk until thoroughly mixed. Pour dressing over the salad or serve it on the side. Mmmmm!!!

MAKES 1 SERVING

Don't let feta get bored in the fridge.

Turn to the cheese listing in the index, find the other feta recipes, and make something soon!

large plate or bowl,
small bowl, skillet,
nonstick spray

PREP:
10 minutes

COOK:
5 minutes

📷 **For a pic
of this recipe,
see the first
photo insert.
Yay!**

MEXI-LiCiOUS SHRiMP & CORN FANDANGO SALAD

Mexican flavors, shrimp, corn . . . and, um, FANDANGO!!!

PER SERVING (entire recipe): 260 calories, 2g fat,
622mg sodium, 39g carbs, 8g fiber, 15g sugars, 24g protein

Ingredients

3 cups chopped romaine lettuce
1 cup dry coleslaw mix
½ cup chopped tomatoes
½ cup chopped cucumber
⅓ cup chopped red onion
2 tablespoons chopped fresh cilantro
1 tablespoon seasoned rice vinegar
½ tablespoon lime juice
1 teaspoon Mexican hot sauce
½ cup frozen yellow corn
3 ounces cooked and chilled ready-to-eat shrimp

Directions

Combine lettuce with slaw mix on a large plate or in a large bowl.
Top with tomato, cucumber, onion, and cilantro. Set aside.

To make the dressing, combine vinegar, lime juice, and hot sauce in
a small bowl, and mix thoroughly. Set aside.

Bring a skillet sprayed with nonstick spray to high heat on the
stove. Add corn and cook until thawed and slightly blackened, about
5 minutes. Transfer to the large plate/bowl.

Add shrimp and drizzle dressing over the salad. Grab a fork and dig in!

MAKES 1 SERVING

ISLAND TIME SALAD

Another fine HG salad overflowing with shrimp and lots of other good stuff. Best part? The MANGO!!! Mmmmmmm . . .

PER SERVING (entire recipe): 275 calories, 2.75g fat, 695mg sodium, 42g carbs, 9.5g fiber, 22.5g sugars, 24.5g protein

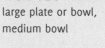

Ingredients

3 cups chopped romaine lettuce
1 cup dry coleslaw mix
½ cup diced mango
¼ cup diced cucumber
¼ cup diced red bell pepper
¼ cup canned black beans, drained and rinsed
3 ounces cooked and chilled ready-to-eat shrimp, chopped
2 tablespoons fat-free mayonnaise
1 tablespoon orange juice
1 teaspoon seasoned rice wine vinegar

Directions

Place lettuce on a large plate or in a large bowl and set aside.

Combine all remaining ingredients in a medium bowl and toss well to mix.

Top lettuce with the mixture and enjoy!

MAKES 1 SERVING

YOU'LL NEED:
large plate or bowl,
small bowl, skillet,
nonstick spray

PREP:
10 minutes

COOK:
5 minutes

ASIAN BBQ SHRIMP SALAD

Crustaceans rock. That's why this salad is packed with shrimp. There's some BBQ yumminess thrown in for good measure too. Weeee!

PER SERVING (entire recipe): 262 calories, 3.75g fat, 643mg sodium, 28.5g carbs, 6.75g fiber, 17g sugars, 28g protein

Ingredients

4 cups mixed field greens
1 cup dry coleslaw mix
½ cup grape or cherry tomatoes, halved
2 tablespoons chopped scallions
2 tablespoons canned tomato sauce
1 tablespoon sweet Asian chili sauce
1 teaspoon crushed dry-roasted peanuts
½ teaspoon brown sugar (not packed)
½ teaspoon seasoned rice vinegar
¼ teaspoon garlic powder
4 ounces raw shrimp, peeled, tails removed, deveined
½ cup sugar snap peas

Directions

Place field greens on a large plate or in a large bowl, and evenly top with coleslaw mix, tomatoes, and scallions. Set aside.

In a small bowl, combine tomato sauce, chili sauce, peanuts, brown sugar, vinegar, garlic powder, and 1 teaspoon water. Mix well and set aside.

Bring a skillet sprayed with nonstick spray to medium-high heat on the stove. Add shrimp and snap peas. Stirring occasionally, cook until shrimp are cooked through and snap peas have slightly softened, about 5 minutes.

Remove skillet from heat. Add sauce mixture to the skillet and mix well.

Place the saucy shrimp and veggies over your salad and enjoy!

MAKES 1 SERVING

HG Tip!

If you like your salad fully dressed, spritz this with some sesame-ginger spray dressing!!

YOU'LL NEED:
large plate or bowl, skillet, nonstick spray, small bowl

PREP:
10 minutes

COOK:
10 minutes

CLASSIC CHEESESTEAK SALAD

If you are Philly cheesesteak-obsessed, you will DIE over this salad. The steak, onions, and gooey cheese might send you over the edge. Be warned . . .

PER SERVING (entire recipe): 275 calories, 8g fat, 785mg sodium, 19g carbs, 4.5g fiber, 11.5g sugars, 32g protein

Ingredients

4 cups chopped romaine lettuce
⅓ cup sliced mushrooms
⅓ cup thinly sliced onion
4 ounces raw lean filet beefsteak, thinly sliced (freeze slightly before slicing)
Dash each salt and black pepper
1 slice fat-free American cheese
1½ tablespoons ketchup
½ tablespoon balsamic vinegar

Directions

Place lettuce on a large plate or in a large bowl and set aside.

Bring a skillet sprayed with nonstick spray to medium-high heat on the stove. Add mushrooms and onion. Stirring occasionally, cook until slightly browned, about 5 minutes.

Add veggies to the lettuce and set aside.

Remove skillet from heat, re-spray with nonstick spray, and return to medium-high heat. Season beef with a dash each of salt and pepper and add to the skillet. Flipping occasionally, cook until desired level of doneness is reached, about 2 minutes.

Break cheese slice into small strips. Place cheese on top of the beef in the skillet and continue to cook until cheese has melted slightly. Transfer the cheese-topped beef to the salad and set aside.

To make the dressing, in a small bowl, combine ketchup, vinegar, and ½ tablespoon of water. Mix thoroughly and drizzle over salad or serve on the side. Enjoy!

MAKES 1 SERVING

large plate or bowl, small bowl, large skillet, nonstick spray

PREP:

10 minutes

COOK:

10 minutes

📷 **For a pic of this recipe, see the first photo insert. Yay!**

HOT & COLD 10-VEGGIE EXPLOSION

There are HOT veggies, there are COLD veggies . . . There are so many gorgeous vegetables in this chopped salad, your eyes may pop right out of your face. Let's hope they don't, though.

PER SERVING (entire recipe): 216 calories, 3.75g fat, 539mg sodium, 41g carbs, 11.5g fiber, 19g sugars, 9.5g protein

Ingredients

4 cups chopped romaine lettuce

1 tomato, chopped

¼ cup canned sliced beets

¼ cup canned hearts of palm, sliced into coins

2 tablespoons sliced black olives

1½ tablespoons orange juice

½ tablespoon balsamic vinegar

½ tablespoon Hellmann's/Best Foods Dijonnaise

¼ cup frozen sweet yellow corn

½ cup chopped asparagus

½ cup sliced onion

½ cup sliced red bell pepper

½ cup sliced mushrooms

Directions

Place lettuce on a large plate or in a large bowl and evenly top with tomato, beets, hearts of palm, and olives. Set aside.

To make the dressing, in a small bowl, combine juice, vinegar, and Dijonnaise. Mix well and set aside.

Bring a large skillet sprayed with nonstick spray to high heat on the stove. Add corn and, stirring occasionally, cook until thawed and slightly blackened, about 3 minutes. Transfer corn to the salad and bring skillet to medium-high heat.

Add asparagus, onion, and bell pepper to the skillet. Stirring occasionally, cook until slightly softened, about 2 minutes.

Add mushrooms to the skillet and, stirring often, continue to cook until all veggies are softened, about 3 minutes.

Transfer cooked veggies to the salad. Top or serve salad with dressing and enjoy!

MAKES 1 SERVING

Whatcha gonna do with those leftover sliced olives?

Flip to olives in the index and check out your options.

grill pan, nonstick spray, large plate or bowl, small bowl

PREP:
10 minutes

COOK:
25 minutes

For the Weight Watchers *PointsPlus*™ values of all the recipes in this book, check out hungry-girl.com/books. Yay!

BBQ GRILLED VEGGIE SALAD

This salad is packed with grilled veggies and topped with a sweet-n-sassy balsamic BBQ dressing. The sun-dried tomatoes are a total added bonus!

PER SERVING (entire recipe): 234 calories, 6g fat, 688mg sodium, 43g carbs, 9.25g fiber, 19.5g sugars, 8.5g protein

Ingredients

1 large slice eggplant

⅛ teaspoon salt

1 small onion, sliced

1 small zucchini, sliced

1 portabella mushroom, sliced

3 cups chopped romaine lettuce

¼ cup sun-dried tomatoes packed in oil, drained and roughly chopped

2 tablespoons BBQ sauce with about 45 calories per 2-tablespoon serving

1 tablespoon balsamic vinegar

Optional: crushed black pepper

Directions

Sprinkle both sides of eggplant with salt and set aside.

Bring a grill pan sprayed with nonstick spray to medium-high heat. Lay onion and zucchini flat in the pan and cook until outsides are charred and insides are slightly soft, about 4 minutes per side. Set aside.

Lay portabella and eggplant flat in the pan and cook until outsides are charred and insides are slightly soft, 1 to 2 minutes per side. Set aside.

Place lettuce on a large plate or in a large bowl and top with tomatoes. Set aside.

In a small bowl combine BBQ sauce and balsamic vinegar and mix thoroughly. Set aside.

Chop grilled veggies into bite-sized pieces and place over the lettuce and tomatoes. Drizzle the BBQ-balsamic mixture over the entire salad and, if you like, sprinkle with crushed black pepper. Enjoy!

MAKES 1 SERVING

Have some extra eggplant?

Slice it up and make EZ Cheesy Lasagna for Two (page 232). YUM!!

YOU'LL NEED:
large plate or bowl,
baking sheet,
nonstick spray

PREP:
10 minutes

COOK:
10 minutes

NACHO-ED UP MEXI-CHOP

This salad is a must-chew for anyone who enjoys nachos. (This means you!)

PER SERVING (entire recipe): 274 calories, 3.75g fat, 1,084mg sodium, 47g carbs, 10.5g fiber, 7g sugars, 14.5g protein

Ingredients

4 cups chopped romaine lettuce
Two 6-inch corn tortillas
⅛ teaspoon salt
1 tablespoon sliced black olives
1 tablespoon jarred jalapeño slices
¼ cup fat-free refried beans
2 tablespoons shredded fat-free cheddar cheese
2 tablespoons fat-free sour cream
2 tablespoons salsa
1 tablespoon chopped scallions
Optional: hot sauce

Directions

Preheat oven to 400 degrees.

Place lettuce on a large plate or in a large bowl and set aside.

Place tortillas on a baking sheet sprayed with nonstick spray. Mist tortillas with nonstick spray and sprinkle with salt. Bake in the oven until crisp, about 4 minutes per side.

Once tortillas are cool enough to handle, break into bite-sized pieces and place over the lettuce.

Top lettuce and baked tortilla pieces evenly with olives and jalapeño slices. Add beans, cheese, sour cream, and salsa, in small evenly spaced spoonfuls.

Top with scallions and, if you like, add a few drops of hot sauce. Serve and enjoy!

MAKES 1 SERVING

Leftover olive alert!

There are SO many more recipes that call for sliced olives—just find olives in the index at the back of the book. See?!

FETA 'N FUJI CHICKEN SALAD

Feta cheese and apples . . . together in a salad?! Uhhhh, yeah. Got a problem with that? If you said "yes," that just means you haven't tried it yet.

PER SERVING (entire recipe): 290 calories, 5.75g fat, 799mg sodium, 31g carbs, 7g fiber, 18g sugars, 30g protein

Ingredients

Salad
4 cups chopped romaine lettuce
3 ounces cooked and chopped skinless lean chicken breast
½ Fuji apple, cored and chopped
¼ cup chopped seedless or seeded cucumber
¼ cup canned sliced beets, drained
3 tablespoons crumbled reduced-fat feta cheese

Dressing
1 tablespoon honey mustard
1 tablespoon fat-free mayonnaise
1 teaspoon cider vinegar
Dash black pepper

Directions

Place lettuce on a large plate or in a large bowl and evenly top with remaining salad ingredients. Set aside.

In a small bowl, combine dressing ingredients and mix well. Drizzle dressing over the salad or serve on the side. Enjoy!

MAKES 1 SERVING

Want MORE . . .

delicious uses for your crumbled cheese? Find feta in the index and have fun!

Egg Mugs and Breakfast Bowls

Super-Sized Berry-nana Oatmeal Parfait, p. 48

It's All Greek to Me Egg Mug, p. 19

Crunchy Beefy Taco Egg Mug, p. 18

S'mores Oatmeal, p. 42

PB&J Oatmeal Heaven, p. 52

Turkey Club B. Bowl, p. 47

Breakfast Plates and No-Cook B-fasts

Rockin' Red Velvet Pancakes, p. 60

Buenos Días Breakfast Fajitas, p. 70

Smokey Salmon Lettuce Wraps, p. 89

Creamy Crab Cakes Benedict, p. 66

Hawaiian B-fast Stacks, p. 92

Ratatouille Frittata, p. 120

Crazy-Delicious Cheesy Cherry Danish, p. 100

Banana Split Bread, p. 116

Breakfast Bruschetta, p. 104

BIG Salads and Return of the Foil Packs

Mexi-licious Shrimp & Corn Fandango Salad, p. 130

Lean 'n Green Fruity Tuna Bowl, p. 143

No-Nonsense Nacho Lettuce Cups, p. 158

Dreamy Butternut Chicken Foil Pack, p. 156

Hot & Cold 10-Veggie Explosion, p. 136

Buffalo Chicken Wing Macaroni & Cheese, p. 186

iHungry Spaghetti Tacos, p. 190

Cheeseburger Mashed Potato Parfaits, p. 174

Lasagna Cupcakes, p. 188

International Favorites

Takes-the-Cake Ziti Bake, p. 230

Sweet & Sour Chicken 1-2-3, p. 220

Nacho-rific Stuffed Chicken, p. 204

BLT Pizza, p. 256

Pizza-fied Grilled Cheese, p. 257

Loaded 'n Oated Spinach & Mushroom Girlfredo Pizza, p. 246

Sandwiches

The Skinny Elvis, p. 294

Grilled Fuji-n-Chick 'Wich, p. 288

Faux-Fried Mozzarella-n-Basil Eggplant Sandwiches, p. 292

Perfect Portabella Club, p. 290

LEAN 'N GREEN FRUiTY TUNA BOWL

This is a perfect light-n-fruity salad for a hot summer day—or even a cold wintery day, really. Basically, this salad ROCKS any time of year.

YOU'LL NEED:
skillet, nonstick spray, large plate or bowl, small bowl

PREP:
5 minutes

COOK:
10 minutes

For a pic of this recipe, see the first photo insert. Yay!

PER SERVING (entire recipe): 295 calories, 6g fat, 616mg sodium, 22.5g carbs, 5g fiber, 14.5g sugars, 37g protein

Ingredients

One 5-ounce raw sushi-grade ahi or yellowfin tuna steak
⅛ teaspoon salt
⅛ teaspoon black pepper
4 cups mixed field greens
½ cup thinly sliced seedless or seeded cucumber
¼ cup sliced strawberries
¼ cup red grapes, halved
1½ tablespoons thinly sliced almonds
1 tablespoon orange juice
1 tablespoon seasoned rice vinegar

Directions

Bring a skillet sprayed with nonstick spray to medium-high heat on stove. Season tuna steak with salt and pepper and add to the skillet. Cook until evenly seared on the outside and cooked through to your liking, at least 2 minutes per side. Set aside.

Place field greens on a large plate or in a large bowl and evenly top with cucumber, strawberries, grapes, and almonds. Set aside.

To make the dressing, combine orange juice with vinegar in a small bowl. Mix well and set aside.

Slice tuna steak and add to the salad. Drizzle the dressing over the salad and enjoy!

MAKES 1 SERVING

YOU'LL NEED:
microwave-safe bowl,
large plate or bowl

PREP:
10 minutes

COOK:
5 minutes

CHILL:
10 minutes

DECONSTRUCTED FALAFEL SALAD

Chickpea lovers and general falafel fans, here's a salad you will LOOOOOOOVE.

PER SERVING (entire recipe): 227 calories, 4g fat, 496mg sodium, 38g carbs, 12g fiber, 11.5g sugars, 13.5g protein

Ingredients

¼ cup thinly sliced red onion
¼ cup fat-free plain yogurt
¾ teaspoon lemon juice
¼ teaspoon ground cumin
¼ teaspoon garlic powder
1 teaspoon chopped fresh parsley
Dash each salt and black pepper, or more to taste
½ cup canned chickpeas, drained and rinsed
4 cups chopped romaine lettuce
¼ cup chopped seedless or seeded cucumber
1 small tomato, chopped
1 teaspoon sesame seeds

Directions

Place onion in a microwave-safe bowl and top with 2 tablespoons water. Cover and microwave for 2 minutes, or until onion has softened. Do not drain water.

To the bowl, add yogurt, lemon juice, cumin, garlic powder, parsley, salt, and pepper. Mix thoroughly. Add chickpeas and toss to coat. Refrigerate for at least 10 minutes.

Meanwhile, place lettuce on a large plate or in a large bowl and evenly top with cucumber and tomato. Once chickpea mixture has chilled, evenly spoon it over the salad. If you like, sprinkle with additional salt and pepper.

Sprinkle sesame seeds over the salad and enjoy!

MAKES 1 SERVING

PREP:

10 minutes

COOK:

5 minutes

CLASSIC CLUB SALAD

BACON!!!!! Now that you're paying attention, here's a decadent salad (which does contain bacon) that you'll likely enjoy immensely.

PER SERVING (entire recipe): 257 calories, 5.5g fat, 981mg sodium, 28.5g carbs, 8.25g fiber, 10.5g sugars, 29g protein

Ingredients

1 slice light white bread, cut into small squares
3 sprays zero-calorie butter spray
Dash garlic powder
4 cups chopped romaine lettuce
1 tomato, chopped
1 cup chopped cucumber
2 ounces cooked and chopped skinless lean turkey breast
2 tablespoons precooked real crumbled bacon
1 tablespoon fat-free mayonnaise
½ tablespoon white wine vinegar
1 teaspoon Dijon mustard

Directions

Preheat oven to 350 degrees.

To make the croutons, place bread squares on a baking sheet sprayed with nonstick spray. Evenly spray with butter spray and sprinkle with garlic powder. Bake in the oven until crispy, 3 to 5 minutes. Set aside.

Meanwhile, place lettuce on a large plate or in a large bowl and evenly top with tomato, cucumber, turkey, and bacon. Set aside.

In a small bowl, combine mayo, vinegar, and mustard. Mix well and drizzle over the salad.

Top salad with croutons and eat!

MAKES 1 SERVING

Need turkey-cooking tips?

Flip to page 167 for poultry-prepping assistance!

YOU'LL NEED:

small bowl, 2 large
bowls, large skillet or
wok, nonstick spray

PREP:

10 minutes

COOK:

10 minutes

✳ For full-color
photos of all the recipes
in this book, check out
hungry-girl.com/books.
Woohoo!

CLASSIC WARM ASIAN CHICKEN SALAD

A total classic . . . warm chicken, tons of veggies, and a sweet 'n spicy dressing. A complete yum-fest!

PER SERVING (½ of recipe): 222 calories, 2g fat, 1,042mg sodium, 18g carbs, 5g fiber, 9g sugars, 34g protein

Ingredients

2 tablespoons reduced-sodium/lite soy sauce
1½ tablespoons seasoned rice vinegar
1 teaspoon red chili sauce
1 teaspoon chopped garlic
6 cups spinach
8 ounces raw boneless skinless lean chicken breast, cubed
Dash each salt and black pepper
1 cup chopped mushrooms
¼ cup shredded carrots
2 cups bean sprouts
¼ cup chopped scallions

Directions

In a small bowl, combine soy sauce, vinegar, chili sauce, and chopped garlic. Mix well and set aside.

Evenly divide spinach between 2 large bowls and set aside.

Spray a large skillet or wok with nonstick spray and bring to medium-high heat on the stove. Season chicken with salt and pepper and add to the skillet/wok. Add mushrooms, carrots, bean sprouts, scallions, and 2 tablespoons water.

Stirring occasionally, cook until veggies have softened and chicken is fully cooked, about 5 minutes.

Give sauce mixture a stir and add to the skillet/wok. Stir and cook until sauce is evenly distributed and has thickened slightly, about 5 minutes.

Evenly divide chicken mixture among the spinach bowls. Allow chicken mixture to cool and spinach to wilt slightly.

Serve and enjoy!

MAKES 2 SERVINGS

CHAPTER 7: RETURN OF THE FOIL PACKS

They're back—and more delicious than EVER. Just assemble, wrap, and bake. Success!!! Stock up on that sturdy heavy-duty aluminum foil, people... It works best for these recipes!

bowl, nonstick spray,
heavy-duty aluminum
foil, baking sheet

For the Weight Watchers
PointsPlus™ values of
all the recipes in this
book, check out
hungry-girl.com/books.
Yay!

TOO-EZ FISH TACO SUPREME

A fish taco in a foil pack? Who says it can't be?! Don't be a non-believer.

PER SERVING (entire recipe, 1 taco): 258 calories, 3.25g fat, 337mg sodium, 30g carbs, 6g fiber, 5.5g sugars, 28.5g protein

Ingredients

4 ounces raw tilapia
⅓ cup thinly sliced onion
⅓ cup thinly sliced bell pepper
½ teaspoon taco seasoning mix
1 teaspoon lime juice
1 large corn tortilla
¼ cup canned black beans, drained and rinsed

Directions

Preheat oven to 400 degrees.

Place fish and sliced veggies in a bowl, and spray with a light mist of nonstick spray. Sprinkle with taco seasoning and lime juice, and then toss to combine. Set aside.

Lay a large piece of heavy-duty foil on a baking sheet and spray with nonstick spray. Transfer fish-veggie mixture to the center of the foil.

Fold together and seal the top and bottom edges of the foil, and then the side edges, to create a well-sealed packet.

Bake in the oven for 15 minutes, or until fish is cooked through. Allow packet to cool for a few minutes, and then cut to release steam before opening it entirely. (Careful—steam will be hot.)

Toast or warm tortilla slightly, and then place beans in the center. Add fish and veggies to the tortilla. Fold tortilla sides up, and then chew away!

MAKES 1 SERVING

YOU'LL NEED:

large bowl, small bowl, heavy-duty aluminum foil, baking sheet, nonstick spray

PREP:

20 minutes

COOK:

30 minutes

ROCKIN' CHICKEN RATATOUILLE

The lovely chicken breast takes ratatouille to a whole new level. Yummmmm!

PER SERVING (½ of recipe, about 2¼ cups): 299 calories, 2g fat, 660mg sodium, 32.5g carbs, 9.75g fiber, 18g sugars, 37.5g protein

Ingredients

10 ounces raw boneless skinless lean chicken breast, cubed
⅛ teaspoon salt, or more to taste
⅛ teaspoon black pepper, or more to taste
1½ cups cubed eggplant
¾ cup chopped red bell pepper
¾ cup sliced and halved zucchini
¾ cup coarsely chopped onion
1 cup canned fire-roasted diced tomatoes, drained
½ cup canned tomato paste
¼ cup finely chopped fresh basil
1 teaspoon chopped garlic
⅛ teaspoon crushed red pepper, or more to taste

Directions

Preheat oven to 375 degrees.

Place chicken in a large bowl and season with salt and black pepper. Add eggplant, bell pepper, zucchini, and onion. Mix well and set aside.

In a small bowl, combine all other ingredients and mix well. Add this mixture to the large bowl and toss to coat. Set aside.

154

Lay a large piece of heavy-duty foil on a baking sheet and spray with nonstick spray. Scoop mixture into the center of the foil.

Place another large piece of foil evenly over the sheet. Fold together and seal all four edges of the two foil pieces, forming a well-sealed packet.

Place baking sheet in the oven and bake for 30 minutes, or until veggies are tender and chicken is fully cooked.

Allow packet to cool for a few minutes, and then cut to release steam before opening it entirely. (Careful—steam will be hot.) If you like, season to taste with additional salt, black pepper, and crushed red pepper. Eat up!

MAKES 2 SERVINGS

What do you do with excess eggplant?

Make a Ratatouille Frittata (page 120). If you love THIS recipe, you'll love THAT one too!

YOU'LL NEED:

large bowl,
heavy-duty aluminum
foil, nonstick spray,
baking sheet

PREP:

15 minutes

COOK:

35 minutes

📷 **For a pic
of this recipe,
see the first
photo insert.
Yay!**

DREAMY BUTTERNUT CHICKEN FOIL PACK

This dish is so super-creamy and decadent, it's hard to believe it has just about 3g of fat per serving. Like magic!!!

PER SERVING (½ of recipe, about 2 cups): 292 calories, 3.25g fat, 575mg sodium, 35.5g carbs, 6g fiber, 10g sugars, 32g protein

Ingredients

½ cup canned 98% fat-free cream of chicken
   condensed soup

¼ cup fat-free sour cream

1 teaspoon chopped garlic

2 cups peeled and sliced butternut squash

1½ cups chopped cauliflower

¾ cup chopped onion

8 ounces raw boneless skinless lean chicken breast,
   cut into bite-sized pieces

⅛ teaspoon salt, or more to taste

⅛ teaspoon black pepper, or more to taste

Directions

Preheat oven to 375 degrees.

In a large bowl, combine condensed soup, sour cream, and
garlic. Mix well. Add squash, cauliflower, and onion, and stir
to coat. Set aside.

Lay a large piece of heavy-duty foil on a baking sheet and
spray with nonstick spray. Lay veggie mixture on the foil
sheet and set aside.

Season chicken with salt and pepper, and place it on top of the veggie mixture.

Place another large piece of foil on top. Fold together and seal all four edges of the two foil pieces, forming a well-sealed packet.

Place baking sheet in the oven and bake for about 35 minutes, until chicken is cooked through and veggies are tender.

Allow packet to cool for a few minutes, and then cut to release steam before opening it entirely. (Careful—steam will be hot.)

Mix well and serve it up! If you like, season with additional salt and black pepper.

MAKES 2 SERVINGS

Are you a squash skeptic?

The tips on page 431 will help you tackle the gourd!

YOU'LL NEED:
large bowl,
heavy-duty aluminum
foil, nonstick spray,
baking sheet

PREP:
20 minutes

COOK:
35 minutes

📷 **For a pic
of this recipe,
see the first
photo insert.
Yay!**

NO-NONSENSE
NACHO LETTUCE CUPS

Nachos in lettuce cups?! How insanely awesome!

PER SERVING (¼th of recipe, 5 lettuce cups): 236 calories, 6.75g fat,
748mg sodium, 19.5g carbs, 4.25g fiber, 4.5g sugars, 22.5g protein

Ingredients

8 ounces raw lean ground turkey
2 teaspoons taco seasoning mix
1 cup fat-free refried beans
½ cup chopped onion
½ cup shredded fat-free cheddar cheese
¼ cup shredded reduced-fat Mexican-blend cheese
¼ cup sliced black olives
2 tablespoons jarred jalapeño slices
20 small leaves butter or romaine lettuce
½ cup chopped tomatoes
½ cup fat-free sour cream

Directions

Preheat oven to 375 degrees.

In a large bowl, combine turkey with taco seasoning and mix well.

Lay a large piece of heavy-duty foil on a baking sheet and spray
with nonstick spray. Spread beans onto the center of the foil.
Use your hands to break up turkey and evenly spread over
beans. Evenly top with onion, both types of cheese, olives,
and jalapeño slices.

Place another large piece of foil over the mixture. Fold together and seal all four edges of the two foil pieces, forming a well-sealed packet.

Bake in the oven for 30 to 35 minutes, until turkey is cooked through.

Allow packet to cool for a few minutes, and then cut to release steam before opening it entirely. (Careful—steam will be hot.)

Evenly distribute nacho mixture among lettuce cups, about 2 tablespoons per lettuce cup, and top with chopped tomatoes and sour cream. Enjoy!

MAKES 4 SERVINGS

YOU'LL NEED:
heavy-duty aluminum
foil, baking sheet,
nonstick spray

PREP:
10 minutes

COOK:
25 minutes

SWEET POTATO APPLE PACK

Sweet potatoes, Fuji apples, and cranberries—together in one cozy foil pack. Comforting, sweet, and incredibly delicious!

PER SERVING (½ of recipe, 1 heaping cup): 256 calories, 4g fat, 288mg sodium, 55g carbs, 7.25g fiber, 29g sugars, 2.5g protein

Ingredients

2 sweet potatoes (about 4½ ounces each), peeled and cut into bite-sized chunks
1 large Fuji apple, cored and cut into bite-sized chunks
2 tablespoons dried sweetened cranberries
1½ tablespoons light whipped butter or light buttery spread
1½ tablespoons brown sugar (not packed)
¼ teaspoon cinnamon, or more to taste
⅛ teaspoon salt, or more to taste
Dash ground nutmeg, or more to taste

Directions

Preheat oven to 350 degrees.

Lay a large piece of heavy-duty foil on a baking sheet and spray with nonstick spray. Place the potato chunks, apple chunks, and cranberries in the center of the foil. Add butter in evenly spaced dollops. Sprinkle with brown sugar, cinnamon, salt, and nutmeg.

Place another large piece of foil over the potato-apple mixture. Fold together and seal all four edges of the two foil pieces, forming a well-sealed packet.

Place baking sheet in the oven and bake for about 25 minutes, until potato chunks and apple chunks are soft.

Let cool slightly. Using oven mitts, carefully flip packet over, allowing butter mixture to coat the veggies, and return to right-side up.

Cut packet to release steam before opening it entirely. (Careful—steam will be hot.) If you like, season to taste with additional cinnamon, salt, and nutmeg. Mmmmm!

MAKES 2 SERVINGS

YOU'LL NEED:

heavy-duty aluminum foil, baking sheet, nonstick spray, bowl, small microwave-safe bowl

PREP:

10 minutes

COOK:

20 minutes

STEAMY CREAMY SQUASH PACKET

Oh! A pack of creamy squash. How, um, interesting. Hey, do NOT knock it. IT'S SOCKS-ROCKIN'LY GOOD!

PER SERVING (½ of recipe, about 1 cup): 80 calories, 2.75g fat, 232mg sodium, 11g carbs, 3g fiber, 5g sugars, 3.5g protein

Ingredients

2 zucchini or yellow summer squash, stem ends removed

½ cup thinly sliced onion

2 teaspoons light whipped butter or light buttery spread

⅛ teaspoon dried oregano

Dash each salt and black pepper, or more to taste

½ teaspoon chopped garlic

1 wedge The Laughing Cow Light Creamy Swiss cheese

Directions

Preheat oven to 375 degrees.

Thinly slice each zucchini/squash lengthwise, forming wide, flat strips. Cut strips in half widthwise and set aside.

Lay a large piece of heavy-duty foil on a baking sheet and spray with nonstick spray. Place sliced zucchini/squash and onion in the center of the foil. Top veggies with two evenly spaced dollops of butter. Sprinkle with oregano, salt, and pepper. Top with garlic.

Place another large piece of foil over the veggies. Fold together and seal all four edges of the two foil pieces, forming a well-sealed packet.

Bake in the oven until veggies are soft and tender, about 20 minutes.

Let cool slightly. Cut packet to release steam before opening it entirely. (Careful—steam will be hot.) Empty into a bowl and set aside.

Place cheese wedge in a small microwave-safe bowl, and microwave for 20 seconds. Stir until smooth, add to veggies, and toss gently to coat. If you like, season to taste with additional salt and pepper. EAT!

MAKES 2 SERVINGS

YOU'LL NEED:

large bowl, small
bowl, heavy-duty
aluminum foil, baking
sheet, nonstick spray

PREP:

10 minutes

COOK:

20 minutes

For the Weight Watchers
PointsPlus™ values of
all the recipes in this
book, check out
hungry-girl.com/books.
Yay!

WOOHOO! BAYOU FiSH PACK

This cajun-seasoned meal's got veggies, beans, AND flounder.
WOOHOO is right!

PER SERVING (½ of recipe, 1 fillet with seasoned beans):
270 calories, 2g fat, 592mg sodium, 32.5g carbs, 9.5g fiber,
8g sugars, 31g protein

Ingredients

1 cup canned red kidney beans, drained and rinsed
½ cup finely chopped green bell pepper
½ cup finely chopped onion
½ cup finely chopped celery
¼ cup tomato paste
½ teaspoon Cajun seasoning, divided
½ teaspoon chopped garlic
⅛ teaspoon ground thyme
⅛ teaspoon salt
⅛ teaspoon black pepper
Two 4-ounce raw flounder fillets
Optional: hot sauce

Directions

Preheat oven to 350 degrees.

Place beans, bell pepper, onion, and celery in a large bowl. Mix
well and set aside.

In a small bowl, combine tomato paste with ¼ teaspoon Cajun
seasoning. Add garlic, thyme, salt, and black pepper, and mix
thoroughly. Transfer seasoned tomato paste to the bean-veggie
mixture, and stir to coat. Set aside.

Lay a large piece of heavy-duty foil on a baking sheet and spray with nonstick spray. Scoop seasoned bean-veggie mixture into the center of the foil, and spread it out a bit. Sprinkle remaining ¼ teaspoon Cajun seasoning on both sides of each fillet, and lay the fillets side by side on top of the bean-veggie mixture.

Place another large piece of foil over the whole thing. Fold together and seal all four edges of the two foil pieces, forming a well-sealed packet.

Bake in the oven for 20 minutes, or until the fillets are cooked through and the veggies are tender. Cut packet to release steam before opening it entirely. (Careful—steam will be hot.)

Serve each fillet with half of the bean-veggie mixture. If you like, add a little hot sauce. Enjoy!

MAKES 2 SERVINGS

medium microwave-
safe bowl, heavy-duty
aluminum foil, baking
sheet, nonstick spray

PREP:

15 minutes

COOK:

25 minutes

WINNER WINNER ONION CHICKEN DINNER

Chicken + onions = PHENOMENAL. Sweet with a hint of spice, this one should be added into regular rotation at your house . . .

PER SERVING (entire recipe): 251 calories, 4.5g fat, 340mg sodium, 16g carbs, 3.75g fiber, 7g sugars, 35.5g protein

Ingredients

One 5-ounce raw boneless skinless lean chicken
    breast cutlet, pounded to ½-inch thickness
1 teaspoon dry onion soup/dip mix, divided
½ tablespoon light whipped butter or light
    buttery spread
¾ cup sliced onion
½ cup sliced mushrooms
1 small yellow summer squash, ends removed, sliced
Optional: salt and black pepper

Directions

Preheat oven to 375 degrees.

Season chicken with ½ teaspoon onion soup/dip mix and set aside.

Place butter in a medium microwave-safe bowl, and heat in the microwave for 15 seconds, or until melted. Add onion, mushrooms, and squash, and toss to mix. Add remaining ½ teaspoon onion soup/dip mix and mix well.

Lay a large piece of heavy-duty foil on a baking sheet and spray with nonstick spray. Place veggies in the center of the foil.

Lay chicken on top of veggies and place another large piece of foil over the top. Fold together and seal all four edges of the two foil pieces, forming a well-sealed packet.

Bake in the oven for about 25 minutes, until chicken is cooked through and veggies are tender. Cut packet to release steam before opening it entirely. (Careful—steam will be hot.) Yum!

MAKES 1 SERVING

Meat Prep 101

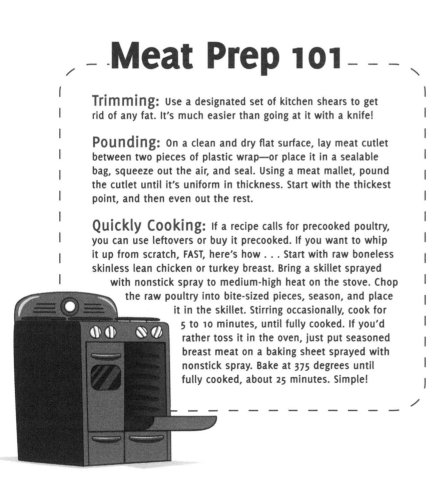

Trimming: Use a designated set of kitchen shears to get rid of any fat. It's much easier than going at it with a knife!

Pounding: On a clean and dry flat surface, lay meat cutlet between two pieces of plastic wrap—or place it in a sealable bag, squeeze out the air, and seal. Using a meat mallet, pound the cutlet until it's uniform in thickness. Start with the thickest point, and then even out the rest.

Quickly Cooking: If a recipe calls for precooked poultry, you can use leftovers or buy it precooked. If you want to whip it up from scratch, FAST, here's how . . . Start with raw boneless skinless lean chicken or turkey breast. Bring a skillet sprayed with nonstick spray to medium-high heat on the stove. Chop the raw poultry into bite-sized pieces, season, and place it in the skillet. Stirring occasionally, cook for 5 to 10 minutes, until fully cooked. If you'd rather toss it in the oven, just put seasoned breast meat on a baking sheet sprayed with nonstick spray. Bake at 375 degrees until fully cooked, about 25 minutes. Simple!

blender or food
processor, large bowl,
skillet, nonstick spray,
heavy-duty aluminum
foil, baking sheet

PREP:

20 minutes

COOK:

30 minutes

*✳ For more recipes,
plus food finds,
tips 'n tricks, and MORE,
sign up for FREE daily
emails at
hungry-girl.com!*

HOT TUNA STUFFED TOMATOES

Don't let the name fool you—these are GREAT cold too!

PER SERVING (¼th of recipe, 1 stuffed tomato): 141 calories, 2g fat, 340mg sodium, 22g carbs, 8.25g fiber, 7g sugars, 13.5g protein

Ingredients

4 large tomatoes, each about 3 inches wide

½ cup Fiber One Original bran cereal

½ cup chopped green bell pepper

¼ cup chopped onion

One 5-ounce can albacore tuna packed in water, drained and flaked

½ cup canned chickpeas, drained and rinsed

2 tablespoons tomato paste

1 teaspoon chopped garlic

½ teaspoon dried basil

Dash each salt and black pepper, or more to taste

2 teaspoons reduced-fat Parmesan-style grated topping

Directions

Preheat oven to 375 degrees.

Carefully slice about ½ inch off the top of each tomato. Gently scoop out and discard insides. Set hollow tomatoes aside.

Using a blender or food processor, grind cereal to a breadcrumb-like consistency. Transfer crumbs to a large bowl and set aside.

Bring a skillet sprayed with nonstick spray to medium-high heat on the stove. Add bell pepper and onion. Stirring occasionally, cook until veggies begin to soften, about 5 minutes. Transfer to the bowl with the crumbs.

To the bowl, add all remaining ingredients *except* Parm-style topping. Stir thoroughly and, if you like, season to taste with additional salt and/or black pepper. Evenly distribute mixture among the hollow tomatoes. Equally sprinkle the tops of the tomatoes with Parm-style topping.

Lay a large piece of heavy-duty foil on a baking sheet. Place tomatoes upright in the center of foil in rows of two with the edges touching. Place another large piece of foil over the tomatoes. Fold together and seal all four edges of the two foil pieces, forming a well-sealed packet without extra room around the tomatoes.

Bake in the oven until tomatoes are hot and mostly softened, about 25 minutes. Allow to cool slightly. Cut packet to release steam before opening it entirely. (Careful—steam will be hot.) Serve 'em up!

MAKES 4 SERVINGS

YOU'LL NEED:

small bowl,
heavy-duty aluminum
foil, baking sheet,
nonstick spray

PREP:

15 minutes

COOK:

35 minutes

COLOSSAL ASiAN VEGGiE 'N CHiCKEN PACK

Yowsa . . . It's a GINORMOUS serving of chicken and veggies with an Asian flair!

PER SERVING (¼th of recipe, about 1½ cups): **222 calories, 1.5g fat, 811mg sodium, 19g carbs, 3.25g fiber, 9.5g sugars, 30.5g protein**

Ingredients

1 tablespoon seasoned rice vinegar
½ tablespoon cornstarch
3 tablespoons oyster sauce
1 teaspoon chopped garlic
⅛ teaspoon ground ginger
3 cups thinly sliced cabbage
2 cups bean sprouts
1½ cups sugar snap peas
1 cup sliced mushrooms
½ cup matchstick-cut carrots
One 8-ounce can sliced water chestnuts, drained
12 ounces raw boneless skinless lean chicken
    breast, cut into bite-sized pieces

Directions

Preheat oven to 375 degrees.

In a small bowl, combine vinegar and cornstarch. Mix until dissolved, and then add in oyster sauce, garlic, and ginger. This is your sauce; set aside.

Lay a large piece of heavy-duty foil on a baking sheet and spray with nonstick spray. Place all veggies into the center of the foil, scattering them out a bit (not important to mix evenly), and lay chicken pieces on top. Pour sauce over chicken and veggies, and place another large piece of foil over the top. Fold together and seal all four edges of the two foil pieces, forming a well-sealed packet.

Bake in the oven for 35 minutes, until veggies are tender and chicken is cooked. Let cool slightly. Using oven mitts, carefully flip packet over, allowing sauce to coat the veggies, and then return to right-side-up. Cut packet to release steam before opening it entirely. (Careful—steam will be hot.) Serve it up!

MAKES 4 SERVINGS

CHAPTER 8: COMFORT FOODS

Everyone LOVES comfort food. These HG-ified favorites are SO decadent. Prepare yourself for INSANE deliciousness . . .

YOU'LL NEED:

large microwave-safe bowl, skillet and nonstick spray *or* microwave-safe plate, 4 parfait glasses

PREP:

15 minutes

COOK:

15 minutes

📷 **For a pic of this recipe, see the first photo insert. Yay!**

CHEESEBURGER MASHED POTATO PARFAITS

A totally unique and incredibly delicious recipe that'll kick any fast-food craving to the curb!

PER SERVING (¼th of recipe, 1 parfait): 168 calories, 1.5g fat, 634mg sodium, 29g carbs, 3.25g fiber, 4g sugars, 10g protein

Ingredients

1⅓ cups instant mashed potato flakes

¼ teaspoon onion powder

¼ teaspoon salt

¼ cup fat-free sour cream

2 frozen meatless hamburger-style patties with about 100 calories each

2 slices fat-free American cheese, broken into small pieces

½ cup chopped tomatoes

¼ cup chopped onion

4 teaspoons ketchup

4 hamburger dill pickle chips

Directions

In a large microwave-safe bowl, combine potato flakes, onion powder, salt, and 2⅓ cups water. Stir until completely moistened. Cover and microwave for 4 minutes, or until hot.

Once cool enough to handle, add sour cream and stir until blended and smooth. Re-cover to keep hot and set aside.

Prepare burger patties on the stove in a skillet sprayed with nonstick spray or on a microwave-safe plate in the microwave. (Refer to package instructions for exact temperature and time.) Once cool enough to handle, chop well. Set aside.

Scoop about ⅓ cup potatoes into each of 4 parfait glasses. Evenly distribute chopped burger patties among the glasses, followed by cheese pieces.

Evenly distribute remaining mashed potatoes among the glasses, followed by tomatoes and onion. Top each with 1 teaspoon ketchup and a pickle chip. Enjoy!

MAKES 4 SERVINGS

YOU'LL NEED:

2 small bowls, large bowl, large baking sheet, aluminum foil (optional), nonstick spray

PREP:

30 minutes

COOK:

20 minutes

CHICKEN POT POCKETS

These pockets are packed with pot pie goodness. They're hard to resist, but why would ANYONE want to resist 'em?

PER SERVING (1/12th of recipe, 1 pocket): 119 calories, 1.25g fat, 280mg sodium, 17g carbs, 1g fiber, 1.5g sugars, 10g protein

Ingredients

1 teaspoon cornstarch

One 10.75-ounce can 98% fat-free cream of celery condensed soup

2 cups frozen bite-sized mixed veggies (like diced carrots, peas, corn, etc.)

12 ounces cooked and finely chopped skinless lean chicken breast

12 large square egg roll wrappers (found in the refrigerated section of the supermarket with the other Asian items)

Optional: salt and black pepper

Directions

Preheat oven to 350 degrees.

In a small bowl, mix cornstarch thoroughly with 1 teaspoon cold water. In a large bowl, combine cornstarch mixture with soup, and mix thoroughly. Add veggies and chicken, mix well, and then season to taste with salt and pepper, if you like. This is your filling. Set aside.

On a large dry surface, lay out three egg roll wrappers. Set out a small bowl of water, dip your finger into it, and then run your finger along all of the wrapper edges—repeat this as needed while preparing your pockets, to help keep them sealed.

Starting about ½ inch from the bottom, place about ⅓ cup filling along the bottom half of each wrapper, leaving a ½-inch border on both sides. Fold the top half of each wrapper over, so that the top edge meets the bottom—the mixture should be completely encased with a ½-inch border on three sides. Dab each border with water, and fold each inward about ¼ inch to lightly seal all sides. Press firmly along the borders with the prongs of a fork to seal completely.

Line a large baking sheet with foil and/or spray with nonstick spray. Using a large spatula, carefully transfer the pockets to the baking sheet. Repeat the entire process 3 more times, so that you have 12 pockets on the baking sheet. If needed, prepare and use an additional baking sheet.

Bake in the oven for 20 minutes. Allow to cool for 5 minutes before serving. Then dig in!

MAKES 12 SERVINGS

Starting with raw chicken?

Go to page 167 for simple cooking techniques!

YOU'LL NEED:

baking sheet,
nonstick spray,
rolling pin (optional)

PREP:

10 minutes

COOK:

15 minutes

CHEESY PiGS iN BACON BLANKiES

Simply put, there are no words to effectively describe just how INCREDIBLE these are . . . You really have to make them. And SOON!

PER SERVING (1/8th of recipe, 1 pig in a blanket): 164 calories, 6.75g fat, 877mg sodium, 16g carbs, 0g fiber, 3.5g sugars, 10.5g protein

Ingredients

1 package Pillsbury Reduced Fat Crescent rolls
    refrigerated dough
4 wedges The Laughing Cow Light Creamy Swiss cheese
8 dashes garlic powder, or more to taste
8 hot dogs with about 40 calories and 1g fat or less each
¼ cup precooked real crumbled bacon
Optional dips: Hellmann's/Best Foods Dijonnaise,
    ketchup, salsa

Directions

Preheat oven to 375 degrees.

Spray a baking sheet with nonstick spray and set aside.

Slightly stretch or roll out 1 of the 8 triangle-shaped pieces of dough to make a larger triangle. Evenly spread with half a wedge of cheese, and then sprinkle with a dash of garlic powder. Place hot dog along the base and gently but firmly roll it up. Squeeze the dough gently to ensure it is secure around the hot dog.

Sprinkle ½ tablespoon bacon on your work surface and roll the dough-wrapped dog in it, so the bacon sticks to the outside. Press any remaining bacon into the dough. Place on the baking sheet.

Repeat with remaining ingredients, so that you have 8 evenly spaced pigs in a blanket on the sheet.

Bake in the oven until dough is lightly browned, 12 to 14 minutes.

Let cool slightly. If you like, dip your dog into one or more of the optional ingredients. Enjoy!

MAKES 8 SERVINGS

YOU'LL NEED:

13-inch by 9-inch baking pan, nonstick spray, strainer, large microwave-safe bowl, kitchen shears (optional), large bowl, large skillet, meat mallet, sealable plastic bag

PREP:

20 minutes

COOK:

50 minutes

Searching for shirataki?

Page 521 tells you where those noodles are hiding . . .

TURKEY TETRAZZINI BAKE

Here's another super-creamy and comforting dish that the entire family will FREAK for.

PER SERVING (⅛th of recipe, about 1½ cups): 285 calories, 9.5g fat, 942mg sodium, 28g carbs, 7g fiber, 6g sugars, 22g protein

Ingredients

3 bags House Foods Tofu Shirataki Spaghetti Shaped Noodle Substitute
One 10.75-ounce can 98% fat-free cream of mushroom condensed soup
¼ cup fat-free sour cream
½ cup light plain soymilk
4 wedges The Laughing Cow Light Creamy Swiss cheese
½ cup reduced-fat Parmesan-style grated topping, divided
1½ teaspoons garlic powder, divided
1 teaspoon onion powder, divided
½ teaspoon plus 1 dash salt, divided
¼ teaspoon plus 1 dash black pepper, divided
2 cups frozen peas
3 cups sliced mushrooms
1 onion, chopped
12 ounces raw lean ground turkey
¼ cup Fiber One Original bran cereal
2 tablespoons panko breadcrumbs
½ teaspoon dried oregano

Directions

Preheat oven to 375 degrees.

Spray a 13-inch by 9-inch baking pan with nonstick spray and set aside.

Use a strainer to rinse and drain noodles well. Pat dry. Place noodles in a large microwave-safe bowl, and microwave for 1 minute. Drain excess liquid. Dry as thoroughly as possible, using paper towels. Cut noodles up a bit with kitchen shears (if you've got 'em), and set aside.

In a large bowl, combine soup, sour cream, soymilk, cheese wedges, and ¼ cup Parm-style topping. Add ½ teaspoon garlic powder, ½ teaspoon onion powder, ¼ teaspoon salt, and ⅛ teaspoon black pepper. Mix until smooth. Stir in peas and set aside.

Bring a large skillet sprayed with nonstick spray to medium-high heat on the stove. Add mushrooms and onion. Stirring occasionally, cook until slightly softened, 3 to 4 minutes. Transfer veggies to the bowl with the soup mixture and set aside.

Remove skillet from heat, re-spray, and return to medium-high heat on the stove. Add turkey and season with ½ teaspoon garlic powder, ½ teaspoon onion powder, ¼ teaspoon salt, and ⅛ teaspoon black pepper. Cook and crumble until browned and cooked through, about 6 minutes.

Transfer turkey to the bowl with the soup mixture. Add noodles and stir thoroughly. Transfer mixture to the baking pan and set aside.

Place cereal in a sealable plastic bag and, removing as much air as possible, seal. Using a meat mallet, carefully crush cereal through the bag. Sprinkle cereal crumbs over the mixture in the pan.

Sprinkle remaining ½ teaspoon garlic powder, dash salt, dash pepper, and ¼ cup Parm-style topping over the cereal crumbs. Sprinkle panko breadcrumbs and oregano over the seasonings.

Bake in the oven until topping is browned and slightly crunchy, 25 to 30 minutes.

Let cool slightly and then serve it up!

MAKES 6 SERVINGS

sealable plastic bag,
meat mallet, 3 plates,
bowl, large skillet,
nonstick spray

PREP:

20 minutes

COOK:

20 minutes

PLATE-LiCKiN'-GOOD CHiCKEN 'N WAFFLES

Slightly weird? Sure! 100 PERCENT DELICIOUS? Absolutely . . . crispy chicken and waffles with sweet maple-y syrup = a combo you won't want to live without.

PER SERVING (½ of recipe, 1 piece of chicken with 1 waffle and syrup): 289 calories, 3.5g fat, 730mg sodium, 34g carbs, 6.5g fiber, 1.5g sugars, 37.5g protein

Ingredients

⅓ cup Fiber One Original bran cereal

¼ teaspoon salt, divided

¼ teaspoon black pepper, divided

⅛ teaspoon garlic powder

Two 5-ounce raw boneless skinless lean chicken
breast cutlets, pounded to ½-inch thickness

2 tablespoons fat-free liquid egg substitute

2 frozen low-fat waffles

½ cup sugar-free pancake syrup

Optional: fat-free chicken gravy

Directions

Place cereal in a sealable plastic bag and seal. Using a meat mallet, crush to a breadcrumb-like consistency. Add ⅛ teaspoon each salt, pepper, and garlic powder. Seal and shake to mix well. Transfer crumbs to a plate and set aside.

Place chicken cutlets in a bowl and evenly season with remaining ⅛ teaspoon salt and ⅛ teaspoon pepper. Top with egg substitute. Flip cutlets over to evenly coat. One at a time, transfer cutlets to the plate of crumbs and evenly coat on both sides.

Bring a large skillet sprayed with nonstick spray to medium-high heat on the stove. Add breaded cutlets and cook until insides are fully cooked and outsides are crispy, about 4 minutes per side.

Meanwhile, toast waffles and place each on a plate. Pour ¼ cup syrup over each waffle, and top with a cooked chicken cutlet.

If you like, serve with gravy for dipping. SO GOOD!

MAKES 2 SERVINGS

New to the world of poultry pounding?

Flip to page 167 for some super-simple tips!

YOU'LL NEED:

2 large pots (1 with a lid), nonstick spray

PREP:

10 minutes

COOK:

15 minutes

FUNKADELIC CHILI MAC

A new guilt-free spin on an old fattening favorite. Be careful—you'll want to scarf down this entire recipe, so portion it out first! Mmmmmm . . .

PER SERVING (¼th of recipe, about 1¾ cups): 297 calories, 2g fat, 637mg sodium, 55.5g carbs, 9.75g fiber, 11.5g sugars, 19g protein

Ingredients

One 14.5-ounce can stewed tomatoes, roughly chopped, juice reserved
1 cup canned red kidney beans, drained and rinsed
1 cup frozen ground-beef-style soy crumbles
1 onion, chopped
1 red or green bell pepper, seeded and chopped
1 cup chopped portabella mushrooms
⅓ cup tomato paste
1 teaspoon chili powder, or more to taste
½ teaspoon chopped garlic
¼ teaspoon ground cumin, or more to taste
5 ounces (about 1¼ cups) uncooked elbow macaroni with at least 2g fiber per 2-ounce serving
¼ cup shredded fat-free cheddar cheese
Optional: cayenne pepper

Directions

To make the chili, bring a large pot sprayed with nonstick spray to medium heat on the stove. Add all ingredients—including the reserved tomato juice—*except* the macaroni, cheese, and optional spice. Stir thoroughly. Cover and cook until veggies are tender, about 15 minutes, occasionally removing the lid to stir.

Meanwhile, in another large pot, prepare macaroni according to package instructions. Drain and set aside.

Once both are cooked, add drained pasta to the pot of chili. Mix thoroughly. Season to taste with cayenne pepper and additional spices, if you like. Evenly top each serving with cheese and enjoy!

MAKES 4 SERVINGS

YOU'LL NEED:

medium-large pot, skillet, nonstick spray, microwave-safe bowl, 8-inch by 8-inch baking pan

PREP:

10 minutes

COOK:

45 minutes

📷 **For a pic of this recipe, see the first photo insert. Yay!**

BUFFALO CHICKEN WING MACARONI & CHEESE

This one's got many favorites rolled into one—cheese, hot sauce, chicken, and veggies. Yee-haaa!

PER SERVING (¼th of recipe): 267 calories, 3.5g fat, 924mg sodium, 35g carbs, 4.5g fiber, 5.5g sugars, 23g protein

Ingredients

4½ ounces (about 1 cup) uncooked elbow macaroni with at least 2g fiber per 2-ounce serving

2 stalks celery, chopped

2 medium carrots, chopped

1 small onion, chopped

8 ounces cooked and shredded skinless lean chicken breast

1 teaspoon chopped garlic

¼ cup Frank's RedHot Original Cayenne Pepper Sauce, divided

½ cup fat-free sour cream

2 wedges The Laughing Cow Light Creamy Swiss cheese

2 teaspoons yellow mustard

1½ tablespoons reduced-fat Parmesan-style grated topping

1 tablespoon chopped fresh parsley

Directions

Preheat oven to 350 degrees.

Cook pasta al dente in a medium-large pot. (Refer to package instructions for exact time.) Drain and set aside.

Bring a skillet sprayed with nonstick spray to medium-high heat on the stove. Add celery, carrots, and onion. Stirring occasionally, cook until veggies have slightly softened, about 5 minutes.

Add chicken, garlic, and 3 tablespoons hot sauce to the skillet. Mix thoroughly and set aside.

In a microwave-safe bowl, combine sour cream, cheese wedges, mustard, and remaining 1 tablespoon hot sauce. Mix well and heat in the microwave for 30 seconds.

Spray an 8-inch by 8-inch baking pan with nonstick spray. Evenly place half of the pasta into the pan. Evenly top with the chicken-veggie mixture followed by the remaining pasta.

Add the sour cream mixture to the pan in an even layer. Sprinkle with Parm-style topping and parsley.

Bake in the oven until hot and bubbly, about 30 minutes.

Serve and enjoy!

MAKES 4 SERVINGS

HG Tip!

Don't miss our EZ Guide to Shredded Chicken on page 211!

YOU'LL NEED:

large skillet, nonstick spray, bowl, 12-cup muffin pan

PREP:

30 minutes

COOK:

30 minutes

📷 **For a pic of this recipe, see the first photo insert. Yay!**

LASAGNA CUPCAKES

Yeah, you read that right—LASAGNA CUPCAKES. And they are A-MAZ-ING and not to be skipped. Add the ingredients to your shopping list NOW!

PER SERVING (1/12th of recipe, 1 cupcake): 165 calories, 4.75g fat, 390mg sodium, 14g carbs, 1.25g fiber, 3g sugars, 15g protein

Ingredients

12 ounces raw lean ground turkey

¼ teaspoon salt, divided

⅛ teaspoon black pepper

1 cup chopped onion

½ cup chopped mushrooms

One 14.5-ounce can crushed tomatoes

1½ teaspoons chopped garlic, divided

½ teaspoon Italian seasoning

One 10-ounce package frozen chopped spinach, thawed and squeezed dry

1½ cups fat-free ricotta cheese

¼ cup fat-free liquid egg substitute

⅛ teaspoon ground nutmeg

24 small square wonton wrappers (often stocked with the tofu in the refrigerated section of the supermarket)

1½ cups shredded part-skim mozzarella cheese

Directions

Preheat oven to 375 degrees.

Bring a large skillet sprayed with nonstick spray to medium-high heat on the stove. Add turkey and season with ⅛ teaspoon salt and pepper. Cook and crumble until no longer pink, about 5 minutes.

Add onion and mushrooms and, stirring often, cook until veggies are soft and turkey is fully cooked, about 6 minutes.

Reduce heat to low. Add crushed tomatoes, 1 teaspoon garlic, and Italian seasoning to the skillet. Stirring occasionally, simmer for 10 minutes. Set aside.

Meanwhile, in a bowl, combine spinach, ricotta cheese, egg substitute, nutmeg, remaining ⅛ teaspoon salt, and remaining ½ teaspoon garlic. Mix well and set aside. Spray a 12-cup muffin pan with nonstick spray, and press a wonton wrapper into each cup of the pan. Evenly distribute about half of the spinach-ricotta mixture among the cups, smoothing the surfaces with the back of a spoon.

Evenly distribute about half of the turkey mixture among the cups, smoothing the surfaces with the back of a spoon. Top each turkey layer with 1 tablespoon mozzarella cheese. Place another wonton wrapper into each cup, lightly pressing it down on the cheese layer and along the sides of the cup, letting the edges fall over the pan. Repeat layering by evenly distributing remaining spinach-ricotta mixture and turkey mixture among the cups. Top each cup with 1 tablespoon mozzarella cheese.

Bake in the oven until cheese has melted and edges are browned, about 10 minutes.

Allow to cool, carefully transfer to a plate, and serve 'em up!

MAKES 12 SERVINGS

YOU'LL NEED:

2 microwave-safe bowls, strainer, kitchen shears (optional)

PREP:

10 minutes

COOK:

5 minutes

📷 **For a pic of this recipe, see the first photo insert. Yay!**

iHUNGRY SPAGHETTI TACOS

> Made famous on *icarly*, spaghetti tacos have become part of American pop culture. Now you can enjoy 'em free of guilt.

PER SERVING (⅓rd of recipe, 2 tacos): 253 calories, 7g fat, 778mg sodium, 29.5g carbs, 6g fiber, 4g sugars, 18g protein

Ingredients

1 cup frozen ground-beef-style soy crumbles

¾ teaspoon taco seasoning mix

1 bag House Foods Tofu Shirataki Spaghetti Shaped Noodle Substitute

1 cup canned crushed tomatoes

6 corn taco shells (flat-bottomed shells, if available)

¾ cup shredded fat-free cheddar cheese

⅓ cup chopped onion

½ cup shredded lettuce

Directions

Place soy crumbles in a microwave-safe bowl and sprinkle with taco seasoning. Microwave for 1 minute, or until hot. Stir and set aside.

Use a strainer to rinse and drain noodles well. Pat dry. Place noodles in a microwave-safe bowl, and microwave for 1 minute. Drain excess liquid. Dry as thoroughly as possible, using paper towels. Cut noodles up a bit with kitchen shears (if you've got 'em).

Add the crushed tomatoes and seasoned crumbles to the bowl of noodles and mix well. Microwave for another minute, until hot.

Give spaghetti mixture a stir and then evenly distribute among the taco shells, about ⅓ cup per shell. Top each evenly with cheese, onion, and lettuce. Tada!

MAKES 3 SERVINGS

YOU'LL NEED:

2 large microwave-safe bowls, potato masher, skillet, nonstick spray, bowl, 8-inch by 8-inch baking pan, nonstick spray

PREP:

30 minutes

COOK:

55 minutes

For the Weight Watchers *PointsPlus*™ values of all the recipes in this book, check out hungry-girl.com/books. Yay!

HUNGRY CHICK SHEPHERD'S PIE

Shepherd's pie is like a giant bear hug in a bowl. A DELICIOUS bear hug . . .

PER SERVING (¼ of pie): 280 calories, 1.75g fat, 576mg sodium, 36.5g carbs, 6g fiber, 7g sugars, 26.5g protein

Ingredients

1 cup instant mashed potato flakes

3 cups frozen cauliflower florets

½ tablespoon light whipped butter or light buttery spread

2 dashes each salt and black pepper, or more to taste

12 ounces raw boneless skinless lean chicken breast cutlets

½ cup fat-free chicken gravy

4 cups frozen mixed vegetables

One 8-ounce can sliced mushrooms, drained

Optional: garlic powder, onion powder, paprika

Directions

Preheat oven to 375 degrees.

In a large microwave-safe bowl, combine potato flakes with 1½ cups hot water, and stir until moistened. Add cauliflower and mix well. Cover and microwave for 3 minutes, or until potatoes have thickened and cauliflower is hot. Once cool enough to handle, mash well with a potato masher or fork. Add butter and a dash each of salt and pepper. Mix well and set aside.

Bring a skillet sprayed with nonstick spray to medium-high heat on the stove. Add chicken and sprinkle with remaining dash each of salt and pepper. If you like, season with garlic powder, onion powder, additional salt, and/or additional pepper. Cook for about 5 minutes per side, until cooked through. Once cool enough to handle, chop into small pieces. Place in a bowl with gravy, stir to coat, and set aside.

Place frozen mixed veggies in a large microwave-safe bowl and microwave for 5 to 6 minutes, until thawed. Drain excess liquid, and then stir in mushrooms. Arrange veggies flat in the bottom of an 8-inch by 8-inch baking pan sprayed with nonstick spray.

Scatter gravy-coated chicken over the veggies. Evenly spoon potato-cauliflower mixture over the chicken in the pan, and smooth surface with the back of the spoon. If you like, sprinkle with paprika.

Bake in the oven for 35 minutes, until potato-cauliflower layer has slightly browned. If you like, season to taste with additional salt and/or pepper. Eat up!

MAKES 4 SERVINGS

YOU'LL NEED:

baking sheet, nonstick spray, blender or food processor, sealable container or plastic bag, 2 small bowls

PREP:

15 minutes

COOK:

20 minutes

FAUX-FRIED GREEN TOMATOES

Yep, these are made with Fiber One . . . and are not actually FRIED. But they ROCK like you wouldn't believe!

PER SERVING (entire recipe): 140 calories, 1.5g fat, 699mg sodium, 34g carbs, 12g fiber, 7g sugars, 8g protein

Ingredients

⅓ cup Fiber One Original bran cereal

1½ tablespoons cornmeal

¼ teaspoon seasoned salt

⅛ teaspoon garlic powder

⅛ teaspoon onion powder

Dash each salt and black pepper

2 tablespoons fat-free liquid egg substitute

2 tablespoons low-fat milk or light plain soymilk

1 green (unripe) tomato, cut into ½-inch-thick slices

Optional dip: ketchup

Directions

Preheat oven to 400 degrees.

Spray a baking sheet with nonstick spray and set aside.

In a blender or food processor, grind cereal to a breadcrumb-like consistency. Transfer to a sealable container or plastic bag. Add cornmeal and spices, and mix well. Set aside.

Pour the egg substitute into one small bowl, and pour milk into another small bowl. Dip a tomato slice in the milk, and place it in the cereal/cornmeal mixture. Seal the container or bag, and shake until the slice is coated.

Remove the slice and set aside, and then repeat with the remaining slices. Next, repeat this entire process using the egg substitute in place of the milk, coating your tomato slices with the crumb mixture a second time. (Before coating the slices in crumbs again, give 'em a shake so they're not dripping with excess egg substitute.)

Place the double-coated slices on the baking sheet. Pop 'em in the oven and bake until outsides are crispy, 15 to 20 minutes, flipping the slices about halfway through cooking. Enjoy! These are great by themselves, but they're also excellent dipped in ketchup!

MAKES 1 SERVING

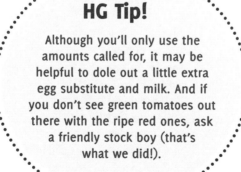

HG Tip!

Although you'll only use the amounts called for, it may be helpful to dole out a little extra egg substitute and milk. And if you don't see green tomatoes out there with the ripe red ones, ask a friendly stock boy (that's what we did!).

YOU'LL NEED:

strainer, large microwave-safe bowl, kitchen shears (optional), bowl, large pie pan, nonstick spray

PREP:

20 minutes

COOK:

30 minutes

SUPER-DUPER SPAGHETTI PIE PART DEUX

The only thing to say is WOW. WOW. WOW. WOW. You MUST try this pie—even if you THINK you're not a fan of tofu shirataki. Just do it . . .

PER SERVING (¼ of pie): 140 calories, 3g fat, 499mg sodium, 16g carbs, 5g fiber, 6g sugars, 13g protein

Ingredients

1 bag House Foods Tofu Shirataki Spaghetti Shaped Noodle Substitute

One 14.5-ounce can crushed tomatoes

½ cup canned pure pumpkin

1 teaspoon reduced-fat Parmesan-style grated topping

½ teaspoon garlic powder

½ teaspoon Italian seasoning

Dash each salt and black pepper, or more to taste

1 cup frozen ground-beef-style soy crumbles, thawed and patted dry

½ cup thinly sliced bell pepper

½ cup thinly sliced onion

½ cup fat-free liquid egg substitute

⅓ cup shredded part-skim mozzarella cheese

Directions

Preheat oven to 425 degrees.

Use a strainer to rinse and drain noodles well. Pat dry. Place noodles in a large microwave-safe bowl, and microwave for 1 minute. Drain excess liquid. Dry as thoroughly as possible, using paper towels. Cut noodles up a bit with kitchen shears (if you've got 'em), and set aside.

In a separate bowl, combine tomatoes, pumpkin, Parm-style topping, garlic powder, Italian seasoning, salt, and black pepper; mix well. If you like, season to taste with additional salt and pepper. Stir in soy crumbles. Transfer about ¾ of the tomato mixture to the bowl with the noodles; set the rest aside.

Add veggies and egg substitute to the bowl with the noodles; mix well. Transfer contents of the bowl to a large pie pan sprayed with nonstick spray.

Bake for approximately 25 minutes, until firm.

Remove pie from the oven and evenly spread with remaining tomato mixture. Sprinkle with mozzarella cheese.

Return pie to the oven and bake until tomato mixture is hot and cheese has melted, about 3 minutes.

Allow to cool for a few minutes and then slice into quarters. Enjoy!

MAKES 4 SERVINGS

YOU'LL NEED:

extra-large pot with a
lid, tongs (optional),
bowl, whisk
(optional), large bowl,
nonstick spray

PREP:

45 minutes

COOK:

70 minutes

FLOOSH'S
STUFFED CABBAGE

Who is FLOOSH, you might ask? She's my mom!!! And her stuffed cabbage is an old family favorite. Now it's been HG-ified, so it's even better!

PER SERVING (1/7th of recipe, 2 cabbage rolls with sauce): 242 calories, 6.5g fat, 610mg sodium, 30.5g carbs, 3g fiber, 22g sugars, 18g protein

Ingredients

1 extra-large head green cabbage, core carefully removed
   with a sharp knife
2 cups low-fat plain marinara sauce
¾ cup jellied cranberry sauce
⅓ cup sugar-free blackberry jam or preserves
⅓ teaspoon salt
1¼ pounds raw lean ground turkey
¾ cup finely chopped onion
⅓ cup ketchup
1½ tablespoons tomato paste
½ tablespoon chopped garlic
1½ no-calorie sweetener packets

Directions

Place cored cabbage head in an extra-large pot of water, and bring water to a boil on the stove. Once boiling, cook for 5 to 7 minutes, rotating cabbage occasionally with tongs or a large heat-resistant spoon, until leaves soften, loosen, and begin to fall off the head. Remove from heat. Carefully remove cabbage head and leaves from the pot, drain, and let cool. Meanwhile, prepare sauce and filling.

To make your sauce, combine marinara sauce, cranberry sauce, jam or preserves, and salt in a bowl, and stir with a whisk or fork until smooth. Set aside.

To make your filling, combine turkey, onion, ketchup, tomato paste, garlic, and sweetener in a large bowl. Knead with your hands until mixture is evenly combined. Set aside.

Once cabbage is cool enough to handle, gently remove 14 large leaves. (Refrigerate the rest for another use.)

Prepare the (empty) extra-large pot used to boil the cabbage by spraying it lightly with nonstick spray. Lay one cabbage leaf on a dry surface and spoon 2 heaping tablespoons of filling into the center of it. Spread filling out slightly and roll cabbage up around the filling like a burrito, folding the sides in first and then rolling it up from the bottom. Place seam-side down in the pot. Repeat with remaining 13 leaves and remaining filling.

Gently place cabbage rolls in the pot, stacking them if needed. Pour sauce over cabbage rolls, covering as much of the exposed cabbage as possible.

Cover the pot and set stove temperature to low heat. Cook for about 1 hour, until filling is cooked through.

Gently remove cabbage rolls and serve topped with sauce!

MAKES 7 SERVINGS

HG Heads-Up!

The recipe stats include a full serving ($\frac{1}{7}$th of the ENTIRE amount) of sauce. So unless you swallow all of the excess sauce (there will be a lot!), chances are each serving of this recipe will have more like 200 calories.

strainer, kitchen
shears (optional),
large skillet, nonstick
spray, bowl

PREP:

5 minutes

COOK:

20 minutes

*✳ For full-color
photos of all the recipes
in this book, check out
hungry-girl.com/books.
Woohoo!*

BEEF STROGATAKI

*Weird name. Anything-but-weird recipe. Noodles & gravy & beef &
mushrooms!? This one's a keeper . . .*

PER SERVING (entire recipe): 291 calories, 10g fat,
955mg sodium, 17g carbs, 5g fiber, 4g sugars, 31g protein

Ingredients

1 bag House Foods Tofu Shirataki Fettuccine
   Shaped Noodle Substitute
4 ounces raw lean filet beefsteak, thinly sliced
   (freeze slightly before slicing)
1 teaspoon dry au jus gravy mix
½ cup sliced mushrooms
½ cup thinly sliced onion
1 wedge The Laughing Cow Light Creamy
   Swiss cheese, room temperature
1 teaspoon fat-free plain yogurt
Optional: salt and black pepper

Directions

Use a strainer to rinse and drain noodles well. Dry as thoroughly as
possible, using paper towels. Cut noodles up a bit with kitchen shears
(if you've got 'em), and set aside.

Bring a large skillet sprayed with nonstick spray to medium-high heat
on the stove. Add beef and cook for about 4 minutes per side, until
fully cooked. Remove and set aside.

In a bowl, combine gravy mix with 1 cup water and stir until dissolved. Carefully pour mixture into the skillet, still over medium-high heat on the stove. Add mushrooms and onion, and cook until veggies are tender and sauce has thickened, about 8 minutes.

Add cheese wedge and stir until melted. Add yogurt and stir well, until sauce appears uniform and ingredients are thoroughly combined.

Add noodles and beef to the skillet, and mix until completely coated and hot. Season to taste with salt and pepper, if you like, and eat up!

MAKES 1 SERVING

CHAPTER 9: INTERNATIONAL FAVORITES

You don't need to go globe-trotting to enjoy favorites from around the world. Chew 'em HG-style right in your own kitchen!

large baking pan, nonstick spray, bowl, blender or food processor, plate, toothpicks, aluminum foil

PREP:

20 minutes

COOK:

35 minutes

📷 **For a pic of this recipe, see the first photo insert. Yay!**

NACHO-RiFiC STUFFED CHiCKEN

It's hard to believe no one thought of making cheesy, bean-stuffed, tortilla chip-encrusted chicken before, isn't it?! YUM!!!

PER SERVING (¼th of recipe, 1 stuffed chicken cutlet): 267 calories, 3.75g fat, 667mg sodium, 17g carbs, 5g fiber, 1.5g sugars, 39.5g protein

Ingredients

½ cup fat-free refried beans

¼ cup shredded fat-free cheddar cheese

4 wedges The Laughing Cow Light Creamy Swiss cheese

½ cup Fiber One Original bran cereal

8 low-fat baked tortilla chips, crushed

1 teaspoon taco seasoning mix

2 dashes cayenne pepper, or more to taste

Four 5-ounce raw boneless skinless lean chicken breast cutlets, pounded to ⅓-inch thickness

¼ cup taco sauce

Optional toppings: fat-free sour cream, salsa

Directions

Preheat oven to 350 degrees.

Spray a large baking pan with nonstick spray and set aside.

To make the filling, combine beans, shredded cheese, and cheese wedges in a bowl. Mix thoroughly and set aside.

In a blender or food processor, grind cereal to a breadcrumb-like consistency. Add crushed chips, taco seasoning, and cayenne pepper. With the lid on, remove processor/blender from the base and give it a good shake to mix. Transfer crumb mixture to a plate and set aside.

Lay cutlets flat on a clean, dry surface. Spoon filling onto the centers of the cutlets, evenly dividing it among them. Carefully roll each cutlet up over the filling (which may ooze a little, but don't worry!) and secure with toothpicks.

Cover each stuffed cutlet with 1 tablespoon taco sauce, using the back of the spoon or your fingers to coat. Carefully roll each cutlet in the crumb mixture, making sure to coat all sides—use a spoon or your fingers, if needed. Gently transfer to the baking pan.

Cover the pan with foil, and bake in the oven for 20 minutes.

Carefully remove foil, and bake in the oven for another 15 minutes, or until chicken is cooked through and outsides are crispy.

Let cool slightly and, if you like, serve with sour cream and/or salsa. Enjoy!

MAKES 4 SERVINGS

Unfamiliar with putting cereal in the blender?

Turn to page 243 for a few quick tips . . . DO IT!

YOU'LL NEED:

skillet, nonstick spray,
bowl, baking pan,
microwave-safe plate

PREP:

10 minutes

COOK:

20 minutes

SURPRISE, IT'S PUMPKIN! ENCHILADAS

Traditionally, enchiladas do NOT include pumpkin. But you already knew that, right?! Despite that fact, these are super-awesome!

PER SERVING (½ of recipe, 1 enchilada): 188 calories, 2g fat, 948mg sodium, 31g carbs, 5g fiber, 8g sugars, 10.5g protein

Ingredients

⅓ cup chopped onion

⅔ cup canned pure pumpkin

1½ tablespoons taco sauce

1 teaspoon taco seasoning mix

2 large corn tortillas

¾ cup red enchilada sauce, divided

1 slice fat-free cheddar cheese, halved

¼ cup shredded fat-free cheddar cheese

Optional: salt, black pepper, fat-free sour cream, chopped scallions

Directions

Preheat oven to 400 degrees.

Bring a skillet sprayed with nonstick spray to medium heat on the stove. Add onion and, stirring occasionally, cook until it begins to brown, about 2 minutes. Transfer to a bowl.

Add pumpkin, taco sauce, and taco seasoning to the bowl. Mix well. If you like, season to taste with salt and pepper. Set aside.

Spray a baking pan with nonstick spray and set aside.

Place tortillas on a microwave-safe plate. Warm slightly in the microwave, about 15 seconds.

Lay tortillas flat, side by side. Spread 2 tablespoons enchilada sauce onto each one. Place a half-slice of cheese in the center of each tortilla. Evenly distribute the pumpkin mixture between the centers of the tortillas.

Wrap tortillas up tightly and place them in the baking pan with the seam sides down. Cover with remaining ½ cup enchilada sauce.

Bake in the oven for about 8 minutes, until enchiladas are hot. Carefully remove pan from the oven, and sprinkle enchiladas with shredded cheese.

Return to the oven and bake for another 5 minutes, or until the cheese has melted. Plate those babies and, if you like, top with sour cream and/or scallions. Enjoy!

MAKES 2 SERVINGS

Extra canned pumpkin needs a purpose.

Whip up a Pumpkin Pie Oatmeal Parfait (page 38) or some Crazy-Good Carrot-Cake Pancakes (page 68)!

YOU'LL NEED:

large bowl, small
bowl, grill or grill pan,
nonstick spray

PREP:

10 minutes

COOK:

10 minutes

GRiLLED GO FiSH! SOFT TACOS

> These are SOOOOO incredible—thanks to that crazy avocado cream. Yum!!!

PER SERVING (½ of recipe, 2 tacos): 273 calories, 5.75g fat, 330mg sodium, 30g carbs, 5g fiber, 5g sugars, 27g protein

Ingredients

Tacos
2 tablespoons lime juice
1 teaspoon garlic powder
1 teaspoon ground cumin
½ teaspoon chili powder
⅛ teaspoon salt
Two 4-ounce raw tilapia fillets (or other flaky white fish)
Four 6-inch corn tortillas
1 cup shredded cabbage or dry coleslaw mix
¼ cup chopped tomato

Avocado Cream
2 tablespoons mashed avocado
2 tablespoons fat-free sour cream
½ teaspoon lime juice
Dash garlic powder, or more to taste
Dash chili powder, or more to taste
Dash salt, or more to taste

Optional topping: fruity salsa

Directions

Combine lime juice and spices for tacos in a large bowl, and mix well. Add fillets and cover both sides of each with seasoned lime juice. Let marinate in the fridge for at least 5 minutes.

Meanwhile, combine all ingredients for avocado cream in a small bowl and mix well. Refrigerate until ready to serve.

Spray a grill or grill pan with nonstick spray and bring to medium heat. Grill fish for 5 minutes, and then very carefully flip. Grill for 3 more minutes, or until cooked through. Set aside.

Place tortillas on the grill/grill pan and grill for 1 minute per side, or until toasty. Plate and spread evenly with avocado cream. Break fish into pieces and evenly divide among tortillas. Top with cabbage, tomatoes and, if you like, some fruity salsa. Fold and enjoy!

MAKES 2 SERVINGS

YOU'LL NEED:

small bowl, grill or
grill pan, nonstick
spray

PREP:

10 minutes

COOK:

5 minutes

SW BBQ CHICKEN QUESADILLA

creamy, cheesy, and packed with BBQ goodness. This quesadilla will become one of your go-to favorites!

PER SERVING (entire recipe): 299 calories, 7.75g fat, 940mg sodium, 35g carbs, 7g fiber, 7g sugars, 27g protein

Ingredients

- 1 tablespoon BBQ sauce with about 45 calories per 2-tablespoon serving
- 1 wedge The Laughing Cow Light Creamy Swiss cheese
- 1 medium-large high-fiber flour tortilla with about 110 calories
- 2 ounces cooked and shredded (or finely chopped) skinless lean chicken breast
- 1 tablespoon canned black beans, drained and rinsed
- 1 tablespoon corn kernels, thawed from frozen
- 2 tablespoons shredded reduced-fat Mexican-blend cheese
- 1 tablespoon chopped scallions
- Optional dips: salsa, fat-free ranch dressing, additional BBQ sauce

Directions

In a small bowl, mix BBQ sauce and cheese wedge until blended. Lay tortilla flat and spread BBQ-cheese mixture on one half. Top mixture with remaining ingredients and set aside.

Spray a grill or grill pan with nonstick spray and bring to medium-high heat. Place the half-loaded tortilla flat on the grill/grill pan, and cook for 2 minutes. Using a spatula, carefully fold the plain half of the tortilla over the filling and press down lightly to seal.

Leftover black beans?

Make a Nice to See Ya! Quesadilla (page 62) or an Amazing Ate-Layer Open-Faced Taco (page 344). YES!!!

Carefully flip and grill for 3 more minutes, or until both sides are crispy.

Once cool enough to handle, slice into wedges. If you like, dunk in salsa, ranch dressing, or additional BBQ sauce. Enjoy!

MAKES 1 SERVING

Better Off Shred

HG's EZ Guide to Shredded Chicken

Shredded chicken is awesome in recipes like our Buffalo Chicken Wing Macaroni Cheese (page 186), Cheesy Chicken Enchiladas (page 212), Southwest Stuffed Tomatoes (page 386), and Chicken Empanadas (page 444). And making it yourself is a SNAP . . .

1. Fill a large pot about two-thirds of the way with water and bring to a boil on the stove.

2. Add raw boneless skinless lean chicken breast and boil until cooked through, about 10 minutes.

3. Drain and transfer chicken to a bowl. Once cool enough to handle, shred using two forks—one to hold the chicken in place and the other to scrape across the meat and shred it.

Tada! BTW, every 8 ounces of raw chicken will yield about 6 ounces of cooked and shredded chicken. So now you know!

YOU'LL NEED:

baking pan, nonstick spray, skillet, bowl, microwave-safe plate

PREP:

10 minutes

COOK:

15 minutes

CHEESY CHiCKEN ENCHiLADAS

You like chicken enchiladas? Look no further. You should eat these today (or at least sometime this week).

PER SERVING (½ of recipe, 1 enchilada): 252 calories, 3.5g fat, 840mg sodium, 20.5g carbs, 2.25g fiber, 4g sugars, 33g protein

Ingredients

¼ cup chopped onion

6 ounces cooked and shredded skinless lean chicken breast

½ cup shredded fat-free cheddar cheese, divided

½ cup plus 2 tablespoons green enchilada sauce, divided

2 large corn tortillas

Optional toppings: fat-free sour cream, chopped scallions

Directions

Preheat oven to 400 degrees.

Spray a baking pan with nonstick spray and set aside.

Bring a skillet sprayed with nonstick spray to medium-high heat on the stove. Add onion and, stirring occasionally, cook until slightly browned, about 2 minutes. Transfer to a bowl.

To the bowl, add chicken, ¼ cup cheese, and 2 tablespoons enchilada sauce. Mix well and set aside.

On a microwave-safe plate, heat tortillas in the microwave for 15 seconds, or until warm.

Evenly distribute chicken mixture between the tortillas. Wrap the tortillas up tightly, and place them in the baking pan with the seam sides down.

Pour remaining ½ cup enchilada sauce over the enchiladas. Bake in the oven until hot, about 10 minutes.

Evenly sprinkle remaining ¼ cup cheese over the enchiladas. Bake in the oven until cheese has melted, about 2 more minutes.

Allow to cool slightly. If you like, top with sour cream and scallions. Enjoy!

MAKES 2 SERVINGS

HG Tip!

Don't miss our EZ Guide to Shredded Chicken on page 211!

YOU'LL NEED:

large skillet, small bowl, microwave-safe plate

PREP:

10 minutes

COOK:

10 minutes

'BELLA ASADA FAJITAS

Vegetarians and carnivores alike will dream of chewing these crazy-amazing mushroom fajitas. Yummmmmmmy!

PER SERVING (½ of recipe, 3 fajitas): 275 calories, 8g fat, 312mg sodium, 47g carbs, 8.5g fiber, 7.5g sugars, 7g protein

For the Weight Watchers *PointsPlus*™ values of all the recipes in this book, check out hungry-girl.com/books. Yay!

Ingredients

1 teaspoon olive oil
2 large portabella mushroom caps, sliced
¾ cup sliced bell peppers
¾ cup sliced onion
¼ teaspoon garlic powder
¼ teaspoon salt, divided
⅛ teaspoon chili powder, or more to taste
⅛ teaspoon ground cumin
Dash black pepper
½ cup chopped tomatoes
¼ cup roughly mashed avocado
2 tablespoons chopped fresh cilantro
½ tablespoon lime juice
Six 6-inch corn tortillas

Directions

Drizzle a large skillet with oil and bring to medium-high heat on the stove. Add sliced mushrooms, bell peppers, and onion, and sprinkle with garlic powder, ⅛ teaspoon salt, chili powder, cumin, and black pepper. Stirring occasionally, cook for 6 minutes, or until veggies are tender. Set aside.

In a small bowl, combine tomatoes, avocado, cilantro, lime juice, and remaining ⅛ teaspoon salt. If you like, season to taste with chili powder. Mix well and set aside.

Place tortillas on a microwave-safe plate, and microwave for 25 seconds, or until slightly warm. Top each tortilla with about ½ cup fajita veggies and a spoonful of the tomato-avocado mixture. Fold and chew!

MAKES 2 SERVINGS

YOU'LL NEED:

microwave-safe
bowl, large bowl,
large baking sheet,
nonstick spray

PREP:

30 minutes

COOK:

35 minutes

SHRIMPYLICIOUS EGG ROLLS

Each egg roll has less than 100 calories. Feel free to do a happy dance. No one's looking . . .

PER SERVING (⅓rd of recipe, 2 egg rolls): 189 calories, 0.75g fat, 949mg sodium, 33.5g carbs, 3.5g fiber, 5g sugars, 12.5g protein

Ingredients

4 cups (about half of a 12-ounce bag) dry coleslaw mix

One 6-ounce can (4 ounces drained) tiny shrimp, drained

½ cup canned water chestnuts, drained and
    sliced into strips

¼ cup bean sprouts, chopped

2 scallions, chopped

1 stalk celery, thinly sliced widthwise

2 tablespoons reduced-sodium/lite soy sauce

1 teaspoon crushed garlic

¼ teaspoon ground ginger

⅛ teaspoon salt

Dash black pepper

6 large square egg roll wrappers (found in the refrigerated
    section of the supermarket with the other Asian items)

Optional dip: sweet & sour sauce

Directions

Preheat oven to 375 degrees.

Place slaw mix in a microwave-safe bowl with 2 tablespoons
of water, cover, and microwave for 2 minutes. Drain any
excess water, and transfer slaw mix to a large bowl. Add all
other ingredients *except* the wrappers, mix well, and set aside.

For more intense flavor, allow mixture to marinate in the fridge for 20 minutes.

Prepare a large baking sheet by spraying it lightly with nonstick spray.

Place two egg roll wrappers on a clean, dry surface. Evenly distribute about ½ cup of the mixture onto each wrapper, in a row a little below the center. Moisten all four edges of each wrapper by dabbing your fingers in water and going over the edges smoothly.

Fold the sides of each wrapper about ¾ inch towards the middle, to keep the mixture from falling out of the sides. Then, roll the bottom of each wrapper up around the mixture, and continue rolling until you reach the top. Seal the outside edge with another dab of water. Carefully transfer egg rolls to the baking sheet.

Repeat process twice with remaining wrappers and filling, making sure you have a clean, dry surface each time.

Spray the tops of the egg rolls with nonstick spray. Bake in the oven for 25 to 30 minutes, until golden brown. Allow to cool slightly. If you like, dip egg rolls in some sweet & sour sauce!

MAKES 3 SERVINGS

HG Alternative!

If you're not into shrimp so much, just swap 'em for ½ cup chopped mushrooms and you'll have fantastic veggie egg rolls. Woohoo!

YOU'LL NEED:

small pot with a lid, whisk, large bowl, large skillet, nonstick spray

PREP:

15 minutes

COOK:

20 minutes

EGG-CELLENT FOO YOUNG

Here's one of those recipes that you're going to have to tell 100 people about. And there are FIVE delicious pancakes per serving. YES!

PER SERVING (½ of recipe, about 5 pancakes with sauce): 286 calories, 2g fat, 1,026mg sodium, 21.5g carbs, 2.5g fiber, 7g sugars, 45g protein

Ingredients

1½ cups fat-free chicken broth

1½ tablespoons cornstarch

1 tablespoon reduced-sodium/lite soy sauce, divided

1 cup fat-free liquid egg substitute

1 cup finely chopped onion

1 cup bean sprouts

½ cup chopped mushrooms

½ teaspoon chopped garlic

4 ounces raw bay shrimp (or medium shrimp, chopped)

4 ounces cooked and shredded (or finely chopped) skinless lean chicken breast

2 scallions, chopped

Directions

To make your sauce, combine broth, cornstarch, and 2 teaspoons soy sauce in a small pot. Whisk until cornstarch has dissolved. Bring to a boil on the stove.

Reduce heat to low and simmer for about 4 minutes, until liquid thickens. Remove pot from heat and cover to keep sauce warm.

In a large bowl, whisk together egg substitute and remaining 1 teaspoon soy sauce until slightly fluffy. Set aside.

Bring a large skillet sprayed with nonstick spray to medium heat on the stove. Add onion, bean sprouts, mushrooms, and garlic. Stirring occasionally, cook for about 3 minutes, until veggies soften slightly.

Add shrimp to the skillet. Continue to cook and stir until veggies are soft and shrimp are opaque, about 2 minutes.

Transfer contents of the skillet to the bowl with the egg mixture. Add chicken and scallions to the bowl, and stir well.

Remove skillet from heat, re-spray, and bring to medium-high heat.

Working in batches, add evenly spaced heaping ¼ cups of the mixture to the skillet to form small pancakes (about 10 total), using a spatula to help the pancakes take shape. Removing and re-spraying the skillet between batches, cook pancakes until golden brown and cooked through, about 1 to 2 minutes per side.

Serve pancakes smothered in warm sauce. Mmmmm!

MAKES 2 SERVINGS

HG Alternative!

Save about 230mg of sodium per serving by using low-sodium chicken broth.

📷 **For a pic of this recipe, see the first photo insert. Yay!**

SWEET & SOUR CHICKEN 1-2-3

It's sweet AND sour (and a little sticky!). And you won't BELIEVE how much it tastes like the uber-fatty kind you get at restaurants.

PER SERVING (⅓rd of recipe, about 2 cups): 295 calories, 2g fat, 730mg sodium, 37g carbs, 5.25g fiber, 27g sugars, 30g protein

Ingredients

12 ounces raw boneless skinless lean chicken breast, cut into bite-sized pieces

⅛ teaspoon salt

⅛ teaspoon black pepper

1½ cups broccoli florets

1 cup chopped red bell pepper

1 cup chopped celery

16 ounces pineapple chunks packed in juice (not drained)

1 tablespoon cornstarch

3 tablespoons seasoned rice vinegar

1 tablespoon ketchup

1 tablespoon reduced-sodium/lite soy sauce

½ teaspoon chopped garlic

¼ teaspoon crushed red pepper

⅛ teaspoon ground ginger

2 cups bean sprouts

Directions

Bring a large skillet or wok sprayed with nonstick spray to medium-high heat on the stove. Season chicken with salt and black pepper and place in the skillet/wok.

Stirring occasionally, cook until chicken is no longer pink on the outside, about 3 minutes. Add broccoli florets, bell pepper, celery, and 2 tablespoons water to the skillet/wok. Cover and cook until veggies are tender, about 8 minutes.

Meanwhile, to make the sauce, drain the juice from the canned pineapple into a small nonstick pot. Add cornstarch and stir to dissolve. Add vinegar, ketchup, soy sauce, garlic, crushed red pepper, and ginger. Mix thoroughly. Bring to medium-high heat on the stove. Stirring frequently, cook until thickened, about 3 minutes.

Add pineapple chunks, bean sprouts and sauce to the skillet/wok. Mix well. Continue to cook and stir until sprouts have softened and chicken is fully cooked, about 4 minutes.

Serve and enjoy!

MAKES 3 SERVINGS

YOU'LL NEED:

strainer, kitchen shears (optional), small bowl, wok or large skillet, nonstick spray, bowl

PREP:

20 minutes

COOK:

10 minutes

CHICKY PAD THAI

This HG take on Pad Thai is awesome. Sweet with a little bit of spiciness, and packed with chicken. Nice!

PER SERVING (½ of recipe, about 2½ cups): 285 calories, 4g fat, 625mg sodium, 32g carbs, 9g fiber, 13g sugars, 34g protein

Ingredients

2 bags House Foods Tofu Shirataki Fettuccine Shaped Noodle Substitute

2 tablespoons ketchup

2 tablespoons lime juice

1 tablespoon sugar-free apricot preserves

2 teaspoons crushed dry-roasted peanuts

2 teaspoons brown sugar (not packed)

1 teaspoon reduced-sodium/lite soy sauce

¼ teaspoon chopped garlic

¼ teaspoon crushed red pepper, or more to taste

½ cup fat-free liquid egg substitute

6 ounces raw boneless skinless lean chicken breast, cut into bite-sized pieces

Dash each salt and black pepper

2 cups chopped broccoli

1½ cups bean sprouts

¾ cup 1-inch scallion pieces

Optional topping: chopped fresh cilantro

Directions

Use a strainer to rinse and drain noodles well. Dry as thoroughly as possible, using paper towels. Cut noodles up a bit with kitchen shears (if you've got 'em), and set aside.

To make the sauce, in a small bowl, combine ketchup, lime juice, preserves, peanuts, brown sugar, soy sauce, garlic, and crushed red pepper. Stir thoroughly and set aside.

Spray a wok or large skillet with nonstick spray and bring to medium-high heat on the stove. Add egg substitute and scramble until fully cooked, about 2 minutes. Transfer to a bowl and set aside.

Remove wok/skillet from heat (if needed, clean it once cooled), re-spray, and return to medium-high heat. Add chicken and season with salt and black pepper. Add broccoli, bean sprouts, scallion pieces, and 2 tablespoons water. Stirring occasionally, cook until chicken is no longer pink and broccoli is tender, about 4 minutes.

Add sauce to wok/skillet, stir to evenly distribute, and continue to cook until sauce is hot, for about 2 minutes. Add scrambled egg substitute and noodles, mix well, and continue to cook until contents are hot and chicken is fully cooked, about 3 minutes.

If you like, season to taste with additional crushed red pepper and/or top with cilantro. Serve and enjoy!

MAKES 2 SERVINGS

Tofu shira-what?

Flip to page 521 for the 411. DO IT!

YOU'LL NEED:

small bowl, large
skillet or wok,
nonstick spray

PREP:

10 minutes

COOK:

10 minutes

WOWOWOW! KUNG PAO

Regular Kung Pao is an oily mess of a dish. This delicious spin slashes TONS of fat and calories but keeps ALL the flavor. Can you say "WOWOWOW"!?

PER SERVING (½ of recipe, about 1½ cups): 245 calories, 4g fat, 720mg sodium, 21g carbs, 3g fiber, 11g sugars, 30g protein

Ingredients

2 tablespoons reduced-sodium/lite soy sauce

1½ tablespoons rice vinegar

2 teaspoons granulated sugar

½ tablespoon cornstarch

1 teaspoon red chili sauce, or more to taste

8 ounces raw boneless skinless lean chicken breast, cubed

⅛ teaspoon salt, or more to taste

⅛ teaspoon black pepper, or more to taste

¾ cup roughly chopped mushrooms

¾ cup roughly chopped bell peppers

½ cup chopped celery

½ cup chopped onion

1 teaspoon minced garlic

¼ cup canned sliced water chestnuts, drained and halved

1 tablespoon chopped dry-roasted unsalted peanuts

Optional: crushed red pepper

Directions

To make the sauce, in a small bowl, combine 2 tablespoons cold water with soy sauce, vinegar, sugar, cornstarch, and chili sauce. Stir until all ingredients have dissolved. Set aside.

Spray a large skillet or wok with nonstick spray, and bring to medium-high heat on the stove. Season chicken with salt and black pepper and add to the skillet or wok. Add mushrooms, bell peppers, celery, onion, garlic, and 2 tablespoons water. Stirring occasionally, cook for about 5 minutes, until chicken is fully cooked but still tender.

Add water chestnuts and peanuts to the skillet/wok. Raise heat to high, give sauce a stir, and add it to the skillet/wok as well.

Mix until sauce has thickened and coated chicken-veggie mixture. If you like, season to taste with salt, black pepper, and crushed red pepper. Enjoy!

MAKES 2 SERVINGS

YOU'LL NEED:

strainer, small bowl, kitchen shears (optional), skillet, nonstick spray (butter flavored, optional)

PREP:

20 minutes

COOK:

15 minutes

For the Weight Watchers *PointsPlus*™ values of all the recipes in this book, check out hungry-girl.com/books. Yay!

SUPER-DELICIOUS SHRIMP SCAMPI WITH FETTUCCINE

Garlicky, buttery shrimp with noodles . . . for less than 300 calories?! It's all true . . .

PER SERVING (½ of recipe, about 1¾ cups): 238 calories, 8.5g fat, 329mg sodium, 14g carbs, 5g fiber, 2g sugars, 26g protein

Ingredients

- 1 small lemon
- 2 bags House Foods Tofu Shirataki Fettuccine Shaped Noodle Substitute
- ¼ cup chopped onion
- 1 teaspoon chopped garlic
- 8 ounces raw shrimp, peeled, tails removed, deveined
- 1 plum tomato, chopped
- 2 tablespoons light whipped butter or light buttery spread
- 2 teaspoons reduced-fat Parmesan-style grated topping
- Optional: salt, black pepper, crushed red pepper, chopped parsley

Directions

Cut lemon in half and, over a strainer, squeeze the juice from one half into a small bowl. Set aside. Cut the other half into wedges, and set those aside as well.

Use a strainer to rinse and drain noodles well. Dry as thoroughly as possible, using paper towels. Cut noodles up a bit with kitchen shears (if you've got 'em), and set aside.

Bring a skillet sprayed with nonstick spray (butter flavored, if you've got it) to medium heat on the stove. Add onion and garlic, and cook until softened, 2 to 3 minutes.

Add shrimp and tomato. Stirring occasionally, cook until shrimp are opaque, about 2 minutes. Add lemon juice and continue to cook and stir for 1 minute.

Raise heat to medium high, add noodles, and mix well. Continue to cook for 1 to 2 minutes, until entire dish is hot and shrimp are cooked through. Add butter and stir.

Plate (or bowl!) your scampi, and top each serving with 1 teaspoon Parm-style topping. Garnish with lemon wedges and, if you like, season to taste with optional ingredients. Enjoy!

MAKES 2 SERVINGS

FAUX-FRIED & FABULOUS CALAMARI

This is one dish you need to make at home instead of chowing down on a deep-fried version at an Italian restaurant. That's the bottom line . . .

PER SERVING (entire recipe): 236 calories, 4g fat, 779mg sodium, 31.5g carbs, 7g fiber, 1g sugars, 23g protein

Ingredients

¼ cup Fiber One Original bran cereal

3 tablespoons panko breadcrumbs

¼ teaspoon garlic powder

¼ teaspoon onion powder

¼ teaspoon Italian seasoning

¼ teaspoon salt

Dash black pepper, or more to taste

4 ounces raw calamari rings (not breaded)

2 tablespoons fat-free liquid egg substitute

Optional: reduced-fat Parmesan-style grated topping, lemon wedges, low-fat marinara sauce

Directions

Preheat oven to 350 degrees.

In a blender or food processor, grind cereal to a breadcrumb-like consistency. Pour crumbs into a sealable container or plastic bag. Add panko, garlic powder, onion powder, Italian seasoning, salt, and pepper. Seal and shake to mix thoroughly.

Make sure calamari rings are as dry as possible. (Blot with paper towels.) Place them in a bowl, and pour egg substitute over them. Toss to coat.

Transfer rings to the crumb mixture, and secure lid or seal bag. Shake until rings are thoroughly coated, and then place rings on a baking sheet sprayed with nonstick spray. Open any rings that are sticking to themselves.

Bake calamari in the oven for 15 minutes, flipping them about halfway through, until firm and fully cooked. If you like, sprinkle with Parm-style topping and serve with lemon wedges and/or marinara sauce. YUM!

MAKES 1 SERVING

Faux-frying for the first time?

Flip to page 243 for a few pointers on grinding up the cereal!

YOU'LL NEED:

large pot, large bowl, extra-large skillet, nonstick spray, 8-inch by 8-inch baking pan

PREP:

10 minutes

COOK:

40 minutes

📷 **For a pic of this recipe, see the first photo insert. Yay!**

TAKES-THE-CAKE ZITI BAKE

Finally . . . an HG-ified classic baked ziti. Make it . . . try it . . . then pinch yourself to prove it isn't just a dream.

PER SERVING (¼ of ziti bake): 286 calories, 7g fat, 455mg sodium, 41g carbs, 5g fiber, 7g sugars, 16.5g protein

Ingredients

5 ounces (about 1½ cups) uncooked whole-wheat or high-fiber ziti or penne pasta
1 cup thinly sliced onion
2 cups chopped brown mushrooms
1 tablespoon chopped garlic
2 cups spinach
¾ cup light or low-fat ricotta cheese
2 tablespoons chopped fresh basil
1½ cups canned crushed tomatoes
½ cup plus 2 tablespoons shredded part-skim mozzarella cheese, divided
2 tablespoons reduced-fat Parmesan-style grated topping

Directions

Preheat oven to 375 degrees.

In a large pot, prepare pasta al dente according to package directions. Drain well, place in a large bowl, and set aside.

Meanwhile, bring an extra-large skillet sprayed with nonstick spray to medium heat on the stove. Add onion and, stirring occasionally, cook until slightly softened, about 3 minutes. Add mushrooms and garlic, and raise temperature to medium high. Continue to cook, stirring often, until mushrooms are soft, about 3 minutes.

Add spinach to the skillet and, stirring often, cook until spinach has wilted and excess moisture has evaporated, about 8 minutes. Remove from heat, and stir in ricotta cheese and basil.

Transfer contents of the skillet to the bowl with the cooked pasta. Add tomatoes and ½ cup mozzarella cheese. Toss gently to mix.

Spray an 8-inch by 8-inch baking pan with nonstick spray, and carefully fill with contents of the bowl. Evenly top with Parm-style topping and remaining 2 tablespoons mozzarella cheese.

Bake in the oven until entire dish is hot and cheese on top has melted, about 15 minutes. Allow to cool slightly, and then serve and enjoy!

MAKES 4 SERVINGS

YOU'LL NEED:

nonstick spray, baking
sheet, medium bowl,
skillet, small bowl,
large loaf pan (about
9 inches by 5 inches)

PREP:

15 minutes

COOK:

50 minutes

EZ CHEESY LASAGNA FOR TWO

AHHHHH . . . this lasagna is sooooo cheesy and fantastic you might be tempted to eat the entire thing. Remember, it's a TWO-SERVING recipe, people!

PER SERVING (½ of lasagna): 238 calories, 4g fat, 845mg sodium, 31.5g carbs, 5g fiber, 10g sugars, 17.5g protein

Ingredients

Two ¼-inch-thick eggplant slices (cut lengthwise
    from a long eggplant), patted dry
1 egg white *or* 2 tablespoons liquid egg whites
½ cup fat-free ricotta cheese
1 tablespoon chopped fresh basil
½ teaspoon chopped garlic
¼ teaspoon salt, or more to taste
Dash ground nutmeg
1 cup chopped mushrooms
½ tablespoon Italian seasoning
1 cup canned crushed tomatoes
2 sheets oven-ready lasagna noodles
¼ cup shredded part-skim mozzarella cheese
1 tablespoon reduced-fat Parmesan-style grated topping
Optional: black pepper

Directions

Preheat oven to 425 degrees.

Spritz both sides of each eggplant slice with nonstick spray and place on a baking sheet. Bake in the oven until browned and softened, about 20 minutes, carefully flipping halfway through.

Meanwhile, in a bowl, combine egg white(s), ricotta cheese, basil, garlic, salt, and nutmeg. Stir well and set aside.

Bring a skillet sprayed with nonstick spray to medium-high heat on the stove. Add mushrooms and, stirring occasionally, cook until softened, about 4 minutes. Stir mushrooms into ricotta mixture and set aside.

In a small bowl, combine Italian seasoning with crushed tomatoes. If you like, season to taste with salt and black pepper. Mix well and set aside.

Spray a large loaf pan with nonstick spray. Pour ¼ cup tomatoes evenly into the bottom of the pan. Top with 1 lasagna sheet. Spread half of the ricotta-mushroom mixture on top, followed by another ¼ cup tomatoes. Top with 1 eggplant slice.

Repeat layering with ¼ cup tomatoes, 1 lasagna sheet, remaining ricotta-mushroom mixture, remaining ¼ cup tomatoes, and remaining eggplant slice.

Evenly top with mozzarella and grated topping. Bake until cheese starts to brown, 20 to 25 minutes. Serve and enjoy!

MAKES 2 SERVINGS

Leftover eggplant alert!

Make yourself a BBQ Grilled Veggie Salad (page 138). Yum!

YOU'LL NEED:

2 large bowls, large skillet, nonstick spray, deep 8-inch by 8-inch baking pan

PREP:

30 minutes

COOK:

1 hour

VEGGIE-RIFIC NOODLE-FREE LASAGNA

Are noodles in lasagna overrated? Um, not really. But it IS entirely possible to make a completely yumtastic lasagna-ish dish without 'em. Here's proof . . .

PER SERVING (¼ of lasagna): 266 calories, 4.75g fat, 926mg sodium, 32.5g carbs, 11g fiber, 13.5g sugars, 24g protein

Ingredients

2 cups canned crushed tomatoes
⅛ teaspoon garlic powder
⅛ teaspoon onion powder
⅛ teaspoon Italian seasoning
3 medium zucchini, ends removed, sliced lengthwise
1 large portabella mushroom, sliced into strips
1 large eggplant, ends removed, sliced lengthwise
One 16-ounce package frozen chopped spinach,
    thawed, thoroughly drained and patted dry
2 tablespoons fat-free liquid egg substitute
1 cup fat-free ricotta cheese
1 tablespoon chopped fresh basil
¼ teaspoon salt
Dash ground nutmeg
1 cup frozen ground-beef-style soy crumbles, thawed
½ cup shredded part-skim mozzarella cheese
1 tablespoon reduced-fat Parmesan-style grated topping

Directions

Preheat oven to 425 degrees.

In a large bowl, combine crushed tomatoes with garlic powder, onion powder, and Italian seasoning. Mix well and set aside.

Lay several paper towels next to the stove; as you cook the veggies, transfer them to the paper towels to drain excess moisture.

Bring a large skillet sprayed with nonstick spray to medium-high heat on the stove. Working in batches, cook zucchini, portabella mushroom, and eggplant until softened, about 2 minutes per side; remove the skillet from heat and re-spray it between batches. Set aside.

In a large bowl, combine spinach, egg substitute, ricotta cheese, basil, salt, and nutmeg. Mix thoroughly and set aside.

Spray a deep 8-inch by 8-inch baking pan with nonstick spray. Evenly spread half of the seasoned crushed tomatoes into the bottom of the pan. Evenly layer half of the sliced veggies over the tomatoes. Spread half of the spinach mixture into an even layer over the veggies. Top evenly with soy crumbles.

Evenly layer remaining veggies into the pan, followed by the remaining spinach mixture. Evenly cover with remaining seasoned crushed tomatoes. Evenly distribute mozzarella cheese and grated topping over the crushed tomatoes.

Bake in the oven until lasagna is hot and mozzarella cheese begins to brown, about 30 minutes.

Allow to cool slightly, cut into quarters, and enjoy!

MAKES 4 SERVINGS

YOU'LL NEED:

microwave-safe bowl, baking pan, nonstick spray, toothpicks, aluminum foil, small bowl, blender or food processor (optional)

PREP:

25 minutes

COOK:

35 minutes

THREE-CHEESE CHICKEN CANNELLONI

THREE AMAZING CHEESES, humans. Count 'em!

PER SERVING (½ of recipe, 1 stuffed cutlet): 274 calories, 3.5g fat, 776mg sodium, 12g carbs, 2g fiber, 6g sugars, 43g protein

Ingredients

¼ cup frozen chopped spinach
¼ cup finely chopped mushrooms
⅓ cup fat-free ricotta cheese
2 teaspoons reduced-fat Parmesan-style grated topping
1 teaspoon chopped garlic, divided
Dash ground nutmeg
2 dashes salt, divided, or more to taste
2 dashes black pepper, divided, or more to taste
Two 5-ounce raw boneless skinless lean chicken
     breast cutlets, pounded to ⅓-inch thickness
¾ cup canned crushed tomatoes
1 teaspoon dried minced onion
½ teaspoon Italian seasoning
1 stick light string cheese

Directions

Preheat oven to 350 degrees.

Place spinach and mushrooms in a microwave-safe bowl. Microwave for 1 minute, until softened. Blot thoroughly, removing excess liquid. Add ricotta cheese, Parm-style topping, ½ teaspoon garlic, nutmeg, and a dash each of salt and pepper. Mix well and set aside.

Spray a baking pan with nonstick spray and set aside.

Season chicken with remaining dash each of salt and pepper. Lay cutlets flat and spread evenly with veggie-cheese mixture. Starting with a longer side, roll up one cutlet (not too tightly or the filling will ooze!), and secure with toothpicks. Place in the baking pan. Repeat with second cutlet. Cover pan with foil.

Bake in the oven for 20 minutes. (Afterward, leave oven on.)

Meanwhile, in a small bowl, combine tomatoes, onion, Italian seasoning, and remaining ½ teaspoon garlic. Mix well and set aside.

Break string cheese into thirds and place in a blender or food processor—blend at high speed until cheese takes on a shredded or grated consistency. (Or just tear string cheese into pieces and roughly chop.) Set aside.

Remove pan from the oven, and carefully remove foil. Spoon seasoned tomatoes equally over chicken, and sprinkle shredded/grated string cheese over tomatoes.

Return to the oven and bake, uncovered, until chicken is cooked through and cheese on top has melted, about 15 minutes. Remove toothpicks and enjoy!

MAKES 2 SERVINGS

Never pounded a chicken cutlet?

No sweat! Check out the tips on page 167 . . .

microwave-safe
bowl, blender or food
processor (optional),
large skillet, nonstick
spray, bowl, baking
sheet, rolling pin

PREP:

25 minutes

COOK:

25 minutes

✳ For more recipes,
plus food finds,
tips 'n tricks, and MORE,
sign up for FREE daily
emails at
hungry-girl.com!

PEPPERONi-POPPiN' VEGGiE CALZONES

Just like the calzones at your local pizza place. The only difference?
You'll still be able to fit into your pants after enjoying these . . .

PER SERVING (⅕th of recipe, 1 calzone with sauce):
279 calories, 5.25g fat, 946mg sodium, 44g carbs, 2.5g fiber,
8g sugars, 14g protein

Ingredients

1 cup canned crushed tomatoes (with basil, if available)
Dash Italian seasoning, or more to taste
2 sticks light string cheese
2 cups chopped brown mushrooms
½ cup thinly sliced onion
2 cups roughly chopped spinach leaves
½ tablespoon chopped garlic
25 slices turkey pepperoni, chopped
1 package Pillsbury Classic Pizza Crust refrigerated dough
Whole-wheat flour, for dusting
5 teaspoons reduced-fat Parmesan-style grated topping
Optional: garlic powder, onion powder, crushed red pepper

Directions

Preheat oven to 375 degrees.

In a microwave-safe bowl, season tomatoes with Italian seasoning
and any optional spices. Set aside.

Break string cheese sticks into thirds, place in a blender/food
processor, and blend at high speed until shredded/grated. (Or just
tear into pieces and roughly chop.) Set aside.

Bring a large skillet sprayed with nonstick spray to medium-high heat on the stove. Add mushrooms and onion. Stirring occasionally, cook until softened, about 4 minutes. Transfer to a bowl lined with paper towels to absorb moisture. Set aside.

Add spinach and garlic to the skillet. Stirring frequently, cook until wilted, about 1 minute. Add to the bowl with mushrooms and onion. Remove paper towels. Blot veggies with more towels to remove excess liquid.

Add pepperoni and half of seasoned tomatoes to veggies. Mix well. This is your filling. Set aside. Spray a baking sheet with nonstick spray. Set aside.

Roll out dough into a large rectangle of even thickness. Slice into 5 strips, each about 3 inches by 9 inches.

Sprinkle workspace with flour, and place one dough strip in the center. Fold strip in half twice, and flatten with your palm. Use a rolling pin dusted with flour to roll dough into a large oval-ish shape, with longer sides on top and bottom. Place one-fifth of filling in the center. Top with one-fifth of grated/shredded cheese and 1 teaspoon Parm. Stretch and pull the top of dough over filling to meet the bottom, forming a crescent. Use your fingers or a fork to firmly seal edges. (Doesn't need to look perfect!) Carefully transfer to baking sheet. Repeat four times with remaining ingredients, re-sprinkling space with flour, if needed.

Poke a few slits in each calzone, to let steam escape. Bake in the oven for 16 to 18 minutes, until golden brown.

Meanwhile, heat remaining tomatoes in the microwave. Let calzones cool slightly; serve with tomatoes for dipping!

MAKES 5 SERVINGS

YOU'LL NEED:

large bowl, potato masher, baking sheet, blender or food processor

PREP:

20 minutes

COOK:

35 minutes

FALAFEL PITA POCKETS WITH DILL-ICIOUS YOGURT DIP

No deep-fried falafel here . . . just a tasty calorie-friendly sandwich pocket you'll want to make 'n eat over and over and over.

PER SERVING (⅕th of recipe, 1 pita pocket with 3 falafel balls and 3 tablespoons dip): 198 calories, 2.25g fat, 863mg sodium, 37g carbs, 8.5g fiber, 5g sugars, 10g protein

Ingredients

HG Alternative!

Enjoy your falafel 'n dip pita-free (wrapped in lettuce, over a salad, or straight from a plate!). A pita-less serving has 139 calories, 2g of fat, 718mg of sodium, 24g of carbs, 6g of fiber, 5g of sugars, and 7.5g of protein. Woohoo!

Falafel Pockets

One 15-ounce can chickpeas, drained and rinsed
1 onion, very finely chopped
¼ cup whole-wheat flour
3 tablespoons finely chopped fresh parsley
1½ tablespoons chopped garlic
1 tablespoon chopped fresh cilantro
½ tablespoon ground cumin
¾ teaspoon salt
½ teaspoon baking powder
¼ teaspoon lemon juice
⅛ teaspoon paprika
Dash black pepper
Two 2-second sprays olive oil nonstick spray
2½ whole-wheat or high-fiber pitas

Dip

One 6-ounce container fat-free plain yogurt
1 small seedless cucumber, peeled and chopped
1 teaspoon dried dill
¾ teaspoon crushed garlic
¼ teaspoon salt
Black pepper, to taste

240

Directions

Preheat oven to 375 degrees.

Place all ingredients for falafel *except* the pitas and nonstick spray in a large bowl, and give them a good stir. Using a potato masher, mash well. Mixture should remain slightly chunky, not smooth.

Spray a baking sheet thoroughly with a 2-second spray of olive oil nonstick spray.

One at a time, take spoonfuls of the mixture in your hands and form 15 balls, each about the size of a ping-pong ball, and gently place them on the baking sheet. Spray the top of each ball with olive oil nonstick spray, for a total of about a 2-second spray.

Bake in the oven for 15 minutes. Meanwhile, combine all ingredients for dip in a blender or food processor, and pulse until just blended. Season to taste with black pepper and refrigerate until ready to serve.

Remove baking sheet from the oven, and carefully turn each ball over, gently reshaping if the bottoms have flattened. Return to the oven and bake until golden brown and slightly crisp, an additional 10 to 15 minutes. Allow to cool and set for at least 5 minutes.

Cut the whole pitas into halves, toast or warm all pita halves slightly, and then fill each with three falafel balls and 3 tablespoons dip. Enjoy!

MAKES 5 SERVINGS

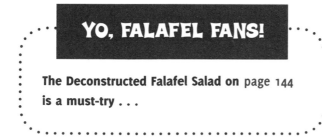

YO, FALAFEL FANS!

The Deconstructed Falafel Salad on page 144 **is a must-try . . .**

YOU'LL NEED:
large pot with a lid

PREP:
20 minutes

COOK:
45 minutes

POW! SOCK! BAM! JAMBALAYA

Yeah, jambalaya is American, but there's no "Intranational Favorites" chapter, so I just put it here. Don't judge; just enjoy . . .

PER SERVING (¼ᵗʰ of recipe, about 1½ cups):
256 calories, 5.5g fat, 688mg sodium, 30.5g carbs, 3.5g fiber,
6.5g sugars, 20g protein

Ingredients

6 ounces (about 2 links) fully cooked chicken sausage, sliced into coins
One 14.5-ounce can fire-roasted diced tomatoes (not drained)
1 onion, chopped
1 green bell pepper, seeded and chopped
1 cup chopped celery
1 cup low-sodium fat-free chicken broth
½ cup uncooked brown rice
1 tablespoon chopped garlic
1 teaspoon Cajun seasoning
½ teaspoon hot sauce, or more to taste
¼ teaspoon dried oregano
¼ teaspoon ground thyme
6 ounces raw shrimp, peeled, tails removed, deveined, chopped
Optional: salt and black pepper

Directions

Add all ingredients *except* the shrimp to a large pot on the stove. Mix thoroughly. Bring to a boil.

Reduce heat to medium low. Cover and simmer until veggies are tender and rice is fluffy, about 35 minutes. Add shrimp and re-cover. Continue to cook until shrimp are tender and cooked through, about 6 minutes.

If you like, season to taste with salt, black pepper, and additional hot sauce. Serve and enjoy!!!

MAKES 4 SERVINGS

Grind Luck
The 411 on
Fiber One Crushing...

* Blenders and food processors are both great at pulverizing Fiber One Original bran cereal into crumbs. Smaller blenders, like the Magic Bullet, work especially well.

* If your appliance of choice isn't capable of grinding small amounts, you may want to try this method when a recipe calls for grinding ⅓ cup of cereal or less . . . Put the cereal in a sealable bag, remove air, and seal; then carefully crush the cereal through the bag with a meat mallet (or a heavy can).

* Another option? Blend up a bunch of cereal at once, and keep a batch of the crumbs in an airtight container for future recipes. The crumbs measure out to half the volume of the cereal itself. So if a recipe calls for ½ cup cereal, use ¼ cup of the crumbs.

CHAPTER 10: ALL THiNGS PiZZA

Face it: There are few things better than pizza. The recipes in this chapter are all pizza-fied, yum-ified, and HG-ified . . . YES!

YOU'LL NEED:

baking sheet,
nonstick spray,
blender or food
processor, bowl,
microwave-safe bowl,
skillet

PREP:

15 minutes

COOK:

20 minutes

📷 **For a pic
of this recipe,
see the first
photo insert.
Yay!**

LOADED 'N OATED SPINACH & MUSHROOM GIRLFREDO PIZZA

There's something super-satisfying about making your own pizza crust. And no worries, it's REALLY easy to do. check it out . . .

PER SERVING (entire recipe): 282 calories, 8.75g fat, 745mg sodium, 34.5g carbs, 10g fiber, 4g sugars, 20g protein

Ingredients

¼ cup Fiber One Original bran cereal
¼ cup old-fashioned oats
¼ cup fat-free liquid egg substitute
1 wedge The Laughing Cow Light Creamy Swiss cheese
1 teaspoon fat-free sour cream
¼ teaspoon crushed garlic
Dash each salt and black pepper, or more to taste
½ cup roughly chopped spinach
⅓ cup chopped brown mushrooms
¼ cup shredded part-skim mozzarella cheese
4 thin rings red onion
Dash paprika

Directions

Preheat oven to 400 degrees.

Spray a baking sheet with nonstick spray and set aside.

In a blender or food processor, grind cereal and oats to a breadcrumb-like consistency. Transfer crumbs to a bowl. Add egg substitute, mix well, and set aside.

To make the sauce, in a microwave-safe bowl, combine cheese wedge, sour cream, garlic, salt, and pepper.

Microwave for 15 seconds, or until warm. Add ½ tablespoon water, stir thoroughly, and set aside.

Bring a skillet sprayed with nonstick spray to medium heat on the stove. Add cereal-egg mixture and, using the back of a spoon, smooth into a circular shape of desired thickness to form the crust.

Raise heat to medium high. Spray a spatula on both sides with nonstick spray. Cook crust until lightly browned, about 2 minutes per side, gently flipping it with the spatula. Transfer crust to the baking sheet and set aside.

Remove skillet from heat, re-spray, and return to medium heat. Add spinach and mushrooms and cook until spinach has wilted and mushrooms have softened slightly, about 1 minute. Remove from heat and set aside.

Evenly spread sauce onto the crust, leaving a half-inch border of crust uncovered. Evenly distribute spinach-mushroom mixture and mozzarella cheese over the sauce. Evenly top with red onion and paprika.

Place baking sheet in the oven and bake until mozzarella cheese has melted and onion has softened, about 10 minutes.

Allow to cool slightly, cut into quarters, and devour!

MAKES 1 SERVING

baking sheet,
nonstick spray, small
bowl, rolling pin
(optional)

* For full-color photos of all the recipes in this book, check out hungry-girl.com/books. Woohoo!

PEPPERONi PiZZA PiNWHEELS

Weeee . . . pizza PINWHEELS. How cute and delicious!

PER SERVING (⅛th of recipe, 1 pinwheel): 125 calories, 6.25g fat, 405mg sodium, 13g carbs, <0.5g fiber, 2.5g sugars, 5g protein

Ingredients

2 wedges The Laughing Cow Light Creamy Swiss cheese

2 tablespoons sun-dried tomatoes packed in oil, drained and finely chopped

1 package Pillsbury Crescent Recipe Creations Seamless Dough Sheet

16 slices turkey pepperoni, chopped

½ teaspoon Italian seasoning

¼ teaspoon garlic powder

2 sticks light string cheese, pulled into strings

Optional: seasoned crushed tomatoes, for dipping

Directions

Preheat oven to 350 degrees.

Spray a baking sheet with nonstick spray and set aside.

In a small bowl, combine cheese wedges with sun-dried tomatoes. Mix well and set aside.

Roll out dough into a large rectangle of even thickness, with the shorter sides on the right and left. Spread cheese mixture evenly over the dough, leaving a 2-inch border of exposed dough along the right side only.

Evenly distribute turkey pepperoni over the cheese and sprinkle with Italian seasoning and garlic powder. Evenly place string cheese pieces vertically on the dough sheet. Starting with the left side, roll the dough tightly up into a log, and seal by pinching together the right edge and the roll itself.

Using a sharp serrated knife, slice the log into 8 pinwheels, and lay them flat on the baking sheet, evenly spaced. Bake for 16 to 18 minutes, until lightly golden.

Allow to cool slightly. If you like, serve with crushed tomatoes for dipping. Chew and enjoy!

MAKES 8 SERVINGS

YOU'LL NEED:

skillet, nonstick
spray, blender or food
processor (optional),
baking sheet, small
bowl, rolling pin
(optional)

PREP:

20 minutes

COOK:

20 minutes

PIZZA PUFFS

Great balls of pizza! Here's a recipe for a pizza-ish treat that's totally new and different!

PER SERVING (⅕th of recipe, 3 puffs): 185 calories, 8.5g fat, 461mg sodium, 22.5g carbs, 1g fiber, 4.5g sugars, 5.5g protein

Ingredients

½ cup chopped mushrooms
½ cup chopped onion
½ cup chopped green pepper
2 sticks light string cheese
1 package Pillsbury Crescent Recipe Seamless
    Dough Sheet
1½ teaspoons Italian seasoning
⅛ teaspoon onion powder
⅛ teaspoon garlic powder
1 tablespoon reduced-fat Parmesan-style
    grated topping
Optional dip: low-fat marinara sauce

Directions

Preheat oven to 400 degrees.

Bring a skillet sprayed with nonstick spray to medium-high heat on the stove. Add veggies and, stirring occasionally, cook until slightly softened, about 4 minutes. Set aside.

Break string cheese into thirds and place in a blender or food processor—blend at high speed until cheese takes on a shredded or grated consistency. (Or just tear string cheese into pieces and finely chop.) Set aside.

Spray a baking sheet with nonstick spray and set aside. In a small bowl, combine seasonings and Parm-style topping; mix well and set aside.

Roll out dough into a large rectangle of even thickness. Cut into 15 equally sized squares. Evenly distribute veggies among the dough squares, about 1 tablespoon each. Sprinkle shredded/grated cheese over the veggies.

Carefully fold each dough square around the filling and firmly press dough together to seal and form round "pizza puffs." Evenly place them seam-side down on the baking sheet.

Mist the puffs with nonstick spray and sprinkle with seasoning mixture. Bake in the oven until golden brown, about 12 minutes.

If you like, serve with warm marinara sauce for dipping!

MAKES 5 SERVINGS

YOU'LL NEED:

blender or food processor, baking sheet, nonstick spray, large skillet, bowl

PREP:

45 minutes

COOK:

55 minutes

SUPREMELY STUFFED PIZZA-FIED EGGPLANT

Ya gotta LOVE this recipe. It combines all your favorite pizza ingredients with eggplant and a little Fiber One thrown in . . . The result? HUUUGE pizza-ed-up hunks of eggplant for less than 200 calories a pop.

PER SERVING (¼th of recipe, 1 large piece): 170 calories, 3g fat, 608mg sodium, 26g carbs, 9.75g fiber, 9.5g sugars, 14.5g protein

Ingredients

¼ cup Fiber One Original bran cereal

1 large eggplant

1 cup chopped onion

1 cup chopped red and green bell peppers

1 cup frozen ground-beef-style soy crumbles, slightly thawed

½ cup canned diced tomatoes, drained

¼ cup fat-free liquid egg substitute

2 tablespoons tomato paste

2 tablespoons reduced-fat Parmesan-style grated topping

2 teaspoons chopped garlic

½ teaspoon Italian seasoning

¼ teaspoon salt

½ cup canned crushed tomatoes

2 sticks light string cheese, pulled into strings

Directions

Preheat oven to 350 degrees.

Using a blender or food processor, grind cereal to a breadcrumb-like consistency. Set aside.

Slice about 1 inch off the stem side of the eggplant. Halve the eggplant lengthwise. Carefully cut along the inside of each half, about ½ inch from the skin. Scoop out the insides with a spoon, and chop them into small pieces. Place the hollow eggplant shells, cut-side up, on a baking sheet sprayed with nonstick spray; set aside.

Bring a large skillet sprayed with nonstick spray to medium-high heat on the stove. Add chopped eggplant, onion, and peppers. Stirring often, cook for 7 to 8 minutes, until soft. Transfer to a bowl and let cool slightly.

Add cereal crumbs to the bowl. Add all other ingredients *except* the crushed tomatoes and string cheese to the bowl. Mix thoroughly. Equally divide between the eggplant shells, lightly packing down until even.

Bake in the oven for 35 minutes. Then remove but keep the oven on.

Spoon ¼ cup crushed tomatoes evenly over the top of each stuffed eggplant shell, and lay string cheese pieces over the crushed tomatoes. Return to the oven for another 10 minutes, or until cheese has melted.

Let cool slightly and then cut each piece in half. Now enjoy!

MAKES 4 SERVINGS

YOU'LL NEED:
large baking sheet, nonstick spray, rolling pin (optional)

PREP:
15 minutes

COOK:
15 minutes

✳ For full-color photos of all the recipes in this book, check out hungry-girl.com/books. Woohoo!

JUST VEGGiN' PiZZA

Need to make a full-sized vegged-up pizza (almost) from scratch? Look no further. This recipe will produce a no-guilt pizza that everyone (this means you, your kids, your pals, and your man!) will love.

PER SERVING (⅛th of recipe, 1 slice): 150 calories, 1.5g fat, 572mg sodium, 26.5g carbs, 1g fiber, 4g sugars, 7g protein

Ingredients

1 package Pillsbury Classic Pizza Crust refrigerated dough

¾ cup canned tomato sauce with Italian seasonings

1 small Japanese eggplant, thinly sliced widthwise, ends removed (or 3 ounces regular eggplant, thinly sliced and cut into bite-sized pieces)

1 small zucchini, thinly sliced widthwise, ends removed

¾ cup shredded fat-free mozzarella cheese (or alternative at right)

½ cup sliced brown mushrooms

⅓ cup chopped red bell pepper

Optional toppings: reduced-fat Parmesan-style grated topping, crushed red pepper

Directions

Preheat oven to 425 degrees.

Spray a large baking sheet with nonstick spray. Roll out dough on the sheet into a large rectangle of even thickness.

Spread tomato sauce over the dough, leaving about a half-inch border for the crust. Place the eggplant and zucchini slices evenly over the sauce, and then sprinkle with the mozzarella cheese. Evenly distribute mushrooms and bell pepper over the pizza.

Bake in the oven for about 15 minutes, until the crust is a nice shade of golden brown. Cut into 8 pieces. If you like, top your piece with some reduced-fat Parmesan-style grated topping and/or crushed red pepper. Now dig in!

MAKES 8 SERVINGS

HG Alternative!

No fat-free mozzarella? No worries! Make this with part-skim mozzarella, and each serving will have 165 calories and 3.5g of fat.

YOU'LL NEED:
baking sheet, nonstick spray, rolling pin (optional), skillet, bowl

PREP:
10 minutes

COOK:
25 minutes

Dough you need some tips?

Turn to page 123 for Pillsbury pointers . . . DO IT!

📷 **For a pic of this recipe, see the first photo insert. Yay!**

BLT PiZZA

Yep, it's an unconventional BACON, LETTUCE, and TOMATO pizza. People love BLTs and they love pizza. Why not combine the two?

PER SERVING (⅙th of recipe, 1 slice): 213 calories, 5g fat, 815mg sodium, 35.5g carbs, 1g fiber, 6g sugars, 7.5g protein

Ingredients

1 package Pillsbury Classic Pizza Crust refrigerated dough
6 slices center-cut bacon or turkey bacon
½ cup fat-free mayonnaise
½ teaspoon dry ranch seasoning mix
2 cups shredded lettuce
2 plum tomatoes, chopped

Directions

Preheat oven to 425 degrees.

Spray a large baking sheet with nonstick spray. Roll out dough on the sheet into a large rectangle of even thickness.

Bake in the oven until golden brown, about 15 minutes. Set aside to cool.

Bring a skillet sprayed with nonstick spray to medium heat on the stove. Add bacon and cook until crispy, about 4 minutes per side. Once cool enough to handle, crumble or chop and set aside.

In a bowl, combine mayo with ranch mix and mix well. Spread mixture evenly over the cooled pizza crust. Evenly top with lettuce, tomatoes, and crumbled bacon.

Slice into 6 pieces and enjoy!

MAKES 6 SERVINGS

PIZZA-FIED GRILLED CHEESE

The name says it all. GRILLED CHEESE PIZZA. Uh, there's nothing more to say.

PER SERVING (entire recipe): 185 calories, 5g fat, 900mg sodium, 23.5g carbs, 5.5g fiber, 5g sugars, 13g protein

Ingredients

2 slices light bread
1 wedge The Laughing Cow Light Creamy Swiss cheese
2 tablespoons canned crushed tomatoes
½ teaspoon Italian seasoning
4 slices turkey pepperoni
1 slice fat-free American cheese
1 teaspoon light whipped butter or light buttery spread, room temperature
Optional: additional crushed tomatoes, additional Italian seasoning

Directions

Lay bread slices flat and evenly spread the upward-facing sides with cheese wedge. Evenly top one cheese-covered slice with crushed tomatoes, Italian seasoning, pepperoni slices, and American cheese. Top with other slice of bread, cheese-covered side down.

Evenly spread the upward-facing bread slice with ½ teaspoon butter. Place in a skillet with the buttered side down. Evenly spread remaining ½ teaspoon butter onto the upward-facing slice of bread.

Bring skillet to medium-high heat on the stove. Cook until bread is lightly browned and cheese has melted, about 2 minutes per side, flipping carefully.

If you like, season some additional crushed tomatoes with Italian seasoning and serve as a dip. Enjoy!

MAKES 1 SERVING

YOU'LL NEED:
skillet, nonstick spray

PREP:
10 minutes

COOK:
10 minutes

Don't let extra ingredients get bored in your fridge.

Flip to the index and look up tomatoes. Exciting uses there!

For a pic of this recipe, see the first photo insert. Yay!

YOU'LL NEED:
microwave-safe bowl,
bowl, grill or grill pan,
nonstick spray

PREP:
5 minutes

COOK:
10 minutes

GRiLLED GREEK PiZZA MiNiS

You like pizza? You like Greek food? Whip up a few batches of these and let the chewing begin!

PER SERVING (½ of recipe, 4 mini pizzas): 116 calories, 2.5g fat, 430mg sodium, 16g carbs, 3g fiber, 3g sugars, 9g protein

For the Weight Watchers *PointsPlus*™ values of all the recipes in this book, check out hungry-girl.com/books. Yay!

Ingredients

½ cup chopped mushrooms
½ cup chopped green bell pepper
¼ cup chopped onion
¼ cup canned crushed tomatoes
¼ teaspoon chopped garlic
⅛ teaspoon garlic powder
⅛ teaspoon oregano
Dash black pepper
1 piece lavash bread with about 100 calories
⅓ cup crumbled fat-free feta cheese
2 tablespoons sliced black olives

Directions

In a microwave-safe bowl, combine mushrooms, bell pepper, and onion with 2 tablespoons of water. Cover and microwave for 1 minute, or until veggies are soft. Set aside.

To make the sauce, in another bowl, combine tomatoes, garlic, and all the seasonings. Mix well and set aside.

Bring a grill or grill pan sprayed with nonstick spray to medium heat. Lay lavash bread flat and grill until slightly crispy, 3 to 4 minutes.

Carefully flip lavash bread and sprinkle with cheese. Top lavash with sauce in evenly spaced spoonfuls. Once cheese and sauce are hot, about 2 minutes, evenly top with veggies and olives.

Continue to grill until cheese has melted, about 3 minutes.

Carefully remove from grill, slice into 8 pizza minis, and enjoy!

MAKES 2 SERVINGS

Have extra olives?

Put 'em to work! Skip to the olives section of the index for a SLEW of recipes to use 'em in!

PIZZA-BELLAS

Ooooooooohhhhh . . . exciting! Adorable no-bread-needed pizzas that have mushroom crusts. Who needs all the extra carbs anyway?

PER SERVING (½ of recipe, 1 pizza-bella): 118 calories, 4.75g fat, 487mg sodium, 7.5g carbs, 1.75g fiber, 3g sugars, 11.5g protein

Ingredients

2 large portabella mushrooms
2 sticks light string cheese
¼ cup canned crushed tomatoes
½ teaspoon chopped garlic
Dash Italian seasoning
8 slices turkey pepperoni, chopped
2 tablespoons sliced black olives

Directions

Preheat oven to 400 degrees.

Remove mushroom stems, chop, and set aside. Place mushroom caps on a baking sheet sprayed with nonstick spray, rounded sides down. Bake in the oven for 8 minutes, or until softened.

Meanwhile, break each stick of string cheese into thirds and place in a blender or food processor—blend at high speed until cheese takes on a shredded or grated consistency. (Or just tear string cheese into pieces and roughly chop.) Set aside.

Remove sheet from the oven but leave oven on. Blot excess liquid from mushroom caps and set aside.

In a small bowl, combine crushed tomatoes, garlic, and Italian seasoning. Mix well and equally distribute between mushroom caps; spread until smooth and even. Sprinkle shredded/grated cheese over the saucy layer on each cap. Top with chopped mushroom stems, pepperoni, and olives.

Bake in the oven for 8 to 10 minutes, until cheese has melted. Eat as soon as you can without burning your mouth!

MAKES 2 SERVINGS

HG Alternative!

Don't like olives? Not into turkey pepperoni? Don't use 'em! Each standard saucy 'n cheesy mushroom "pizza" has 89 calories and 2.75g of fat, so feel free to pick your own toppings and add their stats to those numbers.

microwave-safe
bowl, blender or food
processor (optional),
small bowl, baking
sheet, nonstick spray

PREP:

25 minutes

COOK:

15 minutes

HG Tip! ✳

If you're
noshing solo,
only bake two
of the mini
pizzas. Wrap
the others in
plastic wrap
and freeze for
another time—
then just thaw,
bake, and eat!

PURPLE PIZZA EATERS

English muffin pizzas with a purple hue?! Kids freak over the way
they look but EVERYONE flips for the taste. Enjoy!!!

PER SERVING (½ of recipe, 2 mini pizzas): 240 calories, 5g fat,
812mg sodium, 32g carbs, 6.75g fiber, 2g sugars, 20.5g protein

Ingredients

3 ounces purple potato (about 1 small one), thinly sliced
2 sticks light string cheese
¼ cup fat-free ricotta cheese
2 drops purple food coloring (or a drop each of red and blue)
⅛ teaspoon garlic powder
2 dashes salt
2 tablespoons finely chopped red onion
2 light English muffins, split into halves
2 tablespoons precooked real crumbled bacon
Optional: black pepper, additional salt

Directions

Preheat oven to 375 degrees.

Place potato slices in a microwave-safe bowl with 2 tablespoons
water. Cover and nuke for about 2 minutes, until potatoes have
softened slightly. Drain water and set aside.

Break each stick of string cheese into thirds, and place in a
blender or food processor—blend at high speed until cheese takes
on a shredded or grated consistency. (Or tear string cheese into
pieces and roughly chop.) Set aside.

In a small bowl, mix ricotta cheese with food coloring, garlic powder, and salt, and stir until blended. Mix in onion, and then evenly distribute purple ricotta mixture among muffin halves. Chop potato slices into bite-sized pieces, and evenly distribute those as well.

Sprinkle "pizzas" with shredded/grated string cheese and bacon. Place on a baking sheet sprayed with nonstick spray.

Bake in the oven for 10 to 12 minutes, until pizzas are hot and string cheese has melted. If you like, season with pepper and additional salt. Now chew, you crazy thing!

MAKES 2 SERVINGS

HG Alternative!

If you can't find purple spuds, grab a small red-skinned potato. It won't be as beautiful, but it'll work fine.

blender or food processor (optional), small bowl, medium-large skillet, nonstick spray

PREP:

10 minutes

COOK:

10 minutes

CHEESY PiZZA QUESADiLLA

Pizzas rock—as do quesadillas. So why not combine the two for a head-explodingly amazing snack or mini meal?!

PER SERVING (entire recipe): 252 calories, 7.25g fat, 979mg sodium, 31.5g carbs, 7.5g fiber, 5.5g sugars, 18g protein

Ingredients

1 stick light string cheese
¼ cup canned crushed tomatoes, plus more for optional dipping
½ teaspoon Italian seasoning, plus more for optional dip
¼ cup sliced mushrooms
¼ cup chopped green bell pepper
1 medium-large high-fiber flour tortilla with about 110 calories
1 wedge The Laughing Cow Light Creamy Swiss cheese
4 slices turkey pepperoni, chopped

Directions

Break string cheese into thirds and place in a blender or food processor—blend at high speed until cheese takes on a shredded or grated consistency. (Or just tear string cheese into pieces and roughly chop.) Set aside.

In a small bowl, combine tomatoes with Italian seasoning. Mix well and set aside.

Bring a medium-large skillet (at least the size of the tortilla) sprayed with nonstick spray to medium-high heat on the stove. Add mushrooms and bell pepper. Stirring occasionally, cook until softened, about 4 minutes. Remove veggies and set aside.

Remove skillet from heat, re-spray, and bring to medium heat on the stove. Spread one side of the tortilla evenly with cheese wedge. Lay tortilla flat in the skillet. Evenly spread seasoned tomatoes over one half of the upward-facing side of the tortilla.

Evenly top tomatoes with half of the shredded/grated cheese, followed by veggies and turkey pepperoni. Top with remaining half of shredded/grated cheese. Cook for 3 minutes.

Using a spatula, carefully fold the plain half of the tortilla over the filling and press down lightly to seal. Carefully flip and cook until both sides are crispy, about 3 minutes.

Once cool enough to handle, slice into wedges. If you like, mix up some extra seasoned crushed tomatoes for your dipping pleasure and enjoy!

MAKES 1 SERVING

YOU'LL NEED:

large skillet, nonstick spray, large bowl, blender or food processor (optional)

PREP:

10 minutes

COOK:

20 minutes

PIZZA BURGERS A LA HG

Enjoy these Italian-inspired burgers on a light bun or flat roll, over a salad, or just on a plate. YUM!!!

PER SERVING (¼th of recipe, 1 patty with cheese and sauce): 223 calories, 7g fat, 559mg sodium, 9g carbs, 1.5g fiber, 5g sugars, 31g protein

Ingredients

1 cup chopped mushrooms
½ cup chopped green bell pepper
½ cup chopped onion
2 sticks light string cheese
1 pound raw extra-lean ground beef
2 tablespoons ketchup
1 teaspoon garlic powder
½ teaspoon dried oregano
½ teaspoon dried basil
Dash each salt and black pepper
½ cup pizza sauce
12 slices turkey pepperoni
Optional: lettuce leaves, for wrapping

Directions

Bring a large skillet sprayed with nonstick spray to medium-high heat on the stove. Add veggies and, stirring occasionally, cook until softened, about 5 minutes. Transfer to a large bowl and set aside.

Break each string cheese stick into thirds and place in a blender or food processor—blend at high speed until cheese takes on a shredded or grated consistency. (Or just tear string cheese into pieces and roughly chop.) Set aside.

Add beef, ketchup, and spices to the bowl with the cooked veggies. Use your hands to mix thoroughly. Evenly divide and form mixture into four ½-inch-thick patties.

Remove skillet from heat, re-spray, and bring to medium-high heat on the stove. Place patties in the skillet and cook to your liking, at least 3 minutes per side.

Reduce heat to medium low. Carefully top each patty in the skillet with 2 tablespoons sauce, ¼ of the shredded/grated cheese, and 3 slices pepperoni. Continue to cook until sauce is hot and cheese has melted, about 2 minutes.

Plate your patties, maybe wrap them up in some lettuce, and dig in!

MAKES 4 SERVINGS

YOU'LL NEED:

medium bowl,
blender or food
processor (optional),
baking sheet,
nonstick spray

PREP:

20 minutes

COOK:

10 minutes

THE GREAT GREEK PIZZA

Yup, MORE Greek pizza. Why? Because one Greek pizza recipe just isn't enough . . .

PER SERVING (entire recipe): 277 calories, 4.75g fat, 990mg sodium, 38g carbs, 8.5g fiber, 4.5g sugars, 19g protein

Ingredients

½ cup chopped spinach, thawed from frozen, squeezed dry

2 tablespoons crumbled fat-free feta cheese

½ teaspoon crushed garlic

1 stick light string cheese

1 whole-wheat or high-fiber pita

3 tablespoons canned crushed tomatoes

2 thin slices red onion, rings separated and halved

1 tablespoon sliced black olives

4 slices plum tomato

Dash dried oregano *or* ¼ teaspoon fresh oregano

Optional: salt and black pepper

Directions

Preheat oven to 375 degrees.

In a medium bowl, combine spinach, feta cheese, and garlic. Mix well and set aside.

Break string cheese into thirds and place in a blender or food processor—blend at high speed until cheese takes on a shredded or grated consistency. (Or just tear string cheese into pieces and roughly chop.) Set aside.

Spray a baking sheet with nonstick spray, and lay pita in center. Spread crushed tomatoes over the pita, leaving a ½-inch border around the edge. Evenly top with spinach-feta mixture, and then cover with shredded/grated string cheese.

Place onion, olive, and tomato slices on top of your "pizza," and sprinkle with oregano.

Bake in the oven for 8 to 10 minutes, until pizza is hot and string cheese has melted.

If you like, season to taste with salt and pepper. Cut into wedges, and enjoy!

MAKES 1 SERVING

Have leftover olives?

Use them in one of our many other recipes that call for olives—just go to the index and look 'em up under O!

small bowl, medium-large skillet, nonstick spray, baking sheet

PREP:
10 minutes

COOK:
20 minutes

CRISPY CHEESEBURGER PIZZA

This recipe is like the love child of a fast-food burger and a pizza. And that sounds like a baby ANYONE would love!

PER SERVING (entire recipe): 256 calories, 3.75g fat, 1,222mg sodium, 39g carbs, 9g fiber, 9g sugars, 25g protein

HG Sodium Tip!

Save about 300mg sodium with a no-salt-added ketchup, like the kind by Heinz.

Ingredients

1½ tablespoons ketchup

½ tablespoon fat-free mayonnaise

1 teaspoon yellow mustard

½ cup frozen ground-beef-style soy crumbles, thawed

1 medium-large high-fiber flour tortilla with about 110 calories

¼ cup shredded fat-free cheddar cheese

1 tablespoon chopped onion

3 tablespoons shredded lettuce

2 tablespoons chopped tomato

Optional toppings: hamburger dill pickle chips, additional ketchup

Directions

Preheat oven to 375 degrees.

In a small bowl, combine ketchup, mayo, and mustard, and mix until uniform. Add soy crumbles and toss to coat. Set aside.

Lightly spray a medium-large skillet (at least the size of the tortilla) with nonstick spray and bring to medium heat on the stove. Lay tortilla flat in the skillet and cook until slightly crispy, a few minutes on each side.

Transfer tortilla to a baking sheet sprayed with nonstick spray. Scoop soy crumble mixture into the center of the tortilla and spread it out evenly, leaving a ½-inch border around it. Sprinkle with cheese and onion.

Bake in the oven for 11 to 13 minutes, until tortilla border browns and cheese melts.

Top with lettuce and tomato. If you like, add pickles and a squiggle of ketchup. Cut into slices and EAT!

MAKES 1 SERVING

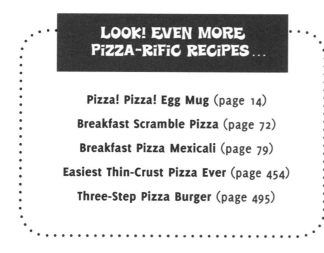

LOOK! EVEN MORE PIZZA-RIFIC RECIPES...

Pizza! Pizza! Egg Mug (page 14)

Breakfast Scramble Pizza (page 72)

Breakfast Pizza Mexicali (page 79)

Easiest Thin-Crust Pizza Ever (page 454)

Three-Step Pizza Burger (page 495)

CHAPTER 11: SANDWICHES

If bread stuffed with items is your thing, check these out . . .

YOU'LL NEED:

wide bowl, skillet,
nonstick spray

PREP:

5 minutes

COOK:

5 minutes

MONTE CRISTO SANDWICH

To "properly" enjoy this sandwich, dip it into some sugar-free preserves before taking a bite. DELISH!

PER SERVING (entire recipe): 232 calories, 7g fat, 954mg sodium, 21g carbs, 5.25g fiber, 3g sugars, 25g protein

Ingredients

2 slices light bread

1 teaspoon yellow mustard

1 ounce (about 2 slices) thickly sliced reduced-sodium lean skinless turkey breast

½ ounce (about 1 slice) thickly sliced 97% to 98% fat-free ham

1 slice reduced-fat Swiss cheese

¼ cup fat-free liquid egg substitute

Dash black pepper

1 teaspoon light whipped butter or light buttery spread

Optional: powdered sugar, sugar-free fruit preserves

Directions

Lay one slice of bread flat and evenly spread mustard onto the upward-facing side. Evenly top with half of the turkey, followed by ham, cheese, remaining turkey, and remaining slice of bread. Slice sandwich in half, diagonally, and set aside.

In a wide bowl, combine egg substitute and pepper. Stir and set aside.

Bring a skillet sprayed with nonstick spray to medium-high heat on the stove. Add butter and move the skillet back and forth to allow butter to coat the bottom.

One at a time, evenly coat sandwich halves in the egg mixture and place in the skillet. Cook until outsides are toasty and the cheese has melted, about 2 minutes per side, flipping carefully.

If you like, top with powdered sugar and preserves. Yum!

MAKES 1 SERVING

YOU'LL NEED:

small microwave-safe
bowl, microwave-safe
plate

PREP:

5 minutes

COOK:

5 minutes

SPiCY MEXiCAN SANDWiCH

The cayenne gives this baby a little heat . . . Add more than a pinch if you dare. *CALIENTE!*

PER SERVING (entire recipe): 228 calories, 5.5g fat, 906mg sodium, 22.5g carbs, 4g fiber, 4g sugars, 23.5g protein

Ingredients

2 tablespoons chopped onion
½ teaspoon chopped garlic
Dash chili powder
Dash cayenne pepper
3 ounces thinly sliced roast beef
1 small hamburger bun (light, if available)
¼ cup shredded lettuce
1 tablespoon salsa
Optional: jarred jalapeño slices

Directions

In a small microwave-safe bowl, combine onion with 1 tablespoon water. Cover and cook in the microwave for 1 minute, or until onion is soft. Once cool enough to handle, drain any excess water. Add garlic, chili powder, and cayenne pepper. Mix and set aside.

Place roast beef on a microwave-safe plate and warm in the microwave for about 30 seconds. Using two forks, shred the roast beef. Add to bowl with the onion mixture and mix well.

Evenly top the bottom half of the bun with the roast beef mixture, lettuce, salsa and, if you like, jalapeño slices. Finish it off with the top of the bun. *Olé!*

MAKES 1 SERVING

A+ AVOCADO BURGER

If you're not a HUGE avocado fan, skip this one. But if you LOVE the stuff, this will likely become your new favorite lunch (or dinner) . . .

YOU'LL NEED:
skillet, nonstick spray

PREP:
5 minutes

COOK:
10 minutes

PER SERVING (entire recipe): 292 calories, 9.5g fat, 728mg sodium, 33.5g carbs, 11g fiber, 5g sugars, 19g protein

Ingredients

One 100-calorie flat sandwich bun
1 wedge The Laughing Cow Light Creamy Swiss cheese
¼ cup shredded lettuce
1 slice tomato
1 slice red onion
1 frozen meatless hamburger-style patty with about 100 calories
1 ounce sliced avocado (about ¼ of an avocado)
Optional toppings: yellow mustard, ketchup

Directions

Split bun into halves and lightly toast. Spread bottom half with cheese wedge and top with lettuce, tomato, and red onion. Set aside.

Bring a skillet sprayed with nonstick spray to medium heat on the stove. Add patty and cook for about 4 minutes per side, until cooked through.

Place patty over the veggie-topped half of the bun. If you like, add a little mustard and ketchup. Top evenly with avocado.

Place the other half of the bun on top and enjoy!

MAKES 1 SERVING

skillet, nonstick spray,
small bowl

PREP:
5 minutes

COOK:
15 minutes

HG Sodium Tip!

Make this with
no-salt-added
skinless lean
turkey breast,
and your
sandwich will
clock in with
about 700mg
of sodium.

GRILLY GIRL CHEESY TURKEY & BACON 'WICH

SO ridiculously decadent—and under 250 calories. How can it be?!?!

PER SERVING (entire recipe): 228 calories, 6g fat,
1,037mg sodium, 22.5g carbs, 5g fiber, 3.5g sugars, 23g protein

Ingredients

1 slice center-cut bacon or turkey bacon
½ tablespoon fat-free mayonnaise
½ tablespoon sun-dried tomatoes packed in oil,
      drained and chopped
⅛ teaspoon Italian seasoning
2 slices light bread
2 ounces (about 4 slices) reduced-sodium skinless
      lean turkey breast
1 slice fat-free cheddar cheese
1 teaspoon light whipped butter or light buttery
      spread, room temperature, divided

Directions

Bring a skillet sprayed with nonstick spray to medium heat on the
stove. Add bacon and cook until crispy, about 4 minutes per side.

Once cool enough to handle, break or cut bacon in half and set aside.

To make the sauce, combine mayo, sun-dried tomatoes, and Italian
seasoning in a small bowl. Mix well. Spread sauce on one slice of
bread and top with bacon, turkey, and cheese. Place the other slice
of bread on top, and press gently to seal. Spread ½ teaspoon butter
on the upward-facing slice of bread. Set aside.

If needed, clean and dry skillet. Re-spray skillet and place sandwich in it with the buttered side down. Spread remaining ½ teaspoon butter on the upward-facing bread slice. Bring the skillet to medium-high heat on the stove. Cook for 2 minutes. Gently flip and cook for 1 additional minute, or until both sides are hot and toasty. Slice in half or bite right in!

MAKES 1 SERVING

YOU'LL NEED:
skillet or grill pan,
nonstick spray

PREP:
5 minutes

COOK:
15 minutes

SO-GOOD GRILLED VEGGIE PANINI

WOW—this could be one of the most delicious sandwiches of all time. You may never purchase premade panini again.

PER SERVING (entire recipe): 204 calories, 7.75g fat, 710mg sodium, 26.5g carbs, 6g fiber, 5.5g sugars, 12g protein

Ingredients

¼ cup sliced zucchini

¼ cup sliced red bell pepper

¼ cup sliced onion

¼ teaspoon Italian seasoning

⅛ teaspoon garlic powder

⅛ teaspoon salt

One 100-calorie flat sandwich bun

1 piece The Laughing Cow Mini Babybel Light cheese, chopped

2 teaspoons light whipped butter or light buttery spread, room temperature, divided

Directions

Bring a skillet or grill pan sprayed with nonstick spray to medium-high heat on the stove. Add zucchini, bell pepper, and onion, and sprinkle with seasonings. Stirring occasionally, cook until veggies have softened, 4 to 5 minutes. Remove from heat and set aside.

Split bun in half, and lay the halves flat, split sides up. Evenly top one half with cooked veggies and chopped cheese. Place the other half on top, split side down. Spread 1 teaspoon butter over the upward-facing side of the bun.

Place sandwich in the skillet/pan with the buttered side down. Evenly spread remaining 1 teaspoon butter over the upward-facing side of the bun. Bring skillet/pan back to medium-high heat.

Using a spatula, press down gently but firmly to seal the sandwich. Cook until lightly browned, 2 to 3 minutes per side, flipping carefully and pressing down with the spatula to seal.

Eat up!

MAKES 1 SERVING

Can't find flat buns?

Go to page 287 for other options!

YOU'LL NEED:

microwave-safe plate,
skillet, nonstick spray

PREP:

5 minutes

COOK:

15 minutes

✳ For full-color photos of all the recipes in this book, check out hungry-girl.com/books. Woohoo!

FLAT-TOP PATTY MELT

A classic ooey-gooey patty melt with less than half the calories of restaurant versions. Nice!

PER SERVING (entire recipe): 259 calories, 3.25g fat,
1,039mg sodium, 38.5g carbs, 10g fiber, 8g sugars, 23.5g protein

Ingredients

2 slices light bread (rye, if available)
2 slices fat-free American cheese
¾ cup sliced onion
1 frozen meatless hamburger-style patty with
    about 100 calories

Directions

Toast bread slices and place on a microwave-safe plate. Top one slice of bread with a slice of cheese, and set aside.

Bring a skillet sprayed with nonstick spray to medium heat on the stove. Add patty and cook for about 4 minutes per side, until cooked through. Place on cheese-topped bread slice and set aside.

Remove skillet from heat, re-spray, and bring to medium-high heat. Add onion and, stirring occasionally, cook until softened, about 5 minutes. Place cooked onion over the cooked patty, and top with remaining cheese slice.

Place the other toasted bread slice over the cheese and press lightly to seal. Microwave until cheese has melted and entire sandwich is hot, about 20 seconds.

Allow to cool slightly and then enjoy!

MAKES 1 SERVING

BLTA CLUB

Bacon . . . lettuce . . . tomato . . . and AVOCADO. A total YUMFEST!!!

YOU'LL NEED:
skillet, nonstick spray

PREP:
5 minutes

COOK:
10 minutes

PER SERVING (entire recipe): 244 calories, 12.75g fat, 782mg sodium, 25.5g carbs, 7.5g fiber, 4.5g sugars, 12g protein

Ingredients

2 slices light bread
3 slices center-cut bacon or turkey bacon
1 tablespoon fat-free mayonnaise
1 ounce mashed avocado (about ¼ of an avocado)
2 leaves lettuce
2 slices tomato

Directions

Lightly toast bread and set aside.

Bring a skillet sprayed with nonstick spray to medium heat on the stove. Add bacon and cook until crispy, about 4 minutes per side. Once cool enough to handle, break or cut bacon in half. Set aside.

Lay both slices of bread flat. Evenly spread mayo onto one slice and avocado onto the other slice.

Evenly top the mayo-covered slice of bread with lettuce, tomato, and bacon. Place the other bread slice on top with the avocado-covered side down.

Eat and enjoy!

MAKES 1 SERVING

2 small
microwave-safe bowls

PREP:
5 minutes

COOK:
5 minutes

For the Weight Watchers
PointsPlus™ values of
all the recipes in this
book, check out
hungry-girl.com/books.
Yay!

THANKSGIVING
TURKEY SANDWICH

This one uses classic holiday ingredients but is great any time of year. So no need to wait 'til late November to whip it up . . .

PER SERVING (entire recipe): 241 calories, 2.5g fat, 881mg sodium, 42g carbs, 6.25g fiber, 10g sugars, 17.5g protein

Ingredients

¼ cup dry stuffing mix
¼ cup sliced onion
1 tablespoon dried sweetened cranberries
2 slices light bread
½ tablespoon fat-free mayonnaise
2 ounces (about 4 slices) reduced-sodium skinless lean turkey breast
2 tablespoons fat-free turkey gravy

Directions

In a small microwave-safe bowl, combine dry stuffing with 2 tablespoons water. Microwave for 45 seconds, or until water has completely absorbed. Fluff with a fork and set aside.

In another small microwave-safe bowl, combine onion with 1 tablespoon water. Cook in the microwave for 1 minute, or until onion has softened. Once cool enough to handle, drain excess water and transfer onion to the bowl with the stuffing. Add cranberries and mix well. Set aside.

Lay one slice of bread flat, and evenly spread mayo onto the upward-facing side. Evenly top with stuffing mixture.

If you like, place turkey slices in the microwave-safe bowl and warm in the microwave for about 20 seconds. Evenly lay turkey over the stuffing mixture.

If you like, place gravy in the microwave-safe bowl and warm in the microwave for about 20 seconds. Drizzle gravy over the turkey.

Complete the sandwich by topping with the remaining slice of bread. Give thanks and eat up!

MAKES 1 SERVING

YOU'LL NEED:

small bowl, large skillet or grill pan, nonstick spray

PREP:

10 minutes

COOK:

15 minutes

RING-MY-BELLA MUSHROOM SANDWICH

Here's a delicious HG take on that classic over-caloried mushroom burger found at a place that rhymes with "The Schmeezecake Hacktory."

PER SERVING (entire recipe): 263 calories, 10.25g fat, 786mg sodium, 32.5g carbs, 7.5g fiber, 7g sugars, 15.5g protein

Ingredients

- 1 large portabella mushroom cap
- 1 teaspoon olive oil
- ⅛ teaspoon salt, or more to taste
- 2 dashes ground thyme, or more to taste
- 1 tablespoon fat-free mayonnaise
- Dash cayenne pepper, or more to taste
- 1 stick light string cheese
- One 100-calorie flat sandwich bun
- 1 teaspoon light whipped butter or light buttery spread, room temperature
- 2 dashes garlic powder
- 1 thick slice red onion, all rings intact
- 1 large slice tomato
- ½ cup shredded lettuce

Directions

Coat both sides of the mushroom cap with oil and sprinkle with salt and thyme. Gently rub the seasonings into the mushroom and set aside.

In a small bowl, season mayo to taste with cayenne pepper. Mix well and set aside. Pull string cheese into pieces and set aside as well.

Split apart the bun and spread the inside with butter. Sprinkle with garlic powder.

Bring a large skillet or grill pan sprayed with nonstick spray to medium-high heat on the stove. Place bun halves in the skillet/pan with the buttered sides down. Once warm and toasty, remove and plate with the buttered sides up.

Place mushroom in the skillet/pan, rounded side up, along with the onion, side by side. Cook for 5 minutes, and then flip both.

Top mushroom evenly with cheese, and cook for another 5 minutes, or until cheese and veggies have softened.

Place mushroom on the bottom half of the bun. Top with onion, tomato, and lettuce. Spread the buttered side of the bun's top half with mayo, and finish off your sandwich with it. Now CHEW!

MAKES 1 SERVING

Flat Bun 411 and Alternatives

If the words "100-calorie flat sandwich bun" in an ingredients list leave you confused, worry not. Just turn to the Recommended Products list on page 6 for specifics. If you can't find any of these on shelves, no worries. You can use a light English muffin, two slices of light bread, or a small hamburger bun (light, if available). Just look for something with around 100 calories that'll hold your sandwich together!

YOU'LL NEED:
skillet, nonstick spray

PREP:
5 minutes

COOK:
15 minutes

📷 For a pic of this recipe, see the first photo insert. Yay!

GRiLLED FUJi-N-ChiCK 'WiCH

sandwiches made with Fuji apples ROCK. There's no way around it. This one's GRILLED . . . and has chicken and cheese too. YAY!!!

PER SERVING (entire recipe): 298 calories, 5.5g fat, 659mg sodium, 30g carbs, 6g fiber, 10g sugars, 33g protein

Ingredients

One 4-ounce raw boneless skinless lean chicken breast cutlet
Dash each salt and black pepper
½ cup peeled and thinly sliced Fuji apple
¼ cup thinly sliced onion
2 dashes ground sage
2 dashes garlic powder
2 slices light bread
1 wedge The Laughing Cow Light Creamy Swiss cheese, room temperature
1 teaspoon light whipped butter or light buttery spread, room temperature, divided

Directions

Bring a skillet sprayed with nonstick spray to medium heat on the stove. Add chicken, season with salt and pepper, and cook for 4 minutes on one side.

Flip chicken in the skillet. Add apple and onion, and sprinkle with sage and garlic powder. Cook until apple and onion have softened and chicken is cooked through, about 4 minutes. Remove from heat.

Once chicken is cool enough to handle, thinly slice and set aside with the apple-onion mixture.

Lay bread slices flat and evenly spread the upward-facing sides with cheese. Evenly top one slice with chicken and apple-onion mixture. Place the other bread slice on top with cheese-covered side down. Press gently to seal.

Spread ½ teaspoon butter on the upward-facing bread slice. Set aside.

Remove skillet from heat, re-spray, and place back on the stove. Place sandwich in the skillet with the buttered side down. Spread remaining ½ teaspoon butter on the upward-facing bread slice.

Bring skillet to medium heat. Cook sandwich until hot and toasty, 1 to 2 minutes per side, flipping it gently.

Allow to cool slightly. Then cut it in half, if you like, or just bite right in! Yummm . . .

MAKES 1 SERVING

YOU'LL NEED:

plate, skillet with a lid, nonstick spray, toothpicks (optional)

PREP:

5 minutes

COOK:

20 minutes

📷 For a pic of this recipe, see the first photo insert. Yay!

PERFECT PORTABELLA CLUB

A mushroom club sandwich is unique for sure . . . but it's arguably better than a classic club sandwich. Try it and see!

PER SERVING (entire recipe): 208 calories, 8.25g fat, 892mg sodium, 27g carbs, 7g fiber, 5.5g sugars, 12g protein

Ingredients

1 large portabella mushroom cap
½ teaspoon olive oil
⅛ teaspoon salt
⅛ teaspoon black pepper
⅛ teaspoon garlic powder
2 slices center-cut bacon or turkey bacon
2 slices light bread
2 teaspoons fat-free mayonnaise
2 slices tomato
2 leaves romaine lettuce

Directions

Place mushroom cap on a plate, and evenly coat both sides with oil. Sprinkle with salt, pepper, and garlic powder.

Bring a skillet sprayed with nonstick spray to medium-high heat on the stove. Add mushroom cap, cover, and cook until soft, about 4 minutes per side. Once cool enough to handle, thinly slice and set aside.

Remove skillet from heat, re-spray, and bring to medium heat. Add bacon and cook until crispy, about 4 minutes per side. Once cool enough to handle, break or cut bacon slices in half and set aside.

Toast bread slices and place side by side on a plate. Evenly spread one slice with mayo and top with sliced mushroom, tomato, lettuce, and bacon. Finish it all off with the other piece of bread.

If you like, slice your sandwich and secure with fancy toothpicks. Get clubbin'!

MAKES 1 SERVING

2 large baking sheets,
nonstick spray,
blender or food
processor, large plate,
wide bowl,
medium pot

PREP:

15 minutes

COOK:

25 minutes

📷 **For a pic of this recipe, see the first photo insert. Yay!**

FAUX-FRIED MOZZARELLA-N-BASIL EGGPLANT SANDWICHES

cheesy, hot, and crispy veggie goodness . . . Mmmmm!

PER SERVING (¼th of recipe, 2 sandwiches with sauce):
147 calories, 3.25g fat, 694mg sodium, 25.5g carbs, 11.75g fiber,
5g sugars, 11g protein

Ingredients

Sandwiches
1 cup Fiber One Original bran cereal
¼ teaspoon salt
3 sticks light string cheese
½ cup fat-free liquid egg substitute
1 long eggplant, sliced widthwise into 16 slices
10 fresh large basil leaves, roughly chopped
1 teaspoon Italian seasoning
1 tablespoon reduced-fat Parmesan-style grated topping

Sauce
2 tablespoons diced onion
2 teaspoons chopped garlic
1 cup canned crushed tomatoes
½ teaspoon Italian seasoning
¼ teaspoon salt, or more to taste
Dash black pepper, or more to taste

Directions

Preheat oven to 350 degrees.

Spray two large baking sheets with nonstick spray and set aside.

Place cereal and salt in a blender or food processor. Grind cereal to a breadcrumb-like consistency. Transfer crumbs to a large plate and set aside.

Break string cheese into thirds and place in a blender or food processor—blend at high speed until cheese takes on a shredded consistency. (Or just tear string cheese into pieces and roughly chop.) Set aside.

Pour egg substitute into a wide bowl and set aside.

Dip one side of an eggplant slice into egg substitute, gently shake to remove excess egg substitute, and lay it in the cereal crumbs with the egg-covered side down. Carefully transfer the slice to a baking sheet with the crumb-covered side up. Repeat with remaining eggplant slices.

Spray the tops of the slices with nonstick spray and bake in the oven until eggplant begins to soften, about 10 minutes.

Remove sheets from the oven, but leave oven on. Carefully flip over *half* of the eggplant slices, so the crumb-covered sides are down, and sprinkle with shredded cheese and chopped basil. Evenly place one of the remaining eggplant slices on top of each of the flipped slices, crumb-coated side up. Sprinkle with Italian seasoning and Parm-style topping.

Return sheet to the oven and bake until cheese has melted and coating is crispy, about 10 minutes.

Meanwhile, to make the sauce, bring a medium pot sprayed with nonstick spray to medium-high heat on the stove. Add onion and garlic and, stirring occasionally, cook until soft, about 2 minutes.

Add all other sauce ingredients to the pot and mix well. Continue to cook and stir until hot, about 2 minutes. If you like, season to taste with additional salt and pepper. Remove from heat and set aside.

Serve eggplant sandwiches with warm sauce for dipping!

MAKES 4 SERVINGS

YOU'LL NEED:

plate, skillet, nonstick
spray

PREP:

5 minutes

COOK:

15 minutes

📷 **For a pic
of this recipe,
see the first
photo insert.
Yay!**

THE SKINNY ELVIS

*A little less conversation, a little more chewing . . . Bet even Elvis himself
would have appreciated this HG-ified version of his favorite sandwich.*

PER SERVING (entire recipe): 286 calories, 11.75g fat,
499mg sodium, 39g carbs, 7.5g fiber, 11g sugars, 11g protein

Ingredients

2 slices light bread
½ tablespoon light whipped butter or light buttery
    spread, room temperature
1 tablespoon reduced-fat peanut butter, room temperature
½ banana, thinly sliced
1 slice center-cut bacon or turkey bacon

Directions

Lay bread slices side by side on a plate, and evenly spread butter
onto both slices. Flip slices over. Evenly spread peanut butter onto
one slice and top with banana slices. Set aside.

Bring a skillet sprayed with nonstick spray to medium heat on the
stove. Add bacon and cook until crispy, about 4 minutes per side.
Once cool enough to handle, break or cut bacon slice in half.

Evenly place bacon over the banana slices. Top with the other
bread slice, buttered side up. Set aside.

If needed, clean and dry skillet. Re-spray skillet and bring to
medium-high heat. Add sandwich and cook until lightly browned
on both sides, about 2 minutes per side.

Serve and enjoy!

MAKES 1 SERVING

OPEN-FACED CHICKEN SALAD MELT

Like a diner chicken salad melt, only this one won't make your pants explode.

YOU'LL NEED:
baking sheet, nonstick spray, small bowl

PREP:
10 minutes

COOK:
5 minutes

PER SERVING (entire recipe): 299 calories, 7.75g fat, 1,224mg sodium, 26g carbs, 5.75g fiber, 4.5g sugars, 31g protein

Ingredients

2 slices light bread
3 ounces (about ⅓ cup) canned 98% fat-free chunk
    white chicken breast in water, drained and flaked
½ tablespoon whole-grain mustard
½ tablespoon fat-free mayonnaise
¼ cup dry broccoli cole slaw, roughly chopped
Squirt of lemon juice
Dash chili powder
Dash black pepper
2 slices 2% milk Swiss cheese

Directions

Preheat broiler.

Lightly toast bread. Set aside on a baking sheet lightly sprayed with nonstick spray.

In a small bowl, combine chicken, mustard, mayo, cole slaw, lemon juice, chili powder, and pepper. Mix well.

Evenly top each slice of bread with the chicken mixture, followed by a slice of cheese. Broil for 1 to 2 minutes, until cheese melts. Plate and enjoy!

MAKES 1 SERVING

YOU'LL NEED:
skillet, nonstick spray

PREP:
5 minutes

COOK:
5 minutes

GRiLLED CHEESE 'N VEGGiE SANDWiCH

Grilled cheese so good, you may start to cry when you bite into it. No exaggeration . . .

PER SERVING (entire recipe): 182 calories, 2.75g fat, 783mg sodium, 29.5g carbs, 7g fiber, 7g sugars, 15g protein

Ingredients

2 slices light bread
2 slices fat-free cheddar cheese
¼ cup thinly sliced onion
2 slices tomato
6 spinach leaves
1 teaspoon light whipped butter or light buttery spread, room temperature, divided
2 dashes garlic powder, divided

Directions

Lay a slice of bread flat and top with one slice of cheese. Evenly top with onion, tomato, and spinach. Top with remaining slice of cheese and slice of bread.

Evenly spread ½ teaspoon butter on the upward-facing slice of bread and sprinkle with a dash of garlic powder.

With the buttered side down, place sandwich in a skillet sprayed with nonstick spray. Spread remaining ½ teaspoon butter on the upward-facing slice of bread and sprinkle with remaining dash of garlic powder.

Bring the skillet to medium heat on the stove. Cook sandwich until cheese has melted and bread is lightly browned, 1 to 2 minutes per side, flipping carefully.

Eat your sandwich and enjoy it!

MAKES 1 SERVING

CHAPTER 12: CROCK-POT FUN

Break out the slow cooker . . .
like RIGHT NOW.

crock pot, bowl

PREP:

15 minutes

COOK:

4 hours *or*

7 to 8 hours

VERY VERY VEGGIE STEW

ooooh—a large pot of veggies that have cooked slowly for your chewing pleasure. Nicely done!

PER SERVING (⅛th of recipe, about 1 cup): 100 calories, 1g fat, 296mg sodium, 20g carbs, 6g fiber, 7g sugars, 4g protein

Ingredients

1 cup canned chickpeas, drained and rinsed

1 eggplant, peeled and cut into ½-inch cubes

2 cups coarsely chopped zucchini

1 cup coarsely chopped carrot

1 cup cubed butternut squash

1 cup chopped onion

1 tomato, coarsely chopped

1½ cups fat-free vegetable broth

One 6-ounce can tomato paste

1 tablespoon chopped garlic

1 teaspoon extra-virgin olive oil

1 teaspoon dried basil

⅓ teaspoon cinnamon

¼ teaspoon salt, or more to taste

⅛ teaspoon paprika

⅛ teaspoon ground ginger

1 no-calorie sweetener packet

Directions

Place the chickpeas and all the veggies in the crock pot.

In a bowl, combine broth, tomato paste, garlic, olive oil, basil, cinnamon, salt, paprika, ginger, and sweetener. Mix well and pour evenly over the contents of the crock pot. Gently stir to allow the sauce to coat the veggies.

Cover and cook on high for about 4 hours *or* on low for 7 to 8 hours. If you like, add additional salt to taste. Enjoy!

MAKES 8 SERVINGS

Need squash-slicing advice?

Page 431 has got you covered!

YOU'LL NEED:

skillet and nonstick
spray *or* microwave-
safe plate, crock pot

PREP:

10 minutes

COOK:

10 minutes plus
3 to 4 hours *or*
7 to 8 hours

For the Weight Watchers
PointsPlus™ values of
all the recipes in this
book, check out
hungry-girl.com/books.
Yay!

CROCK-POT COQ AU VIN

Oh, don't get all intimidated by the fancy name. It's just chicken, bacon, mushrooms, and some other stuff in a big pot . . .

PER SERVING (⅛ th of recipe, about 1 cup): 202 calories, 3g fat, 330mg sodium, 9g carbs, 1.25g fiber, 3.5g sugars, 29g protein

Ingredients

4 slices center-cut bacon or turkey bacon

1 cup fat-free low-sodium chicken broth

½ cup red wine

1 tablespoon cornstarch

½ tablespoon chopped garlic

2 sprigs fresh thyme, chopped

1½ pounds raw boneless skinless lean
    chicken breast tenders

¼ teaspoon salt, or more to taste

¼ teaspoon black pepper, or more to taste

2 cups sliced mushrooms

1½ cups baby carrots

1½ cups sliced onion

Directions

Prepare bacon on the stove in a skillet sprayed with nonstick spray or on a microwave-safe plate in the microwave. (Refer to package instructions for exact temperature and time.) Once cool enough to handle, crumble or chop and set aside.

Combine broth, wine, cornstarch, garlic, and thyme in the crock pot. Stir until completely mixed. Season chicken with salt and pepper, and then add it to the pot. Add bacon and veggies and stir thoroughly.

Cover and cook on high for 3 to 4 hours *or* on low for 7 to 8 hours, until chicken is cooked through.

Stir well and, if you like, season to taste with additional salt and pepper. Enjoy!

MAKES 6 SERVINGS

YOU'LL NEED:

large bowl, crock pot, bowl

PREP:

15 minutes

COOK:

3 hours *or* 7 hours

CROCK-POT CiNNA-APPLES 'N OATS

A delicious slow-cooked b-fast that'll fill you up! Make a pot the night before and just heat 'n eat in the AM. Yes!!!

PER SERVING (⅕ᵗʰ of recipe, 1 heaping cup): 249 calories, 4.5g fat, 320mg sodium, 52g carbs, 7.5g fiber, 26g sugars, 4.5g protein

Ingredients

8 cups chopped Fuji apples (about 6 apples)
2 tablespoons brown sugar (not packed), divided
1½ teaspoons cinnamon, divided
1½ cups old-fashioned oats
1 cup light vanilla soymilk
⅓ cup sugar-free pancake syrup
½ teaspoon salt
2 tablespoons light whipped butter or light buttery spread

Directions

In a large bowl, mix apples with 1 tablespoon brown sugar and ½ teaspoon cinnamon. Stir to coat apples well. Transfer to the crock pot.

In the empty bowl, combine all remaining ingredients *except* the butter (oats, soymilk, 1 tablespoon brown sugar, 1 teaspoon cinnamon, syrup, and salt). Add 1 cup water and mix well.

Add oat mixture to the crock pot, and gently stir. Cover and cook on high for 3 hours *or* on low for 7 hours.

Add butter and mix well. (Do NOT forget this step. Stick a Post-it to your timer if you have to!) Serve and enjoy!

MAKES 5 SERVINGS

CROCK-POT FAKE-BAKED BEANS

Who says you have to BAKE beans? People who are WRONG, that's who!

YOU'LL NEED:
bowl, crock pot

PREP:
20 minutes

COOK:
3 to 4 hours *or*
7 to 8 hours

PER SERVING (⅟₁₀th of recipe, about ¾ cup): 174 calories, 0.75g fat, 473mg sodium, 36.5g carbs, 9g fiber, 12g sugars, 7.5g protein

Ingredients

One 6-ounce can tomato paste
¼ cup molasses
2 tablespoons cider vinegar
1 tablespoon yellow mustard
1 teaspoon chopped garlic
½ teaspoon salt
One 15-ounce can black beans, drained and rinsed
One 15-ounce can pinto beans, drained and rinsed
One 15-ounce can red kidney beans, drained and rinsed
3 cups finely chopped onion
2 cups finely chopped red bell pepper
1 cup finely chopped Fuji apple

Directions

In a bowl, combine tomato paste, molasses, vinegar, mustard, garlic, and salt. Mix thoroughly and set aside.

Place all remaining ingredients in the crock pot. Add the tomato paste mixture and toss to coat.

Cover and cook on high for 3 to 4 hours *or* on low for 7 to 8 hours.

Stir well and then serve it up!

MAKES 10 SERVINGS

'CUE THE PULLED PORK

This unique spin on classic BBQ combines "sensible" pork tenderloin with "indulgent" pork shoulder. The result? A lightened-up yet super-delicious pot of pork BBQ . . . AMAZING!!!

PER SERVING (⅛th of recipe, about ⅔ cup): 220 calories, 6g fat, 637mg sodium, 16g carbs, 1g fiber, 12g sugars, 24g protein

Ingredients

1 cup canned tomato sauce

½ cup ketchup

2 tablespoons plus 2 teaspoons brown sugar (not packed)

2 tablespoons plus 2 teaspoons cider vinegar

2 teaspoons garlic powder

12 ounces raw lean boneless pork tenderloin, trimmed of excess fat

12 ounces raw boneless pork shoulder (the leanest piece you can find), trimmed of excess fat

¼ teaspoon salt

⅛ teaspoon black pepper

2 cups sliced onion, cut into 2-inch strips

Optional: crushed red pepper

Directions

Place tomato sauce, ketchup, sugar, vinegar, and garlic powder in the crock pot. Stir until mixed. Season both types of pork with salt and black pepper, and add pork to the crock pot. Top with onion and gently stir.

Cover and cook on high for 3 to 4 hours *or* on low for 7 to 8 hours, until pork is fully cooked.

Remove all the pork and place it in a large bowl. Shred each piece using two forks—one to hold the pork in place and the other to scrape across the meat and shred it.

Return the shredded pork to the crock pot and mix well with the sauce.

If you're serving a group, keep the crock pot on its lowest setting, so the pork stays warm. If you like, season to taste with crushed red pepper. Yum time!

MAKES 6 SERVINGS

PREP:

5 minutes

COOK:

10 minutes plus
3 to 4 hours *or*
7 to 8 hours

📷 **For a pic
of this recipe,
see the
second photo
insert. Yay!**

CHEESEBURGER MAC ATTACK

There are eight servings in this INCREDIBLE recipe, and you'll likely want to inhale 'em all at once. Don't say you weren't warned. Just invite your friends over and let the chewing begin!

PER SERVING (⅛th of recipe, about 1 cup): 179 calories, 5.75g fat, 512mg sodium, 19g carbs, 2g fiber, 3.5g sugars, 12.5g protein

Ingredients

5 ounces (about 1¼ cups) uncooked elbow macaroni
   with at least 2g fiber per 2-ounce serving
10 ounces raw lean ground turkey
1 teaspoon onion powder
2 tablespoons ketchup
24 ounces (about 6 cups) frozen Green Giant
   Cauliflower & Cheese (or Three Cheese) Sauce
3 wedges The Laughing Cow Light Creamy Swiss cheese
Optional: salt and black pepper

Directions

In a large pot, prepare pasta *very* al dente, cooking for about half of the time indicated on the package. Drain well and set aside.

In a bowl, combine turkey, onion powder, and ketchup. Use your hands to mix well. Transfer mixture to a crock pot.

Add frozen veggies and cooked pasta to the crock pot and gently stir. Cover and cook on high for 3 to 4 hours *or* on low for 7 to 8 hours, until turkey is fully cooked.

Stir mixture and crumble turkey. Add cheese wedges and stir until evenly distributed. Season to taste with salt and pepper, if you like, and dig in!

MAKES 8 SERVINGS

SWEET 'N RED HOT APPLE MASH

It's a great side dish, a delicious dessert, and even a super-duper topping for fro yo! Is there anything this rockin' crock-pot dish CAN'T do?

PER SERVING (⅙th of recipe, a heaping ½ cup): 121 calories, 1g fat, 63mg sodium, 30g carbs, 2.5g fiber, 23.5g sugars, 0.5g protein

Ingredients

8 Fuji apples, peeled, cored, and cut into chunks
3 tablespoons Red Hots cinnamon-flavored candies
1 tablespoon light whipped butter or light buttery spread, room temperature
½ tablespoon lemon juice
1 teaspoon vanilla extract
1 teaspoon cinnamon
¼ teaspoon ground nutmeg
⅛ teaspoon salt

Directions

Place apples and Red Hots in a crock pot.

In a small bowl, combine all other ingredients. Add 2 tablespoons water and mix well. Pour mixture over the contents of the crock pot, and stir to coat.

Cover and cook on high for 3 to 4 hours *or* on low for 7 to 8 hours, until apples have softened and candy has dissolved.

Stir well and serve!

MAKES 6 SERVINGS

YOU'LL NEED:
crock pot, small bowl

PREP:
5 minutes

COOK:
3 to 4 hours *or*
7 to 8 hours

YOU'LL NEED:

crock pot, large bowl

PREP:

10 minutes

COOK:

3 to 4 hours *or*
7 to 8 hours

📷 **For a pic of this recipe, see the second photo insert. Yay!**

CHICKEN AND SAUSAGE GUMBO

A new HG classic. You like gumbo? You'll LOVE this version . . . PROMISE!

PER SERVING (⅒th of recipe, about 1 cup): 117 calories, 3.5g fat, 523mg sodium, 8g carbs, 2g fiber, 3.5g sugars, 13g protein

Ingredients

8 ounces raw boneless skinless lean chicken breast cutlets

⅛ teaspoon salt, or more to taste

⅛ teaspoon black pepper, or more to taste

12 ounces (about 4 links) fully cooked chicken sausage, sliced into ¼-inch coins

One 14.5-ounce can diced tomatoes with green chilies (not drained)

3 cups reduced-sodium fat-free chicken broth

2 cups frozen cut okra

1½ cups chopped celery

1 green bell pepper, seeded and chopped

1 large onion, chopped

1½ teaspoons Cajun seasoning

1 teaspoon chopped garlic

1 teaspoon Worcestershire sauce

1 teaspoon ground thyme

Directions

Season chicken with salt and pepper, and place it in the crock pot. Add all remaining ingredients and lightly stir.

Cover and cook on high for 3 to 4 hours *or* on low for 7 to 8 hours, until chicken is fully cooked.

Remove chicken and place in a large bowl. Shred each piece using two forks—one to hold the chicken in place and the other to scrape across the meat and shred it.

Return shredded chicken to the crock pot, and give your gumbo a stir. If you like, season to taste with additional salt and pepper. Serve it up!

MAKES 10 SERVINGS

large skillet, nonstick spray, crock pot, bowl, whisk

PREP:

20 minutes

COOK:

10 minutes plus 3 to 4 hours *or* 7 to 8 hours

📷 **For a pic of this recipe, see the second photo insert. Yay!**

OUTSIDE-IN TURKEY TAMALE PIE

Here's a crazy-delicious, stick-to-your-ribs recipe that anyone will FLIP for. Especially kids and husbands . . .

PER SERVING (¹⁄₇ᵗʰ of recipe, about 1 cup): 230 calories, 7.5g fat, 481mg sodium, 21g carbs, 3g fiber, 3g sugars, 19g protein

Ingredients

1¼ pounds raw lean ground turkey

¾ cup yellow cornmeal

1 cup fat-free chicken or vegetable broth

One 14.5-ounce can diced tomatoes with chilies (not drained)

1 small onion, chopped

¾ cup canned sweet corn, drained

½ cup canned red kidney beans, drained and rinsed

½ cup sliced black olives, drained

2 teaspoons chili powder

1 teaspoon ground cumin

Optional toppings: fat-free shredded cheddar cheese, fat-free sour cream

Directions

Bring a large skillet sprayed with nonstick spray to medium-high heat on the stove. Add turkey and spread it around to break it up a bit. Cook and crumble until meat is brown and cooked through, about 6 minutes. Drain any excess liquid and add turkey to the crock pot.

In a bowl, combine cornmeal with broth and whisk thoroughly. Let stand for 5 minutes.

Add cornmeal mixture to the crock pot along with all other ingredients. Mix thoroughly.

Cover and cook on high for 3 to 4 hours *or* on low for 7 to 8 hours.

Serve and, if you like, top each serving with cheese and/or sour cream. Mmmmmm!!!

MAKES 7 SERVINGS

HG Tip!

If you have one of those fancy-pants immersion blenders, you can puree your soup right in the crock pot. SUPER-EASY!

VERY VEGGIE BiSQUE

A thick and tasty six-veggie soup. It won't win any beauty pageants, but it's REALLY delicious!

PER SERVING (⅛th of recipe, 1 generous cup): 78 calories, 1g fat, 460mg sodium, 15g carbs, 2.5g fiber, 4.5g sugars, 4g protein

Ingredients

3 cups chopped broccoli
2 cups chopped cauliflower
2 cups chopped zucchini or other summer squash
2 cups sliced mushrooms
1 cup chopped onion
1 medium russet potato (about 7 ounces), peeled and cubed
1 tablespoon chopped garlic
3 cups fat-free vegetable broth
1 cup light plain soymilk
2 tablespoons reduced-fat Parmesan-style grated topping
½ teaspoon salt, or more to taste
½ teaspoon black pepper
¼ teaspoon ground thyme

Directions

Add all ingredients to the crock pot along with 1 cup water. Mix well.

Cover and cook on high for about 4 hours *or* on low for 7 to 8 hours, until veggies are tender enough to puree.

Allow to cool slightly. Working in batches, transfer soup to a blender and puree until smooth, transferring the pureed batches to a large bowl.

Serve it up—reheating in the pot, if needed—and enjoy!

MAKES 8 SERVINGS

TEN-ALARM
SOUTHWESTERN CORN CHOWDER

This thick 'n yummy chowder is sweet, but it's also hot, Hot, HOT! Don't say you weren't warned . . .

PER SERVING (⅛th of recipe, 1 generous cup): 119 calories, 1g fat, 367mg sodium, 24.5g carbs, 2.75g fiber, 7g sugars, 4g protein

Ingredients

Two 14.5-ounce cans (about 3½ cups) fat-free chicken broth
One 14.75-ounce can cream-style corn
2 cups frozen sweet corn kernels
2 plum tomatoes, chopped
1 red bell pepper, seeded and chopped
1 green bell pepper, seeded and chopped
1 onion, finely chopped
½ cup light plain soymilk
1 tablespoon canned chopped chipotle peppers in adobo sauce
1 teaspoon chopped garlic
¼ teaspoon ground cumin
¾ cup instant mashed potato flakes
¼ cup fat-free sour cream
Optional: salt, black pepper, chopped fresh cilantro

Directions

Place all ingredients *except* the potato flakes, sour cream, and optional ingredients in the crock pot. Mix well.

Cover and cook on high for 3 to 4 hours *or* on low for 7 to 8 hours.

Add potato flakes and sour cream. Stir thoroughly. If you like, season to taste with salt and black pepper and sprinkle with cilantro.

Slurpin' time!

MAKES 8 SERVINGS

YOU'LL NEED:
crock pot

PREP:
15 minutes

COOK:
3 to 4 hours *or*
7 to 8 hours

HG Tip!

For no-alarm chowder, leave out the chipotle peppers in sauce . . .

YOU'LL NEED:

large bowl, crock pot

PREP:

15 minutes

COOK:

3 to 4 hours *or*

7 to 8 hours

✳ For full-color photos of all the recipes in this book, check out hungry-girl.com/books. Woohoo!

ALL THE RAGE BOLOGNESE

Use it as a sauce, top salads with it, or just enjoy it straight. AWE. SOME. And it's super-easy to make, too . . .

PER SERVING (¹⁄₁₀th of recipe, 1 heaping cup):
150 calories, 4g fat, 391mg sodium, 14.5g carbs, 3.25g fiber, 8g sugars, 13.5g protein

Ingredients

One 28-ounce can crushed tomatoes

One 6-ounce can tomato paste

1 tablespoon chopped garlic

1 tablespoon balsamic vinegar

½ tablespoon Worcestershire sauce

1 teaspoon dried oregano, or more to taste

1 teaspoon dried basil, or more to taste

Dash crushed red pepper, or more to taste

One 14.5-ounce can diced tomatoes, lightly drained

2 carrots, finely chopped

1 onion, finely chopped

1 red bell pepper, seeded and finely chopped

1 green pepper, seeded and finely chopped

1¼ pounds raw lean ground turkey

⅛ teaspoon salt, or more to taste

Directions

In a large bowl, combine crushed tomatoes, tomato paste, garlic, vinegar, Worcestershire sauce, oregano, basil, and crushed red pepper. Stir until thoroughly mixed.

Add diced tomatoes and all the veggies. Stir to coat. Set aside.

Place turkey in the bottom of the crock pot and sprinkle with salt. Mix well to break up the meat and distribute the salt. (Using your hands is the easiest way.) Add the mixture in the bowl to the crock pot. Stir gently. Cover and cook on high for 3 to 4 hours *or* on low for 7 to 8 hours.

Once ready to serve, stir thoroughly. If you like, season to taste with additional herbs and salt. Eat up!

MAKES 10 SERVINGS

CHICKEN CHILI SURPRISE

It's part chili—part soup . . . SURPRISE!

PER SERVING (1/10th of recipe, about 1 cup): 175 calories, 1.25g fat, 531mg sodium, 19g carbs, 4.75g fiber, 2g sugars, 22g protein

Ingredients

Two 15-ounce cans white kidney beans, drained and rinsed, divided

4 cups fat-free chicken broth, divided

1½ pounds raw boneless skinless lean chicken breast cutlets

¼ teaspoon salt

¼ teaspoon black pepper

One 7-ounce can diced green chilies, lightly drained

1 small onion, chopped

1 cup finely chopped celery

1 cup frozen white corn

1 tablespoon chopped garlic

1 teaspoon chili powder

½ teaspoon ground cumin

½ teaspoon hot pepper sauce, or more to taste

½ teaspoon dried oregano

Optional toppings: salsa, fat-free sour cream

Directions

Place half of the beans in a blender or food processor. Add 1 cup broth and puree until smooth. Transfer pureed beens to the crock pot.

Season chicken with salt and pepper and add to the crock pot. Add remaining beans, broth, and all remaining ingredients *except* the optional toppings to the crock pot.

Cover and cook on high for 3 to 4 hours *or* on low for 7 to 8 hours, until chicken is fully cooked.

Remove the chicken pieces and place them in a large bowl. Shred each piece using two forks—one to hold the chicken in place and the other to scrape across the meat and shred it. Return the shredded chicken to the crock pot, and stir into the chili.

Top a bowlful with salsa and fat-free sour cream, if you like. Eat up!

MAKES 10 SERVINGS

CHAPTER 13:
STIR-FRYS & SKILLET MEALS

Bust out that skillet, YOU, and get cookin'!

YOU'LL NEED:

large skillet with a lid,
nonstick spray, small
bowl

PREP:

5 minutes

COOK:

15 minutes

HG'S CARIBBEAN SHRIMP SURPRISE

Mmmmm . . . mango, shrimp, black beans, and broccoli?! And you get two full cups of it for less than 300 calories. THAT is a calorie bargain!

PER SERVING (½ of recipe, about 2 cups): 292 calories, 3.25g fat, 795mg sodium, 35.5g carbs, 9.25g fiber, 12g sugars, 32g protein

For the Weight Watchers
PointsPlus™ values of
all the recipes in this
book, check out
hungry-girl.com/books.
Yay!

Ingredients

3 cups broccoli florets
⅓ cup mango nectar
1 tablespoon ketchup
½ tablespoon lime juice
½ tablespoon chopped garlic
½ teaspoon cornstarch
½ teaspoon chili powder
⅛ teaspoon salt, or more to taste
⅛ teaspoon black pepper, or more to taste
1 red bell pepper, seeded, sliced
8 ounces raw shrimp, peeled, deveined, tails removed
¾ cup canned black beans, lightly drained

Directions

Bring a large skillet sprayed with nonstick spray to medium heat on the stove. Add broccoli and ¼ cup water. Cover and cook until broccoli has slightly softened, about 5 minutes.

Meanwhile, to make sauce, in a small bowl combine mango nectar, ketchup, lime juice, garlic, cornstarch, chili powder, salt, and black pepper. Mix well and set aside.

Add bell pepper and shrimp to the skillet. Stirring often, cook until shrimp are cooked through, about 5 minutes.

Add black beans and sauce and mix well. Continue to cook until sauce is evenly distributed and black beans are hot, about 1 minute.

Serve and enjoy!

MAKES 2 SERVINGS

extra-large skillet,
nonstick spray

PREP:

5 minutes

COOK:

15 minutes

For full-color
photos of all the recipes
in this book, check out
hungry-girl.com/books.
Woohoo!

SKILLET-SEARED SCALLOPS FRA DiAVOLO

Here's a seafood-packed Italian dish that's LOADED with flavor and protein but not fat.

PER SERVING (½ of recipe, about 2¼ cups): 244 calories, 1.5g fat, 910mg sodium, 24g carbs, 4.5g fiber, 10.5g sugars, 31.5g protein

Ingredients

12 ounces raw large scallops
⅛ teaspoon salt, or more to taste
⅛ teaspoon black pepper, or more to taste
1 onion, chopped
½ cup chopped red bell pepper
2 teaspoons chopped garlic
1 cup canned fire-roasted diced tomatoes, drained
¾ cup canned crushed tomatoes
1 teaspoon dried oregano
¼ teaspoon crushed red pepper, or more to taste
¼ teaspoon Frank's RedHot Original Cayenne
        Pepper Sauce, or more to taste

Directions

Bring an extra-large skillet sprayed well with nonstick spray to medium-high heat on the stove. Season scallops with salt and black pepper, and place them in the skillet. Cook until evenly seared, 1 to 2 minutes per side.

Reduce heat to medium. Add onion, bell pepper, and garlic. Gently stirring occasionally, cook until veggies have softened, about 4 minutes.

Add all other ingredients to the skillet and carefully mix. Gently stirring occasionally, cook until tomatoes are hot and scallops are cooked through, 3 to 4 minutes.

Serve and, if you like, season to taste with additional salt, black pepper, crushed red pepper, and hot sauce. Enjoy!

MAKES 2 SERVINGS

YOU'LL NEED:

large skillet,
nonstick spray, small
microwave-safe bowl

PREP:

10 minutes

COOK:

15 minutes

THE CLUB SKILLET

An interesting and incredibly delicious take on a classic "club." It takes the original from a sandwich to a full-on meal!

PER SERVING (½ of recipe): 299 calories, 6.5g fat, 773mg sodium, 16g carbs, 3g fiber, 7g sugars, 41g protein

Ingredients

3 slices center-cut bacon or turkey bacon

10 ounces raw boneless skinless lean turkey breast,
     cut into bite-sized pieces

⅛ teaspoon salt

⅛ teaspoon black pepper

1 small red onion, sliced

1 wedge The Laughing Cow Light Creamy Swiss cheese

2 tablespoons honey mustard

1 tablespoon fat-free mayonnaise

6 cups spinach leaves

½ teaspoon chopped garlic

1 small tomato, chopped

Directions

Bring a large skillet sprayed with nonstick spray to medium heat on the stove. Add bacon and cook until crispy, about 4 minutes per side. Once cool enough to handle, crumble or chop and set aside.

Remove skillet from heat and, if needed, clean and dry. Re-spray and bring to medium-high heat. Season turkey with salt and pepper and add to the skillet.

Add onion and, stirring occasionally, cook until onion is soft and turkey is cooked through, about 5 minutes.

Meanwhile, in a small microwave-safe bowl, combine cheese wedge, honey mustard, and mayo. Microwave for 30 seconds, or until hot, and stir until smooth. Set aside.

Add spinach and garlic to the skillet. Cook and stir until spinach has mostly wilted, about 1 minute. Add cheese-mustard mixture and toss to coat.

Remove skillet from heat and stir in tomato and bacon. Serve it up!

MAKES 2 SERVINGS

large skillet, nonstick
spray, bowl

PREP:
10 minutes

COOK:
15 minutes

CHEESY BURGER SKILLET

> You can use it as a sandwich filler, a salad topper, or a
> center-plate entrée. Totally your call . . . and it's TOTALLY delicious.

PER SERVING (½ of recipe, about 1¾ cups): 267 calories, 6.25g fat,
854mg sodium, 29.5g carbs, 9.5g fiber, 11g sugars, 21g protein

Ingredients

3 frozen meatless hamburger-style patties with about
    100 calories each
1½ cups sliced onion
1½ cups chopped tomatoes
½ cup canned crushed tomatoes
1 teaspoon yellow mustard
2 wedges The Laughing Cow Light Creamy Swiss cheese

Directions

Bring a large skillet sprayed with nonstick spray to medium-
high heat on the stove. Add burger patties and onion. Cook until
patties are hot and slightly blackened on both sides and onion has
softened, about 6 minutes, stirring onion occasionally.

Meanwhile, combine chopped tomatoes, crushed tomatoes, and
mustard in a bowl. Mix well and set aside.

Using a spatula, carefully break patties into bite-sized pieces while
still in the skillet.

Add tomato-mustard mixture and cheese wedges to the skillet,
breaking cheese wedges into pieces as you add them. Stirring
continually, cook until cheese is melted and evenly distributed,
about 5 minutes.

Serve it up and devour!

MAKES 2 SERVINGS

SWEET APPLE & CHICKEN STIR-FRY

Apples and chicken, together again. Toss in a little onion and you've got a sweet 'n savory skillet meal! Yummmmm . . .

YOU'LL NEED:
large skillet or wok, nonstick spray

PREP:
10 minutes

COOK:
10 minutes

PER SERVING (½ of recipe, about 2 cups): 285 calories, 2.25g fat, 406mg sodium, 24.5g carbs, 4g fiber, 15.5g sugars, 40.5g protein

Ingredients

12 ounces raw boneless skinless lean
    chicken breast, thinly sliced
¼ teaspoon onion powder
¼ teaspoon dried oregano
¼ teaspoon garlic powder
¼ teaspoon salt, divided
Dash black pepper, or more to taste
1 teaspoon chopped garlic
1 large Fuji apple, cored and thinly sliced
1 large onion, thinly sliced
½ tablespoon balsamic vinegar

Directions

Bring a large skillet or wok sprayed with nonstick spray to medium-high heat on the stove. Add chicken and sprinkle with onion powder, oregano, garlic powder, ⅛ teaspoon salt, and pepper. Add chopped garlic and mix well. Stirring often, cook until chicken begins to brown, about 3 minutes.

Add apple, onion, remaining ⅛ teaspoon salt, and vinegar. Stirring frequently, cook until apple and onion have softened and chicken is fully cooked, about 6 minutes.

Remove from heat, divvy it up, and dig in!

MAKES 2 SERVINGS

YOU'LL NEED:
large skillet or wok, nonstick spray, large pot

PREP:
5 minutes

COOK:
20 minutes

📷 **For a pic of this recipe, see the second photo insert. Yay!**

TEMPTING TERIYAKI TRIFECTA

Hmmm . . . should you whip up shrimp teriyaki, chicken teriyaki, or beef teriyaki? Ummm, the answer is YES. Why choose just one protein when you can enjoy all three?!

PER SERVING (⅓rd of recipe, about 2 cups):
296 calories, 7g fat, 1,132mg sodium, 25g carbs, 4.25g fiber, 13g sugars, 30g protein

Ingredients

4 ounces raw lean filet beefsteak, sliced

4 ounces raw boneless skinless lean
    chicken breast, sliced

Dash each salt and black pepper, or more to taste

6 cups frozen Asian-style stir-fry vegetables

6 ounces raw shrimp, peeled, deveined, tails removed

¼ cup low-fat sesame ginger dressing

2 tablespoons thick teriyaki sauce/marinade

Directions

Bring a large skillet or wok sprayed with nonstick spray to medium-high heat on the stove. Season beef and chicken with salt and pepper and add to the skillet/wok. Stirring occasionally, cook until mostly cooked through, about 6 minutes.

Meanwhile place frozen veggies in a large pot on the stove. Set temperature to medium. Stirring occasionally, cook until just thawed, about 5 minutes. Remove from heat and set aside.

Once beef and chicken are mostly cooked, add shrimp to the skillet/wok. Stirring occasionally, continue to cook until shrimp is cooked through, about 4 minutes.

Add thawed veggies, dressing, and teriyaki sauce/marinade to the wok/skillet. Cook and stir until sauce/marinade and dressing are evenly distributed and veggies are hot, about 2 minutes.

Serve and enjoy!

MAKES 3 SERVINGS

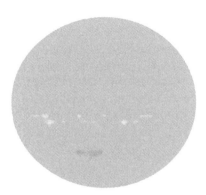

BREAKFAST FOR DINNER SKILLET

You can enjoy this breakfast-y skillet at dinnertime, or even in the AM. So calling it "Dinner for Breakfast" would have been equally appropriate.

PER SERVING (½ of recipe): 291 calories, 2.5g fat, 758mg sodium, 8.5g carbs, 1g fiber, 3g sugars, 54.5g protein

Ingredients

1¼ cups fat-free liquid egg substitute

2 tablespoons chopped scallions

1 tablespoon precooked real crumbled bacon

10 ounces raw boneless skinless lean chicken breast, cut into bite-sized pieces

⅛ teaspoon salt, or more to taste

⅛ teaspoon black pepper, or more to taste

½ cup chopped mushrooms

½ cup chopped onion

1 teaspoon chopped garlic

¼ cup shredded fat-free cheddar cheese

Directions

In a bowl, combine egg substitute, scallions, and bacon. Mix well and set aside.

Bring a skillet sprayed with nonstick spray to medium heat on the stove. Add chicken and season with salt and pepper. Stirring occasionally, cook until chicken is cooked through, about 6 minutes. Remove from skillet and set aside.

Remove skillet from heat, re-spray, and bring to medium-high heat.

Add mushrooms, onion, and garlic and, stirring occasionally, cook until veggies are soft, about 4 minutes.

Reduce heat to medium. Add egg mixture and scramble until fully cooked, about 4 minutes.

Mix cooked chicken into the scramble, still in the skillet, and sprinkle with cheese. Cover and cook until cheese has melted, about 1 minute.

Plate and, if you like, season to taste with salt and pepper. Enjoy!

MAKES 2 SERVINGS

YOU'LL NEED:

strainer, kitchen shears (optional), large skillet, nonstick spray, small microwave-safe bowl

PREP:

15 minutes

COOK:

15 minutes

For more recipes, plus food finds, tips 'n tricks, and MORE, sign up for FREE daily emails at hungry-girl.com!

ROCKiN' CREAMY BROC 'N CHiCKEN

WOW . . . yet another creamy noodle dish. This one's loaded with chicken and broccoli—and lots of other veggies too.

PER SERVING (½ of recipe): 277 calories, 5.5g fat, 722mg sodium, 21.5g carbs, 7g fiber, 6.5g sugars, 34.5g protein

Ingredients

2 bags House Foods Tofu Shirataki Spaghetti Shaped Noodle Substitute

8 ounces raw boneless skinless lean chicken breast, chopped

¼ teaspoon salt, divided

¼ teaspoon black pepper, divided

1 cup chopped broccoli

¾ cup sliced mushrooms

½ cup chopped red bell pepper

½ cup chopped onion

1 teaspoon chopped garlic

2 wedges The Laughing Cow Light Creamy Swiss cheese

2 tablespoons fat-free sour cream

1 tablespoon reduced-fat Parmesan-style grated topping

Directions

Use a strainer to rinse and drain noodles well. Dry as thoroughly as possible, using paper towels. Cut noodles up a bit with kitchen shears (if you've got 'em), and set aside.

Bring a large skillet sprayed with nonstick spray to medium-high heat on the stove. Add chicken and season with ⅛ teaspoon salt and ⅛ teaspoon black pepper. Stirring occasionally, cook until chicken is no longer pink on the outside, about 2 minutes.

Add broccoli, mushrooms, bell pepper, onion, and garlic to the skillet. Stirring occasionally, cook until veggies are tender and chicken is fully cooked, about 8 minutes.

Meanwhile, place cheese in a small microwave-safe bowl, and microwave until soft, about 20 seconds. Stir until smooth. Add sour cream and mix well. Set aside.

Add noodles to the skillet and, stirring often, cook until hot, 1 to 2 minutes.

Add cheese/sour cream mixture, Parm-style topping, remaining ⅛ teaspoon salt, and remaining ⅛ teaspoon black pepper to the skillet. Thoroughly mix and then serve it up!

MAKES 2 SERVINGS

PREP:

5 minutes

COOK:

15 minutes

**Trouble finding
tofu shirataki?**

Turn to page 521
for tips on where
to locate!

📷 **For a pic
of this recipe,
see the
second photo
insert. Yay!**

CHEESY BACON NOODLE SKILLET

Tofu shirataki noodles work so incredibly well in this dish, you'll think you're eating cheesy, creamy, bacon-packed pasta. Weeee!

PER SERVING (½ of recipe, about 1 cup): 149 calories, 7g fat, 658mg sodium, 9g carbs, 4.5g fiber, 2.5g sugars, 8.5g protein

Ingredients

2 bags House Foods Tofu Shirataki Spaghetti
   Shaped Noodle Substitute
3 slices center-cut bacon or turkey bacon
½ cup chopped tomatoes
3 wedges The Laughing Cow Light Creamy Swiss cheese
¼ teaspoon black pepper
Dash salt, or more to taste
Dash cayenne pepper, or more to taste

Directions

Use a strainer to rinse and drain noodles well. Dry as thoroughly as possible, using paper towels. Cut noodles up a bit with kitchen shears (if you've got 'em), and set aside.

Bring a large skillet sprayed with nonstick spray to medium heat on the stove. Add bacon and cook until crispy, about 4 minutes per side. Once cool enough to handle, crumble or chop and set aside.

Remove skillet from heat and, if needed, clean and dry. Re-spray and bring to medium-high heat. Add noodles, bacon, and all other ingredients. Stirring frequently, cook until hot, about 5 minutes.

Eat up!

MAKES 2 SERVINGS

HEY, YOU! There are even more stir-frys and skillet dishes to be chewed and enjoyed. Check out . . .

Balsamic BBQ Chick Skillet (page 436)

Super-Speedy Chinese Stir-Fry (page 448)

Sloppy Joe Stir-Fry Slaw (page 474)

Broccoli Beef Stir-Fry (page 479)

Sweet Spinach Stir-Fry (page 492)

Hot Dog Stir-Fry (page 510)

Quickie-yaki Stir-Fry (page 528)

CHAPTER 14: FAST-FOOD/ DRIVE-THRU MAKEOVERS

Love the taste and the FUN of fast food? You're not alone. These mini meals will have you passing right by the drive-thru. Woohoo!

YOU'LL NEED:

small microwave-safe
bowl, microwave-safe
plate, skillet, nonstick
spray

PREP:

10 minutes

COOK:

10 minutes

SPICY CHICKEN CRUNCHTASTIC SUPREME

This is a fun swap for that oddly shaped Taco Bell offering you dream about . . . Try making it at home. It's really good!

PER SERVING (entire recipe): 240 calories, 3.75g fat,
897mg sodium, 33.5g carbs, 7g fiber, 3g sugars, 23.5g protein

Ingredients

¼ cup canned 98% fat-free chunk white chicken
    breast packed in water, drained and flaked

¼ cup shredded fat-free cheddar cheese

½ teaspoon taco seasoning mix

2 dashes cayenne pepper, or more to taste

1 medium-large high-fiber flour tortilla with
    about 110 calories

3 low-fat baked tortilla chips

1 tablespoon fat-free sour cream

¼ cup shredded lettuce

⅓ plum tomato, diced

Directions

In a small microwave-safe bowl, combine chicken, cheese, taco
seasoning, and cayenne pepper, and mix well. If you like, season to
taste with extra cayenne pepper. Microwave for 30 seconds, or until
cheese begins to melt. Set aside.

Place tortilla on a microwave-safe plate and microwave for 10 seconds, or
until warm. Place the chicken mixture in the center of the tortilla. Flatten
the mixture into a circle, keeping it about 2 inches from the outer edge
of the tortilla. Next, layer the tortilla chips on top of the chicken mixture.
Evenly top with sour cream, lettuce, and tomato.

FOLDING INSTRUCTIONS: Starting at the bottom of the tortilla, fold edge up a few inches to the tortilla's center. Then, going around the edge of the tortilla, repeatedly fold, overlapping sections to meet in the center for a total of about six folds, until filling is completely enclosed. (Trust us, it's easy!)

Bring a skillet sprayed with nonstick spray to medium heat, and carefully place the folded tortilla in the center with the folded side down. Heat for 4 to 5 minutes, until the tortilla is browned. Carefully flip it with a spatula, and heat for another 30 to 60 seconds. Now chew it up!

MAKES 1 SERVING

YOU'LL NEED:

bowl or sealable
plastic bag, skillet,
nonstick spray,
microwave-safe plate

PREP:

5 minutes

MARINATE:

10 minutes

COOK:

10 minutes

For more recipes,
plus food finds,
tips 'n tricks, and MORE,
sign up for FREE daily
emails at
hungry-girl.com!

CHICKEN FAJITA BURRITO

You like fajitas. You like burritos. You like big fat food items with under 300 calories. So what are you waiting for? MAKE THIS!

PER SERVING (entire recipe): 274 calories, 4g fat, 833mg sodium, 34g carbs, 16g fiber, 3.5g sugars, 36g protein

Ingredients

3 ounces raw boneless skinless lean chicken
breast, cut into bite-sized pieces

¼ cup thinly sliced onion

¼ cup thinly sliced bell pepper

½ teaspoon fajita seasoning mix

1 La Tortilla Factory Smart & Delicious Low Carb
High Fiber Large Tortilla

¼ cup fat-free refried beans

2 tablespoons shredded fat-free cheddar cheese

1 tablespoon chopped fresh cilantro

Directions

In a bowl or sealable plastic bag, combine chicken, onion, bell pepper, fajita seasoning mix, and 2 teaspoons water. Mix well. Cover or seal and place in the fridge to marinate for 10 minutes.

Bring a skillet sprayed with nonstick spray to medium-high heat on the stove. Add chicken mixture along with all the marinade. Stirring occasionally, cook until marinade has been absorbed and chicken is cooked through, about 5 minutes. Set aside.

Place tortilla on a microwave-safe plate and warm in the microwave, about 10 seconds. Evenly spread refried beans onto the tortilla. Add chicken mixture, cheese, and cilantro to the center.

Wrap tortilla up like a burrito, folding the sides in first, and then rolling it up from the bottom. Place burrito seam-side down on the microwave-safe plate, and microwave for 30 seconds, or until hot. Enjoy!

MAKES 1 SERVING

YOU'LL NEED:

baking sheet,
nonstick spray,
2 microwave-safe
bowls, plate

PREP:

10 minutes

COOK:

15 minutes

📷 **For a pic of this recipe, see the second photo insert. Yay!**

AMAZING ATE-LAYER OPEN-FACED TACO

Eight layers of Mexican-inspired goodness on a corn tortilla. Delicioso!!!

PER SERVING (entire recipe): 256 calories, 2.25g fat, 795mg sodium, 46.5g carbs, 8.75g fiber, 8.5g sugars, 17g protein

Ingredients

1 large corn tortilla
1 cup cubed butternut squash
Dash salt
Dash cayenne pepper
½ teaspoon ground cumin
¼ teaspoon onion powder
¼ teaspoon garlic powder
¼ cup frozen ground-beef-style soy crumbles
¼ teaspoon taco seasoning mix
½ cup shredded lettuce
2 tablespoons canned black beans, drained and rinsed
2 tablespoons shredded fat-free cheddar cheese
2 tablespoons salsa
2 tablespoons fat-free sour cream
1 tablespoon jarred jalapeño slices or mild
　　banana pepper slices

Directions

Preheat oven to 400 degrees.

Place tortilla on a baking sheet sprayed with nonstick spray. Lightly mist the top of the tortilla with nonstick spray. Bake in the oven until crispy, about 8 minutes.

Place squash in a microwave-safe bowl with 1 tablespoon water. Cover and microwave for 6 minutes, or until soft. Once cool enough to handle, drain excess water, and then add salt, cayenne pepper, cumin, onion powder, and garlic powder. Mash well and set aside.

Place frozen crumbles in another microwave-safe bowl and heat for 25 seconds. Stir in taco seasoning, and heat for an additional 25 seconds.

Set crispy tortilla on a plate, and layer ingredients on top in this order: mashed squash, lettuce, black beans, soy crumbles, and then cheese. Heat in the microwave for 30 seconds.

Top with salsa, sour cream, and pepper slices. Now stuff your face!

MAKES 1 SERVING

HG Sodium Tip!

Save around 350mg of sodium in this recipe by simply skipping the dash of salt and using diced fresh tomatoes & onions in place of salsa.

2 small
microwave-safe
bowls, microwave-
safe plate

PREP:

5 minutes

COOK:

5 minutes

TWICE-AS-NICE GUAPO TACO

Yes, guapo taco means "handsome taco"—and with its snazzy beans 'n extra shell, this taco certainly IS handsome!

PER SERVING (entire recipe): 185 calories, 4.75g fat, 569mg sodium, 26.5g carbs, 10.75g fiber, 0.5g sugars, 15g protein

Ingredients

¼ cup frozen ground-beef-style soy crumbles
⅛ teaspoon taco seasoning mix
2 tablespoons fat-free refried beans
1 medium-small high-fiber flour tortilla with about 60 calories
1 corn taco shell
¼ cup shredded lettuce
1 tablespoon shredded fat-free cheddar cheese

Directions

Place soy crumbles in a small microwave-safe bowl and sprinkle with taco seasoning. Microwave until hot, about 30 seconds. Stir and set aside.

In another small microwave-safe bowl, nuke beans until hot, about 15 seconds. Stir and set aside.

Place tortilla on a microwave-safe plate and microwave for 10 seconds, or until warm. Spread beans evenly over the exposed side of the tortilla. Set aside.

Warm shell in the microwave for 30 seconds. Place shell over the bean-covered tortilla—line up the shell's bottom with the tortilla's center, and align the right side of the shell with the right side of the tortilla.

Gently press on the inside of the shell's right side to seal. Pick up the entire right half of the taco-tortilla, and fold it over so the left sides align. Gently press on the inside of the shell's left side to seal. (If it cracks a little, that's okay!)

Fill shell with seasoned crumbles, lettuce, and cheese. Enjoy!

MAKES 1 SERVING

Use those leftover beans for something fun . . .

NOT a food fight! Go to page 65 for our Cheesy Bean Breakfast Quesadilla recipe.

bowl, skillet, nonstick
spray

PREP:
10 minutes

COOK:
10 minutes

For the Weight Watchers
PointsPlus™ values of
all the recipes in this
book, check out
hungry-girl.com/books.
Yay!

FLAT-TASTIC RANCHY BACON WRAP

How can something this decadent and delicious be soooo calorie-friendly? It's the magic of HG, people!

PER SERVING (entire recipe): 260 calories, 6.75g fat, 727mg sodium, 30.5g carbs, 7.5g fiber, 3.5g sugars, 24.5g protein

Ingredients

1 tablespoon fat-free ranch dressing
1 tablespoon mashed avocado
2 ounces cooked and chopped skinless
    lean chicken breast
¼ cup shredded lettuce
2 tablespoons chopped tomato
1 tablespoon precooked real crumbled bacon
1 medium-large high-fiber flour tortilla with
    about 110 calories

Directions

To make the filling, combine dressing with avocado in a bowl and mix well. Add all other ingredients *except* the tortilla. Toss to coat.

Lay tortilla flat on a clean, dry surface. Spoon filling onto the center. Carefully fold the tortilla sides toward the center, followed by the top and bottom, overlapping to enclose the filling and form a square. Press gently to seal.

Bring a skillet sprayed with nonstick spray to medium heat on the stove. Carefully place the wrap in the skillet, seam-side down, and cook for 3 to 4 minutes. Gently flip and cook for an additional 2 to 3 minutes, until lightly browned.

Slice in half diagonally or just bite right in. TADA!

MAKES 1 SERVING

SNACK-TASTIC BURGER WRAP

Lookin' for a cute little snack? Avoid the drive-thru and whip this up in the privacy of your own kitchen. You've got it—why not use it?!

YOU'LL NEED:
small bowl, microwave-safe plate, skillet, nonstick spray

PREP:
5 minutes

COOK:
10 minutes

PER SERVING (entire recipe): 192 calories, 5.25g fat, 913mg sodium, 24.5g carbs, 11.25g fiber, 4g sugars, 20g protein

Ingredients

2 teaspoons fat-free mayonnaise
1 teaspoon light French dressing
1 medium-large high-fiber flour tortilla with about 110 calories
2 tablespoons chopped onion
¼ cup shredded lettuce
1 slice fat-free American cheese
1 frozen meatless hamburger-style patty with about 100 calories
Optional: hamburger dill pickle chips

Directions

In a small bowl, combine mayo with dressing. Mix well and set aside.

Place tortilla on a microwave-safe plate and warm in the microwave, about 10 seconds. Evenly spread dressing-mayo mixture onto the tortilla. Lay onion and lettuce along the center of the tortilla and top with cheese slice. Set aside.

Bring a skillet sprayed with nonstick spray to medium heat on the stove. Add patty and cook for about 4 minutes per side, until cooked through. Once cool enough to handle, cut patty in half and place on top of the cheese.

If you like, add a few pickle chips. Wrap it all up, and bite it!

MAKES 1 SERVING

YOU'LL NEED:

skillet, nonstick spray,
microwave-safe plate

PREP:

5 minutes

COOK:

15 minutes

BiG BAD BREAKFAST BURRiTO

It's called BIG and BAD, but don't be afraid of this crazy-amazing breakfast swap. Mmmm, mmm, mmm!

PER SERVING (entire recipe): 292 calories, 5.25g fat, 946mg sodium, 34g carbs, 8g fiber, 5g sugars, 32.5g protein

Ingredients

⅓ cup sliced bell pepper
¼ cup sliced onion
½ cup fat-free liquid egg substitute
1 frozen meatless or turkey sausage patty with about 80 calories
1 medium-large high-fiber flour tortilla with about 110 calories
2 tablespoons shredded fat-free cheddar cheese
Optional: salsa

Directions

Bring a skillet sprayed with nonstick spray to medium heat on the stove. Add bell pepper and onion and cook until softened, about 4 minutes. Add egg substitute and scramble until fully cooked, about 3 minutes. Set aside.

If needed, clean and dry skillet. Remove skillet from heat, re-spray, and bring to medium heat. Add patty and cook for about 4 minutes per side, until cooked through. Once cool enough to handle, crumble or chop and set aside.

Place tortilla on a microwave-safe plate and warm in the microwave, about 10 seconds.

Scoop veggie-egg scramble into the center of the tortilla, and top with sausage pieces. Add cheese and, if you like, salsa. Wrap it all up and eat!

MAKES 1 SERVING

NEAT-O CHILI-FRITO BURRITO

YOU'LL NEED:

microwave-safe bowl,
microwave-safe plate

PREP:

5 minutes

COOK:

5 minutes

Who else would not only tell you that Fritos are okay every now and then but also offer up a drive-thru swap featuring these salty corn chips?! NO ONE!

PER SERVING (entire recipe): 248 calories, 5.75g fat, 790mg sodium, 39g carbs, 8.5g fiber, 3.5g sugars, 15.5g protein

Ingredients

⅓ cup low-fat turkey or veggie chili
1 medium-large high-fiber flour tortilla with about 110 calories
2 tablespoons shredded fat-free cheddar cheese
½ package Fritos Original Corn Chips 100 Calorie Pack
   (or alternative at right)
Optional: 2 tablespoons diced onion

Directions

Place chili in a microwave-safe bowl, cover, and microwave until hot, 45 to 60 seconds. Set aside.

Lay tortilla flat on a microwave-safe plate, and warm in the microwave for about 10 seconds. Spoon chili down the center of the tortilla. Cover the chili with cheese, and then top with Fritos. If you like, sprinkle with onion.

Wrap tortilla up like a burrito, folding the sides in first, and then rolling it up from the bottom. (Or serve it wrap-style, with one end left open.) Place burrito seam-side down on the plate, and microwave until hot, about 30 seconds.

Now CHEW!

MAKES 1 SERVING

HG Alternative!

If you can't find 100-calorie packs of Fritos, you could just use 10 Fritos from a regular bag. But we don't trust ourselves around a giant bag of Fritos—so we'd just use 50 calories' worth of crushed baked tortilla chips instead!

YOU'LL NEED:

bowl, blender or food processor, plastic container with an airtight lid *or* sealable plastic bag, skillet, nonstick spray

PREP:

10 minutes

COOK:

15 minutes

TOTALLY STACKED STEAK-STYLE HG BURGER

Ooooh—a saucy burger topped with faux-fried onion strings?!? You are so welcome!

PER SERVING (entire recipe): 280 calories, 4.5g fat, 1,026mg sodium, 45g carbs, 13g fiber, 9g sugars, 22g protein

Ingredients

¼ cup thinly sliced onion

1 tablespoon fat-free liquid egg substitute

¼ cup Fiber One Original bran cereal

¼ teaspoon onion powder, or more to taste

Dash each salt and black pepper, or more to taste

1 frozen meatless hamburger-style patty with about 100 calories

One 100-calorie flat sandwich bun

1 slice fat-free American cheese

½ tablespoon A.1. Thick & Hearty Steak Sauce

2 slices tomato

2 small lettuce leaves

Optional: fat-free mayonnaise

Directions

Place onion "strings" in a bowl and cover with egg substitute. Toss to coat and set aside.

Using a blender or food processor, grind cereal to a breadcrumb-like consistency. Transfer crumbs to a plastic container with an airtight lid or a sealable plastic bag. Add onion powder, salt, and pepper (use extra, if you like) and mix well.

Remove onion strings from the egg substitute, shake gently to remove excess liquid, and transfer to the container/bag with the seasoned crumbs. Cover or seal and shake until onion strings are completely coated in crumbs.

Bring a skillet sprayed with nonstick spray to medium-high heat on the stove. Evenly disperse crumb-coated onion strings in the skillet. (Discard excess crumbs—you'll only use about half.) Flipping occasionally with a spatula, cook for about 5 minutes, until slightly browned and softened.

Remove skillet from heat and, if needed, clean and dry skillet. Re-spray skillet and bring to medium heat. Add patty and cook for about 4 minutes per side, until cooked through. Set aside.

Split bun in half and, if you like, lightly toast. Place patty over the bottom half of the bun, and top with cheese.

Spread A.1. sauce over the cheese. Top with crispy onion strings, tomato, and lettuce. If you like, spread the inside of the bun's top half with mayo. Finish off your burger with the top half of the bun. Now CHEW!

MAKES 1 SERVING

No flat buns?

No problem. Flip to page 287 for a few alternatives . . .

YOU'LL NEED:

baking sheet, nonstick spray, blender or food processor, sealable plastic bag, wide bowl

PREP:

15 minutes

COOK:

40 minutes

📷 **For a pic of this recipe, see the second photo insert. Yay!**

CRISPITY CRUNCHITY DRUMSTICKS

Forget greasy fried chicken . . . FOREVER. These crispy things will satisfy all cravings for KFC. Really!!!

PER SERVING (⅓rd of recipe, 2 drumsticks): 184 calories, 5g fat, 567mg sodium, 10.5g carbs, 5g fiber, <0.5g sugars, 28g protein

Ingredients

6 raw chicken drumsticks, skin removed
½ teaspoon salt, divided
½ cup Fiber One Original bran cereal
1¼ teaspoons black pepper
¾ teaspoon garlic powder
¾ teaspoon onion powder
¾ teaspoon dried oregano
¼ teaspoon chili powder
¼ cup fat-free liquid egg substitute
Optional: additional seasonings

Directions

Preheat oven to 400 degrees.

Spray a baking sheet with nonstick spray and set aside.

Season chicken with ¼ teaspoon salt and set aside.

Using a blender or food processor, grind cereal to a breadcrumb-like consistency. Transfer crumbs to a large sealable plastic bag. Add remaining ¼ teaspoon salt and all other seasonings. Seal bag and shake to mix. Open bag and, if you like, season crumbs to taste with additional seasonings. Set aside.

Place egg substitute in a wide bowl. Two at a time, coat drumsticks in egg substitute, gently shake to remove excess liquid, and place in the bag with the crumbs. Seal and shake to coat. Transfer crumb-coated drumsticks to the baking sheet and repeat with remaining drumsticks.

Bake in the oven for 20 minutes and then carefully flip. Bake for another 15 to 20 minutes, until crispy and cooked through. Enjoy!

MAKES 3 SERVINGS

YOU'LL NEED:

toothpicks, large
skillet or grill pan,
nonstick spray

PREP:

10 minutes

COOK:

15 minutes

📷 For a pic
of this recipe,
see the
second photo
insert. Yay!

LOADED BACON-WRAPPED HOT DOGS

Bacon-wrapped dogs are famous in Los Angeles. These yum-ilicious HG-ified pups are as good as the ones served in Hollywood . . . and they have a fraction of the fat and calories. Take THAT, full-fat-fatty-fat bacon dogs!

PER SERVING (¼th of recipe, 1 fully dressed hot dog): 186 calories, 4.5g fat, 850mg sodium, 28g carbs, 5.5g fiber, 6g sugars, 13g protein

Ingredients

4 hot dogs with about 40 calories and
    1g fat or less each

4 slices center-cut bacon or turkey bacon

1 cup sliced onion

1 cup sliced red bell pepper

1 jalapeño pepper, seeded and sliced
    into strips (not rings)

2 tablespoons fat-free mayonnaise

4 light hot dog buns

4 teaspoons yellow mustard

Directions

Carefully break 4 toothpicks in half. Wrap each hot dog in a strip of bacon and secure with a toothpick half at each end. Set aside.

Bring a large skillet or grill pan sprayed with nonstick spray to medium-high heat on the stove. Add onion, bell pepper, and jalapeño pepper and cook until softened, about 4 minutes. Remove from skillet/pan and set aside.

Remove skillet/pan from heat, re-spray, and bring to medium heat. Add bacon-wrapped hot dogs and cook until bacon is crisp and fully cooked and hot dogs are heated through, about 6 minutes, rotating the hot dogs several times to evenly cook the bacon. Set aside.

Evenly spread mayo inside the buns. Remove toothpicks from hot dogs and place a bacon-wrapped dog in each bun. Top each dog with a teaspoon of mustard.

Evenly distribute veggie mixture among the dogs. Eat up!

MAKES 4 SERVINGS

FAST-FOOD FREAKS!

Check out the Fast-Food Hamburger Scramble (page 497) **and the Sausage, Egg 'n Cheese ChickGriddle** (page 58)!

STARTERS, SOUPS & SIDES

The items in this section are called starters, soups, and sides—but really, they can be amazing snacks and mini meals too. Use 'em however you wish. Just love them for what they are: DELICIOUS.

CHAPTER 15:
STARTERS

Come on, get appy!

Directions

Preheat oven to 450 degrees.

Tear lightly toasted bread into pieces and place in a blender or food processor. Pulse until reduced to breadcrumbs, and then transfer to a medium bowl.

Add crabmeat, parsley, garlic, salt, and black pepper to the bowl, and gently mix until combined. Add onion and celery, lightly mix again, and set aside.

Break cheese wedge into pieces and place in a small bowl. Add egg substitute, mayo, Dijonnaise, lemon juice, butter, Worcestershire sauce, and hot sauce. Whisk until smooth, and pour over the crabmeat mixture. Using a rubber spatula, gently fold the liquid mixture into the crabmeat mixture.

Prepare a medium-large baking pan by spraying with butter-flavored nonstick spray. Take one-third of the crab cake mixture (about ¾ cup) from the bowl. Gently form it into a ball, place it in the baking pan, and flatten it into a cake about 1-inch thick—repeat twice with remaining crab mixture so that you have 3 cakes in the baking pan.

Bake in the oven for 14 to 15 minutes, until the cakes are slightly firm and cooked through. Remove carefully from the pan and serve with additional Dijonnaise for dipping and/or lemon wedges for squirting!

MAKES 3 SERVINGS

YOU'LL NEED:

small bowl, nonstick spray, grill or grill pan, large serving platter

PREP:

20 minutes

COOK:

25 minutes

GRiLLY-GOOD EGGPLANT BiTES

Yum! These veggie treats are so good, you might find yourself gobbling up the entire batch. No harm, though . . . The whole recipe has just 220 calories!

PER SERVING (⅕th of recipe, 3 pieces): 44 calories, 0.5g fat, 144mg sodium, 9g carbs, 4g fiber, 3.5g sugars, 1.5g protein

Ingredients

1 small onion

1 large eggplant

3 large firm plum tomatoes

¾ teaspoon dried oregano

½ teaspoon garlic powder

¼ teaspoon salt

Dash black pepper

½ cup chopped fresh basil

1 tablespoon reduced-fat Parmesan-style grated topping

Directions

Slice off and discard both ends of the onion. Cut onion into two thick rings, keeping the inner rings of each intact. Set aside.

Slice off and discard both ends of the eggplant.

Cut eggplant widthwise into 15 evenly sized slices. Set aside.

Cut each tomato widthwise into 5 evenly sized slices, for a total of 15 slices. Set aside.

In a small bowl, combine oregano, garlic powder, salt, and pepper.

Spray eggplant slices lightly with nonstick spray. Sprinkle both sides of the eggplant slices with the seasoning mixture.

Bring a grill or grill pan sprayed with nonstick spray to medium-high heat. Working in batches if needed, grill eggplant slices until soft, about 4 minutes per side. Evenly place on a serving platter and set aside.

Grill onion rings until soft, about 5 minutes per side. Grill tomatoes until slightly soft, 1 to 2 minutes per side. Remove from heat. Once cool enough to handle, slice onion rings in half. Set aside.

Evenly top eggplant slices with basil, Parm-style topping, onion, and tomato. Serve eggplant flat, tostada-style, or fold 'em up, taco-style!

MAKES 5 SERVINGS

YOU'LL NEED:

skillet, nonstick spray, medium bowl, potato masher (optional), blender or food processor (optional), large baking sheet

PREP:

20 minutes

COOK:

40 minutes

📷 **For a pic of this recipe, see the second photo insert. Yay!**

ROCKiN' ROASTED CORN GUAC 'N CHiPS

Here's an HG take on the roasted corn guacamole found at Chili's.

PER SERVING (⅛th of recipe, about ⅓ cup guacamole with 9 chips): 160 calories, 4g fat, 456mg sodium, 27.5g carbs, 4.75g fiber, 4.5g sugars, 5g protein

Ingredients

Guac

1 cup frozen sweet yellow corn

One 15-ounce can early/young peas, drained

½ cup mashed avocado (about 1 medium-small avocado's worth)

¼ cup fat-free plain Greek yogurt

1 tablespoon plus 1 teaspoon lime juice

½ teaspoon chopped garlic

¼ teaspoon salt, or more to taste

⅛ teaspoon black pepper, or more to taste

⅛ teaspoon ground cumin

⅛ teaspoon chili powder

¾ cup chopped cherry or grape tomatoes

¼ cup finely chopped onion

Optional: chopped fresh cilantro, chopped jarred jalapeño slices

Chips

Twelve 6-inch corn tortillas

¼ teaspoon salt, divided

Directions

Preheat oven to 400 degrees.

Bring a skillet sprayed with nonstick spray to high heat on the stove. Add corn and cook until thawed and slightly blackened, about 8 minutes. Set aside to cool.

Place peas in a medium bowl and mash thoroughly with a potato masher or fork. (Or puree peas in a small blender or food processor and transfer to a medium bowl.) Add avocado, yogurt, lime juice, garlic, and dry seasonings. Continue to mash until blended.

Stir in corn, tomatoes, and onion. If you like, mix in cilantro and/or jalapeño. Refrigerate until ready to serve.

To make the chips, divide tortillas into two stacks and cut each in half. Cut each stack of halves into three triangles, for a total of 72 pieces.

Spray a large baking sheet with nonstick spray. Evenly lay about one-third of the tortilla triangles flat on the sheet.

Cover triangles with a generous mist of nonstick spray, spraying for about 2 seconds. Evenly sprinkle with $\frac{1}{8}$ teaspoon salt. Flip triangles over and sprinkle with another $\frac{1}{8}$ teaspoon salt.

Bake in the oven for 5 minutes. Carefully flip tortilla triangles over on the sheets. Continue to bake in the oven until crispy, about 5 minutes longer.

Repeat baking process until all the chips are baked. (If you have extra baking sheets and a large oven, feel free to do it all at once!)

Once cool enough to handle, transfer chips to a serving bowl. Serve with chilled guac and enjoy!

MAKES 8 SERVINGS

YOU'LL NEED:

deep square baking pan or loaf pan, nonstick spray, bowl, microwave-safe bowl, baking sheet

PREP:

5 minutes

COOK:

10 minutes

For the Weight Watchers *PointsPlus*™ values of all the recipes in this book, check out hungry-girl.com/books. Yay!

SASSY WONTON TACOS

Are these sassy-licious things more like wontons or tacos? YOU decide . . .

PER SERVING (½ of recipe, 4 wonton tacos): 191 calories, 2g fat, 605mg sodium, 25g carbs, 1g fiber, 7.5g sugars, 17g protein

Ingredients

8 small square wonton wrappers (often stocked near the tofu in the refrigerated section of the market)

4 ounces cooked and shredded (or finely chopped) skinless lean chicken breast

2 tablespoons BBQ sauce with about 45 calories per 2-tablespoon serving

¾ cup dry coleslaw mix

2 tablespoons low-fat sesame ginger dressing

2 tablespoons chopped fresh cilantro

Directions

Preheat oven to 400 degrees.

To make the wonton shells, spray the inside and outside walls of a deep square or rectangular baking pan with nonstick spray. Evenly drape wonton wrappers over the pan's walls on a diagonal, making triangle-shaped "shells." (Use two pans, if needed, to keep wontons from overlapping.) Bake until just crispy enough to hold their shape, 3 to 4 minutes. Remove pan from the oven and set aside to cool.

Combine chicken with BBQ sauce in a bowl and mix well. Set aside.

In a microwave-safe bowl, combine coleslaw mix, dressing, and cilantro. Mix well. Microwave until slightly softened, about 45 seconds. Set aside.

Spray a baking sheet with nonstick spray. One at a time, carefully remove wonton shells from the pan and fill each with a heaping tablespoon of BBQ chicken and a heaping teaspoon of cilantro slaw. Lay filled wontons gently on their sides on the baking sheet.

Spray the upward-facing sides of the wonton shells lightly with nonstick spray (for added crispiness) and bake for about 5 minutes, until warm and crunchy. Let cool slightly and serve!

MAKES 2 SERVINGS

large skillet, nonstick
spray, large bowl

20 minutes

20 minutes

*✱ For more recipes,
plus food finds,
tips 'n tricks, and MORE,
sign up for FREE daily
emails at
hungry-girl.com!*

MEXi-LiCiOUS POT STiCKERS

These pot stickers are head-explodingly delicious. You may want to make a meal out of 'em . . .

PER SERVING (⅙th of recipe, 4 pot stickers): 175 calories,
3g fat, 459mg sodium, 21.5g carbs, 1.75g fiber, 1.5g sugars, 13.5g protein

Ingredients

8 ounces raw lean ground turkey

½ tablespoon taco seasoning mix

1 small onion, chopped

¼ cup taco sauce

½ cup fat-free refried beans

½ cup shredded fat-free cheddar cheese

24 small square wonton wrappers (often
stocked near the tofu in the refrigerated
section of the market)

Optional toppings: salsa, fat-free sour cream

Directions

Spray a large skillet with nonstick spray, and bring to
medium-high heat on the stove. Add turkey, and cook and
crumble until browned and fully cooked, about 5 minutes.

Reduce heat to medium and sprinkle turkey with taco seasoning.
Add onion and taco sauce. Stirring occasionally, continue to cook
until onion has softened, about 5 minutes.

Transfer mixture to a large bowl. Add beans and cheese and stir to
combine. Allow to cool completely. Meanwhile, wash skillet.

Lay two wrappers flat on a clean, dry surface. Spoon a heaping tablespoon of filling into the center of each wrapper. Moisten all four edges of each wrapper by dabbing your fingers in water and going over the edges smoothly. Fold the bottom left corner of each wrapper to meet the top right corner, forming a triangle and enclosing the filling.

Press firmly on the edges to seal. Repeat with remaining wrappers and filling.

Once all wontons are assembled, spray skillet with nonstick spray and return to medium-high heat on the stove. Working in batches and beginning with the flatter sides down, cook wontons until crispy, 3 to 4 minutes per side. (Between batches, remove skillet from heat and re-spray.)

Serve and, if you like, top with salsa and sour cream. Enjoy!

MAKES 6 SERVINGS

YOU'LL NEED:

large bowl, blender
or food processor,
baking sheet,
nonstick spray

PREP:

20 minutes

COOK:

20 minutes

SO-GOOD SPiNACH BiTES

Each of these flavor-packed little spinach balls has less than 25 calories. So start poppin' 'em, people!

PER SERVING (⅛ᵗʰ of recipe, about 3 spinach bites): 70 calories, 2g fat, 341mg sodium, 8.5g carbs, 2.5g fiber, 1g sugars, 4.5g protein

Ingredients

One 10-ounce package frozen chopped spinach,
     thawed and thoroughly patted dry
½ cup finely chopped onion
¼ cup reduced-fat Parmesan-style grated topping
¼ cup fat-free liquid egg substitute
3 tablespoons fat-free cream cheese, room temperature
1 tablespoon light whipped butter or light
     buttery spread, room temperature
¾ teaspoon chopped garlic
¾ teaspoon Italian seasoning
¼ teaspoon salt
⅛ teaspoon black pepper
⅓ cup Fiber One Original bran cereal

Directions

Preheat oven to 350 degrees.

In a large bowl, combine all ingredients *except* the cereal, and stir until completely mixed. Set aside.

In a blender or food processor, grind cereal to a breadcrumb-like consistency. Add crumbs to the large bowl and mix until integrated.

Prepare a baking sheet by lightly spraying it with nonstick spray. Scoop out about 1 tablespoon mixture, form it into a ball with your hands, and place it on the baking sheet.

Repeat with the rest of the mixture, yielding a total of about 18 balls.

Bake in the oven for 20 minutes. Allow to cool slightly, and then have a ball (or several)!

MAKES 6 SERVINGS

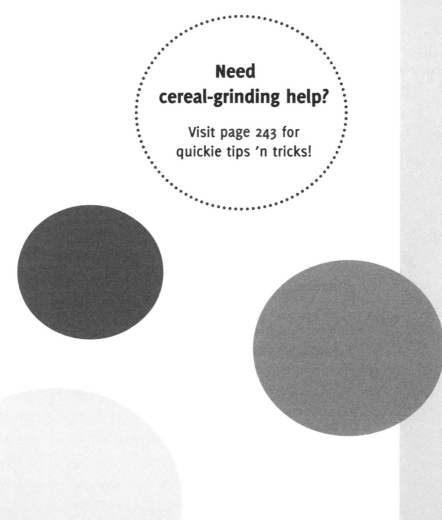

Need cereal-grinding help?

Visit page 243 for quickie tips 'n tricks!

YOU'LL NEED:

large baking sheet,
nonstick spray, skillet,
large bowl

PREP:

30 minutes

COOK:

50 minutes

✳ For full-color
photos of all the recipes
in this book, check out
hungry-girl.com/books.
Woohoo!

CHEESY CHICKEN EGG ROLLS

spinachy, cheesy chicken egg rolls that'll make your face happy!

PER SERVING (⅛th of recipe, 1 egg roll): 112 calories, 1.5g fat, 334mg sodium, 17g carbs, 1g fiber, 1.5g sugars, 8.5g protein

Ingredients

½ tablespoon light whipped butter or light buttery spread

1 sweet onion, thinly sliced

¼ teaspoon salt

2 cups spinach leaves

½ tablespoon chopped garlic

4 ounces cooked and chopped skinless lean chicken breast

2 wedges The Laughing Cow Light Creamy Swiss cheese

6 large square egg roll wrappers (stocked with the refrigerated Asian items in the supermarket)

Directions

Preheat oven to 375 degrees.

Prepare a large baking sheet by spraying it lightly with nonstick spray; set aside.

Place butter in a skillet and bring to medium-high heat on the stove. Once butter has coated the bottom of the skillet, add onion and salt. Stirring often, sauté onion until softened and slightly browned, about 6 minutes.

Reduce heat to medium low. Stirring occasionally, continue to cook onion until browned and caramelized, about 15 minutes. Transfer to a large bowl and set aside.

Return skillet to medium-high heat on the stove. Add spinach and garlic and cook until the spinach has wilted, 1 to 2 minutes. Transfer mixture to the large bowl.

Add chicken and cheese to the bowl, breaking the cheese wedges into pieces as you add them. Mix thoroughly and set aside.

Place two egg roll wrappers on a clean, dry surface. Evenly distribute ⅛th of the mixture (about ⅓ cup) in a horizontal row a little below the center of each wrapper.

Moisten all four edges of each wrapper by dabbing your fingers in water and going over the edges smoothly.

Fold in the sides of each wrapper about an inch toward the middle, over the filling to prevent it from escaping. Roll the bottom of each wrapper up around the mixture; continue rolling until you reach the top. Seal the outside edge with another dab of water. Carefully transfer egg rolls to the baking sheet.

Repeat with remaining wrappers and filling, making sure you have a clean, dry surface each time. Spray the tops of the egg rolls with nonstick spray.

Bake in the oven until golden brown, about 25 minutes.

Allow to cool slightly. Slice into halves, if you like, and dig in!

MAKES 6 SERVINGS

YOU'LL NEED:

large microwave-safe
bowl

PREP:

10 minutes

COOK:

5 minutes

AB-FAB
ARTICHOKE CRAB DIP

This dip is great on veggies, on low-fat chips, or even over tofu shirataki noodles. Yum!

PER SERVING (⅛th of recipe, about ⅓ cup): 79 calories, 1.5g fat, 544mg sodium, 9g carbs, 0.75g fiber, 3.5g sugars, 6.5g protein

Ingredients

¼ cup fat-free cream cheese
2 wedges The Laughing Cow Light Creamy Swiss cheese
One 14-ounce can artichoke hearts, drained and chopped
8 ounces (about 1½ cups) roughly chopped imitation
        crabmeat or high-quality real crabmeat
½ cup fat-free sour cream
1 teaspoon chopped garlic
½ teaspoon garlic powder
½ teaspoon onion powder
¼ teaspoon black pepper, or more to taste
⅛ teaspoon salt, or more to taste
⅛ teaspoon cayenne pepper, or more to taste
2 tablespoons reduced-fat Parmesan-style grated topping

Directions

Place cream cheese and cheese wedges in a large microwave-safe bowl. Microwave until soft, for 30 to 45 seconds. Stir until blended.

Add all other ingredients *except* Parm-style topping to the bowl. Mix thoroughly.

Microwave for 1 minute; stir well. Top with Parm-style topping and microwave until dip is warm, or for 1 additional minute. Dig in!

MAKES 8 SERVINGS

HOT DOG–HOT POTATO HOTCAKES

This is HANDS DOWN one of the best recipes in the book. THESE. ROCK. HARD. Make batches to share and your popularity will likely increase by 36 percent.

PER SERVING (½ of recipe, 3 hotcakes): 192 calories, 1.5g fat, 982mg sodium, 28g carbs, 1.75g fiber, 2g sugars, 16.5g protein

Ingredients

3 hot dogs with about 40 calories and 1g fat each, chopped
¼ cup chopped onion
⅔ cup instant mashed potato flakes
½ cup fat-free liquid egg substitute
1 tablespoon whole-wheat flour
⅛ teaspoon salt
⅛ teaspoon black pepper
⅛ teaspoon garlic powder
½ teaspoon dried minced onion

Directions

Bring a skillet sprayed with nonstick spray to medium-high heat on the stove. Add chopped hot dogs and onion. Stirring occasionally, cook until browned, about 5 minutes. Transfer to a medium bowl and set aside.

In a large bowl, combine potato flakes with ½ cup water and stir thoroughly. (Mixture will be slightly stiff.) Add all remaining ingredients and mix well. Add hot dog/onion mixture and stir to combine.

Re-spray skillet (away from the heat), and return to medium-high heat. Working in batches, drop potato mixture into the skillet to form six cakes, flattening each slightly with the back of a spoon. Cook until evenly browned, about 1 to 2 minutes per side.

Plate and enjoy!

MAKES 2 SERVINGS

YOU'LL NEED:
skillet, nonstick spray, medium bowl, large bowl

PREP:
5 minutes

COOK:
15 minutes

For more recipes, plus food finds, tips 'n tricks, and MORE, sign up for FREE daily emails at hungry-girl.com!

YOU'LL NEED:

small microwave-safe bowl

PREP:

5 minutes

COOK:

5 minutes

MiNi NACHO DiPPERS

so cute . . . and DEE-LICIOUS!!!

PER SERVING (entire recipe, 10 pieces): 200 calories, 3.5g fat, 940mg sodium, 33g carbs, 4.5g fiber, 6.5g sugars, 9g protein

Ingredients

¼ cup fat-free refried beans
10 cheese-flavored soy crisps or mini rice cakes
¼ cup fat-free sour cream
¼ cup salsa
Optional: jarred jalapeño slices, sliced black olives

Directions

Place beans in a small microwave-safe bowl and microwave until hot, about 30 seconds. Stir and evenly distribute among soy crisps/mini rice cakes.

If you like, top each crisp/cake with a slice of jalapeño or olive. Serve with sour cream and salsa for dipping!

MAKES 1 SERVING

SWEET COCONUT CRUNCH SHRIMP

crunchy, sweet, and coconutty, this shrimp absolutely lives up to its name. Mmmmmm!

YOU'LL NEED: sealable plastic bag, meat mallet, large plate, large baking sheet, nonstick spray, bowl

PREP: 20 minutes

COOK: 15 minutes

PER SERVING (¼th of recipe, about 5 shrimp): 164 calories, 4.5g fat, 266mg sodium, 12g carbs, 2g fiber, 3.5g sugars, 19.5g protein

Ingredients

¼ cup Fiber One Original bran cereal
⅓ cup shredded sweetened coconut
3 tablespoons panko breadcrumbs
¼ teaspoon chili powder
⅛ teaspoon garlic powder
⅛ teaspoon black pepper
Dash salt
12 ounces (about 20) raw large shrimp, peeled, tails removed, deveined
3 tablespoons fat-free liquid egg substitute

📷 For a pic of this recipe, see the second photo insert. Yay!

Directions

Preheat oven to 400 degrees.

Place cereal in a sealable plastic bag and, removing as much air as possible, seal. Using a meat mallet, carefully crush cereal through the bag. Add sweetened coconut, panko breadcrumbs, chili powder, garlic powder, black pepper, and salt to the bag; seal and shake to mix. Transfer mixture to a large plate and set aside.

Spray a large baking sheet with nonstick spray and set aside. Pat shrimp with paper towels to ensure they are completely dry.

Combine shrimp with egg substitute in a bowl and toss lightly to coat. One at a time, shake excess egg from shrimp and transfer to the coconut-crumb mixture, gently patting and flipping to coat. Evenly place coated shrimp on the baking sheet.

Bake in the oven until outsides are crispy and lightly browned and insides are cooked through, 10 to 12 minutes. Serve and enjoy!

MAKES 4 SERVINGS

kitchen shears
(optional), large
microwave-safe bowl,
small bowl, small
microwave-safe bowl

PREP:

5 minutes

COOK:

10 minutes

SASSY 'N STEAMY ARTICHOKE

Here's a recipe for a simple steamed artichoke (plus a couple of fun sauces). You'd be surprised how many HGers have been asking for this over the years . . .

PER SERVING (entire recipe): 163 calories, 7.75g fat, 444mg sodium, 19.5g carbs, 9g fiber, 1.5g sugars, 7.5g protein

Ingredients

1 large artichoke

Creamy Salsa Dipping Sauce
1½ tablespoons fat-free plain Greek yogurt
1½ tablespoons salsa

Lemon Butter Dipping Sauce
1½ tablespoons light whipped butter or light buttery spread
¼ teaspoon lemon juice
¼ teaspoon chopped garlic

Directions

Cut stem off artichoke and remove small, tough leaves at the base. Slice an inch off the top of the artichoke and, if you like, trim the tips of the leaves with kitchen shears (if you've got 'em).

Place artichoke in a large microwave-safe bowl, base down, and add about ½ inch of water to the bowl. Cover and microwave for 6 to 8 minutes. Let stand for 1 to 2 minutes before uncovering. Leaves should detach easily from artichoke. Drain water and allow to cool slightly.

To make the creamy salsa, combine yogurt with salsa in a small bowl and mix well.

To make the lemon butter sauce, combine all ingredients in a small microwave-safe bowl. Microwave for 10 seconds, or until melted, and mix well.

Serve your steamed 'choke with dipping sauce(s). Here's the 1-2-3 on how to eat it:

1. Pull off a leaf and dip the base in sauce.

2. Place the base in your mouth, dip side up, and gently close your teeth around it.

3. Scrape it along your top teeth to consume the soft, delicious part (YUM!), and then discard the leaf.

Now repeat! And when all the leaves are gone, scoop out and discard the thistle-like choke, and enjoy the artichoke bottom (the BEST part)!

MAKES 1 SERVING

HG FYI:

The steamed artichoke itself has 76 calories, less than 0.5g of fat, and 8.5g of fiber; the creamy salsa has 18 calories, 0g of fat, and less than 0.5g of fiber; and the lemon butter sauce has 69 calories, 7.5g of fat, and 0g of fiber.

YOU'LL NEED:

large microwave-safe
bowl, potato masher
(optional), medium
pot, nonstick spray,
1 to 2 large ovenproof
plates or baking
sheets

PREP:

10 minutes

COOK:

20 minutes

UNiTED WE CHEW!
RED, WHiTE & BLUE NACHOS

What's better than a delicious app? A PATRIOTIC delicious app! These crunchy nachos are perfect for Independence Day or any of the other 364 days of the year.

PER SERVING (⅛th of recipe, about 15 loaded nachos):
198 calories, 3.5g fat, 745mg sodium, 33.5g carbs, 5.5g fiber,
3.5g sugars, 11g protein

Ingredients

2¼ cups cauliflower florets

One 15-ounce can cannellini (white kidney)
     beans, drained and rinsed

⅓ cup finely chopped onion

1½ teaspoons chopped garlic

3 wedges The Laughing Cow Light Creamy Swiss cheese

¾ teaspoon ground cumin

One 7-ounce bag low-fat baked blue corn tortilla chips

¾ cup shredded fat-free jalapeño jack cheese,
     or alternative at right

1 cup salsa

Optional topping: fat-free sour cream

Directions

Preheat oven to 350 degrees.

Place cauliflower in a large microwave-safe bowl with
3 tablespoons water. Cover and microwave for 5 minutes, or
until cauliflower is tender enough to mash. Once cool enough to
handle, add beans and, using a potato masher or a fork, mash
thoroughly. Set aside.

Bring a medium pot sprayed with nonstick spray to medium heat on the stove. Add onion and garlic, and sauté until soft and fragrant. Reduce heat to low. Add mashed cauliflower/bean mixture, cheese wedges, and cumin. Stir until ingredients are completely integrated. Raise heat to medium high, and cook and stir for 2 to 3 additional minutes. Remove from heat and set aside.

Spread out tortilla chips on a large ovenproof plate or baking sheet. (Use two plates or sheets, if needed.) Spoon cheesy bean mixture over the chips. Sprinkle with shredded cheese.

Bake in the oven for 5 to 10 minutes, until chips are crispy and shredded cheese has melted.

Top with salsa (or serve salsa on the side to keep chips crispy). If you like, top or serve with sour cream. Enjoy!!!

MAKES 8 SERVINGS

HG Alternative!

If you can't find (or don't like) fat-free jalapeño jack cheese, go for reduced-fat cheese—any white variety. Then each serving of the nachos will have about 212 calories and 5.25g of fat. And yellow corn chips work too—they're just not as festive!

baking sheet,
protective glove
(optional), medium
microwave-safe
bowl, blender or food
processor

PREP:

45 minutes

COOK:

15 minutes

For the Weight Watchers
PointsPlus™ values of
all the recipes in this
book, check out
hungry-girl.com/books.
Yay!

BAKED CLAM HALFSIES

Restaurant baked clams are WAY fattier and WAY higher in calories, but they don't taste any better. So make this clam-tastic app at home ... It's worth the effort!

PER SERVING (¼th of recipe, 5 clams): 150 calories, 5.5g fat, 245mg sodium, 16g carbs, 3.5g fiber, 0g sugars, 11g protein

Ingredients

20 littleneck clams in the shell
2 tablespoons light whipped butter or light buttery spread
¼ cup low-sodium chicken broth
½ cup Fiber One Original bran cereal
¼ cup panko breadcrumbs
¼ cup reduced-fat Parmesan-style grated topping
1 teaspoon finely chopped fresh parsley
1 teaspoon chopped garlic

Directions

Preheat oven to 450 degrees.

Place clams on a baking sheet and bake in the oven for 2 to 4 minutes, just until they begin to open. Remove from the oven and reduce temperature to 400 degrees.

Once cool enough to handle, prepare to open clams by ensuring that your hands are dry. If you like, wear a protective glove or drape a kitchen towel on your non-dominant hand. Holding a clam in that hand over a bowl or the sink, carefully run a sharp knife between the two shells. Gently pry the clam open (don't mind the liquid!), and then remove and discard the top shell. Carefully run the knife under the clam meat to detach it, and let it sit loosely in the bottom shell.

Place clam (in the half shell) back on the baking sheet, and repeat with remaining clams. Set aside.

Nuke butter in a medium microwave-safe bowl until melted, about 10 seconds. Add chicken broth and set aside.

Using a blender or food processor, grind cereal to a breadcrumb-like consistency. Add cereal crumbs to the butter-broth mixture, along with all other ingredients. Mix well. Evenly top clams with this mixture, about ½ tablespoon each, and firmly pack down the topping.

Bake in the oven for 8 minutes, or until clams are fully cooked and topping is a little crisp. Let cool slightly and enjoy!

MAKES 4 SERVINGS

YOU'LL NEED:

baking sheet, nonstick spray, large bowl

PREP:

20 minutes

COOK:

25 minutes

SOUTHWEST STUFFED TOMATOES

These packed tomatoes have it all—chicken, corn, chips, and TONS of flavor. Yee-haa!

PER SERVING (⅙th of recipe, 1 stuffed tomato): 123 calories, 1.5g fat, 192mg sodium, 10g carbs, 2.5g fiber, 5.5g sugars, 18g protein

Ingredients

6 large tomatoes

12 ounces cooked and shredded (or finely chopped) skinless lean chicken breast

½ cup chopped mushrooms

¼ cup frozen sweet yellow corn, slightly thawed

2 tablespoons chopped onion

2 tablespoons chopped fresh cilantro

1 teaspoon taco seasoning mix

6 low-fat baked tortilla chips, slightly crushed

3 tablespoons shredded fat-free cheddar cheese

Optional: salt and black pepper

Optional topping: salsa

Directions

Preheat oven to 350 degrees.

Spray a baking sheet with nonstick spray and set aside.

Carefully slice off the top half-inch of the tomatoes and set aside. Scoop out and discard the insides. Place the hollow tomatoes on the baking sheet. Remove and discard stems from tomato tops. Chop the tomato tops and transfer to a large bowl.

To the bowl, add chicken, mushrooms, corn, onion, cilantro, and taco seasoning. Mix well. If you like, season to taste with salt and pepper. Evenly distribute mixture into the tomatoes on the baking sheet.

Bake in the oven for 15 minutes.

Remove sheet from the oven and evenly top tomatoes with crushed chips and cheese.

Return to the oven and bake until tomatoes are soft and cheese has melted, about 10 minutes.

Serve and enjoy!

MAKES 6 SERVINGS

HG Tip!

Don't miss our EZ Guide
to Shredded Chicken
on **page 211**!

YOU'LL NEED:
bowl, baking sheet, nonstick spray

PREP:
20 minutes

COOK:
15 minutes

THE CRAB RANGOONIES

These are fabulous. And not just because they're named after one of our favorite '80s movies . . .

PER SERVING (¼th of recipe, 4 crab rangoonies): 140 calories, 1.25g fat, 593mg sodium, 20g carbs, 1g fiber, 2g sugars, 8.5g protein

Ingredients

4 ounces imitation crabmeat, flaked
¼ cup fat-free cream cheese, room temperature
2 wedges The Laughing Cow Light Creamy Swiss cheese
1 teaspoon reduced-sodium/lite soy sauce
½ teaspoon chopped garlic
2 scallions, finely chopped
16 small square wonton wrappers (often stocked near
    the tofu in the fridge section of the market)
Optional dips: sweet & sour sauce, Chinese-style hot mustard

Directions

Preheat oven to 375 degrees.

To make your filling, combine all ingredients *except* the wonton wrappers in a bowl, breaking up the cheese wedges as you add them. Mix until uniform. Set aside. Spray a baking sheet with nonstick spray and set that aside as well.

Lay two wrappers flat on a clean, dry surface. Spoon a heaping ½ tablespoon filling into the center of each wrapper. Moisten all four edges of each wrapper by dabbing your fingers in water and going over the edges smoothly. Fold the bottom left corner of each wrapper to meet the top right corner, forming a triangle and enclosing the filling. Press firmly on the edges to seal.

Repeat with all remaining wrappers and filling, gently placing each rangoon flat on the baking sheet.

Spray the tops of the wontons with nonstick spray. Bake in the oven for about 12 minutes, carefully flipping halfway through, until golden brown. Allow to cool slightly.

If you like, dip your rangoonies in some sweet & sour sauce or hot mustard!

MAKES 4 SERVINGS

blender or food
processor, plastic
container with an
airtight lid or large
sealable plastic
bag, large bowl,
large baking sheet,
nonstick spray, small
bowl

PREP:

15 minutes

COOK:

20 minutes

CRISPY-LICIOUS FAUX-FRIED FRENZY

AHHHH! This wacky appetizer is so delicious, you'll want to inhale the entire thing. But share it with at least one friend. Come on . . .

PER SERVING (⅓ʳᵈ of recipe, about 1⅓ cups veggies with 2 tablespoons sauce): 175 calories, 1.25g fat, 612mg sodium, 43g carbs, 12g fiber, 11.5g sugars, 8.5g protein

Ingredients

1 cup Fiber One Original bran cereal
½ teaspoon seasoned salt
¼ teaspoon garlic powder
⅛ teaspoon black pepper
1 jumbo sweet onion
5 fresh jalapeño peppers
½ cup fat-free liquid egg substitute
3 tablespoons fat-free ranch dressing
3 tablespoons fat-free sour cream
1½ teaspoons green pepper sauce (like the kind by Tabasco)

Directions

Preheat oven to 375 degrees.

In a blender or food processor, grind cereal to a breadcrumb-like consistency. Pour crumbs into a plastic container with an airtight lid or a large sealable plastic bag. Add seasoned salt, garlic powder, and black pepper. Cover container/seal bag and shake to mix thoroughly. Set aside.

Slice the ends off the onion and remove the outer layer. Cut onion in half, and slice into very thin strips. Separate individual pieces and place in a large bowl. Set aside.

Handling the jalapeños carefully (wash your hands often—or wear gloves—and don't touch your eyes), slice off the tops. Cut jalapeños into rings, and then remove the seeds (or don't, if you like things really spicy).

Add jalapeños to the bowl with the onion, and cover the veggies with egg substitute. Toss to coat, and then drain excess egg substitute.

Transfer the eggy veggies to the container/bag with the cereal crumbs. Cover/seal and shake until veggies are coated with the crumb mixture. (They may not be perfectly coated—this is OK.)

Spray a large baking sheet (use two, if needed) with nonstick spray, and spread out crumb-coated veggies on the sheet. Mist the veggies with nonstick spray.

Bake in the oven until crispy, about 17 to 20 minutes, and then allow to cool slightly. Meanwhile, combine ranch dressing, sour cream, and green pepper sauce in a small bowl, and mix well.

Plate your crunchy goodies and dunk them into the creamy sauce. YUM!

MAKES 3 SERVINGS

YOU'LL NEED:
small pot, nonstick
spray, fun bowl

PREP:
5 minutes

COOK:
10 minutes

GOOEY-GOOD QUESO DIP 'N CHIPS

Queso means "cheese," but queso DIP typically contains both cheese and meat—and other stuff too. This HG-ified queso dip is loaded with flavor and creamy goodness . . .

PER SERVING (⅓rd of recipe, about ⅓ cup dip and 10 chips):
195 calories, 3.25g fat, 730mg sodium, 21g carbs, 2.75g fiber,
1.5g sugars, 20g protein

Ingredients

1 cup frozen ground-beef-style soy crumbles
¾ teaspoon taco seasoning mix, divided
¾ teaspoon ground cumin, divided
⅓ cup light plain soymilk
⅔ cup shredded fat-free cheddar cheese
2 wedges The Laughing Cow Light Creamy Swiss cheese
1½ tablespoons fat-free cream cheese, room temperature
⅛ teaspoon chili powder, or more to taste
2 ounces (about 30) low-fat baked tortilla chips

Directions

Bring a small pot sprayed with nonstick spray to medium-high heat on the stove. Add frozen crumbles and sprinkle with ½ teaspoon taco seasoning and ¼ teaspoon cumin. Cook for about 4 minutes, mixing occasionally, until thawed and hot. Remove seasoned crumbles and set aside. Remove pot from heat and let cool slightly.

To the pot, add soymilk, all three cheeses, chili powder, remaining ¼ teaspoon taco seasoning, and remaining ½ teaspoon cumin. Add ¼ cup water and bring to medium-low heat.

Stirring frequently, heat until cheeses have melted and mixture has a smooth, sauce-like consistency.

Add seasoned crumbles to the pot, and continue to cook and stir until hot. If you like, warm chips in the microwave. Place dip in a fun bowl, and serve with chips!

MAKES 3 SERVINGS

CHAPTER 16:
SOUPS

Soup is a filler-upper, which means that it, um, FILLS YOU UP. This is a very good thing. Of course, what's even better is how incredibly AMAZING the soups in this chapter are. By the way, for even more soupy goodness, definitely check out the crock-pot chapter, starting on page 298!

YOU'LL NEED:

large pot

PREP:

10 minutes

COOK:

10 minutes

★ For full-color photos of all the recipes in this book, check out hungry-girl.com/books. Woohoo!

THE WHOLE ENCHILADA CHICKEN SOUP

This is one of the most popular HG soups of all time. And with good reason. It's AMAZING!!!

PER SERVING (⅑th of recipe, about 1 cup): 105 calories, 1.75g fat, 641mg sodium, 12.5g carbs, 2g fiber, 4g sugars, 11g protein

Ingredients

3 cups fat-free chicken broth
1¼ cups finely chopped celery
½ cup diced sweet yellow onion
3 cups green enchilada sauce
One 15-ounce can pure pumpkin
10 ounces cooked and shredded (or finely chopped) skinless lean chicken breast
1 cup frozen corn
Optional: dash hot sauce
Optional toppings: shredded fat-free cheddar cheese, crushed low-fat baked tortilla chips

Directions

In a large pot, bring broth to a low boil on the stove. Add celery and onion and simmer until slightly tender, about 5 minutes.

Stir in enchilada sauce and pumpkin. Once soup returns to a low boil, add chicken and corn, and mix well. Cook for an additional 3 to 5 minutes, until soup is heated throughout.

Add a dash or more hot sauce. (Or not. It's your soup.) Serve and, if you like, top with shredded cheese and/or crushed chips.

Enjoy!!!

MAKES 9 SERVINGS

I'LL TAKE MANHATTAN CLAM CHOWDER

Load up on this chunky, veggie-packed soup. You can have TWO full cups of it for around 200 calories. That's crazy and wonderful at the same time!

YOU'LL NEED:
large pot with a lid

PREP:
15 minutes

COOK:
40 minutes

PER SERVING (1/12th of recipe, about 1 cup): 100 calories, 1.5g fat, 407mg sodium, 14g carbs, 1.5g fiber, 5.5g sugars, 8.5g protein

Ingredients

1 large onion, chopped
2 carrots, chopped
1½ cups chopped celery
1 medium russet potato (about 7 ounces), peeled and cubed
One 14.5-ounce can diced tomatoes (not drained)
Two 14.5-ounce cans reduced-sodium tomato soup
1 cup fat-free low-sodium chicken broth
1 teaspoon ground thyme
¼ teaspoon black pepper
Two 10-ounce cans baby clams (not drained)
Optional: crushed red pepper, salt

Directions

Place all ingredients *except* the clams and optional spices in a large pot on the stove. Mix well and bring to a boil.

Reduce heat and let simmer for 10 minutes.

Add clams, cover, and let simmer for an additional 20 to 25 minutes, until all veggies are tender.

If you like, season to taste with crushed red pepper and salt. Enjoy!

MAKES 12 SERVINGS

YOU'LL NEED:

fork, microwave-safe plate, medium pot, nonstick spray, 5 bowls

PREP:

5 minutes

COOK:

15 minutes

📷 **For a pic of this recipe, see the second photo insert. Yay!**

FULLY LOADED BAKED POTATO SOUP

It's like a loaded baked potato in a bowl. That you can eat with a spoon. YES!!!

PER SERVING (⅕th of recipe, about 1 cup with toppings):
130 calories, 1g fat, 564mg sodium, 22g carbs, 2g fiber, 2.5g sugars, 7.5g protein

Ingredients

Soup

1 large potato (about 14.5 ounces)
2 tablespoons chopped onion
½ teaspoon minced garlic
3 cups fat-free chicken broth
1 cup light plain soymilk
¼ cup all-purpose flour
2 tablespoons shredded fat-free cheddar cheese
2 tablespoons fat-free sour cream
1 tablespoon precooked real crumbled bacon
¾ teaspoon garlic powder
¾ teaspoon onion powder
¼ teaspoon salt
⅛ teaspoon black pepper

Topping

5 teaspoons shredded fat-free cheddar cheese
5 teaspoons fat-free sour cream
5 teaspoons diced scallions
2½ teaspoons precooked real crumbled bacon

Directions

Pierce potato with a fork in multiple places, and then place it on a microwave-safe plate. Microwave for 8 to 10 minutes, until potato is soft. Once cool enough to handle, remove and discard the skin (either by peeling skin off or cutting potato open and scooping out the insides). Mash the potato pulp with a fork and set aside.

Bring a medium pot sprayed with nonstick spray to medium-high heat on the stove. Add chopped onion and minced garlic and cook for 1 to 2 minutes, until onion has softened. Add broth and soymilk. Slowly add the flour, continuously stirring until it has completely dissolved.

Add mashed potato and stir until fully blended. Add all other ingredients for soup. Mix well, reduce heat, and simmer for 2 minutes.

Top each serving with 1 teaspoon each of cheese, sour cream, and scallions. Sprinkle each serving with ½ teaspoon crumbled bacon. Enjoy!

MAKES 5 SERVINGS

HG Tip!

Feel free to load up your baked potato soup with even more potato toppings like salsa, chopped tomato, and spinach. Yum!

baking sheet,
aluminum foil,
nonstick spray,
blender, large
nonstick pot

PREP:

15 minutes

COOK:

40 minutes

BiG APPLE BUTTERNUT SQUASH SOUP

This soup screams FALL . . . Well, not literally. (If I had a recipe for talking soup I'd be WAY more famous.)

PER SERVING (¼th of recipe, about 1½ cups): 115 calories, 1g fat, 492mg sodium, 26.5g carbs, 4.5g fiber, 10g sugars, 3g protein

Ingredients

3½ cups cubed butternut squash
2 cups peeled and chopped Fuji apples
½ cup chopped carrots
1 small onion, chopped
½ tablespoon chopped garlic
¼ teaspoon salt, or more to taste
¼ teaspoon black pepper, or more to taste
2 cups fat-free chicken broth, divided
1 cup Unsweetened Original Almond Breeze
¼ teaspoon cinnamon
¼ teaspoon ground ginger
Optional: cayenne pepper

Directions

Preheat oven to 400 degrees.

Line a baking sheet with foil and mist with nonstick spray. Evenly place squash, apples, carrots, and onion on the sheet and top with garlic, salt, and pepper. Bake in the oven until soft, 25 to 30 minutes.

Once veggies and apples have cooled slightly, transfer to a blender. Add 1 cup broth and puree until smooth.

Pour pureed mixture into a large nonstick pot on the stove. Add remaining 1 cup broth, Almond Breeze, cinnamon, and ginger. Mix well and bring to a boil.

Reduce heat, stir, and let simmer for 10 minutes.

If you like, season to taste with additional salt, additional black pepper, and cayenne pepper. Enjoy!

MAKES 4 SERVINGS

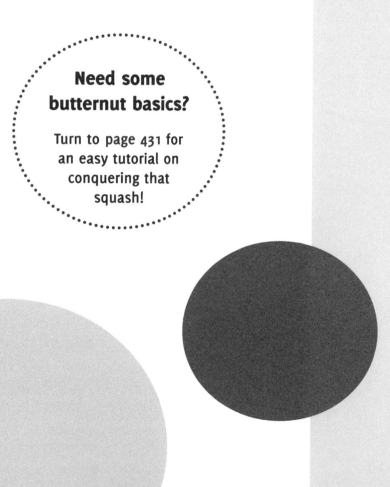

Need some butternut basics?

Turn to page 431 for an easy tutorial on conquering that squash!

YOU'LL NEED:

large nonstick pot,
blender

PREP:

10 minutes

COOK:

20 minutes

✱ For full-color
photos of all the recipes
in this book, check out
hungry-girl.com/books.
Woohoo!

CREAMY CARROT SOUP

so sweet . . . so creamy . . . so CARROTY . . . AHHHHHH!

PER SERVING (¼th of recipe, about 1¼ cups): 125 calories,
1.25g fat, 582mg sodium, 26.5g carbs, 5.5g fiber, 8g sugars, 4g protein

Ingredients

1 large onion, chopped

4 cups chopped carrots

1 medium potato (about 7 ounces),
   peeled and cubed

2 cups fat-free chicken broth

¼ teaspoon salt, or more to taste

¼ teaspoon black pepper, or more to taste

¼ teaspoon ground nutmeg

1 cup Unsweetened Original Almond Breeze

Directions

Bring a large nonstick pot to medium-high heat on the stove.
Add onion, carrots, and potato. Stirring occasionally, cook until
veggies are tender, about 10 minutes.

Add chicken broth and seasonings to the pot and bring to a boil.
Reduce heat to low and let simmer until veggies are soft, about
10 minutes.

Remove from heat and allow to cool slightly.

Carefully transfer contents of the pot to a blender. Add Almond Breeze and puree until smooth.

If needed, return soup to the pot and bring to desired temperature on the stove.

Season with additional salt and pepper, if you like, and enjoy!

MAKES 4 SERVINGS

YOU'LL NEED:

medium bowl, large
pot

PREP:

25 minutes

COOK:

15 minutes

📷 **For a pic
of this recipe,
see the
second photo
insert. Yay!**

WOWOWOW!
WONTON SOUP

Feeling ambitious? Make your own wonton soup . . . come on—don't
be afraid. Your Chinese food delivery guy will forgive you . . .

PER SERVING (⅛th of recipe, about 1 cup with 2 wontons):
115 calories, 3g fat, 541mg sodium, 12g carbs, 1.5g fiber,
1g sugars, 9.5g protein

Ingredients

Wontons

9 ounces raw lean ground turkey

2 teaspoons reduced-sodium/lite soy sauce

2 teaspoons dried minced onion

½ teaspoon garlic powder

⅛ teaspoon black pepper

16 small square wonton wrappers (often
stocked near the tofu in the refrigerated
section of the market)

Soup

6 cups fat-free chicken broth

2 cups dry broccoli cole slaw

⅓ cup canned bamboo shoots, drained

½ cup canned straw mushrooms, drained
and roughly chopped

1 teaspoon finely chopped fresh ginger

1 teaspoon chopped garlic

½ cup chopped scallions

Directions

To make the wonton filling, combine all wonton ingredients
except the wrappers in a medium bowl. Mix by hand until evenly
combined. Set aside (and, duh, wash your hands).

In a large pot, combine all soup ingredients *except* the scallions. Bring to a boil on the stove. Reduce heat to low and allow soup to simmer for 10 minutes.

Lay three wonton wrappers flat on a clean, dry surface. Scoop a spoonful (about 2 teaspoons) of filling into the center of each wrapper. Moisten all wrapper edges by dabbing with water. Fold the bottom left corner of each wrapper to meet the top right corner, forming a triangle and enclosing the filling. Press firmly on the edges to seal. Set aside, and repeat with remaining wrappers and filling.

Stir scallions into the simmering soup. One at a time, carefully add wontons. Make sure they're submerged, but don't stir. Simmer for 5 minutes, adjusting temperature if soup begins to boil, until wonton centers are firm. (Don't worry if the wontons fall apart a little. They'll still taste delicious!)

Carefully serve up wontons and broth. Slurp 'n chew, people!

MAKES 8 SERVINGS

ZAZZLED-UP ZUPPA

This soup starts with the best canned soup on the planet—Amy's Chunky Tomato Bisque. Add a few key ingredients and you've got something even better!

PER SERVING (½ of recipe, about 1 cup): 182 calories, 4g fat, 542mg sodium, 27g carbs, 5.75g fiber, 12g sugars, 10g protein

Ingredients

One 14.5-ounce can Amy's Organic Light in
    Sodium Chunky Tomato Bisque
½ cup frozen ground-beef-style soy crumbles
⅓ cup canned cannellini (white kidney) beans,
    drained and rinsed
¼ teaspoon Italian seasoning
¼ teaspoon garlic powder
1 teaspoon reduced-fat Parmesan-style grated topping
Optional garnish: chopped parsley

Directions

Add all ingredients *except* Parm-style topping and optional garnish to a nonstick pot, and bring to medium-high heat on the stove. Stirring occasionally, cook until crumbles have thawed and soup is hot, about 4 minutes.

Top each serving with ½ teaspoon Parm-style topping and, if you like, garnish with a little chopped parsley. Slurp!

MAKES 2 SERVINGS

MMM-MMM MiNESTRONE

Pasta . . . veggies . . . beans . . . This super-filling soup has it ALL.

PER SERVING (¹⁄₁₀ᵗʰ of recipe, 1 generous cup): 105 calories, 0.5g fat, 512mg sodium, 19.5g carbs, 4.5g fiber, 4g sugars, 5g protein

Ingredients

Two 14-ounce cans (3½ cups) fat-free vegetable broth
Two 14.5-ounce cans diced tomatoes, drained
One 15-ounce can cannellini (white kidney) beans, drained and rinsed
One 10-ounce package frozen spinach, mostly thawed
1 cup frozen cut green beans
1 cup frozen peas and carrots
1 cup uncooked whole-wheat-blend rotini or penne pasta
1 tablespoon dried minced onion
2 teaspoons chopped garlic
1 teaspoon Italian seasoning
1 bay leaf
Optional: salt and black pepper

Directions

Combine all ingredients in a large pot on the stove. Add 1 cup water and stir it up. Cover and bring to a boil.

Reduce heat to low and allow soup to simmer, covered, for 10 minutes. Remove bay leaf. If you like, add salt and pepper to taste, and serve!

MAKES 10 SERVINGS

YOU'LL NEED:
large pot with a lid,
nonstick spray

PREP:
15 minutes

COOK:
50 minutes

NO-BUNS-ABOUT-IT CHILI DOG CHILI

This chili is loaded with chunks of hot dogs . . . but not their buns. Hence the name.

PER SERVING (⅛th of recipe, about 1 cup): 129 calories, 1.25g fat, 834mg sodium, 22g carbs, 5g fiber, 8g sugars, 9.5g protein

Ingredients

Two 14.5-ounce cans stewed tomatoes, Mexican-style
    if available (not drained)
2 green bell peppers, chopped
1 large onion, chopped
1 large tomato, chopped
7 hot dogs with about 40 calories and 1g fat each, chopped
One 15-ounce can red kidney beans, drained and rinsed
1½ tablespoons yellow mustard
½ teaspoon chili powder
½ teaspoon ground cumin
⅛ teaspoon garlic powder
Optional: salt, black pepper, cayenne pepper
Optional topping: shredded fat-free cheddar cheese

Directions

Roughly chop the stewed tomatoes, reserving all juice. Set aside.

Bring a large pot sprayed with nonstick spray to medium-high heat on the stove. Add chopped bell peppers and onion. Stirring occasionally, cook until softened, about 5 minutes. Add chopped (fresh) tomato, give mixture a stir, and continue to cook for 1 minute.

Add stewed tomatoes and the reserved juice to the pot. Add all remaining ingredients *except* the optional spices and topping and mix well. Raise heat to high and bring to a boil.

Once boiling, reduce heat to medium low. Cover and allow to simmer for 20 minutes, removing the lid occasionally to stir.

Remove pot from heat and remove the lid. Allow chili to thicken for about 20 minutes.

If you like, season to taste with salt, black pepper, and/or cayenne pepper. Top each serving with cheese, if you like, and enjoy!

MAKES 8 SERVINGS

CHAPTER 17:
SiDES

They're not center-plate foods, people—but that doesn't make them any less enjoyable or important. These creative and yum-tastic dishes are sides (or snacks!) and PROUD!

YOU'LL NEED:

microwave-safe
bowl, potato masher
(optional)

PREP:

15 minutes

COOK:

10 minutes

LOADED MiRACLE MASHiES

What are they loaded with? cheese . . . bacon . . . sour cream . . . chives . . . but NOT fat and calories. Good deal!

PER SERVING (entire recipe): 181 calories, 2g fat, 758mg sodium, 28g carbs, 5g fiber, 7g sugars, 13.5g protein

Ingredients

3 ounces cubed red potatoes (about 1 to 2 small
    potatoes), not peeled

1½ cups chopped cauliflower

1 tablespoon fat-free non-dairy liquid creamer

1½ tablespoons fat-free sour cream

Dash salt

1 slice fat-free American cheese

1 tablespoon precooked real crumbled bacon

1 teaspoon chopped chives

Optional: black pepper, additional salt

Directions

Place potatoes and cauliflower in a microwave-safe bowl with 2 tablespoons water. Cover and microwave for 6 minutes, until very tender.

Once the bowl is cool enough to handle, drain any excess water.

Add creamer, sour cream, and salt. Using a potato masher or fork, mash until completely blended. If you like, season to taste with pepper and additional salt.

Lay cheese slice over the potato-cauliflower mixture. Microwave for 30 seconds, or until the cheese has melted.

Top with crumbled bacon and chives. Enjoy!

MAKES 1 SERVING

YOU'LL NEED:
large pot, large bowl, medium bowl

PREP:
10 minutes

COOK:
15 minutes

CHILL:
1 hour

CREAMY DREAMY MACARONI SALAD

This pasta-packed salad is INCREDIBLE. You get a huuuge serving for just 126 calories. How can it be? Macaroni MAGIC, that's how . . . well, that and egg whites.

PER SERVING (⅛th of recipe, 1 heaping cup): 126 calories, 1g fat, 393mg sodium, 23g carbs, 2g fiber, 3.5g sugars, 6g protein

Ingredients

Salad
6 ounces (about 1½ cups) uncooked elbow macaroni with at least 2g fiber per 2-ounce serving

2 cups dry broccoli cole slaw

1 cup chopped celery

1 cup chopped red bell pepper

¼ cup chopped onion

2 tablespoons sweet relish

6 large hard-boiled egg whites, chopped

Dressing
¼ cup plus 2 tablespoons fat-free mayonnaise

¼ cup Dijon mustard

1½ tablespoons white vinegar

⅛ teaspoon black pepper, or more to taste

⅛ teaspoon salt, or more to taste

1 no-calorie sweetener packet

Directions

In a large pot, prepare macaroni according to package instructions. Drain well and transfer to a large bowl. Allow to cool completely.

Combine all ingredients for dressing in a medium bowl and mix until blended. Set aside.

Add all remaining salad ingredients to the bowl with the cooked macaroni. Add dressing and toss to coat. Refrigerate for at least 1 hour, until completely chilled. Enjoy!

MAKES 8 SERVINGS

YOU'LL NEED:

9-inch by 13-
inch baking pan,
nonstick spray, large
microwave-safe bowl

PREP:

5 minutes

COOK:

40 minutes

INSANELY IRRESISTIBLE CORN PUDDING

This corn pudding truly is irresistible. So if you make it, have plenty of other people to share it with. This may be one of the best pieces of advice anyone ever gives you.

PER SERVING (¹⁄₁₂th of recipe, about one 3-inch square): 116 calories, 2.25g fat, 235mg sodium, 20.5g carbs, 1g fiber, 6.5g sugars, 3.5g protein

Ingredients

2 tablespoons light whipped butter or light buttery spread
1 cup fat-free sour cream
½ cup fat-free liquid egg substitute
1 tablespoon brown sugar (not packed)
One 6.5-ounce package cornbread mix
1 cup canned cream-style corn
1 cup frozen sweet corn kernels, thawed

Directions

Preheat oven to 375 degrees.

Spray a 9-inch by 13-inch baking pan with nonstick spray and set aside.

Put butter in a large microwave-safe bowl. Heat in the microwave for 20 seconds, or until melted. Add sour cream, egg substitute, and brown sugar. Mix well.

Add cornbread mix, cream-style corn, and corn kernels to the bowl. Stir thoroughly.

Evenly transfer mixture to the baking pan. Bake in oven until firm, about 40 minutes.

Serve it up and enjoy!

MAKES 12 SERVINGS

COLD DOG SLAW

> Are you a fan of classic hot dogs, mustard, and sauerkraut? If you excitedly nodded your head YES, then this recipe will likely find a way into your heart pretty quickly. Enjoy . . .

PER SERVING (¼th of recipe, about 1¼ cups): 96 calories, 1g fat, 806mg sodium, 13.5g carbs, 4g fiber, 4.5g sugars, 8g protein

Ingredients

¾ cup chopped onion
4 hot dogs with about 40 calories and 1g fat
    or less each, chopped
1½ tablespoons Hellmann's/Best Foods Dijonnaise
1½ tablespoons yellow mustard
One 12-ounce bag (4 cups) dry broccoli cole slaw
¾ cup sauerkraut

Directions

Bring a skillet sprayed with nonstick spray to medium-high heat on the stove. Add onion and, stirring occasionally, cook until softened, about 5 minutes.

Add chopped hot dogs and, stirring occasionally, cook until slightly browned, about 5 more minutes. Remove from heat and allow to cool.

Meanwhile, in a small bowl, combine Dijonnaise with yellow mustard and mix well. Set aside.

In a large bowl or container, combine broccoli cole slaw, sauerkraut, and onionhot dog mixture. Mix well. Add Dijonnaise-mustard mixture and toss to coat. Serve and enjoy!

MAKES 4 SERVINGS

YOU'LL NEED:
skillet, nonstick spray, small bowl, large bowl or container

PREP:
10 minutes

COOK:
10 minutes

small bowl;
vegetable peeler
(optional); crinkle
cutter (optional);
aluminum foil; broiler
pan, baking rack
and baking sheet,
or baking sheet;
nonstick spray; skillet

PREP:

25 minutes

COOK:

40 minutes

RANCH-TASTIC BUTTERNUT FRIES WITH BACON

Because, um, sometimes you just need fries smothered in ranch and bacon.

PER SERVING (½ of recipe): 235 calories, 5.5g fat, 880mg sodium, 39g carbs, 5.5g fiber, 10g sugars, 8.5g protein

Ingredients

⅓ cup fat-free sour cream
½ tablespoon dry ranch dressing/dip mix
1 butternut squash (about 2 pounds—large enough
    to yield 20 ounces once peeled and sliced)
⅛ teaspoon coarse salt
4 slices turkey bacon
Optional topping: chopped scallions

Directions

Preheat oven to 425 degrees.

In a small bowl, combine sour cream with ranch mix and stir thoroughly. Refrigerate until ready to serve.

Slice ends off squash, and then cut it in half widthwise. Peel squash carefully with a vegetable peeler or knife. Cut the round bottom piece in half lengthwise and remove seeds.

Using a crinkle cutter or knife, carefully cut squash into spears/French-fry shapes. (For exact nutritionals, weigh spears and use 20 ounces.) Pat firmly with paper towels to absorb excess moisture. Sprinkle with salt.

Lay spears on a layer of paper towels, and let stand for at least 5 minutes, to allow salt to draw out excess moisture. Pat with paper towels.

Spray a broiler pan, a baking rack placed over a baking sheet, or a baking sheet with nonstick spray, and lay spears flat on it. (Use two pieces of bakeware, if needed.)

Bake in the oven for 20 minutes. Carefully flip fries, and bake for about 20 minutes longer, until tender on the inside and crispy on the outside.

Meanwhile, bring a skillet sprayed with nonstick spray to medium-high heat on the stove. Cook bacon until crispy, about 4 minutes per side, and set aside to cool. Then cut each slice in half widthwise, and cut each half into very thin strips lengthwise.

Mix bacon strips with fries and drizzle or serve with ranch mixture. If you like, sprinkle with scallions as well. Eat up!

MAKES 2 SERVINGS

YOU'LL NEED:

baking sheet,
nonstick spray,
microwave-safe
bowl, potato masher
(optional), large bowl

PREP:

15 minutes

COOK:

35 minutes

SWEET 'N SQUASHED BISCUITS

These are weird (and sorta flat) little things, but hey, can't the same thing be said about some of your best friends?

PER SERVING (1/12th of recipe, 1 biscuit): 80 calories, 1.25g fat, 135mg sodium, 16g carbs, 2.5g fiber, 2g sugars, 2.5g protein

Ingredients

2½ cups cubed butternut squash

⅔ cup light vanilla soymilk

2 tablespoons light whipped butter or light buttery spread, room temperature

1½ cups whole-wheat flour

1½ tablespoons brown sugar (not packed)

½ teaspoon baking powder

½ teaspoon salt

Directions

Preheat oven to 450 degrees.

Spray a baking sheet with nonstick spray and set aside.

Put squash in a microwave-safe bowl with 2 tablespoons of water. Cover and cook in the microwave for 6 minutes, or until soft enough to mash.

Once cool enough to handle, mash squash with a fork or potato masher. Add soymilk and butter and mix well. Set aside.

In a large bowl, combine flour, brown sugar, baking powder, and salt. Add squash mixture and mix thoroughly.

Evenly place squash batter on the baking sheet in 12 evenly sized mounds.

Bake in the oven until slightly browned and cooked through, 25 to 28 minutes.

Allow to cool slightly and then enjoy!

MAKES 12 SERVINGS

Need squash-slicing advice?

Page 431 has got you covered!

YOU'LL NEED:

vegetable peeler (optional); crinkle cutter (optional); aluminum foil; broiler pan, baking rack and baking sheet, or baking sheet; nonstick spray; small microwave-safe bowl

PREP:

25 minutes

COOK:

40 minutes

FOR THE LOVE OF SWEET GARLIC BUTTERNUT FRIES

More b-nut fries for you because they're A-MAZING. And so are you . . .

PER SERVING (½ of recipe): 189 calories, 1.5g fat, 453mg sodium, 45g carbs, 6g fiber, 13g sugars, 3.5g protein

Ingredients

1 butternut squash (about 2 poundslarge enough to yield 20 ounces once peeled and sliced)

¼ teaspoon coarse salt, divided

½ head of garlic

½ teaspoon olive oil

2 tablespoons sweet Asian chili sauce

Optional: additional coarse salt

Directions

Preheat oven to 425 degrees.

Slice ends off squash, and then cut it in half widthwise. Peel squash carefully with a vegetable peeler or knife. Cut the round bottom piece in half lengthwise and remove seeds.

Using a crinkle cutter or knife, carefully cut squash into spears/French-fry shapes. (For exact nutritionals, weigh spears and use 20 ounces.) Pat firmly with paper towels to absorb excess moisture. Sprinkle with ⅛ teaspoon salt.

Lay spears on a layer of paper towels, and let stand for at least 5 minutes, to allow salt to draw out excess moisture. Pat with paper towels. If you like, sprinkle with more salt.

Remove the outer layer of garlic, leaving the skins around the cloves intact. Slice ¼ inch off the top of the garlic, exposing the tops of the cloves. Place garlic on a piece of foil, drizzle with oil, and use your fingers to make sure it's coated. Wrap foil tightly around the garlic, enclosing it completely.

Spray a broiler pan, a baking rack placed over a baking sheet, or a baking sheet with nonstick spray, and lay spears flat on it. (Use two pieces of bakeware, if needed.) Place foil-wrapped garlic on it as well (or directly on oven rack).

Bake in the oven for 20 minutes. Carefully flip fries, and then bake fries and garlic for 10 minutes longer.

Carefully remove foil-wrapped garlic and set aside. Bake fries for 10 more minutes, or until tender on the inside and crispy on the outside.

Once cool enough to handle, unwrap garlic, remove cloves (discard skin), and place in a small microwave-safe bowl. Add remaining ⅛ teaspoon salt and mash with a fork until mostly smooth. Add chili sauce and mix well. Nuke for about 10 seconds, until softened.

Plate fries and top or serve with garlic sauce. Consume immediately!

MAKES 2 SERVINGS

YOU'LL NEED:

large microwave-safe
bowl, large skillet,
nonstick spray,
microwave-safe bowl

PREP:

10 minutes

COOK:

25 minutes

For the Weight Watchers
PointsPlus™ values of
all the recipes in this
book, check out
hungry-girl.com/books.
Yay!

GERMAN-iSH POTATO-iSH SALAD

This recipe is only LOOSELY based on German potato salad. It's named "German-ish" for a reason. But German or not, it is completely delicious . . .

PER SERVING (⅛th of recipe, a heaping ¾ cup): 85 calories, 0.75g fat, 324mg sodium, 16g carbs, 3.25g fiber, 6g sugars, 3.5g protein

Ingredients

1 head cauliflower, cored and roughly chopped
10 ounces baby red potatoes, roughly chopped
3 cups dry coleslaw mix
1 cup chopped onion
¼ cup seasoned rice vinegar
3 tablespoons precooked real crumbled bacon
2 tablespoons Hellmann's/Best Foods Dijonnaise
½ tablespoon granulated sugar
⅛ teaspoon salt
Dash black pepper
¼ cup chopped scallions

Directions

Place cauliflower and potatoes in a large microwave-safe bowl with ⅓ cup water. Cover and microwave for 6 minutes. Stir, re-cover, and microwave for 8 minutes, or until tender. Once cool enough to handle, drain excess water and set aside.

Meanwhile, bring a large skillet sprayed with nonstick spray to medium-high heat on the stove. Add coleslaw mix and onion. Stirring frequently, cook until soft and slightly browned, about 8 minutes. Add contents of the skillet to the bowl with the cauliflower and potatoes. Set aside.

To make the dressing, combine all remaining ingredients *except* the scallions in a microwave-safe bowl. Add 2 tablespoons water, stir, and microwave for 1 minute, or until warm. Mix thoroughly.

Add dressing to the large bowl with veggies and potatoes, and toss to coat. Add scallions, gently mix, and serve! (P.S. If you're making this ahead of time, refrigerate and then warm it up just before serving.)

MAKES 8 SERVINGS

PSSST! There are some super side dishes hangin' out in the LUNCH & DINNER section . . .

Sweet Potato Apple Pack (page 160)

Steamy Creamy Squash Packet (page 162)

Crock-Pot Fake-Baked Beans (page 305)

Sweet 'n Red Hot Apple Mash (page 309)

large pot, large bowl,
small bowl

PREP:
15 minutes

COOK:
15 minutes

CHILL:
1 hour

📷 **For a pic of this recipe, see the second photo insert. Yay!**

VEGGED-OUT POTATO SALAD

This tater salad is totally veggie loaded. Hope you LOVE it as much as we all do here at the HG HQ!

PER SERVING (⅛th of recipe, about ¾ cup): 72 calories, 0.5g fat, 166mg sodium, 15.5g carbs, 1.5g fiber, 3g sugars, 2.25g protein

Ingredients

Salad
1 pound potatoes, chopped
½ cup chopped bell pepper
½ cup chopped celery
½ cup chopped cucumber
½ cup cherry tomatoes, halved
½ cup frozen petite peas and carrots, thawed
¼ cup chopped scallions

Dressing
¼ cup fat-free mayonnaise
¼ cup fat-free sour cream
1 tablespoon yellow mustard
1 tablespoon sweet relish
⅛ teaspoon salt

Directions

Put potatoes in a large pot and fill with enough water to cover potatoes. Bring water to a boil.

Once boiling, continue to cook until potatoes are soft, about 10 minutes. Carefully drain, transfer potatoes to a large bowl, and set aside.

Combine all dressing ingredients in a small bowl and mix well. Set aside.

Once potatoes are cool, add all remaining salad ingredients to the large bowl. Add dressing and lightly toss to coat.

Refrigerate for at least an hour before serving. Then eat up!

MAKES 8 SERVINGS

YOU'LL NEED:
large pot, large bowl, medium bowl, whisk

PREP:
15 minutes

COOK:
5 minutes

CHILL:
1 hour

For more recipes, plus food finds, tips 'n tricks, and MORE, sign up for FREE daily emails at hungry-girl.com!

BEAN THERE, YUM THAT SALAD

Beans, beans, and more beans. And each cup has a nice amount of protein and fiber. Coolio!

PER SERVING (¹⁄₁₀th of recipe, about 1 cup): 122 calories, 2g fat, 338mg sodium, 20.5g carbs, 6g fiber, 5g sugars, 6g protein

Ingredients

Salad

2 cups fresh green beans, trimmed and cut into 1-inch segments

2 cups bite-sized broccoli florets

One 15-ounce can red kidney beans, drained and rinsed

One 15-ounce can garbanzo beans (chickpeas), drained and rinsed

1 red or yellow bell pepper, seeded, thinly sliced, cut into 1-inch segments

1 small red onion, thinly sliced

3 tablespoons chopped fresh parsley

Dressing

2 oranges

¼ cup seasoned rice vinegar

1 tablespoon lemon juice

1 tablespoon olive oil

1 teaspoon chopped garlic

Dash each salt and black pepper, or more to taste

Directions

Bring a large pot of lightly salted water to a rapid boil. Meanwhile, fill a large bowl with cold water and ice; set aside.

Add green beans and broccoli to boiling water, and cook for 5 minutes, or until just tender. Drain water and immediately transfer veggies to the bowl of water and ice to stop the cooking. (Congratulations—you just blanched the veggies!) Set aside.

To make the dressing, squeeze the juice from both oranges into a medium bowl. Remove any seeds. Add all other ingredients for the dressing, and whisk until uniform and blended. Set aside.

Drain ice and water from the large bowl, so only the blanched veggies remain. Add kidney beans, garbanzo beans, bell pepper, onion, and parsley. Top with dressing and toss well, ensuring all veggies and beans are coated.

Let marinate in the refrigerator for at least 1 hour before eating. (Okay . . . If you REALLY can't wait, go ahead and dig in!)

MAKES 10 SERVINGS

YOU'LL NEED:

extra-large bowl,
small bowl

PREP:

15 minutes

CHILL:

1 hour

HG Tip!

Can't locate
pineapple
tidbits? (It
happens!) Just
buy the chunks
and slice 'em
in half. EZ!

For a pic
of this recipe,
see the
second photo
insert. Yay!

CRAZY-DELICIOUS CARIBBEAN BLACK BEAN BROCCOLI SLAW

Islandy-good slaw you can serve to anyone. It's particularly perfect for summer cookouts (and travels well too!).

PER SERVING ($\frac{1}{7}$th of recipe, about 1 cup): 146 calories, <0.5g fat, 325mg sodium, 31g carbs, 7.25g fiber, 15.5g sugars, 5g protein

Ingredients

One 15-ounce can black beans, drained and rinsed
One 12-ounce bag (4 cups) dry broccoli cole slaw
One 8-ounce can pineapple tidbits packed in juice (not drained)
2 cups peeled and chopped mango (about 2 mangoes)
2 cups peeled and chopped jicama (about 1 jicama)
$\frac{1}{3}$ cup fat-free plain yogurt
2 tablespoons seasoned rice vinegar
2 tablespoons Hellmann's/Best Foods Dijonnaise
$\frac{1}{2}$ tablespoon granulated sugar
2 drops coconut extract
$\frac{1}{8}$ teaspoon chili powder, or more to taste
$\frac{1}{8}$ teaspoon salt, or more to taste
$\frac{1}{8}$ teaspoon black pepper, or more to taste

Directions

In an extra-large bowl, combine black beans, broccoli cole slaw, pineapple, mango, and jicama. Mix well and set aside.

In a small bowl, combine all other ingredients and stir until blended. Pour mixture over the contents of the large bowl, and stir to coat. Refrigerate for at least 1 hour. Mix well before serving. If you like, season to taste with additional chili powder, salt, and pepper. Enjoy!

MAKES 7 SERVINGS

Crock-Pot Fun

Cheeseburger Mac Attack, p. 308

Chicken and Sausage Gumbo, p. 310

Outside-In Turkey Tamale Pie, p. 312

Stir-Frys & Skillet Meals, Fast-Food/Drive-Thru Makeovers, and Starters

Loaded Bacon-Wrapped Hot Dogs, p. 356

Rockin' Roasted Corn Guac 'n Chips, p. 366

Cheesy Bacon Noodle Skillet, p. 336

Crispity Crunchity Drumsticks, p. 354

Tempting Teriyaki Trifecta, p. 330

Sweet Coconut Crunch Shrimp, p. 379

Amazing Ate-Layer Open-Faced Taco, p. 344

Soups, Sides, Chicken Trios, and Tortilla Trios

Fully Loaded Baked Potato Soup, p. 398

WOWOWOW! Wonton Soup, p. 404

Vegged-Out Potato Salad, p. 426

Crazy-Delicious Caribbean Black Bean Broccoli Slaw, p. 430

Garlic Shrimp Tostada, p. 459

World's Easiest Chicken Empanadas, p. 444

Tuna Trios and Ground Meat Trios

Looney Tuna-Stuffed Pepper, p. 463

Tuna Mushroom Cups, p. 468

OMG! Burgers (Onion Mushroom Goodness Burgers), p. 477

Simply Sweet Meatballs, p. 481

Meatless Burger Patty Trios

Burgs in a Blanket, p. 490

Cheesy Noodles 'n Burgs!, p. 496

Burger-ific Mushroom Melt, p. 499

Hot Dogs, Hot Trios and Noodle Trios

Hot Doggy Home Fries, p. 507

EZ Chili Mac, p. 517

Sweetness, Spice & 3-Things Nice Noodles, p. 516

Fresh 'n Fruity Skewer Dogs, p. 509

Squash It!

Hungry Girl's Guide to Mastering the Butternut Squash

When a recipe calls for cubed squash, you can sometimes find the pre-cubed kind in the produce section of the supermarket. If you plan to break down the tough-skinned gourd yourself, here are a few things you should know . . .

Choose it! Go for a long squash with a short round section—the round part is mostly hollow (with seeds and fibers that need to be removed); the long part is all flesh.

Hack it! Cut off the ends with a sharp knife, and then slice the squash in two widthwise, just above the round part—you'll have two easy-to-work-with pieces with flat ends and no awkward angles.

Peel it! Use a vegetable peeler to remove the skin. Drag it firmly down the length of the squash, repeating until you get to the bright orangey-yellow part. Be aggressive, but watch your fingers!

Slice it! Once you're done peeling, cut the pieces in half lengthwise. If your squash is super firm and tough to slice, try nuking it in the microwave for about 45 seconds to soften it.

Scoop it! Carefully scoop out or slice off and discard the seeds and fibers. Now you're ready to chop, slice, or cube away!

TRIOS

What on EARTH are TRIOS?
They're super-simple recipes consisting of
three little ingredients that come together to
create taste sensations that please mouths
across the globe. They're like HG couples, only
with someone else crashing the party. You get
the idea . . . BTW, you'll notice that spices
do NOT count as ingredients for these.
Just go with it . . .

CHAPTER 18: CHICKEN TRIOS

Poultry alert! Here are some creative ways to use everyone's favorite bird . . .

YOU'LL NEED:
skillet, nonstick spray, small bowl, plate

PREP:
5 minutes

COOK:
10 minutes

BALSAMiC BBQ ChiCK SKiLLET

Pair it with veggies or toss it on a salad . . .

PER SERVING (entire recipe): 218 calories, 2g fat, 422mg sodium, 7.5g carbs, 0g fiber, 5.5g sugars, 39g protein

Ingredients

6 ounces raw boneless skinless lean chicken breast
1 tablespoon BBQ sauce with about 45 calories per 2-tablespoon serving
½ tablespoon balsamic vinegar

Spices: salt, black pepper

Directions

Bring a skillet sprayed with nonstick spray to medium heat on the stove. Season chicken with a dash each of salt and pepper. Cook in the skillet for about 5 minutes, flipping chicken as needed, until fully cooked.

Meanwhile, in a small bowl, combine BBQ sauce with vinegar and mix well.

Once fully cooked, while still in the skillet, brush or top chicken with sauce-vinegar mixture. Flip to coat.

Continue to cook until sauce mixture is hot, about 30 seconds. Plate chicken and drizzle with any excess sauce. Enjoy!

MAKES 1 SERVING

BASIL-icious CHICKEN

so simple and totally yummy!

YOU'LL NEED: baking pan, nonstick spray, plate

PREP: 5 minutes

COOK: 25 minutes

PER SERVING (entire recipe): 197 calories, 2g fat, 448mg sodium, 1g carbs, 0.5g fiber, 0g sugars, 39.5g protein

Ingredients

One 6-ounce raw boneless skinless lean chicken
    breast cutlet, pounded to ½-inch thickness
1 teaspoon Dijon mustard
⅓ cup chopped fresh basil or your herb of choice

Spices: salt, black pepper, garlic powder

Directions

Preheat oven to 350 degrees.

Spray a baking pan with nonstick spray. Season chicken with ⅛ teaspoon of each of the spices. Lay cutlet in the baking pan.

Bake in the oven until chicken is fully cooked, 20 to 25 minutes.

Plate chicken and evenly top with mustard. Cover with basil and eat up!

MAKES 1 SERVING

For the Weight Watchers *PointsPlus*™ values of all the recipes in this book, check out hungry-girl.com/books. Yay!

YOU'LL NEED:

small bowl,
toothpicks, baking
pan, nonstick spray,
aluminum foil

PREP:

10 minutes

COOK:

35 minutes

✳ For full-color
photos of all the recipes
in this book, check out
hungry-girl.com/books.
Woohoo!

TOMATO-INFUSED CHiCKEN ROLLUP

sun-dried tomatoes make this rollup ROCK!

PER SERVING (entire recipe): 206 calories, 4.5g fat,
470mg sodium, 2.5g carbs, 0.5g fiber, 1g sugars, 35g protein

Ingredients

1 wedge The Laughing Cow Light Original Swiss cheese
1 tablespoon sun-dried tomatoes packed in oil, drained and chopped
One 5-ounce raw boneless skinless lean chicken
       breast cutlet, pounded to ¼-inch thickness

Spices: Italian seasoning, salt, black pepper

Directions

Preheat oven to 350 degrees.

In a small bowl, combine cheese with tomatoes and mix well. If you like,
mix in a dash of Italian seasoning. Set aside.

Season chicken with a dash each of salt and pepper. Lay chicken cutlet
flat and evenly spread with cheese/tomato mixture.

Starting with one of the longer sides (or any side, if it's square), tightly
roll up the chicken cutlet and secure with toothpicks.

Place chicken roll in a baking pan sprayed with nonstick spray, and then
cover the pan with foil.

Bake in the oven for 20 minutes.

Carefully remove foil. Bake, uncovered, until chicken is cooked through,
about 15 minutes. Enjoy!

MAKES 1 SERVING

CRISPY NACHO CHICKEN

Crunchy with a Mexi-licious twist!

YOU'LL NEED:
baking pan,
nonstick spray

PREP:
10 minutes

COOK:
20 minutes

PER SERVING (entire recipe): 261 calories, 3.5g fat, 755mg sodium, 13.5g carbs, 2g fiber, 2g sugars, 41g protein

Ingredients

One 6-ounce raw boneless skinless lean chicken breast, pounded to ½-inch thickness
¼ cup salsa
½ ounce (about 8) low-fat baked tortilla chips, crushed

Spices: salt, black pepper

Directions

Preheat oven to 375 degrees.

Spray a baking pan with nonstick spray. Season chicken with a dash each of salt and pepper and place in the pan.

Evenly top chicken with salsa and crushed chips, gently pressing the chips into the salsa.

Bake in the oven until chicken is cooked through, about 20 minutes.

Serve and enjoy!

MAKES 1 SERVING

YOU'LL NEED:

large skillet, nonstick spray, small bowl

PREP:

5 minutes

COOK:

10 minutes

FRUITY BBQ CHICKEN FOR TWO

BBQ apricot chicken that ROCKS HARD!

PER SERVING (½ of recipe): 219 calories, 2g fat, 411mg sodium, 10.5g carbs, 0g fiber, 4.5g sugars, 39g protein

Ingredients

12 ounces raw boneless skinless lean chicken breast, cubed
2 tablespoons BBQ sauce with about 45 calories per 2-tablespoon serving
2 tablespoons sugar-free apricot preserves

Spices: salt, black pepper

Directions

Bring a large skillet sprayed with nonstick spray to medium-high heat on the stove. Add chicken and season with ⅛ teaspoon salt and ⅛ teaspoon pepper. Stirring occasionally, cook for 5 minutes.

Meanwhile, in a small bowl, combine sauce with preserves and mix well.

Add sauce-preserves mixture to the skillet and stir to coat. Continue to cook for 5 minutes, or until chicken is fully cooked.

Serve it up and eat it up!

MAKES 2 SERVINGS

SWEET 'N SPiCY CHiCKEN LETTUCE CUPS

As good as restaurant versions, only 100 times easier to make and totally guilt-free!

YOU'LL NEED:
skillet, nonstick spray, bowl

PREP:
5 minutes

COOK:
5 minutes

PER SERVING (entire recipe, 2 lettuce cups): 166 calories, 1g fat, 611mg sodium, 18g carbs, 1g fiber, 14g sugars, 20g protein

Ingredients

3 ounces raw boneless skinless lean chicken breast, cubed
2 tablespoons sweet Asian chili sauce
2 leaves romaine, butter, or green leaf lettuce

Spices: salt, black pepper

Directions

Bring a skillet sprayed with nonstick spray to medium-high heat on the stove. Season chicken with a dash each of salt and pepper and add to the skillet. Stirring occasionally, cook chicken until fully cooked, about 4 minutes.

Transfer chicken to a bowl, top with chili sauce, and toss to coat.

Evenly distribute chicken among the lettuce "cups" and eat up!

MAKES 1 SERVING

YOU'LL NEED:

baking pan, nonstick spray

PREP:

5 minutes

COOK:

25 minutes

For full-color photos of all the recipes in this book, check out hungry-girl.com/books. Woohoo!

BACON-WRAPPED BBQ CHICKEN

Bacon-snuggled chicken . . . Mmmmmm!

PER SERVING (entire recipe): 267 calories, 6.75g fat, 802mg sodium, 11g carbs, og fiber, 10g sugars, 37g protein

Ingredients

One 5-ounce raw boneless skinless lean chicken breast cutlet
2 tablespoons BBQ sauce with about 45 calories per 2-tablespoon serving
2 slices center-cut bacon or turkey bacon

Spices: salt, black pepper

Directions

Preheat oven to 375 degrees.

Spray a baking pan with nonstick spray. Season chicken with a dash each of salt and pepper and coat with BBQ sauce. Wrap bacon around chicken and place in the pan.

Bake in the oven until chicken is fully cooked, about 20 minutes.

Set oven to broil and broil chicken until bacon is crispy, about 4 minutes.

Serve and enjoy!

MAKES 1 SERVING

CHICKEN A LA POT PIE

Just like the creamy insides of your favorite chicken pot pie . . .

YOU'LL NEED:
baking pan, nonstick spray

PREP:
5 minutes

COOK:
20 minutes

PER SERVING (entire recipe): 258 calories, 3.75g fat, 680mg sodium, 11g carbs, 2.5g fiber, 2g sugars, 42g protein

Ingredients

6 ounces raw boneless skinless lean chicken breast
⅓ cup 98% fat-free cream of mushroom condensed soup
¼ cup frozen peas

Spices: salt, black pepper

Directions

Preheat oven to 375 degrees.

Spray a baking pan with nonstick spray. Season chicken with a dash each of salt and pepper and place in the pan. Cover chicken with soup and flip to coat. Top with peas.

Bake in the oven until chicken is cooked through, about 20 minutes.

Time to chew!

MAKES 1 SERVING

YOU'LL NEED:
baking sheet,
nonstick spray,
medium bowl, rolling
pin (optional)

PREP:
15 minutes

COOK:
15 minutes

📷 For a pic
of this recipe,
see the
second photo
insert. Yay!

WORLD'S EASIEST CHICKEN EMPANADAS

Baked and beautiful . . . not to mention DEE-LISH!

PER SERVING (⅙th of recipe, 1 empanada): 157 calories, 6.5g fat, 465mg sodium, 16.5g carbs, 0.5g fiber, 3g sugars, 9.5g protein

Ingredients

6 ounces cooked and shredded (or finely chopped)
  skinless lean chicken breast

¼ cup salsa

1 package Pillsbury Crescent Recipe Creations Seamless Dough Sheet

Spices: salt, black pepper

Directions

Preheat oven to 375 degrees.

Spray a baking sheet with nonstick spray and set aside.

Combine chicken with salsa in a medium bowl. Add ⅛ teaspoon salt and ⅛ teaspoon pepper. Mix well and set aside.

Roll out dough into a large rectangle of even thickness. Cut lengthwise into two even pieces. Cut each piece widthwise into thirds, leaving you with 6 rectangular pieces of dough. Stretch or roll out each rectangle a bit.

Evenly distribute chicken mixture among the centers of dough. Arrange one of the pieces of dough so that the shorter sides are on the right and left. Fold and stretch the lower left corner to meet the upper right corner.

Press edges firmly to enclose the chicken mixture. Using a fork dipped in water, press edges to crimp and seal. Transfer to the baking sheet and repeat with remaining ingredients.

Bake in the oven until dough is golden brown, about 12 minutes.

Allow to cool slightly and enjoy!

MAKES 6 SERVINGS

YOU'LL NEED:
sealable plastic bag or container, baking pan, nonstick spray

PREP:
5 minutes

MARINATE:
10 minutes

COOK:
25 minutes

EZ PINEAPPLE CHICKEN

sweet, salty & satisfying!

PER SERVING (entire recipe): 228 calories, 2g fat, 676mg sodium, 10g carbs, 0.5g fiber, 8g sugars, 40g protein

Ingredients

6 ounces raw boneless skinless lean chicken breast
¼ cup pineapple chunks packed in juice (not drained)
½ tablespoon reduced-sodium/lite soy sauce

Spices: salt, black pepper, garlic powder

Directions

Preheat oven to 350 degrees.

Season chicken with ⅛ teaspoon of each of the spices. Put chicken in a sealable plastic bag or container. Add pineapple, with juice, and soy sauce. Seal or cover and let marinate for 10 minutes.

Spray a baking pan with nonstick spray. Transfer contents of the bag or container, including excess marinade, to the baking pan.

Bake in the oven until chicken is fully cooked, 20 to 25 minutes.

Grab a fork!

MAKES 1 SERVING

NAKED CHICKEN PARM

You won't even miss the breadcrumbs . . .

YOU'LL NEED:
blender or food processor (optional), skillet with a lid, nonstick spray

PREP:
5 minutes

COOK:
10 minutes

PER SERVING (entire recipe): 247 calories, 5.25g fat, 685mg sodium, 6.5g carbs, 1g fiber, 4g sugars, 40g protein

Ingredients

1 stick light string cheese
One 5-ounce raw boneless skinless lean chicken
    breast cutlet, pounded to ⅓-inch thickness
¼ cup low-fat marinara sauce

Spices: salt, black pepper, garlic powder

For the Weight Watchers *PointsPlus*™ values of all the recipes in this book, check out hungry-girl.com/books. Yay!

Directions

Break string cheese into thirds and place in a blender or food processor—blend at high speed until cheese takes on a shredded or grated consistency. (Or just tear string cheese into pieces and roughly chop.) Set aside.

Bring a skillet sprayed with nonstick spray to medium-high heat on the stove. Season chicken with a dash of each of the spices. Add chicken to the skillet and cook about 4 minutes per side, until fully cooked.

Reduce heat to low. Top chicken with sauce while still in the skillet. Top with cheese. Cover skillet and continue to cook until sauce is hot and cheese has melted, about 1 minute.

Tada!

MAKES 1 SERVING

skillet, nonstick spray

PREP:
5 minutes

COOK:
15 minutes

HG Cheat Sheet! ✳

This recipe is great with reduced-sodium/lite soy sauce or thick teriyaki sauce/marinade thrown in!

SUPER-SPEEDY CHINESE STIR-FRY

Too easy for words . . . and TASTY too!

PER SERVING (½ of recipe): 295 calories, 4.5g fat, 680mg sodium, 23.5g carbs, 4.75g fiber, 13g sugars, 38.5g protein

Ingredients

10 ounces raw boneless skinless lean chicken breast, cut into bite-size pieces
4 cups frozen Asian-style stir-fry vegetables
½ cup mandarin oranges packed in juice, drained

Spices: salt, black pepper, crushed red pepper

Directions

Bring a skillet sprayed with nonstick spray to medium-high heat on the stove. Season chicken with ⅛ teaspoon salt and ⅛ teaspoon black pepper and add to the skillet. Stirring occasionally, cook until chicken is no longer pink, about 5 minutes.

Add veggies to the skillet. Stirring occasionally, cook until chicken is fully cooked, veggies are hot, and any excess water has evaporated, about 8 minutes.

Add mandarin oranges and mix well. If you like, top with a dash or two of crushed red pepper. Enjoy!

MAKES 2 SERVINGS

EASY BBQ CHICKEN NACHOS

Yay! You get to eat the whoooooole thing!

PER SERVING (entire recipe, about 15 nachos): 257 calories, 4g fat, 578mg sodium, 30g carbs, 1.75g fiber, 6.5g sugars, 24g protein

Ingredients

3 ounces cooked and shredded skinless lean chicken breast

1½ tablespoons BBQ sauce with about 45 calories per 2-tablespoon serving, divided

1 ounce (about 15) low-fat baked tortilla chips

Directions

Mix chicken with 1 tablespoon BBQ sauce in a small microwave-safe bowl. Heat in the microwave for 30 seconds, or until warm.

Lay chips on a microwave-safe plate and evenly top with chicken mixture. Heat in the microwave for another 30 seconds, until chicken is hot and chips are warm.

Drizzle with remaining ½ tablespoon BBQ sauce and dig in!

MAKES 1 SERVING

CHAPTER 19: TORTILLA TRIOS

Tortillas. They can do it all!
Check out these easy-peasy
threesomes, and let the fiesta
in your face begin!

YOU'LL NEED:
skillet, nonstick spray

PREP:
5 minutes

COOK:
5 minutes

FRUITY QUESADILLA

creamy cheese & mango make this an AMAZING little snack! This ROCKS even more when dunked in fat-free sour cream or salsa. Mmmmm!

PER SERVING (entire recipe): 199 calories, 4g fat, 512mg sodium, 39g carbs, 7.25g fiber, 14.5g sugars, 8g protein

Ingredients

1 medium-large high-fiber flour tortilla with about 110 calories
1 wedge The Laughing Cow Light Creamy Swiss cheese
½ cup chopped mango

Spices: cayenne pepper

Directions

Lay tortilla flat and evenly spread with cheese. Evenly distribute mango over one half of the cheese-covered tortilla. If you like, sprinkle with a dash of cayenne pepper. Fold the cheese-only half of the tortilla over the mango-topped side and press gently to seal and form the quesadilla.

Bring a skillet sprayed with nonstick spray to medium-high heat on the stove. Add quesadilla and cook until the outside is slightly crispy and the inside is hot, about 2 minutes per side.

Cut into triangles and eat!

MAKES 1 SERVING

SPEEDY BEANY-RiTO

A classic that'll become a staple in your life if you're a Mexican-food fan . . .

YOU'LL NEED:
microwave-safe bowl, microwave-safe plate

PREP:
5 minutes

COOK:
5 minutes

PER SERVING (entire recipe): 260 calories, 3.75g fat, 1,017mg sodium, 46.5g carbs, 12g fiber, 3g sugars, 14.5g protein

Ingredients

½ cup fat-free refried beans
1 wedge The Laughing Cow Light Creamy Swiss cheese
1 medium-large high-fiber flour tortilla with about 110 calories

Spices: chili powder, garlic powder, onion powder, ground cumin

Directions

Combine beans and cheese in a microwave-safe bowl and mix well. Microwave for 1 minute, until hot. Stir thoroughly. Season with a dash of each of the spices. Mix well and set aside.

Lay tortilla flat on a microwave-safe plate, and warm in the microwave for about 10 seconds. Spoon cheesy beans onto the center of the tortilla.

Wrap tortilla up like a burrito, folding the sides in first, and then rolling it up from the bottom.

Place burrito seam-side down on the plate, and microwave for 30 seconds, or until hot.

Eat it!

MAKES 1 SERVING

YOU'LL NEED:
baking sheet,
nonstick spray

PREP:
5 minutes

COOK:
10 minutes

* For full-color
photos of all the recipes
in this book, check out
hungry-girl.com/books.
Woohoo!

EASIEST THIN-CRUST PIZZA EVER

Pizza doesn't get easier—or more guilt-free—than this!

PER SERVING (entire recipe): 181 calories, 5g fat, 657mg sodium, 27g carbs, 6.5g fiber, 2.5g sugars, 12.5g protein

Ingredients

1 medium-large high-fiber flour tortilla with about 110 calories
2 tablespoons pizza sauce
1 stick light string cheese

Spices: Italian seasoning, garlic powder, onion powder

Directions

Preheat oven to 375 degrees.

Place tortilla on a baking sheet sprayed with nonstick spray. Bake in the oven until slightly crispy, about 5 minutes.

Remove sheet from the oven and evenly spread sauce over the tortilla, leaving a ½-inch border around the edge. Sprinkle sauce with a dash of each of the spices. Pull string cheese into shreds and place over the sauce.

Bake in the oven until cheese has melted and tortilla is crisp, about 5 minutes. Cut into slices and eat!

MAKES 1 SERVING

LEAN 'N GREEN SHRIMP-CHILADA

A fun little thing for you to chew . . .

PER SERVING (½ of recipe, 1 enchilada): 184 calories, 3.5g fat, 510mg sodium, 18g carbs, 2g fiber, 3g sugars, 19g protein

Ingredients

6 ounces raw shrimp, peeled, tails removed, deveined, chopped
½ cup plus 1 tablespoon green enchilada sauce, divided
2 large corn tortillas

Directions

Preheat oven to 400 degrees.

Spray a baking pan with nonstick spray and set aside.

In a small bowl, combine shrimp with 1 tablespoon enchilada sauce and toss to coat. Set aside.

Place tortillas on a microwave-safe plate and warm in the microwave for about 15 seconds. Lay tortillas flat and evenly distribute shrimp mixture between the centers.

Wrap each tortilla up tightly, and place it in the baking pan with the seam-side down.

Pour remaining ½ cup enchilada sauce over the enchiladas.

Bake in the oven until hot, about 15 minutes. Serve 'em up!

MAKES 2 SERVINGS

YOU'LL NEED:
baking pan, nonstick spray, small bowl, microwave-safe plate

PREP:
5 minutes

COOK:
15 minutes

* **HG Cheat Sheet!**

Top these with shredded fat-free cheese or fat-free sour cream!

YOU'LL NEED:

baking sheet,
nonstick spray, small
microwave-safe bowl

PREP:

5 minutes

COOK:

10 minutes

EZ CHEESY TOSTADA

Crispy and delicious . . . A no-brainer if you like beef 'n cheese. (And there's NO BEEF IN IT!)

PER SERVING (entire recipe): 196 calories, 3.5g fat, 794mg sodium, 31g carbs, 8.5g fiber, 2.5g sugars, 20g protein

Ingredients

1 medium-large high-fiber flour tortilla with about 110 calories
½ cup frozen ground-beef-style soy crumbles
1 slice fat-free American cheese, torn into pieces

Spices: chili powder, garlic powder, onion powder, ground cumin

Directions

Preheat oven to 400 degrees.

Place tortilla on a baking sheet sprayed with nonstick spray. Bake in the oven until crispy, about 5 minutes.

Meanwhile, place soy crumbles in a small microwave-safe bowl and season with a dash of each of the spices. Microwave for 1 minute, or until hot. Set aside.

Remove baking sheet from the oven and flip tortilla over. Evenly cover with soy crumbles and top with cheese.

Bake in the oven until cheese has melted, 2 to 4 minutes.

Slice into pieces or just bite right in!

MAKES 1 SERVING

AMAZIN' ONION QUESADILLA

There's something about caramelized onions . . . This thing is just plain screamworthy—AHHHHHHH!!!!

PER SERVING (entire recipe): 179 calories, 3.75g fat, 667mg sodium, 33g carbs, 7g fiber, 6g sugars, 8g protein

Ingredients

½ cup chopped onion
1 medium-large high-fiber flour tortilla with about 110 calories
1 wedge The Laughing Cow Light Creamy Swiss cheese

Spices: salt, black pepper

Directions

Bring a skillet sprayed with nonstick spray to medium heat on the stove. Add onion and sprinkle with a dash each of salt and pepper. Stirring occasionally, cook until softened, about 4 minutes.

Reduce heat to medium low, and continue to cook and stir until browned, 6 to 8 minutes. Remove from heat and set aside.

Lay tortilla flat and evenly spread with cheese. Evenly distribute onion over one half of the cheese-covered tortilla. Fold the cheese-only side of the tortilla over the onion-topped side and press gently to seal and form the quesadilla.

Remove skillet from heat, re-spray, and bring to medium-high heat. Add quesadilla to the skillet and cook until the outside is crispy and the inside is hot, 1 to 2 minutes per side.

Cut into triangles and eat!

MAKES 1 SERVING

YOU'LL NEED:
skillet, nonstick spray

PREP:
5 minutes

COOK:
15 minutes

For more recipes, plus food finds, tips 'n tricks, and MORE, sign up for FREE daily emails at hungry-girl.com!

RAW APPLE ROLLUP

No cooking required for this sweet 'n savory snack . . . Just chewing.

PER SERVING (entire recipe): 192 calories, 4g fat, 526mg sodium, 37.5g carbs, 8g fiber, 12g sugars, 8g protein

Ingredients

1 medium-large high-fiber flour tortilla with about 110 calories
1 wedge The Laughing Cow Light Creamy Swiss cheese
½ apple (preferably Fuji), cored and cut into matchstick-size pieces

Directions

Lay tortilla flat and evenly spread with cheese. Top evenly with apple, laying the pieces vertically, and pressing gently so the pieces adhere to the cheese.

Roll the tortilla up, from left to right. Grab 'n eat!

MAKES 1 SERVING

GARLIC SHRIMP TOSTADA

WOW . . . creamy-good garlicky shrimp on a crunchy bottom. AWESOME!

PER SERVING (entire recipe): 231 calories, 4.5g fat, 715mg sodium, 25.5g carbs, 6g fiber, 2.5g sugars, 25.5g protein

Ingredients

1 medium-large high-fiber flour tortilla with about 110 calories
3 ounces cooked ready-to-eat small shrimp
1 wedge The Laughing Cow Light Creamy Swiss cheese

Spices: garlic powder, black pepper, salt

Directions

Preheat oven to 375 degrees.

Place tortilla on a baking sheet sprayed with nonstick spray. Bake in the oven until somewhat crispy, about 4 minutes per side.

Place shrimp in a small bowl and season with ¼ teaspoon garlic powder, a dash of pepper and, if you like, a dash of salt. Set aside.

Remove sheet from oven. Once cool enough to handle, evenly spread cheese over the tortilla. Evenly top with shrimp.

Return to oven until cheese and shrimp are hot, about 4 minutes.

MAKES 1 SERVING

YOU'LL NEED:
baking sheet, nonstick spray, small bowl

PREP:
5 minutes

COOK:
15 minutes

📷 For a pic of this recipe, see the second photo insert. Yay!

CHAPTER 20:
TUNA TRIOS

"Tuna is NOT boring. Tuna is NOT boring." You can try to convince yourself by repeating this line 400 times, or you can simply whip up some of these trios for proof.

YOU'LL NEED:
microwave-safe bowl

PREP:
5 minutes

COOK:
5 minutes

BROC 'N GINGER TUNA BOWL

Infuse your tuna with some snazziness and ginger-y fun!

PER SERVING (entire recipe): 270 calories, 5g fat, 930mg sodium, 23g carbs, 7g fiber, 8.5g sugars, 36.5g protein

Ingredients

3 cups broccoli florets
One 5-ounce can albacore tuna packed in water, drained and flaked
2 tablespoons low-fat sesame ginger dressing

Directions

Put broccoli in a microwave-safe bowl with 2 tablespoons water. Cover and microwave until slightly softened, 2½ to 3 minutes.

Once cool enough to handle, drain excess liquid. Add tuna and dressing. Toss to mix. Enjoy warm or chilled!

MAKES 1 SERVING

LOONEY TUNA-STUFFED PEPPER

So easy and delicious, YOU'D be looney not to try it!

PER SERVING (entire recipe): 188 calories, 3g fat, 662mg sodium, 8.5g carbs, 2.5g fiber, 5g sugars, 30g protein

Ingredients

1 red bell pepper
One 5-ounce can albacore tuna packed in water, drained and flaked
1 tablespoon Hellmann's/Best Foods Dijonnaise

Directions

Preheat oven to 375 degrees.

Spray a baking pan with nonstick spray and set aside.

Carefully slice off the top of the pepper, removing the stem and seeds. Set aside.

In a bowl, combine tuna with Dijonnaise. Mix thoroughly. Scoop mixture into the bell pepper.

Place stuffed pepper in the baking pan and bake in the oven until pepper has softened, about 25 minutes.

Serve and enjoy!

MAKES 1 SERVING

HAWAiiAN TUNA SALAD

say "aloha" to fruity tuna goodness . . .

PER SERVING (entire recipe): 199 calories, 2.5g fat, 961mg sodium, 13.5g carbs, 0.5g fiber, 11.5g sugars, 29g protein

Ingredients

One 5-ounce can albacore tuna packed in water, drained and flaked
¼ cup crushed pineapple packed in juice, lightly drained
1 tablespoon thick teriyaki sauce/marinade

Directions

Combine all ingredients in a bowl and mix well.

That's it!

MAKES 1 SERVING

CHEESY TUNA MUFFIN 'WICH

So simple you may kick yourself for not thinking of it first!

YOU'LL NEED:
plate, small bowl

PREP:
5 minutes

COOK:
5 minutes

PER SERVING (entire recipe): 206 calories, 3.75g fat, 645mg sodium, 22.5g carbs, 5.75g fiber, 1g sugars, 22g protein

Ingredients

1 light English muffin
Half a 5-ounce can albacore tuna packed in water, drained and flaked (about ¼ cup)
1 wedge The Laughing Cow Light Creamy Swiss cheese

Spices: salt, black pepper

Directions

Split muffin into halves and lightly toast. Transfer to a plate and set aside.

In a small bowl, combine tuna with cheese, breaking the cheese wedge into pieces as you add it. Mix thoroughly, making sure cheese is evenly distributed. If you like, season to taste with salt and pepper.

Evenly distribute cheesy tuna between the toasty muffin halves, and enjoy your open-faced sandwich treat!

MAKES 1 SERVING

For the Weight Watchers
PointsPlus™ values of
all the recipes in this
book, check out
hungry-girl.com/books.
Yay!

SUN-DRIED TOMATO TUNA SALAD

A must-chew for sun-dried tomato fans . . .

PER SERVING (entire recipe): 177 calories, 4.5g fat, 699mg sodium, 6g carbs, 0.5g fiber, 2g sugars, 29g protein

Ingredients

One 5-ounce can albacore tuna packed in water, drained and flaked
2 tablespoons fat-free mayonnaise
1 tablespoon sun-dried tomatoes packed in oil, drained and chopped

Directions

Combine all ingredients in a bowl and stir until well mixed.

Then eat it . . . straight, wrapped in lettuce leaves, on light bread, WHATEVER!

MAKES 1 SERVING

SALSA TO THE TUNA SALAD!

creamy yogurt and salsa add zazzle to your tuna bowl!

PER SERVING (entire recipe): 168 calories, 2.5g fat, 851mg sodium, 4.5g carbs, 1g fiber, 2.5g sugars, 31g protein

Ingredients

One 5-ounce can albacore tuna packed in water, drained and flaked
¼ cup salsa
1 tablespoon fat-free plain Greek yogurt

Directions

Combine all ingredients in a bowl and stir until well mixed.

TADA!

MAKES 1 SERVING

YOU'LL NEED:

12-cup muffin pan,
nonstick spray, rolling
pin (optional), bowl

PREP:

10 minutes

COOK:

15 minutes

📷 For a pic
of this recipe,
see the
second photo
insert. Yay!

TUNA MUSHROOM CUPS

Hot, creamy, and fun . . . Just the way you like your snacks!

PER SERVING (¹⁄₁₂th of recipe, 1 mushroom cup): 93 calories,
3.75g fat, 345mg sodium, 9g carbs, <0.5g fiber, 1.5g sugars, 6g protein

Ingredients

1 package Pillsbury Crescent Recipe Creations Seamless Dough Sheet
Two 5-ounce cans albacore tuna packed in water, drained and flaked
¾ cup 98% fat-free cream of mushroom condensed soup

Spices: salt, black pepper

Directions

Preheat oven to 375 degrees.

Spray a 12-cup muffin pan with nonstick spray and set aside.

Roll out dough into a large rectangle of even thickness. Cut into
12 equally sized squares. Place a square of dough into each cup of
the muffin pan, pressing it into the bottom and up along the sides.

Combine tuna, soup, ¼ teaspoon salt, and ¼ teaspoon pepper in a
bowl. Mix thoroughly.

Evenly distribute tuna mixture among the cups. Bake in the oven
until golden brown, 10 to 12 minutes.

Time to eat!

MAKES 12 SERVINGS

SALSA-FiED TUNA STACKS

crunchy and protein packed . . . PERFECT!

PER SERVING (entire recipe, 2 stacks): 154 calories, 1.25g fat, 552mg sodium, 17g carbs, 0.75g fiber, 1.5g sugars, 17g protein

Ingredients

Half a 5-ounce can albacore tuna packed in water, drained and flaked (about ¼ cup)

3 tablespoons salsa

2 lightly salted rice cakes

Directions

Combine tuna with salsa in a medium bowl. Mix well.

Evenly divide tuna-salsa mixture between the rice cakes and enjoy your open-faced snack!

MAKES 1 SERVING

✳ For full-color photos of all the recipes in this book, check out hungry-girl.com/books. Woohoo!

FANCY-PANTS FAST TUNA 'N BEANS

Ignore the name; you could really eat this while wearing sweats . . . YUMMY stuff here!

PER SERVING (entire recipe): 248 calories, 4.75g fat, 738mg sodium, 15.5g carbs, 4g fiber, 3.5g sugars, 33.5g protein

Ingredients

One 5-ounce can albacore tuna packed in water, drained and flaked
⅓ cup canned white beans (like cannellini), drained and rinsed
1 tablespoon light raspberry vinaigrette

Spices: dried basil

Directions

Combine all ingredients in a bowl and mix well. If you like, mix in a dash of basil.

YOU'RE DONE! We didn't call it "fast" because it takes a long time to make, people . . .

MAKES 1 SERVING

BEST-EVER TUNA SLAW

It's actually true. This tuna slaw is the BEST EVER.

PER SERVING (⅕th of recipe, about 1 cup): 130 calories, 3.75g fat, 363mg sodium, 7.5g carbs, 2.5g fiber, 5g sugars, 13g protein

Ingredients

One 12-ounce bag (about 4 cups) dry broccoli cole slaw
Two 5-ounce cans albacore tuna packed in water, drained and flaked
½ cup light honey mustard dressing

Directions

Combine all ingredients in a medium bowl and stir to coat. Cover and refrigerate for at least 30 minutes.

Done!

MAKES 5 SERVINGS

YOU'LL NEED:
medium bowl

PREP:
5 minutes

CHILL:
30 minutes

CHAPTER 21: GROUND MEAT TRiOS

Meat lovers, you won't believe how incredibly simple and crazy-amazing these are . . .

YOU'LL NEED:
skillet, nonstick spray

PREP:
5 minutes

COOK:
15 minutes

SLOPPY JOE STIR-FRY SLAW

Veggie-infused and sooo saucy!

PER SERVING (¼th of recipe, about 1 cup): 136 calories, 3.75g fat, 527mg sodium, 12g carbs, 4g fiber, 7g sugars, 14g protein

* For full-color photos of all the recipes in this book, check out hungry-girl.com/books. Woohoo!

Ingredients

8 ounces raw lean ground turkey
One 12-ounce bag (about 4 cups) dry broccoli cole slaw
1 cup Hunt's Manwich Original Sloppy Joe Sauce

Spices: salt, black pepper

Directions

Bring a skillet sprayed with nonstick spray to medium-high heat on the stove. Add turkey and season with ⅛ teaspoon salt and ⅛ teaspoon pepper. Cook and crumble until browned and fully cooked, about 8 minutes.

Add slaw and sauce to the skillet and mix well. Stirring occasionally, continue to cook until sauce is hot and slaw has softened, about 6 minutes.

Serve and enjoy!

MAKES 4 SERVINGS

GRAVY-GOOD BEEF CASSEROLE

some of the easiest-to-whip-up comfort food around!

PER SERVING (¼ of casserole): 191 calories, 5g fat, 831mg sodium, 7.5g carbs, 0.75g fiber, 1g sugars, 27g protein

Ingredients

1 pound raw extra-lean ground beef
4 cups sliced mushrooms
One 12-ounce can fat-free beef or chicken gravy

Spices: salt, black pepper

Directions

Preheat oven to 350 degrees.

Spray an 8-inch by 8-inch baking pan with nonstick spray and set aside.

Bring a skillet sprayed with nonstick spray to medium-high heat on the stove. Add beef and sprinkle with ½ teaspoon salt and ½ teaspoon pepper. Cook and crumble until fully cooked, 6 to 8 minutes.

Drain any excess liquid and transfer beef to the baking pan. Top with mushrooms and gravy and gently mix.

Cover with foil and cook for 30 minutes, or until mushrooms are tender and gravy is bubbly.

Mmmm!!!

MAKES 4 SERVINGS

YOU'LL NEED:
8-inch by 8-inch baking pan, nonstick spray, skillet, aluminum foil

PREP:
5 minutes

COOK:
40 minutes

YOU'LL NEED:
large skillet, nonstick spray

PREP:
5 minutes

COOK:
15 minutes

HG Cheat Sheet! ✸

Let some shredded lettuce, diced tomatoes, fat-free sour cream, and shredded fat-free cheddar cheese join the taco party!

CRUNCHY TURKEY TACOS

A three-ingredient taco party . . . YAY!

PER SERVING (⅙th of recipe, 2 tacos): 258 calories, 12g fat, 220mg sodium, 16g carbs, 1.25g fiber, <0.5g sugars, 20.5g protein

Ingredients

1¼ pounds raw lean ground turkey
2 teaspoons taco seasoning mix
12 corn taco shells

Directions

Bring a large skillet sprayed with nonstick spray to medium-high heat on the stove. Add turkey and cook and crumble until mostly cooked, about 8 minutes.

Add ¼ cup water and taco seasoning and mix well. Continue to cook, stirring occasionally, until water has evaporated and turkey is fully cooked, about 3 minutes.

Allow seasoned turkey to cool slightly and then evenly distribute among taco shells, about ¼ cup each.

Dig in!

MAKES 6 SERVINGS

OMG! BURGERS (ONION MUSHROOM GOODNESS BURGERS)

Head-explodingly delicious!

PER SERVING (⅕th of recipe, 1 burger): 185 calories, 8.25g fat, 535mg sodium, 4.5g carbs, 0.75g fiber, 1.5g sugars, 23.5g protein

Ingredients

2 cups chopped mushrooms
1¼ pounds lean ground turkey
One 1-ounce packet dry onion soup/dip mix

Directions

Bring a skillet sprayed with nonstick spray to medium-high heat on the stove. Add mushrooms and, stirring occasionally, cook until softened, about 5 minutes. Transfer to a large bowl.

Add turkey to the bowl and sprinkle with onion soup/dip mix. Mix thoroughly with your hands. (Don't be squeamish—it's the easiest way!) Evenly and firmly form mixture into 5 patties.

Re-spray skillet and return to medium-high heat. Place burgers in the skillet, working in batches as needed. Cover and cook until cooked through, about 6 minutes per side.

Serve and enjoy!

MAKES 5 SERVINGS

YOU'LL NEED:
skillet with a lid, nonstick spray, large bowl

PREP:
10 minutes

COOK:
30 minutes

HG Cheat Sheet!

Top your burgers with ketchup and pickles. Wrap 'em in lettuce leaves. Eat 'em between 100-calorie flat sandwich buns. YUM!

For a pic of this recipe, see the second photo insert. Yay!

YOU'LL NEED:

large skillet, nonstick spray

PREP:

5 minutes

COOK:

10 minutes

VEGGED-UP GROUND BEEF

Beefy fun for everyone . . .

PER SERVING (⅓ʳᵈ of recipe, about 1½ cups): 175 calories, 4.75g fat, 478mg sodium, 6.5g carbs, 2g fiber, 3.5g sugars, 25g protein

Ingredients

1 small onion, sliced
12 ounces raw extra-lean ground beef
4 cups dry coleslaw mix

Spices: salt, black pepper, garlic powder

Directions

Bring a large skillet sprayed with nonstick spray to medium-high heat on the stove. Add onion and cook until slightly softened, about 5 minutes.

Add beef to the skillet and season with ¼ teaspoon of each of the spices. Cook and crumble until beef begins to brown, about 3 minutes.

Add coleslaw mix and continue to cook and stir until beef is fully cooked and coleslaw mix has wilted, about 3 minutes.

Remove skillet from heat. Season with an additional ¼ teaspoon salt and ¼ teaspoon garlic powder.

Divide (into 3 servings) and conquer!

MAKES 3 SERVINGS

BROCCOLi BEEF STiR-FRY

SO simple it's embarrassing . . .

PER SERVING (½ of recipe, about 1¼ cups): 237 calories, 5.5g fat, 870mg sodium, 19.5g carbs, 4.75g fiber, 9g sugars, 29g protein

YOU'LL NEED:
large skillet or wok with a lid, nonstick spray

PREP:
5 minutes

COOK:
15 minutes

Ingredients

8 ounces raw extra-lean ground beef
4 cups broccoli florets
3 tablespoons thick teriyaki sauce/marinade

Directions

Bring a large skillet or wok sprayed with nonstick spray to medium-high heat on the stove. Add beef and broccoli and stir-fry until beef is crumbled and browned and broccoli has softened, about 8 minutes.

Add teriyaki sauce/marinade and mix well. Cover and cook until broccoli is fully cooked, about 3 additional minutes.

Eat up!

MAKES 2 SERVINGS

MEXI-BOLOGNESE

Eat it as a sandwich filling, on top of veggies or tofu shirataki noodles . . . whatever!

PER SERVING (¼th of recipe, about 1 cup): 214 calories, 5g fat, 840mg sodium, 13g carbs, 2.25g fiber, 5g sugars, 26g protein

Ingredients

1 pound raw extra-lean ground beef
One 20-ounce can crushed tomatoes
One 1-ounce packet taco seasoning mix

Directions

Bring a large nonstick pot to medium-high heat on the stove. Add beef and cook and crumble until no longer pink, about 10 minutes.

Add tomatoes and taco seasoning to the pot and stir well to combine. Stirring occasionally, cook until mixture is thick and saucy, about 5 minutes.

Fiesta time!

MAKES 4 SERVINGS

SIMPLY SWEET MEATBALLS

Even your mom would approve of these . . .

YOU'LL NEED:
baking sheet,
nonstick spray,
large bowl

PREP:
5 minutes

COOK:
20 minutes

PER SERVING (⅕th of recipe, 4 meatballs): 199 calories, 8g fat, 390mg sodium, 8g carbs, 1g fiber, 6.5g sugars, 23g protein

📷 For a pic of this recipe, see the second photo insert. Yay!

Ingredients

1¼ pounds raw lean ground turkey
¾ cup canned crushed tomatoes
One 8-ounce can pineapple tidbits packed in juice, drained

Spices: salt, black pepper

Directions

Preheat oven to 350 degrees. Spray a baking sheet with nonstick spray and set aside.

In a large bowl, combine all ingredients, including ½ teaspoon salt and ¼ teaspoon pepper.

Use your hands to firmly form mixture into 20 evenly sized balls, placing them evenly on the sheet. Cook for 15 minutes.

Gently flip meatballs and return sheet to the oven. Bake until meatballs are cooked through, about 5 more minutes.

Enjoy!

MAKES 5 SERVINGS

YOU'LL NEED:

large skillet, nonstick
spray

PREP:

5 minutes

COOK:

15 minutes

BBQUICK SAUCY TURKEY

spoon it over veggies, have it sloppy joe-style on a light bun, or just fork it straight into your face!

PER SERVING (⅕th of recipe, about ⅔ cup): 244 calories, 8g fat, 707mg sodium, 19g carbs, <0.5g fiber, 14.5g sugars, 23g protein

Ingredients

1¼ pounds raw lean ground turkey
1 small onion, chopped
1 cup BBQ sauce with about 45 calories per 2-tablespoon serving

Spices: salt, black pepper

Directions

Bring a large skillet sprayed with nonstick spray to medium-high heat on the stove. Add turkey and sprinkle with ¼ teaspoon salt and ¼ teaspoon pepper. Add onion and, stirring frequently, cook and crumble until turkey is browned and onion is soft, about 6 minutes.

Reduce heat to medium. Stir in BBQ sauce. Stirring occasionally, cook until thickened, 5 to 7 minutes.

Eat up!

MAKES 5 SERVINGS

VEGGiE-RiFiC MEATLOAF

> The world's easiest meatloaf . . . and it's SUPER-DELICIOUS too!

YOU'LL NEED:
loaf pan, nonstick spray, large bowl

PREP:
5 minutes

COOK:
1 hour and
20 minutes

PER SERVING (⅕th of recipe, 1 thick slice): 211 calories, 8g fat, 436mg sodium, 10g carbs, 2g fiber, 3.5g sugars, 24.5g protein

Ingredients

1¼ pounds raw lean ground turkey
2 cups frozen petite mixed vegetables
1 cup canned crushed tomatoes, divided

Spices: salt, black pepper

✳ For more recipes, plus food finds, tips 'n tricks, and MORE, sign up for FREE daily emails at hungry-girl.com!

Directions

Preheat oven to 375 degrees.

Spray a loaf pan with nonstick spray and set aside.

In a large bowl, combine turkey, vegetables, ¾ cup crushed tomatoes, ½ teaspoon salt, and ¼ teaspoon pepper. Mix well. Transfer mixture to the loaf pan. Top with remaining ¼ cup crushed tomatoes.

Bake in the oven until meatloaf is cooked through, about 1 hour and 20 minutes.

Time for meatloaf!

MAKES 5 SERVINGS

YOU'LL NEED:

skillet or grill pan
with a lid, nonstick
spray

PREP:

5 minutes

COOK:

15 minutes

BACON CHEESEBURGER PATTY

Bacon-infused and cheesed-up. Just the way a burger should be . . .

PER SERVING (entire recipe): 205 calories, 7.75g fat,
650mg sodium, 1g carbs, 0g fiber, 1g sugars, 28.5g protein

Ingredients

4 ounces raw extra-lean ground beef
1 tablespoon precooked real crumbled bacon
1 wedge The Laughing Cow Light Creamy Swiss cheese

Spices: salt, black pepper

Directions

Season beef with a dash each of salt and pepper. Add bacon and
knead to evenly distribute. Form into a ball and, using your thumb,
make a large, hollow indentation in the ball (past the center but not
all the way through).

Fill the hole with cheese and squeeze the meat to seal, making sure
no cheese is exposed. Flatten slightly into a thick patty.

Bring a skillet or grill pan sprayed with nonstick spray to medium-
high heat on the stove. Place patty in the skillet/pan, cover, and
cook until done to your liking, 4 to 7 minutes per side. (Don't press
on the patty with your spatula—your patty might ooze cheese!)

Serve and enjoy!

MAKES 1 SERVING

CHAPTER 22: MEATLESS BURGER PATTY TRiOS

Soy burgers and veggie patties are so good, they deserve their very own haiku. Here it is:

Meatless patties rock . . .
Where have you been all my life?
Sometimes I'll eat two.

Now that the HG creative juices are flowing, check out our fantabulous trios featuring these protein-packed circles!

YOU'LL NEED:

skillet, nonstick spray

PREP:

5 minutes

COOK:

20 minutes

BACON BLEU BURGER

Tastes super-fattening but isn't. That's always fun!

PER SERVING (entire recipe): 229 calories, 12.5g fat, 957mg sodium, 9g carbs, 4g fiber, 1g sugars, 18g protein

✳ For full-color photos of all the recipes in this book, check out hungry-girl.com/books. Woohoo!

Ingredients

1 frozen meatless hamburger-style patty with about 100 calories
1 tablespoon light blue cheese dressing
3 slices center-cut bacon or turkey bacon

Directions

Bring a skillet sprayed with nonstick spray to medium heat on the stove. Add patty and cook for about 4 minutes per side, until cooked through. Plate, top with dressing, and set aside.

Add bacon to the skillet and cook until crispy. (Refer to package instructions for exact temperature and time.)

Once cool enough to handle, break or cut each bacon slice in half. Place bacon halves over dressing-topped patty and dig in!

MAKES 1 SERVING

FRUITIYAKI PATTY

It's like a tropical vacation on a plate . . .

YOU'LL NEED:
skillet, nonstick spray

PREP:
5 minutes

COOK:
10 minutes

PER SERVING (entire recipe): 140 calories, 2.75g fat, 582mg sodium, 17g carbs, 4g fiber, 9g sugars, 11g protein

Ingredients

1 frozen meatless hamburger-style patty with about 100 calories
1 pineapple ring packed in juice, drained
½ tablespoon thick teriyaki sauce/marinade

Directions

Bring a skillet sprayed with nonstick spray to medium heat on the stove. Add patty and cook for about 4 minutes per side, until cooked through. Cook pineapple alongside the patty until hot, about 2 minutes per side.

Plate your patty, drizzle with teriyaki sauce/marinade, and top with pineapple. Chomp!

MAKES 1 SERVING

YOU'LL NEED:
rolling pin (optional),
large baking sheet,
nonstick spray

PREP:
15 minutes

COOK:
15 minutes

📷 **For a pic
of this recipe,
see the
second photo
insert. Yay!**

BURGS IN A BLANKET

snuggly burger fun!

PER SERVING (⅛th of recipe, 2 burgs in a blanket): 196 calories,
7.25g fat, 550mg sodium, 20.5g carbs, 4.25g fiber, 3.5g sugars, 12.5g protein

Ingredients

1 package Pillsbury Reduced Fat Crescent rolls refrigerated dough
8 frozen meatless hamburger-style patties with
    about 100 calories each, thawed, halved
1 cup thinly sliced onion

Directions

Preheat oven to 375 degrees.

Slightly stretch or roll out one of the triangle-shaped portions of
dough, forming a larger triangle. Cut dough into two long narrow
triangles. Repeat with remaining dough, yielding 16 triangles.

Lay a burger half widthwise across the center of each triangle, so
that the top and bottom of each triangle are mostly exposed.
Evenly top each burger half with onion.

Bring the top and bottom of each triangle in toward the center,
over the onion-topped burger halves, and press to seal.

Place dough-covered burgers on a large baking sheet sprayed
with nonstick spray.

Bake in the oven until dough is slightly browned, about 12 minutes. Eat!

MAKES 8 SERVINGS

HG Cheat Sheet!
Dunk 'em in ketchup; it's REALLY good!

YOU'LL NEED:

large skillet,
nonstick spray

PREP:

5 minutes

COOK:

10 minutes

SWEET SPINACH STIR-FRY

This is pretty awesome . . . And if you want to add something else to the mix, pour in some egg substitute and turn it into a scramble!

PER SERVING (entire recipe): 263 calories, 9.25g fat, 849mg sodium, 24g carbs, 9g fiber, 8g sugars, 17g protein

Ingredients

1 frozen meatless veggie-burger patty with about 100 calories
8 cups spinach
3 tablespoons light honey mustard dressing

Spices: salt, black pepper

Directions

Bring a large skillet sprayed with nonstick spray to medium heat on the stove. Add patty and cook for about 4 minutes per side, until cooked through. Once cool enough to handle, chop into bite-sized pieces and set aside.

Remove skillet from heat, re-spray, and return to medium heat. Add spinach and, stirring often, cook until just slightly wilted, about 1 minute.

Add dressing and burger patty pieces and mix well. Continue to cook until spinach has fully wilted and mixture is hot, about 1 minute.

Serve and, if you like, season to taste with salt and pepper. Chew!

MAKES 1 SERVING

CURRY iN A HURRY TRiO

The flavors of India, right there on your patty. Yay!

YOU'LL NEED:
skillet, nonstick spray

PREP:
5 minutes

COOK:
10 minutes

PER SERVING (entire recipe): 225 calories, 5.5g fat,
598mg sodium, 30.5g carbs, 9g fiber, 3g sugars, 17g protein

Ingredients

1 frozen meatless hamburger-style patty with about 100 calories
One 100-calorie flat sandwich bun
1 tablespoon hummus

Spice: curry powder

Directions

Bring a skillet sprayed with nonstick spray to medium heat on
the stove. Add patty and cook for about 4 minutes per side,
until cooked through.

Meanwhile, split sandwich bun into halves and, if you like,
lightly toast. Plate the bun halves and evenly spread hummus
on the inside of bun's top half. Sprinkle hummus with a dash
of curry powder. Set aside.

Place patty over bottom half of the sandwich bun. Place the
other half on top and eat up!

MAKES 1 SERVING

YOU'LL NEED:
microwave-safe bowl

PREP:
5 minutes

COOK:
5 minutes

GRINDER LETTUCE CUPS

A great calorie-bargain recipe for burger lovers . . .

PER SERVING (entire recipe, 3 lettuce cups): 230 calories, 5.75g fat, 810mg sodium, 20g carbs, 8.75g fiber, 3.5g sugars, 23g protein

Ingredients

2 frozen meatless hamburger-style patties with about 100 calories each
⅓ cup canned crushed tomatoes
3 leaves butter lettuce

Spices: Italian seasoning, garlic powder, onion powder

Directions

Prepare patties in a microwave-safe bowl in the microwave. (Refer to package instructions for exact temperature and time.)

Using a fork, crumble patties into bite-sized pieces while still in the bowl. Add tomatoes and a dash of each of the seasonings to the bowl. Mix well.

Microwave for 30 seconds, or until hot.

Divide mixture among the lettuce "cups" and eat!

MAKES 1 SERVING

THREE-STEP PIZZA BURGER

Three steps . . . three ingredients . . . and three times as good as a plain old patty!

YOU'LL NEED:
skillet with a lid, nonstick spray

PREP:
5 minutes

COOK:
10 minutes

PER SERVING (entire recipe): 166 calories, 5.25g fat, 597mg sodium, 9g carbs, 4g fiber, 1g sugars, 17.5g protein

Ingredients

1 frozen meatless hamburger-style patty with about 100 calories
1 tablespoon pizza sauce
1 stick light string cheese

Directions

In a skillet sprayed with nonstick spray, prepare patty on the stove for just *half* the cook time stated on the package. (Refer to package instructions for exact temperature and time.)

Flip patty and evenly top with sauce while still in the skillet. Pull cheese into shreds and lay the pieces over the patty.

Cover skillet and cook for remaining half of the cook time, or until patty is cooked through and cheese has melted. Eat it!

MAKES 1 SERVING

skillet and nonstick spray *or* microwave-safe plate, strainer, microwave-safe bowl, kitchen shears (optional)

PREP:

5 minutes

COOK:

15 minutes

For a pic of this recipe, see the second photo insert. Yay!

CHEESY NOODLES 'N BURGS!

cheese . . . noodles . . . and burger bites—for less than 200 calories?! Yup!

PER SERVING (entire recipe): 175 calories, 5.25g fat, 720mg sodium, 14g carbs, 7.75g fiber, 1.5g sugars, 15g protein

Ingredients

1 frozen meatless hamburger-style patty with about 100 calories
1 bag House Foods Tofu Shirataki Fettuccine Shaped Noodle Substitute
1 wedge The Laughing Cow Light Creamy Swiss cheese

Spices: salt, black pepper

Directions

Prepare patty on the stove in a skillet sprayed with nonstick spray or on a microwave-safe plate in the microwave. (Refer to package instructions for exact temperature and time.) Once cool enough to handle, chop or crumble into bite-sized pieces and set aside.

Use a strainer to rinse and drain noodles well. Pat dry. Place noodles in a microwave-safe bowl, and microwave for 1 minute. Drain excess liquid. Dry as thoroughly as possible, using paper towels. Cut noodles up a bit with kitchen shears (if you've got 'em).

Add cheese wedge to noodles, breaking it into pieces as you add it. Stir until mostly blended. Add patty pieces and mix well.

Microwave for 1 minute, or until hot. Season with a dash each of salt and pepper and mix well. Enjoy!

MAKES 1 SERVING

FAST-FOOD HAMBURGER SCRAMBLE

cheeseburgers for breakfast . . . Yee-haa!

YOU'LL NEED:
skillet, nonstick spray

PREP:
5 minutes

COOK:
15 minutes

PER SERVING (entire recipe): 185 calories, 2.75g fat, 960mg sodium, 11g carbs, 3.75g fiber, 2.5g sugars, 27g protein

Ingredients

1 frozen meatless hamburger-style patty with about 100 calories
½ cup fat-free liquid egg substitute
1 slice fat-free American cheese, broken into pieces

Spices: salt, black pepper

For the Weight Watchers *PointsPlus*™ values of all the recipes in this book, check out hungry-girl.com/books. Yay!

Directions

Bring a skillet sprayed with nonstick spray to medium heat on the stove. Add patty and cook for about 4 minutes per side, until cooked through. Once cool enough to handle, chop into bite-sized pieces and set aside.

Remove skillet from heat, re-spray, and bring to medium heat on the stove. Add egg substitute and scramble until mostly cooked, about 2 minutes.

Add patty pieces and cheese pieces and continue to scramble until egg is fully cooked and cheese has melted, about 2 minutes.

Season with a dash each of salt and pepper. Now enjoy!

MAKES 1 SERVING

YOU'LL NEED:
skillet with a lid,
nonstick spray

PREP:
5 minutes

COOK:
15 minutes

BUNLESS MEDITERRANEAN BURGER

Clever and delicious—with or without a bun . . .

PER SERVING (entire recipe): 125 calories, 3.75g fat, 495mg sodium, 8.5g carbs, 3.75g fiber, 1g sugars, 12.5g protein

Ingredients

1 frozen meatless hamburger-style patty with about 100 calories
1 large piece jarred roasted red pepper
1 tablespoon crumbled reduced-fat feta cheese

Directions

Bring a skillet sprayed with nonstick spray to medium heat on the stove. Add patty and cook for about 4 minutes per side, until cooked through.

Still in the skillet, carefully top patty with roasted red pepper and sprinkle with feta cheese. Cover and continue to cook until pepper and cheese are hot, about 2 minutes.

Eat and enjoy!

MAKES 1 SERVING

BURGER-iFiC MUSHROOM MELT

All that protein and flavor—you'll wanna eat this one ALL THE TIME (and you should) . . .

PER SERVING (entire recipe): 175 calories, 5.75g fat, 717mg sodium, 13g carbs, 5g fiber, 2.5g sugars, 17.5g protein

📷 **For a pic of this recipe, see the second photo insert. Yay!**

Ingredients

1 portabella mushroom cap
1 frozen meatless hamburger-style patty with about 100 calories
1 slice 2% milk Swiss cheese

Spices: salt, black pepper

Directions

Preheat oven to 375 degrees.

Spray a baking sheet with nonstick spray. Lay mushroom cap on the sheet, rounded side down. Sprinkle with a dash each of salt and pepper. Place burger over the mushroom and lay cheese on top.

Bake until mushroom is soft, burger is hot, and cheese has melted, about 20 minutes.

Chew and enjoy!

MAKES 1 SERVING

CHAPTER 23:
HOT DOGS, TRIOS

There's a reason why hot dogs are as popular as they are. But don't let everyone else have all the fun; start doing crazy stuff to your dogs. . . . Need ideas? You're in the right place!

YOU'LL NEED:

heavy-duty aluminum foil, baking sheet, nonstick spray, 2 bowls

PREP:

5 minutes

COOK:

25 minutes

"WRAP THE DOG" FOIL PACK

Smothered dogs in a foil pack. Awesomeness!

PER SERVING (½ of recipe, about ¾ cup): 100 calories, 1.5g fat, 760mg sodium, 8.5g carbs, 0.5g fiber, 3g sugars, 12.5g protein

Ingredients

3 hot dogs with about 40 calories and 1g fat or less each, cut into bite-sized pieces
1 small onion, chopped
¼ cup shredded fat-free cheddar cheese

Directions

Preheat oven to 350 degrees.

Lay a large piece of heavy-duty foil on a baking sheet. Spray with nonstick spray.

Place chopped hot dogs and onion on the foil. Place another large piece of foil over the mixture. Fold together and seal all four edges of the two foil pieces, forming a well-sealed packet.

Bake in the oven for 25 minutes, or until onion is soft. Let cool slightly.

Cut packet to release steam before opening it entirely. (Careful—steam will be hot.)

Divide mixture between two bowls and top evenly with cheese!

MAKES 2 SERVINGS

PIGS ON A STICK IN A BACON-WRAPPED BLANKET

Awwww . . . how snuggly and delicious is THIS?! And the stick just adds to the fun.

PER SERVING (⅛th of recipe, 1 pig on a stick): 163 calories, 7.75g fat, 799mg sodium, 15g carbs, <0.5g fiber, 3g sugars, 9g protein

Ingredients

8 hot dogs with about 40 calories and 1g fat or less each
1 package Pillsbury Reduced Fat Crescent rolls refrigerated dough
8 slices center-cut bacon or turkey bacon

Directions

Preheat oven to 375 degrees.

Spray a baking sheet with nonstick spray and set aside. Skewer each hot dog lengthwise and set aside as well.

One at a time, slightly stretch or roll out each of the 8 triangle-shaped pieces of dough to make larger triangles. Place a hot dog along the base of each and gently but firmly roll it up. Squeeze the dough gently to ensure it is secure around the hot dog.

Carefully wrap and spiral a slice of bacon around the length of each dough-covered hot dog. Evenly place blanketed pups on the baking sheet.

Bake in the oven until dough is lightly browned, about 15 minutes.

Let cool slightly. Enjoy!

MAKES 8 SERVING

YOU'LL NEED:
baking sheet,
nonstick spray,
8 skewers, rolling pin
(optional)

PREP:
15 minutes

COOK:
15 minutes

HG Cheat Sheet!

Dip your dogs in mustard, ketchup, or relish!

YOU'LL NEED:
microwave-safe plate

PREP:
5 minutes

COOK:
5 minutes

YO! CHILI DOG WRAP

Chili dog wrap . . . sounds like a new song. But alas, it is a tasty snack.

PER SERVING (entire recipe): 200 calories, 3.5g fat, 939mg sodium, 35g carbs, 8g fiber, 3.5g sugars, 14.5g protein

Ingredients

1 hot dog with about 40 calories and 1g fat or less
1 medium-large high-fiber flour tortilla with about 110 calories
¼ cup low-fat veggie or turkey chili

Directions

Warm hot dog in microwave, about 20 seconds.

Lay tortilla flat on a microwave-safe plate. Place hot dog in the center and top with chili. Wrap tortilla up like a burrito, folding the sides in first, and then rolling it up from the bottom. Place burrito seam-side down on the plate, and microwave for 30 seconds.

Time to chew!

MAKES 1 SERVING

HOT DOG STROGANOFF

This dish is crazy-insane-amazing—just a heads-up!

YOU'LL NEED:
skillet, nonstick spray

PREP:
5 minutes

COOK:
15 minutes

PER SERVING (⅓rd of recipe, about 1 cup): 156 calories, 3g fat, 1,169mg sodium, 18g carbs, 0.25g fiber, 7.5g sugars, 16g protein

Ingredients

1 small onion, thinly sliced
7 hot dogs with about 40 calories and 1g fat or less each, cut into coins
¾ cup fat-free sour cream

Spices: salt, black pepper

For more recipes, plus food finds, tips 'n tricks, and MORE, sign up for FREE daily emails at hungry-girl.com!

Directions

Bring a skillet sprayed with nonstick spray to medium-high heat on the stove. Add onion and hot dogs and, stirring occasionally, cook until browned, 8 to 10 minutes.

Add sour cream, ⅛ teaspoon salt, ⅛ teaspoon pepper, and ¼ cup water to the skillet. Stir well and reduce heat to low.

Stirring occasionally, simmer until thick and creamy, about 5 minutes.

Eat up!

MAKES 3 SERVINGS

YOU'LL NEED:

large baking sheet,
nonstick spray, rolling
pin (optional)

PREP:

10 minutes

COOK:

15 minutes

PiGS ON A MATTRESS

What DOESN'T taste good sitting on this dough?!

PER SERVING (1/10th of recipe, 1 rectangle): 108 calories, 1.25g fat, 368mg sodium, 20g carbs, <0.5g fiber, 3g sugars, 4g protein

Ingredients

1 package Pillsbury Classic Pizza Crust refrigerated dough
2 hot dogs with about 40 calories and 1g fat or less each, cut into coins
½ cup thinly sliced onion

Spices: garlic powder, Italian seasoning

Directions

Preheat oven to 425 degrees.

Spray a large baking sheet with nonstick spray and set aside.

Roll out dough on the sheet into a large rectangle of even thickness.

Sprinkle dough evenly with ½ teaspoon garlic powder and ½ teaspoon Italian seasoning. Evenly place hot dog coins and sliced onion on the dough, gently pressing down so they stick.

Bake in the oven until lightly browned, about 12 minutes. Let cool slightly. Cut into 10 rectangles—each about 4½ inches by 3 inches—and enjoy!

MAKES 10 SERVINGS

HOT DOGGY HOME FRIES

How come no one ever thought of this before? BRILLIANT!

PER SERVING (⅓rd of recipe, about 1⅓ cups): 145 calories,
1g fat, 640mg sodium, 29g carbs, 3.75g fiber, 9g sugars, 7g protein

Ingredients

4 cups cubed butternut squash
3 hot dogs with about 40 calories and 1g fat or less each, cut into coins
3 tablespoons ketchup

Directions

Bring a large skillet sprayed with nonstick spray to medium-high heat on the stove. Add squash, cover, and cook until it begins to soften, about 12 minutes, removing the lid often to stir.

Add hot dog coins to skillet and cook until hot, about 2 minutes. Remove skillet from heat, mix in ketchup, and toss to coat. Serve it up!

MAKES 3 SERVINGS

YOU'LL NEED:
large skillet with a lid, nonstick spray

PREP:
5 minutes

COOK:
15 minutes

For a pic of this recipe, see the second photo insert. Yay!

YOU'LL NEED:
loaf pan, nonstick
spray, medium bowl

PREP:
5 minutes

COOK:
30 minutes

HOT DIGGITY DOG CASSEROLE

This one's good for breakfast (don't knock it), lunch, dinner, or a snack!

PER SERVING (⅓rd of casserole): 157 calories, 2g fat,
1,040mg sodium, 19g carbs, 2.75g fiber, 2.5g sugars, 17.5g protein

Ingredients

5 hot dogs with about 40 calories and 1g fat or less each, cut into coins
2 light hot dog buns, torn into pieces
¾ cup fat-free liquid egg substitute

Spices: salt, black pepper, onion powder

Directions

Preheat oven to 350 degrees.

Spray a loaf pan with nonstick spray and set aside.

Combine hot dog pieces, buns, and egg substitute in a medium bowl.
Add ⅛ teaspoon salt, ⅛ teaspoon pepper, and ¼ teaspoon onion
powder. Stir well, making sure the bun pieces are saturated with the
egg substitute.

Pour mixture into the loaf pan. Bake in the oven until firm and cooked
through, 25 to 30 minutes.

Doggone good!

MAKES 3 SERVINGS

FRESH 'N FRUITY SKEWER DOGS

Hot dog skewers—a simple yet brilliant idea. The pineapple here makes all the difference . . . YUM!!!

PER SERVING (entire recipe, 2 skewers): 172 calories, 2g fat, 880mg sodium, 26g carbs, 2.5g fiber, 18g sugars, 12g protein

Ingredients

2 hot dogs with about 40 calories and 1g fat
 or less each, each cut into 5 segments
8 cherry tomatoes
8 chunks pineapple

Directions

Prepare 2 skewers; if using wooden ones, soak in water for 20 minutes to prevent burning.

Skewer hot dog pieces, tomatoes, and pineapple chunks alternately onto the 2 skewers.

Spray grill pan lightly with nonstick spray, and bring to medium-high heat.

Cover and cook kebabs for 4 minutes. Then carefully flip kebabs with barbecue tongs. Re-cover and cook for another 3 to 4 minutes, until tomatoes and pineapple have softened and are slightly blackened.

Once cool enough to handle, pull food off the sticks and eat!

MAKES 1 SERVING

YOU'LL NEED:
2 skewers, grill pan with a lid, nonstick spray, barbecue tongs

PREP:
10 minutes

COOK:
10 minutes

For a pic of this recipe, see the second photo insert. Yay!

skillet, nonstick spray

PREP:

5 minutes

COOK:

10 minutes

For full-color photos of all the recipes in this book, check out hungry-girl.com/books. Woohoo!

HOT DOG STiR-FRY

This stuff ROCKS on top of a chopped salad!

PER SERVING (½ of recipe): 100 calories, 2g fat, 704mg sodium, 11g carbs, 1.5g fiber, 4.5g sugars, 11.5g protein

Ingredients

3 cups sliced mushrooms
½ onion, sliced
3 hot dogs with about 40 calories and 1g fat
or less each, cut into bite-sized pieces

Spices: salt, black pepper

Directions

Bring a skillet sprayed with nonstick spray to medium-high heat on the stove. Add veggies and a dash each of salt and pepper. Cook until softened, about 8 minutes.

Add hot dog pieces and cook until heated through, about 2 additional minutes.

Enjoy!

MAKES 2 SERVINGS

SLOPPY BEANS 'N FRANKS

A totally delicious no-brainer of a dish!

PER SERVING (entire recipe): 218 calories, 2.75g fat, 910mg sodium, 39g carbs, 7g fiber, 9g sugars, 13g protein

Ingredients

1 hot dog with about 40 calories and 1g fat or less, chopped
⅓ cup baked beans
1 light hot dog bun

Directions

In a microwave-safe bowl, combine chopped hot dog and baked beans. Microwave 1 minute, and stir. If needed, return to microwave for another 30 seconds, until hot.

Place bun on a plate (you're gonna need it!) and spoon hot dog–bean mixture into bun. Grab a napkin, and eat!

MAKES 1 SERVING

YOU'LL NEED:
microwave-safe bowl, plate

PREP:
5 minutes

COOK:
5 minutes

YOU'LL NEED:
skillet, nonstick spray

PREP:
5 minutes

COOK:
5 minutes

HOT, HOT, HOT DOG!

A little heat and some cool ranch, and you're good to go!

PER SERVING (entire recipe): 60 calories, 2.25g fat, 618mg sodium, 4.5g carbs, og fiber, 1.5g sugars, 5.5g protein

Ingredients

1 hot dog with around 40 calories and 1g fat, cut into bite-sized pieces
1 teaspoon hot sauce
½ tablespoon light ranch dressing

Directions

Bring a skillet sprayed with nonstick spray to medium-high heat on the stove. Add hot dog and hot sauce, and toss to coat. Cook until heated through, about 2 minutes.

Serve with ranch dressing as a dipping sauce. Yum!

MAKES 1 SERVING

CHAPTER 24: NOODLE TRIOS

In HG Land, the word *noodles* pretty much always means "Tofu Shirataki." Take a look at these jaw-droppingly amazing trios. Then whip 'em up and prepare to be noodled!

YOU'LL NEED:

strainer, kitchen shears (optional), skillet, nonstick spray

PREP:

5 minutes

COOK:

10 minutes

📷 **For a pic of this recipe, see the second photo insert. Yay!**

SWEETNESS, SPICE & 3-THINGS NICE NOODLES

sassy and packed with steak . . . good stuff!

PER SERVING (entire recipe): 247 calories, 8.5g fat, 439mg sodium, 14.5g carbs, 4g fiber, 7g sugars, 27g protein

Ingredients

1 bag House Foods Tofu Shirataki Fettuccine Shaped Noodle Substitute
4 ounces raw lean filet beefsteak, thinly sliced (freeze slightly before slicing)
1 tablespoon sweet Asian chili sauce

Spices: salt, black pepper

Directions

Use a strainer to rinse and drain noodles well. Dry as thoroughly as possible, using paper towels. Cut noodles up a bit with kitchen shears (if you've got 'em), and set aside.

Bring a skillet sprayed with nonstick spray to medium-high heat on the stove. Season beef with a dash each of salt and pepper. Cook beef until mostly cooked through, about 4 minutes, stirring occasionally.

Transfer noodles to the skillet. Stir occasionally and continue to cook until noodles are no longer squishy in texture, about 2 minutes. Add the chili sauce. Stir to coat. Heat until sauce is warmed, about 1 additional minute. Enjoy!

MAKES 1 SERVING

EZ CHiLi MAC

The fastest chili mac you'll ever eat. Tasty, too!

PER SERVING (entire recipe): 269 calories, 4.25g fat, 990mg sodium, 37g carbs, 13g fiber, 7g sugars, 19g protein

Ingredients

1 bag House Foods Tofu Shirataki Spaghetti Shaped Noodle Substitute
1 wedge The Laughing Cow Light Creamy Swiss cheese
1 cup canned low-fat veggie chili

Spices: salt, black pepper

Directions

Use a strainer to rinse and drain noodles well. Pat dry. Place noodles in a microwave-safe bowl, and microwave for 1 minute. Drain excess liquid. Dry as thoroughly as possible, using paper towels. Cut noodles up a bit with kitchen shears (if you've got 'em).

Add cheese to the bowl, breaking it into pieces as you add it. Mix thoroughly and microwave for 1 minute. Stir thoroughly, making sure cheese has melted and coated the noodles.

Add chili and microwave for 1 minute, until hot. Mix well and, if you like, season to taste with salt and pepper. Eat up!

MAKES 1 SERVING

YOU'LL NEED:
strainer, microwave-safe bowl, kitchen shears (optional)

PREP:
5 minutes

COOK:
5 minutes

📷 **For a pic of this recipe, see the second photo insert. Yay!**

YOU'LL NEED:
strainer, kitchen
shears (optional),
skillet, nonstick spray

PREP:
5 minutes

COOK:
10 minutes

For full-color
photos of all the recipes
in this book, check out
hungry-girl.com/books.
Woohoo!

CREAMY CHICKEN & NOODLES

An instant classic. Truly!

PER SERVING (½ of recipe, about 1¾ cups): 272 calories, 6.5g fat, 993mg sodium, 16g carbs, 5.25g fiber, 1g sugars, 36g protein

Ingredients

2 bags House Foods Tofu Shirataki Fettuccine Shaped Noodle Substitute
10 ounces raw boneless skinless lean chicken breast, cut into bite-sized pieces
One 10.75-ounce can 98% fat-free cream of celery condensed soup

Spices: salt, black pepper

Directions

Use a strainer to rinse and drain noodles well. Dry as thoroughly as possible, using paper towels. Cut noodles up a bit with kitchen shears (if you've got 'em), and set aside.

Bring a skillet sprayed with nonstick spray to medium-high heat on the stove. Season chicken with ⅛ teaspoon each salt and pepper. Transfer chicken to the skillet. Heat until almost cooked through, about 5 minutes, stirring occasionally.

Add the noodles to the skillet. Continue to cook for about 3 minutes, or until chicken is fully cooked and noodles are no longer squishy in texture. Add the soup. Stir well and continue to cook until heated through, about an additional 2 minutes.

So good!

MAKES 2 SERVINGS

NOT-QUITE-HOMEMADE CHICKEN NOODLE SOUP

Not QUITE as good as Grandma's, though even she would approve!

PER SERVING (½ of recipe, about 2 cups): 81 calories, 0.5g fat, 1,042mg sodium, 11.5g carbs, 4.25g fiber, 3.5g sugars, 6.5g protein

Ingredients

1 bag House Foods Tofu Shirataki Fettuccine Shaped Noodle Substitute
Two 14.5-ounce cans (about 3½ cups) fat-free chicken broth
1 cup frozen peas and carrots

Spices: salt, black pepper

Directions

Use a strainer to rinse and drain noodles well. Pat dry. Cut noodles up a bit with kitchen shears (if you've got 'em).

Place all ingredients in a large pot on the stove. Add ⅛ teaspoon salt and ⅛ teaspoon pepper, mix well, and bring to a boil.

Reduce heat to low and cover. Allow soup to simmer for 10 minutes.

Grab a spoon!

MAKES 2 SERVINGS

YOU'LL NEED:
strainer, kitchen shears (optional), large pot with a lid

PREP:
5 minutes

COOK:
15 minutes

baking sheet,
nonstick spray,
strainer, microwave-
safe bowl, kitchen
shears (optional),
small microwave-safe
bowl, blender or food
processor

PREP:

15 minutes

COOK:

25 minutes

CHEESY SQUASHATAKI

Sweet 'n savory all at once. Toss in some chicken for a protein fix!

PER SERVING (entire recipe): 140 calories, 2.5g fat,
401mg sodium, 24g carbs, 7g fiber, 4g sugars, 5.5g protein

Ingredients

1 cup cubed butternut squash
1 bag House Foods Tofu Shirataki Fettuccine Shaped Noodle Substitute
1 wedge The Laughing Cow Light Creamy Swiss cheese

Spices: salt, black pepper, garlic powder, cinnamon, cayenne pepper

Directions

Preheat oven to 400 degrees.

Place squash cubes on a baking sheet sprayed with nonstick spray. Lightly mist the squash with nonstick spray. Sprinkle with a dash each of salt, black pepper, and garlic powder.

Bake in the oven until soft, about 20 minutes. Allow to cool.

Meanwhile, use a strainer to rinse and drain noodles well. Pat dry. Place noodles in a microwave-safe bowl, and microwave for 1 minute. Drain excess liquid. Dry as thoroughly as possible, using paper towels. Cut noodles up a bit with kitchen shears (if you've got 'em), and set aside.

In a small microwave-safe bowl, microwave cheese for about 15 seconds, until warm. Stir until smooth.

Place squash and cheese in a blender or a food processor. Add a dash of cinnamon, a dash of cayenne pepper, and 3 tablespoons water. Puree until smooth.

Add squash mixture to the noodles and mix well. Microwave for about 1 minute, until hot.

If you like, season to taste with additional spices. Enjoy!

MAKES 1 SERVING

Where in the World Is Tofu Shirataki?

Look for **House Foods Tofu Shirataki** (the best-ever low-calorie noodle swap!) with the Asian items in the refrigerated section of the grocery store. It'll be near the wonton wrappers and blocks of tofu, floating in liquid inside a clear bag. Don't be afraid; it's awesome. If your store doesn't carry it, request it . . . or order some online!

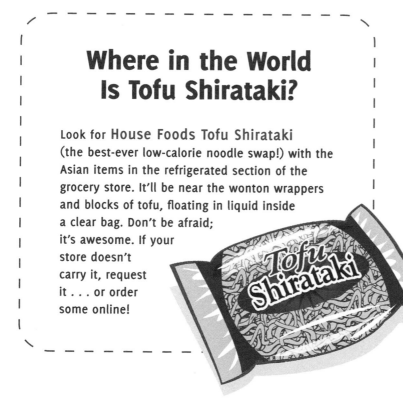

For the Weight Watchers
PointsPlus™ values of
all the recipes in this
book, check out
hungry-girl.com/books.
Yay!

"YO QUIERO TACO BOWL" NOODLES

A noodled-up bowl of Mexi-tasticness!

PER SERVING (entire recipe): 208 calories, 5.75g fat,
711mg sodium, 11g carbs, 4g fiber, 0g sugars, 26g protein

Ingredients

1 bag House Foods Tofu Shirataki Fettuccine Shaped Noodle Substitute
4 ounces raw extra-lean ground beef
1 tablespoon taco seasoning mix, divided

Directions

Use a strainer to rinse and drain noodles well. Dry as thoroughly
as possible, using paper towels. Cut noodles up a bit with kitchen
shears (if you've got 'em), and set aside.

Bring a skillet sprayed with nonstick spray to medium-high heat on
the stove. Add the beef and 2 teaspoons taco seasoning to the skillet.
Stirring occasionally to break up the beef, cook for 2 minutes.

Add the noodles to the skillet and continue to cook until beef is no
longer pink and noodles no longer have a squishy texture, about
3 minutes. Sprinkle with remaining 1 teaspoon taco seasoning, mix
well, and serve!

MAKES 1 SERVING

TUNA NOODLE CASSE-BOWL

> Like Mom's creamy tuna noodle casserole—only in a bowl. And less scary . . .

YOU'LL NEED:
strainer, large microwave-safe bowl, kitchen shears (optional)

PREP:
10 minutes

COOK:
5 minutes

PER SERVING (½ of recipe): 255 calories, 6g fat, 913mg sodium, 12.5g carbs, 4.75g fiber, 0g sugars, 38g protein

Ingredients

2 bags House Foods Tofu Shirataki Fettuccine Shaped Noodle Substitute
Two 5-ounce cans albacore tuna packed in water, drained and flaked
¾ cup 98% fat-free cream of mushroom condensed soup

Spices: salt, black pepper, garlic powder

Directions

Use a strainer to rinse and drain noodles well. Pat dry. Place noodles in a large microwave-safe bowl, and microwave for 1 minute. Drain excess liquid. Dry as thoroughly as possible, using paper towels. Cut noodles up a bit with kitchen shears (if you've got 'em).

Add tuna and soup to the bowl. Mix thoroughly. Microwave for 2 minutes, or until hot.

Mix well and, if you like, season to taste with spices. Serve it up!

MAKES 2 SERVINGS

YOU'LL NEED:
strainer, kitchen
shears (optional),
microwave-safe bowl

PREP:
5 minutes

COOK:
5 minutes

EZ MOCK VODKA PASTA

Here's the fastest and simplest way to nip a craving for vodka sauce in the bud. Make this SOON . . .

PER SERVING (entire recipe): 123 calories, 4g fat,
813mg sodium, 14.5g carbs, 5.25g fiber, 6g sugars, 5g protein

Ingredients

1 bag House Foods Tofu Shirataki Fettuccine Shaped Noodle Substitute
1 wedge The Laughing Cow Light Original Swiss cheese
⅓ cup low-fat marinara sauce

Spices: salt, black pepper

Directions

Use a strainer to rinse and drain noodles well. Pat dry. Place noodles in a microwave-safe bowl, and microwave for 1 minute. Drain excess liquid. Dry as thoroughly as possible, using paper towels. Cut noodles up a bit with kitchen shears (if you've got 'em).

Add cheese to the bowl, breaking cheese wedge into pieces as you add it. Stir, and then mix in marinara sauce. Microwave for 1 minute.

Stir well and then season to taste with salt and pepper. YUM!

MAKES 1 SERVING

BBQ SPAGHETTI

A total yum-fest. Toss in some meatless crumbles for added protein and deliciousness!

YOU'LL NEED:
strainer, large microwave-safe bowl, kitchen shears (optional)

PREP:
5 minutes

COOK:
5 minutes

PER SERVING (entire recipe): 145 calories, 1g fat, 999mg sodium, 24g carbs, 4g fiber, 13g sugars, 8.5g protein

Ingredients

1 bag House Foods Tofu Shirataki Spaghetti Shaped Noodle Substitute
3 tablespoons BBQ sauce with about 45 calories per 2-tablespoon serving
3 tablespoons shredded fat-free cheddar cheese

Spices: salt, black pepper

Directions

Use a strainer to rinse and drain noodles well. Pat dry. Place noodles in a large microwave-safe bowl, and microwave for 1 minute. Drain excess liquid. Dry as thoroughly as possible, using paper towels. Cut noodles up a bit with kitchen shears (if you've got 'em).

Add BBQ sauce, cheese, and a dash each of salt and pepper to the bowl. Mix well.

Microwave for 2 to 3 minutes, until noodles are hot and cheese has melted. Stir and enjoy!

MAKES 1 SERVING

YOU'LL NEED:
strainer, kitchen
shears (optional),
skillet, nonstick spray

PREP:
5 minutes

COOK:
10 minutes

THAI PEANUT NOODLE TRIO

Ez peasy peanut noodles—and sooo low in fat and calories!

PER SERVING (entire recipe): 195 calories, 7g fat, 678mg sodium, 25g carbs, 7.75g fiber, 11g sugars, 7g protein

Ingredients

1 bag House Foods Tofu Shirataki Fettuccine Shaped Noodle Substitute
1 cup frozen Asian-style stir-fry vegetables
3 tablespoons low-fat Thai peanut salad dressing or sauce

Spices: salt, black pepper, crushed red pepper

Directions

Use a strainer to rinse and drain noodles well. Dry as thoroughly as possible, using paper towels. Cut noodles up a bit with kitchen shears (if you've got 'em), and set aside.

Bring a skillet sprayed with nonstick spray to medium heat on the stove. Add veggies and, stirring occasionally, cook until thawed and hot, about 4 minutes

Add noodles to the skillet and cook and stir until hot, 1 to 2 minutes.

Remove skillet from heat and stir in dressing or sauce. Season to taste with spices. Yum time!

MAKES 1 SERVING

QUICK 'N SPICY FETTUCCINE HUNGRY BUFF-REDO

Spicy AND creamy . . . Toss in some chicken to satisfy a craving for hot wings!

YOU'LL NEED: strainer, microwave-safe bowl, kitchen shears (optional)

PREP: 5 minutes

COOK: 5 minutes

PER SERVING (entire recipe): 76 calories, 2.5g fat, 525mg sodium, 7g carbs, 4g fiber, 1g sugars, 4g protein

Ingredients

1 bag House Foods Tofu Shirataki Spaghetti Shaped Noodle Substitute
1 wedge The Laughing Cow Light Original Swiss cheese
½ tablespoon Frank's RedHot Original Cayenne Pepper Sauce

Spices: salt, black pepper

Directions

Use a strainer to rinse and drain noodles well. Pat dry. Place noodles in a microwave-safe bowl, and microwave for 1 minute. Drain excess liquid. Dry as thoroughly as possible, using paper towels. Cut noodles up a bit with kitchen shears (if you've got 'em).

Add cheese and hot sauce to the bowl, breaking cheese wedge into pieces as you add it. Stir and microwave for 1 minute.

Stir well and season to taste with salt and pepper. Enjoy!

MAKES 1 SERVING

For more recipes, plus food finds, tips 'n tricks, and MORE, sign up for FREE daily emails at hungry-girl.com!

YOU'LL NEED:

strainer, kitchen
shears (optional),
skillet with a lid,
nonstick spray

PREP:

5 minutes

COOK:

10 minutes

QUICKIE-YAKI STIR-FRY

A super snack or side dish! Add extra crushed red pepper for some spicy fun . . .

PER SERVING (½ of recipe, about 2 cups): 165 calories, 3g fat, 949mg sodium, 26g carbs, 6.75g fiber, 11.5g sugars, 6.5g protein

Ingredients

1 bag House Foods Tofu Shirataki Fettuccine Shaped Noodle Substitute
4 cups frozen Asian-style stir-fry vegetables
2 tablespoons thick teriyaki sauce/marinade

Spices: salt, black pepper, crushed red pepper

Directions

Use a strainer to rinse and drain noodles well. Dry as thoroughly as possible, using paper towels. Cut noodles up a bit with kitchen shears (if you've got 'em), and set aside.

Bring a skillet sprayed with nonstick spray to medium-high heat on the stove. Add veggies, cover, and cook until hot, about 8 minutes, uncovering and stirring occasionally.

Add noodles and sauce/marinade to the skillet and toss to coat. Cook until hot, about 2 minutes. Season to taste with spices and dig in!

MAKES 2 SERVINGS

There you have it.
300 recipes for you to whip up
and swallow. This should keep you
SUPER-BUSY for a while. And fret not,
because I'll be back before you know it with
more, more, MORE incredibly delicious and
super-creative guilt-free foods. 'Til next time,
CHEW THE RIGHT THING!

HUNGRY5

INDEX

A

A+ Avocado Burger, 277

Ab-Fab Artichoke Crab Dip, 376

All the Rage Bolognese, 316

All-American Egg Mug, 24

Almond Breeze, Unsweetened Original, 400, 402

Almond Breeze, Unsweetened Vanilla, 32, 33, 34, 35, 38, 42, 43, 44, 48, 52

   HG and the Growing Oatmeal . . . Tips & Tricks!, 53

Amazin' Onion Quesadilla, 457

Amazing Ate-Layer Open-Faced Taco, 344

Amy's Organic Light in Sodium Chunky Tomato Bisque, 406

appetizers. *See* **starters**

apples

   Apple Pie Oatmeal Bonanza, 33

   Big Apple Butternut Squash Soup, 400

   Cinn-a-nilla Apple Oatmeal Parfait, 44

   Crock-Pot Cinna-Apples 'n Oats, 304

   Fuji, 142, 160, 288, 304, 305, 309, 329, 400, 458

   Raw Apple Rollup, 458

   Sweet Apple & Chicken Stir-Fry, 329

   Sweet 'n Red Hot Apple Mash, 309

   Sweet Potato Apple Pack, 160

artichokes, 376, 380

Asian foods

   Asian BBQ Shrimp Salad, 132

   Broc 'n Ginger Tuna Bowl, 462

   Chicky Pad Thai, 222

   Classic Warm Asian Chicken Salad, 148

   Colossal Asian Veggie 'n Chicken Pack, 170

   Curry in a Hurry Trio, 493

   Egg-Cellent Foo Young, 218

   Quickie-yaki Stir-Fry, 528

   Sassy Wonton Tacos, 368

   Shrimpylicious Egg Rolls, 216

   Super-Speedy Chinese Stir-Fry, 448

   Sweet & Sour Chicken 1-2-3, 220

   Tempting Teriyaki Trifecta, 330

   Thai Peanut Noodle Trio, 526

   WOWOWOW! Kung Pao, 224

   WOWOWOW! Wonton Soup, 404

asparagus, 23, 136

avocado, 15, 17, 208, 214, 277, 283, 348, 366

B

bacon, Canadian, 54, 82, 92

bacon, precooked real crumbled, 7, 47, 64, 80, 146, 262, 332, 398, 412, 424

   Bacon Cheeseburger Patty, 484

   BTA (Bacon, Tomato, Avocado) Egg Mug, 15

   Cheesy Pigs in Bacon Blankies, 178

   Flat-tastic Ranchy Bacon Wrap, 348

bacon, turkey or center-cut, 62, 72, 78, 290, 294, 302, 326

   Bacon Bleu Burger, 488

   Bacon-Wrapped BBQ Chicken, 442

   BLT Pizza, 256

   BLTA Club, 283

   Cheesy Bacon Noodle Skillet, 336

   Grilly Girl Cheesy Turkey & Bacon 'Wich, 278

   Loaded Bacon-Wrapped Hot Dogs, 356

   Pigs on a Stick in a Bacon-Wrapped Blanket, 503

   Quiche Me Bacon Tarts, 108

   Ranch-tastic Butternut Fries with Bacon, 418

Baked Clam Halfsies, 384

Balsamic BBQ Chick Skillet, 436

bananas, 48, 86, 90, 294

   Banana Split Bread, 116

   Banana Split Growing Oatmeal, 32

basil, fresh, 19, 104, 120, 154, 230, 232, 234, 292, 364

   Basil-icious Chicken, 437

BBQ Grilled Veggie Salad, 138

BBQ Spaghetti, 525

BBQuick Saucy Turkey, 482

Bean 'n Cheesy Soft Taco in an Egg Mug, 25

bean sprouts, 148, 170, 216, 218, 220, 222

beans

baked, 511

Bean There, Yum That Salad, 428

black, canned, 62, 131, 152, 210, 322, 344, 430

Crock-Pot Fake-Baked Beans, 305

kidney, canned red, 164, 184, 312, 408

refried, 25, 65, 140, 158, 204, 342, 346, 370, 378, 453

white, canned, 318, 382, 406, 407, 470

beef, 134, 266, 330, 475, 480, 484, 516, 522. *See also* **meatless hamburger-style patties; soy crumbles, ground-beef-style**

Beef Strogataki, 200

Broccoli Beef Stir-Fry, 479

Crunchy Beefy Taco Egg Mug, 18

Meat Prep 101, 167

roast beef, 276

Vegged-Up Ground Beef, 478

bell pepper, 20, 22, 54, 62, 64, 70, 72, 98, 108, 110, 120, 131, 136, 152, 154, 164, 168, 184, 196, 214, 220, 224, 242, 250, 252, 254, 258, 264, 266, 280, 305, 310, 315, 316, 322, 324, 334, 342, 350, 356, 408, 414, 426, 428, 463

'Bella Asada Fajitas, 214

Best-Ever Tuna Slaw, 471

Big Apple Butternut Squash Soup, 400

Big Bad Breakfast Burrito, 350

black beans, canned, 62, 131, 152, 210, 305, 322, 344, 430

black olives, sliced, 136, 140, 158, 258, 260, 268, 312, 378

BLT Pizza, 256

BLTA Club, 283

Blue Diamond Unsweetened Vanilla Almond Breeze. *See* **Almond Breeze, Unsweetened Vanilla**

Boca products, 7

bran cereal. *See* **Fiber One Original bran cereal**

bread, 6, 47, 66, 104, 278

100-calorie flat sandwich buns, 6, 82, 277, 280, 286, 352, 477, 493

Banana Split Bread, 116

English muffins, 26, 92, 110, 262, 279, 465

Flat Bun 411 and Alternatives, 279

hamburger buns, light, 276, 279

hot dog buns, light, 356, 508, 511

light bread, 8, 146, 257, 274, 278, 282, 283, 284, 288, 290, 294, 295, 296, 362

pitas, whole-wheat or high-fiber, 240, 268

Sweet and Savory Breakfast Bread Pudding Bowl, 40

breakfast, 10. *See also* **crowd pleasers, breakfast; egg mugs; no-cook b-fasts; oatmeal; pancakes**

Big Bad Breakfast Burrito, 350

Breakfast Bruschetta, 104

Breakfast for Dinner Skillet, 332

Breakfast Pizza Mexicali, 79

Breakfast Rice Pudding, 50

Breakfast Scramble Pizza, 72

Breakfast Sundae Supreme, 86

Buenos Días Breakfast Fajitas, 70

Cheesy Bean Breakfast Quesadilla, 65

Creamy Crab Cakes Benedict, 66

Erin-Go-Breakfast Boxty, 80

Gimme S'more Pancakes, 76

HG Hash Scramble, 54

HG's Big Breakfast Casserole, 98

Hola Breakfast Tostada, 64

Hot Dog & Scramble, 46

Hot Stack Morning Sliders, 82

The Morning Waffle Dip, 78

Nice to See Ya! Quesadilla, 62

Sausage, Egg 'n Cheese ChickGriddle, 58

Sweet and Savory Breakfast Bread Pudding Bowl, 40

Turkey Club B. Bowl, 47

Very Veggie-Eggy Explosion, 36

Broc 'n Ginger Tuna Bowl, 462

broccoli, 220, 222, 314, 322, 428, 462

Broccoli Beef Stir-Fry, 479

Rockin' Creamy Broc 'n Chicken, 334

broccoli cole slaw, 295, 404, 414, 417, 430, 471, 474

BTA (Bacon, Tomato, Avocado) Egg Mug, 15

Buenos Días Breakfast Fajitas, 70

Buffalo Chicken Egg Mug, 16

Buffalo Chicken Wing Macaroni & Cheese, 186

Bunless Mediterranean Burger, 498

buns. See **bread**

Burger-ific Mushroom Melt, 499

burgers. *See also* **meatless burger patty trios; meatless hamburger-style patties**

Bacon Cheeseburger Patty, 484

Cheeseburger Mac Attack, 308

Crispy Cheeseburger Pizza, 270

OMG! Burgers (Onion Mushroom Goodness Burgers), 477

Pizza Burgers a la HG, 266

Burgs in a Blanket, 490

butter

light whipped or light buttery spread, 7, 50, 58, 66, 96, 104, 114, 160, 162, 166, 192, 226, 257, 274, 278, 280, 286, 288, 294, 296, 304, 309, 362, 372, 374, 380, 384, 416, 420

spray, zero-calorie, 118, 146

butternut squash, 300, 344, 400, 507, 520

Dreamy Butternut Chicken Foil Pack, 156

For the Love of Sweet Garlic Butternut Fries, 422

Ranch-tastic Butternut Fries with Bacon, 418

Squash It! Hungry Girl's Guide to Mastering the Butternut Squash, 431

Sweet 'n Squashed Biscuits, 420

C

cabbage, 170, 198, 208

calamari, 228

California Love Mug, 17

Canadian bacon, 54, 82, 92

canned beets, sliced, 136, 142

canned black beans, 62, 131, 152, 210, 305, 322, 344, 430 canned chickpeas, 144, 168, 240, 300, 428

canned corn, 112, 312, 315, 416

canned cream of celery soup, 98% fat-free condensed, 176, 518

canned cream of chicken soup, 98% fat-free condensed, 156

canned cream of mushroom soup, 98% fat-free condensed, 180, 443, 468, 523

canned crushed pineapple, 68, 90, 464

canned crushed tomatoes, 14, 29, 72, 120, 188, 190, 196, 230, 232, 234, 236, 238, 248, 252, 257, 258, 260, 264, 268, 292, 316, 324, 328, 480, 481, 483, 494

canned pumpkin, 38, 68, 196, 206, 396

canned red kidney beans, 164, 184, 305, 312, 408, 428

canned sliced beets, 136, 142

canned tomato sauce, 132, 254, 306

canned tomatoes, diced, 120, 154, 242, 252, 316, 324, 407

canned tuna, albacore, in water, 168, 462, 463, 464, 465, 466, 467, 468, 469, 470, 471, 523

canned white beans, 318, 382, 406, 407, 470

cannellini beans. See canned white beans

carrots, 68, 148, 170, 186, 300, 302, 316, 397, 400, 402, 407, 426, 519

cauliflower, 80, 156, 192, 308, 314, 382, 412, 424

celery, 164, 186, 216, 220, 224, 242, 310, 318, 362, 396, 397, 414, 426

cream of, 98% fat-free condensed soup, 176, 518

cereal, bran. See **Fiber One Original bran cereal**

cheese. See also **Laughing Cow Light Creamy Swiss cheese; Parmesan-style grated topping**

American, 24, 58, 78, 82, 122, 134, 174, 257, 282, 349, 352, 412, 456, 497

cheddar, 18, 20, 22, 25, 54, 62, 64, 70, 80, 98, 110, 128, 140, 158, 184, 190, 204, 206, 212, 270, 278, 296, 312, 332, 340, 342, 344, 346, 350, 351, 370, 386, 392, 396, 398, 408, 476, 502, 525

cottage cheese, fat-free, 86, 91

cream cheese, fat-free, 60, 68, 89, 92, 100, 106, 372, 376, 388, 392

feta, fat-free, 129, 258, 268

feta, reduced-fat, 19, 142, 498

Mexican-blend, reduced-fat, 79, 158, 210

mozzarella, part-skim or fat-free, 120, 188, 196, 230, 232, 234, 246, 254

ricotta, fat-free, 188, 232, 234, 236, 262

ricotta, light or low-fat, 27, 29, 230

string, light, 29, 72, 236, 238, 248, 250, 252, 260, 262, 264, 266, 268, 286, 292, 447, 454, 495

Swiss, reduced fat or 2% milk, 274, 295, 499

Cheeseburger Mac Attack, 308

Cheeseburger Mashed Potato Parfaits, 174

Cheesy Bacon Noodle Skillet, 336

Cheesy Bean Breakfast Quesadilla, 65

Cheesy Burger Skillet, 328

Cheesy Chicken Egg Rolls, 374

Cheesy Chicken Enchiladas, 212

Cheesy Noodles 'n Burgs!, 496

Cheesy Pigs in Bacon Blankies, 178

Cheesy Pizza Quesadilla, 264

Cheesy Squashataki, 520

Cheesy Tuna Muffin 'Wich, 465

cherries, 100

chicken, 218, 224, 242, 330, 332, 348, 368, 386. See also **shredded chicken**

Better Off Shred: HG's EZ Guide to Shredded Chicken, 211

Buffalo Chicken Egg Mug, 16

Buffalo Chicken Wing Macaroni & Cheese, 186

Cheesy Chicken Egg Rolls, 374

Cheesy Chicken Enchiladas, 212

Chicken and Sausage Gumbo, 310

Chicken Chili Surprise, 318

Chicken Fajita Burrito, 342

Chicken Fajita Scramble Mug, 20

Chicken Pot Pockets, 176

Chicky Pad Thai, 222

Classic Warm Asian Chicken Salad, 148

Colossal Asian Veggie 'n Chicken Pack, 170

Creamy Chicken & Noodles, 518

Crispity Crunchity Drumsticks, 354

Crock-Pot Coq Au Vin, 302

Dreamy Butternut Chicken Foil Pack, 156

Feta 'n Fuji Chicken Salad, 142

Grilled Fuji-n-Chick 'Wich, 288

Hungry Chick Shepherd's Pie, 192

Meat Prep 101, 167

Nacho-rific Stuffed Chicken, 204

Not-Quite-Homemade Chicken Noodle Soup, 519

Open-Faced Chicken Salad Melt, 295

Plate-Lickin'-Good Chicken 'n Waffles, 182

Rockin' Chicken Ratatouille, 154

Rockin' Creamy Broc 'n Chicken, 334

Spicy Chicken Crunchtastic Supreme, 340

SW BBQ Chicken Quesadilla, 210

Sweet & Sour Chicken 1-2-3, 220

Sweet Apple & Chicken Stir-Fry, 329

Sweet 'n Spicy Chicken Lettuce Cups, 441

Three-Cheese Chicken Cannelloni, 236

The Whole Enchilada Chicken Soup, 396

Winner Winner Onion Chicken Dinner, 166

chicken sausage, 242, 310

chicken trios, 434

Bacon-Wrapped BBQ Chicken, 442

Balsamic BBQ Chick Skillet, 436

Basil-icious Chicken, 437

Chicken a la Pot Pie, 443

Crispy Nacho Chicken, 439

Easy BBQ Chicken Nachos, 449

EZ Pineapple Chicken, 446

Fruity BBQ Chicken for Two, 440

Naked Chicken Parm, 447

Super-Speedy Chinese Stir-Fry, 448

Sweet 'n Spicy Chicken Lettuce Cups, 441

Tomato-Infused Chicken Rollup, 438

World's Easiest Chicken Empanadas, 444

chickpeas, canned, 144, 168, 240, 300, 428

Chicky Pad Thai, 222

chili, 184, 318, 351, 408, 504, 517

chilies, green, 65, 310, 318

chocolate, 6, 32, 34, 35, 42, 43, 60, 76, 86, 106, 116

    Chocolate-Chippy Cheese Danish, 106

    PB & Chocolate Oatmeal Blitz, 43

chorizo, soy, 79

cilantro, fresh, 62, 130, 214, 222, 240, 315, 342, 366, 368, 386

Cinn-a-nilla Apple Oatmeal Parfait, 44

clams

    Baked Clam Halfsies, 384

    I'll Take Manhattan Clam Chowder, 397

Classic Cheesesteak Salad, 134

Classic Club Salad, 146

Classic Warm Asian Chicken Salad, 148

The Club Skillet, 326

Coffee Cake Scones, 114

Cold Dog Slaw, 417

coleslaw mix, 130, 131, 132, 216, 368, 424, 478

Colossal Asian Veggie 'n Chicken Pack, 170

comfort foods, 172

    Beef Strogataki, 200

    Buffalo Chicken Wing Macaroni & Cheese, 186

    Cheeseburger Mashed Potato Parfaits, 174

    Cheesy Pigs in Bacon Blankies, 178

    Chicken Pot Pockets, 176

    Faux-Fried Green Tomatoes, 194

    Floosh's Stuffed Cabbage, 198

    Funkadelic Chili Mac, 184

    Hungry Chick Shepherd's Pie, 192

    iHungry Spaghetti Tacos, 190

    Lasagna Cupcakes, 188

    Plate-Lickin'-Good Chicken 'n Waffles, 182

    Super-Duper Spaghetti Pie Part Deux, 196

    Turkey Tetrazzini Bake, 180

corn

    canned cream-style, 112, 315, 416

    canned sweet, 312

    Corn MegaMuffins, 112

    Insanely Irresistible Corn Pudding, 416

cottage cheese, fat-free, 86, 91

crab

    Ab-Fab Artichoke Crab Dip, 376

    The Crab Rangoonies, 388

    Crabby Patties, 362

    Creamy Crab Cakes Benedict, 66

    imitation, 376, 388

cranberry sauce, 129, 198

Crazy-Delicious Caribbean Black Bean Broccoli Slaw, 430

Crazy-Delicious Cheesy Cherry Danish, 100

Crazy-Good Carrot-Cake Pancakes, 68

cream of celery condensed soup, 98% fat-free, 178, 518

cream of chicken condensed soup, 98% fat-free, 156

cream of mushroom condensed soup, 98% fat-free, 180, 468, 523

Creamy Carrot Soup, 402

Creamy Chicken & Noodles, 518

Creamy Crab Cakes Benedict, 66

Creamy Dreamy Macaroni Salad, 414

Crispity Crunchity Drumsticks, 354

Crispy Cheeseburger Pizza, 270

Crispy Nacho Chicken, 439

Crispy-licious Faux-Fried Frenzy, 390

crock pot, 298

    All the Rage Bolognese, 316

    Cheeseburger Mac Attack, 308

    Chicken and Sausage Gumbo, 310

    Chicken Chili Surprise, 318

    Crock-Pot Cinna-Apples 'n Oats, 304

    Crock-Pot Coq Au Vin, 302

    Crock-Pot Fake-Baked Beans, 305

    'Cue the Pulled Pork, 306

    Outside-In Turkey Tamale Pie, 312

    Sweet 'n Red Hot Apple Mash, 309

    Ten-Alarm Southwestern Corn Chowder, 315

    Very Veggie Bisque, 314

    Very VERY Veggie Stew, 300

crowd pleasers, breakfast, 94

    Banana Split Bread, 116

    Breakfast Bruschetta, 104

    Chocolate-Chippy Cheese Danish, 106

    Coffee Cake Scones, 114

    Corn MegaMuffins, 112

    Crazy-Delicious Cheesy Cherry Danish, 100

    Early-Riser Pigs in a Blanket, 118

    Egg Cups a la Hungry, 102

    Egga-Pinwheels, 122

    Fluffy-Good Zucchini Nut Muffins, 96

    Ham & Cheese Egg Strata Bake, 110

    HG's Big Breakfast Casserole, 98

    Quiche Me Bacon Tarts, 108

    Ratatouille Frittata, 120

Crunchy Beefy Taco Egg Mug, 18

Crunchy Turkey Tacos, 476

crushed pineapple, 68, 90, 464

crushed tomatoes. See **canned crushed tomatoes**

cucumber, 130, 131, 146, 426

    seedless, 89, 142, 143, 144, 240

'Cue the Pulled Pork, 306

Curry in a Hurry Trio, 493

D

Deconstructed Falafel Salad, 144

Denver Omelette in a Mug, 22

Double-0-Strawberry Quickie Kiwi Smoothie, 87

dough. See **Pillsbury refrigerated dough**

Dreamy Butternut Chicken Foil Pack, 156

E

Early-Riser Pigs in a Blanket, 118

Easiest Thin-Crust Pizza Ever, 454

Easy BBQ Chicken Nachos, 449

Egg Cups a la Hungry, 102

egg mugs, 12

    All-American Egg Mug, 24

    Bean 'n Cheesy Soft Taco in an Egg Mug, 25

    BTA (Bacon, Tomato, Avocado) Egg Mug, 15

    Buffalo Chicken Egg Mug, 16

    California Love Mug, 17

    Chicken Fajita Scramble Mug, 20

    Crunchy Beefy Taco Egg Mug, 18

    Denver Omelette in a Mug, 22

    Egg Mugs 101, 21

    Eggs Bene-chick Mug, 26

    The HG Special Egg Mug, 28

    It's All Greek to Me Egg Mug, 19

    Lasagna-Like Egg Mug, 29

    Pizza! Pizza! Egg Mug, 14

    Say Cheese! Egg Mug, 27

    Veggie Eggs-plosion Mug, 23

egg roll wrappers, 176, 216, 374

egg substitute, fat-free liquid, 40, 50, 54, 58, 60, 62, 64, 65, 68, 70, 72, 74, 76, 78, 79, 80, 82, 96, 104, 108, 112, 114, 116, 182, 188, 194, 196, 222, 228, 234, 246, 252, 274, 292, 350, 352, 354, 362, 372, 377, 379, 390, 416, 497, 508. *See also* **egg mugs**

    Breakfast for Dinner Skillet, 332

    Creamy Crab Cakes Benedict, 66

    Ham & Cheese Egg Strata Bake, 110

    HG's Big Breakfast Casserole, 98

    Hot Dog & Scramble, 46

    Ratatouille Frittata, 120

    Turkey Club B. Bowl, 47

    Very Veggie-Eggy Explosion, 36

egg whites, 232, 414

Egga-Pinwheels, 122

Egg-cellent Foo Young, 218

eggplant, 120, 138, 154, 232, 234, 254, 300

    Faux-Fried Mozzarella-n-Basil Eggplant Sandwiches, 292

    Grilly-Good Eggplant Bites, 364

    Supremely Stuffed Pizza-fied Eggplant, 252

Eggs Bene-Chick Mug, 26

English muffins, 26, 92, 110, 262, 279, 465

Erin-Go-Breakfast Boxty, 80

EZ Cheesy Lasagna for Two, 232

EZ Cheesy Tostada, 456

EZ Chili Mac, 517

EZ Mock Vodka Pasta, 524

EZ Pineapple Chicken, 446

F

Fage Total 0% fat-free Greek yogurt, 7

Falafel Pita Pockets with Dill-icious Yogurt Dip, 240

Fancy-Pants Fast Tuna 'n Beans, 470

fast-food/drive-thru makeovers, 338

    Amazing Ate-Layer Open-Faced Taco, 344

    Big Bad Breakfast Burrito, 350

    Chicken Fajita Burrito, 342

    Crispity Crunchity Drumsticks, 354

    Flat-tastic Ranchy Bacon Wrap, 348

    Loaded Bacon-Wrapped Hot Dogs, 356

    Neat-O Chili-Frito Burrito, 351

    Snack-tastic Burger Wrap, 349

    Spicy Chicken Crunchtastic Supreme, 340

    Totally Stacked Steak-Style HG Burger, 352

    Twice-as-Nice *Guapo* Taco, 346

Fast-Food Hamburger Scramble, 497

fat-free cheese. *See* **cheese**

fat-free liquid egg substitute. *See* **egg substitute, fat-free liquid**

fat-free refried beans, 25, 140, 158, 204, 342, 346, 370, 378, 453

faux-fried

    Baked Clam Halfsies, 384

    Crispity Crunchity Drumsticks, 354

    Crispy-licious Faux-Fried Frenzy, 390

    Faux-Fried & Fabulous Calamari, 228

    Faux-Fried Green Tomatoes, 194

    Faux-Fried Mozzarella-n-Basil Eggplant Sandwiches, 292

    Plate-Lickin'-Good Chicken 'n Waffles, 182

    Sweet Coconut Crunch Shrimp, 379

    Totally Stacked Steak-Style HG Burger, 352

feta cheese

    fat-free, 129, 258, 268

    reduced-fat, 19, 142, 498

    Feta 'n Fuji Chicken Salad, 142

Fiber One Original bran cereal, 86, 114, 168, 180, 182, 194, 204, 228, 246, 252, 292, 352, 354, 372, 379, 384, 390. *See also* **faux-fried**

    The 411 on Fiber One Crushing . . ., 243

fish. *See also* **clams; crab; shrimp; tuna; tuna trios**

    Faux-Fried & Fabulous Calamari, 228

    Grilled Go Fish! Soft Tacos, 208

    Lean 'n Green Fruity Tuna Bowl, 143

    scallops, 324

    Smokey Salmon Lettuce Wraps, 89

    tilapia, 152, 208

    Too-EZ Fish Taco Supreme, 152

    Woohoo! Bayou Fish Pack, 164

Flat-tastic Ranchy Bacon Wrap, 348

Flat-Top Patty Melt, 282

Floosh's Stuffed Cabbage, 198

Fluffy-Good Zucchini Nut Muffins, 96

foil packs, 150

    Colossal Asian Veggie 'n Chicken Pack, 170

    Dreamy Butternut Chicken Foil Pack, 156

    Hot Tuna Stuffed Tomatoes, 168

    No-Nonsense Nacho Lettuce Cups, 158

    Rockin' Chicken Ratatouille, 154

    Steamy Creamy Squash Packet, 162

    Sweet Potato Apple Pack, 160

    Too-EZ Fish Taco Supreme, 152

    Winner Winner Onion Chicken Dinner, 166

foil packs (continued)

Woohoo! Bayou Fish Pack, 164

"Wrap the Dog" Foil Pack, 502

For the Love of Sweet Garlic Butternut Fries, 422

freezer staples, 8

Fresh 'n Fruity Skewer Dogs, 509

fridge staples, 7

fruit preserves

apricot, sugar-free, 222, 440

blackberry, sugar-free, 198

strawberry, sugar-free, 32, 52, 74, 116

sugar-free, 274

Fruitiyaki Patty, 489

Fruity BBQ Chicken for Two, 440

Fruity Quesadilla, 452

Fuji apples. See **apples**

Fully Loaded Baked Potato Soup, 398

Funkadelic Chili Mac, 184

G

garlic, chopped, 66, 120, 148, 154, 156, 162,164,
168, 170, 184, 186, 188, 198, 218, 220, 222, 226,
230, 232, 236, 242, 252, 258, 260, 276, 292, 300,
302, 305, 310, 314, 315, 316, 318, 322, 324, 326,
329, 332, 334, 362, 364, 372, 374, 376, 380, 382,
384, 388, 400, 404, 407, 428

Garlic Shrimp Tostada, 459

German-ish Potato-ish Salad, 424

Gimme S'more Pancakes, 76

Gooey-Good Queso Dip 'n Chips, 392

Gravy-Good Beef Casserole, 475

The Great Greek Pizza, 268

Greek foods

The Great Greek Pizza, 268

Grilled Greek Pizza Minis, 258

It's All Greek to Me Egg Mug, 19

yogurt, 7, 112, 380, 467

Grilled Cheese 'n Veggie Sandwich, 296

Grilled Fuji-n-Chick 'Wich, 288

Grilled Go Fish! Soft Tacos, 208

Grilled Greek Pizza Minis, 258

Grilly Girl Cheesy Turkey & Bacon 'Wich, 278

Grilly-Good Eggplant Bites, 364

Grinder Lettuce Cups, 494

ground meat trios, 472

Bacon Cheeseburger Patty, 484

BBQuick Saucy Turkey, 482

Broccoli Beef Stir-Fry, 479

Crunchy Turkey Tacos, 476

Gravy-Good Beef Casserole, 475

Mexi-Bolognese, 480

OMG! Burgers (Onion Mushroom Goodness
Burgers), 477

Simply Sweet Meatballs, 481

Sloppy Joe Stir-Fry Slaw, 474

Vegged-Up Ground Beef, 478

Veggie-rific Meatloaf, 483

ground-beef-style soy crumbles. See **soy
crumbles, ground-beef-style**

H

ham, 22, 26, 122, 274

Ham & Cheese Egg Strata Bake, 110

hamburger buns, light, 276, 279

Hawaiian B-fast Stacks, 92

Hawaiian Tuna Salad, 464

HG Hash Scramble, 54

The HG Special Egg Mug, 28

HG's Big Breakfast Casserole, 98

HG's Caribbean Shrimp Surprise, 322

Hola Breakfast Tostada, 64

HOT, HOT, HOT Dog!, 512

Hot & Cold 10-Veggie Explosion, 136

hot dog buns, light, 46, 356, 508, 511

hot dogs, 7

Cheesy Pigs in Bacon Blankies, 178

Cold Dog Slaw, 417

Hot Dog & Scramble, 46

Hot Dog Stir-Fry, 510

Hot Dog Stroganoff, 505

Hot Doggy Home Fries, 507

Hot Dog–Hot Potato Hotcakes, 377

Loaded Bacon-Wrapped Hot Dogs, 356

No-Buns-About-It Chili Dog Chili, 408

hot dogs, hot trios, 500

Fresh 'n Fruity Skewer Dogs, 509

HOT, HOT, HOT Dog!, 512

Hot Diggity Dog Casserole, 508

Hot Dog Stir-Fry, 510

Hot Dog Stroganoff, 505

Hot Doggy Home Fries, 507

Pigs on a Mattress, 506

Pigs on a Stick in a Bacon-Wrapped
Blanket, 503

Sloppy Beans 'n Franks, 511

"Wrap the Dog" Foil Pack, 502

Yo! Chili Dog Wrap, 504

Hot Stack Morning Sliders, 82

Hot Tuna Stuffed Tomatoes, 168

Hungry Chick Shepherd's Pie, 192

I

iHungry Spaghetti Tacos, 190

I'll Take Manhattan Clam Chowder, 397

In-N-Outrageous Animal-Style Salad, 128

Insanely Irresistible Corn Pudding, 416

international favorites, 202. See also **Asian
foods; Greek foods; Italian foods;
Mexican foods**

Island Time Salad, 131

Italian foods. See also **pizza**

EZ Cheesy Lasagna for Two, 232

Faux-Fried & Fabulous Calamari, 228

Pepperoni-Poppin' Veggie Calzones, 238

Takes-the-Cake Ziti Bake, 230

Three-Cheese Chicken Cannelloni, 236

Veggie-rific Noodle-Free Lasagna, 234

It's All Greek to Me Egg Mug, 19

J

jalapeño pepper, 356, 390

    slices, jarred, 140, 158, 276, 344, 366, 378

Just Veggin' Pizza, 254

K

kidney beans

    canned red, 164, 184, 305, 312, 408, 428

    canned white, 318, 382, 406, 407

kiwi, 87, 91

L

La Tortilla Factory tortillas, 6, 62, 342

Large & In Charge Neapolitan Oatmeal, 34

Lasagna Cupcakes, 188

Lasagna-Like Egg Mug, 29

Laughing Cow Babybel Light cheese, 27, 280

Laughing Cow Light Creamy Swiss cheese, 14, 17, 23, 36, 47, 65, 66, 102, 108, 162, 178, 180, 186, 200, 204, 210, 246, 248, 257, 264, 277, 288, 308, 326, 328, 334, 336, 362, 374, 376, 382, 388, 392, 438, 452, 453, 457, 458, 459, 465, 484, 496, 517, 520, 524, 527

Lean 'n Green Fruity Tuna Bowl, 143

Lean 'n Green Shrimp-chilada, 455

lemon, 226, 228, 362

lettuce, 190, 256, 266, 270, 276, 277, 283, 286, 340, 344, 346, 348, 349, 352, 476, 477

    butter, 158, 441, 494

    green leaf, 441

    mixed field greens, 132, 143

    romaine, 89, 128, 129, 130, 131, 134, 136, 138, 140, 142, 144, 146, 158, 290, 441

light bread. *See* **bread**

light cheese wedges. *See* **Laughing Cow Light Creamy Swiss cheese**

light whipped butter/light buttery spread. *See* **butter**

light/low-fat salad dressing, 7

Loaded Bacon-Wrapped Hot Dogs, 356

Loaded Miracle Mashies, 412

Loaded 'n Oated Spinach & Mushroom Girlfredo Pizza, 246

Looney Tuna-Stuffed Pepper, 463

M

Major Mocha Cappuccino Oatmeal, 35

mango, 131, 322, 430, 452

marinara sauce, low-fat, 198, 228, 250, 447, 524

meat. *See also* **beef; chicken; ground meat trios; pork; turkey**

    Meat Prep 101, 167

meatless burger patty trios, 486

    Bacon Bleu Burger, 488

    Bunless Mediterranean Burger, 498

    Burger-ific Mushroom Melt, 499

    Burgs in a Blanket, 490

    Cheesy Noodles 'n Burgs!, 496

    Curry in a Hurry Trio, 493

    Fast-Food Hamburger Scramble, 497

    Fruitiyaki Patty, 489

    Grinder Lettuce Cups, 494

    Sweet Spinach Stir-Fry, 492

    Three-Step Pizza Burger, 495

meatless hamburger-style patties, 8, 174, 328, 352, 489, 490, 492, 493, 494, 495, 496, 497, 499

    A+ Avocado Burger, 277

    Bacon Bleu Burger, 488

    Bunless Mediterranean Burger, 498

    Flat-Top Patty Melt, 282

    In-N-Outrageous Animal-Style Salad, 128

    Snack-tastic Burger Wrap, 349

    Totally Stacked Steak-Style HG Burger, 352

meatless sausage, 8, 24, 40, 70, 102, 118, 350

    Sausage, Egg 'n Cheese ChickGriddle, 58

Mexi-Bolognese, 480

Mexican foods, 351, 368, 382, 452

    Amazing Ate-Layer Open-Faced Taco, 344

    Bean 'n Cheesy Soft Taco in an Egg Mug, 25

    'Bella Asada Fajitas, 214

    Big Bad Breakfast Burrito, 350

    Breakfast Pizza Mexicali, 79

    Buenos Días Breakfast Fajitas, 70

    Cheesy Bean Breakfast Quesadilla, 65

    Cheesy Chicken Enchiladas, 212

    Cheesy Pizza Quesadilla, 264

    Chicken Fajita Burrito, 342

    Chicken Fajita Scramble Mug, 20

    Crispy Nacho Chicken, 439

    Crunchy Beefy Taco Egg Mug, 18

    Gooey-Good Queso Dip 'n Chips, 392

    Grilled Go Fish! Soft Tacos, 208

    Hola Breakfast Tostada, 64

    iHungry Spaghetti Tacos, 190

    Nacho-ed Up Mexi-Chop, 140

    Nacho-rific Stuffed Chicken, 204

    Nice to See Ya! Quesadilla, 62

    No-Nonsense Nacho Lettuce Cups, 158

    Rockin' Roasted Corn Guac 'n Chips, 366

    Southwest Stuffed Tomatoes, 386

    Spicy Mexican Sandwich, 276

    Surprise, It's Pumpkin! Enchiladas, 206

    SW BBQ Chicken Quesadilla, 210

    Twice-as-Nice *Guapo* Taco, 346

    The Whole Enchilada Chicken Soup, 396

    World's Easiest Chicken Empanadas, 444

Mexi-licious Pot Stickers, 370

Mexi-licious Shrimp & Corn Fandango Salad, 130

Mini Nacho Dippers, 378

Mmm-mmm Minestrone, 407

Monte Cristo Sandwich, 274

The Morning Waffle Dip, 78

Morningstar Farms products, 8

muffins

    Cheesy Tuna Muffin 'Wich, 465

    Corn MegaMuffins, 112

    English muffins, 26, 92, 110, 262

    Fluffy-Good Zucchini Nut Muffins, 96

mushrooms, 17, 23, 36, 98, 110, 134, 136, 148, 166, 170, 180, 188, 200, 218, 224, 230, 232, 236, 238, 246, 250, 254, 258, 264, 266, 302, 314, 332, 334, 386, 468, 475, 510

   canned, 192, 404

   OMG! Burgers (Onion Mushroom Goodness Burgers), 477

   portabella, 138, 184, 214, 260, 286, 290, 499

N

Nacho-ed Up Mexi-Chop, 140

Nacho-rific Stuffed Chicken, 204

Naked Chicken Parm, 447

Neat-O Chili-Frito Burrito, 351

Nice to See Ya! Quesadilla, 62

No-Buns-About-It Chili Dog Chili, 408

no-cook b-fasts, 84

   Breakfast Sundae Supreme, 86

   Double-O-Strawberry Quickie Kiwi Smoothie, 87

   Hawaiian B-fast Stacks, 92

   PB&J Yogurt Parfait, 88

   Smokey Salmon Lettuce Wraps, 89

   Tropical AM Smoothie, 90

   Tropical Wonder B-fast Bowl, 91

No-Nonsense Nacho Lettuce Cups, 158

noodles

   lasagna, 232

   macaroni, 184, 186, 308, 414

   rotini, penne, or ziti, 230, 407

   Tofu Shirataki, 180, 190, 196, 200, 222, 226, 334, 336, 521

   Cheesy Bacon Noodle Skillet, 336

   Cheesy Noodles 'n Burgs!, 496

noodle trios, 514

   BBQ Spaghetti, 525

   Cheesy Squashataki, 520

   Creamy Chicken & Noodles, 518

   EZ Chili Mac, 517

   EZ Mock Vodka Pasta, 524

Not-Quite-Homemade Chicken Noodle Soup, 519

Quick 'n Spicy Fettuccine Hungry Buff-redo, 527

Quickie-yaki Stir-Fry, 528

Sweetness, Spice & 3-Things Nice Noodles, 516

Thai Peanut Noodle Trio, 526

Tuna Noodle Casse-Bowl, 523

"Yo Quiero Taco Bowl" Noodles, 522

Not-Quite-Homemade Chicken Noodle Soup, 519

O

oatmeal

   Apple Pie Oatmeal Bonanza, 33

   Banana Split Growing Oatmeal, 32

   Cinn-a-nilla Apple Oatmeal Parfait, 44

   Crock-Pot Cinna-Apples 'n Oats, 304

   HG and the Growing Oatmeal . . . Tips & Tricks!, 53

   Large & In Charge Neapolitan Oatmeal, 34

   Major Mocha Cappuccino Oatmeal, 35

   PB & Chocolate Oatmeal Blitz, 43

   PB&J Oatmeal Heaven, 52

   Pumpkin Pie Oatmeal Parfait, 38

   S'mores Oatmeal, 42

   Super-Sized Berry-nana Oatmeal Parfait, 48

olives, black, sliced, 136, 140, 158, 258, 260, 268, 312, 378

OMG! Burgers (Onion Mushroom Goodness Burgers), 477

onion, 20, 22, 23, 46, 54, 62, 64, 65, 66, 70, 72, 98, 108, 120, 128, 134, 136, 138, 152, 154, 156, 158, 162, 166, 168, 174, 180, 184, 186, 188, 190, 196, 198, 200, 206, 212, 214, 218, 224, 226, 230, 236, 238, 240, 242, 250, 252, 258, 266, 270, 276, 280, 282, 284, 288, 292, 296, 300, 302, 305, 306, 310, 312, 314, 315, 316, 318, 324, 328, 329, 332, 334, 342, 349, 350, 351, 352, 356, 362, 364, 366, 370, 372, 374, 382, 386, 390, 396, 397, 398, 400, 402, 404, 407, 408, 414, 417, 424, 457, 478, 482, 490, 502, 505, 506, 510

   red, 19, 130, 144, 246, 262, 268, 277, 286, 326, 428

   Winner Winner Onion Chicken Dinner, 166

Open-Faced Chicken Salad Melt, 295

orange juice, 131, 136, 143

oranges, 428, 448

Outside-In Turkey Tamale Pie, 312

P

pancakes

   Crazy-Good Carrot-Cake Pancakes, 68

   Gimme S'more Pancakes, 76

   Rockin' Red Velvet Pancakes, 60

   Strawberry Short Stack, 74

pantry staples, 6

parfaits

   Cheeseburger Mashed Potato Parfaits, 174

   Cinn-a-nilla Apple Oatmeal Parfait, 44

   PB&J Yogurt Parfait, 88

   Pumpkin Pie Oatmeal Parfait, 38

   Super-Sized Berry-nana Oatmeal Parfait, 48

Parmesan-style grated topping, 14, 16, 27, 72, 168, 180, 186, 196, 226, 228, 230, 232, 234, 236, 238, 250, 252, 254, 292, 314, 334, 364, 372, 376, 384, 406

parsley, fresh, 144, 186, 226, 240, 362, 384, 406, 428

pasta. *See* **noodles**

PB & Chocolate Oatmeal Blitz, 43

PB&J Oatmeal Heaven, 52

PB&J Yogurt Parfait, 88

peanut butter, 43, 52, 88, 294

pepperoni, turkey, 7, 14, 257, 260, 264, 266

   Pepperoni Pizza Pinwheels, 248

   Pepperoni-Poppin' Veggie Calzones, 238

peppers. *See* **bell pepper**; **jalapeño pepper**

Perfect Portabella Club, 290

Pigs on a Mattress, 506

Pigs on a Stick in a Bacon-Wrapped Blanket, 503

Pillsbury refrigerated dough

Dough the Right Thing . . . Tips for Working with Refrigerated Dough, 123

Classic Pizza Crust, 238, 254, 256, 506

Crescent Recipe Creations Seamless Dough Sheet, 100, 102, 106, 108, 122, 248, 250, 444, 468

Reduced Fat Crescent rolls, 118, 123, 178, 490, 503

pineapple

chunks, 220, 446, 509

crushed, 68, 90, 464

rings, 92, 489

tidbits, 430, 481

pitas, whole-wheat or high-fiber, 240, 268

pizza, 244

BLT Pizza, 256

Breakfast Pizza Mexicali, 79

Breakfast Scramble Pizza, 72

Cheesy Pizza Quesadilla, 264

Crispy Cheeseburger Pizza, 270

Easiest Thin-Crust Pizza Ever, 454

The Great Greek Pizza, 268

Grilled Greek Pizza Minis, 258

Just Veggin' Pizza, 254

Loaded 'n Oated Spinach & Mushroom Girlfredo Pizza, 246

Pepperoni Pizza Pinwheels, 248

Pizza Burgers a la HG, 266

Pizza! Pizza! Egg Mug, 14

Pizza Puffs, 250

Pizza-bellas, 260

Pizza-fied Grilled Cheese, 257

Purple Pizza Eaters, 262

Supremely Stuffed Pizza-fied Eggplant, 252

Three-Step Pizza Burger, 495

Plate-Lickin'-Good Chicken 'n Waffles, 182

pork. *See also* **bacon; ham**

'Cue the Pulled Pork, 306

potatoes, 36, 54, 262, 398, 402, 426

red, 262, 412, 424

russet, 80, 314, 397

sweet potatoes, 160

Pow! Sock! Bam! Jambalaya, 242

precooked real crumbled bacon. *See* **bacon**

preserves, fruit. *See* **fruit preserves**

pudding, 38

Breakfast Rice Pudding, 50

Insanely Irresistible Corn Pudding, 416

Sweet and Savory Breakfast Bread Pudding Bowl, 40

pumpkin

canned, 68, 196, 396

Pumpkin Pie Oatmeal Parfait, 38

Surprise, It's Pumpkin! Enchiladas, 206

Purple Pizza Eaters, 262

Q

Quiche Me Bacon Tarts, 108

Quick 'n Spicy Fettuccine Hungry Buff-redo, 527

Quickie-yaki Stir-Fry, 528

R

Ranch-tastic Butternut Fries with Bacon, 418

Ratatouille Frittata, 120

Raw Apple Rollup, 458

reduced-fat feta cheese, 19, 142, 498

refried beans, fat-free, 25, 65, 140, 158, 204, 342, 346, 370, 378, 453

refrigerated dough. *See* **Pillsbury refrigerated dough**

Ring-My-Bella Mushroom Sandwich, 286

roast beef, 276

Rockin' Chicken Ratatouille, 154

Rockin' Creamy Broc 'n Chicken, 334

Rockin' Red Velvet Pancakes, 60

Rockin' Roasted Corn Guac 'n Chips, 366

S

salads, 126

Asian BBQ Shrimp Salad, 132

BBQ Grilled Veggie Salad, 138

Bean There, Yum That Salad, 428

Classic Cheesesteak Salad, 134

Classic Club Salad, 146

Classic Warm Asian Chicken Salad, 148

Creamy Dreamy Macaroni Salad, 414

Deconstructed Falafel Salad, 144

Feta 'n Fuji Chicken Salad, 142

German-ish Potato-ish Salad, 424

Hawaiian Tuna Salad, 464

Hot & Cold 10-Veggie Explosion, 136

In-N-Outrageous Animal-Style Salad, 128

Island Time Salad, 131

Lean 'n Green Fruity Tuna Bowl, 143

Mexi-licious Shrimp & Corn Fandango Salad, 130

Nacho-ed Up Mexi-Chop, 140

Open-Faced Chicken Salad Melt, 295

Salsa to the Tuna Salad!, 467

Sun-Dried Tomato Tuna Salad, 466

Thanksgiving in a Salad Bowl, 129

Vegged-Out Potato Salad, 426

salad dressings, 7, 128, 349, 470, 526

blue cheese, light, 16, 488

honey mustard, light, 471, 492

ranch, fat-free or light, 210, 348, 390, 512

sesame-ginger, low-fat, 330, 368, 462

Salsa to the Tuna Salad!, 467

Salsa-fied Tuna Stacks, 469

Salt-Slashing Swaps for Recipe Ingredients, 71

sandwich buns. *See* **bread**

sandwiches, 272

A+ Avocado Burger, 277

BLTA Club, 283

Cheesy Tuna Muffin 'Wich, 465

sandwiches *(continued)*

Faux-Fried Mozzarella-n-Basil Eggplant
  Sandwiches, 292

  Flat-Top Patty Melt, 282

  Grilled Cheese 'n Veggie Sandwich, 296

  Grilled Fuji-n-Chick 'Wich, 288

  Grilly Girl Cheesy Turkey & Bacon 'Wich, 278

  Hawaiian B-fast Stacks, 92

  Monte Cristo Sandwich, 274

  Open-Faced Chicken Salad Melt, 295

  Perfect Portabella Club, 290

  Ring-My-Bella Mushroom Sandwich, 286

  The Skinny Elvis, 294

  So-Good Grilled Veggie Panini, 280

  Spicy Mexican Sandwich, 276

  Thanksgiving Turkey Sandwich, 284

Sassy 'n Steamy Artichoke, 380

Sassy Wonton Tacos, 368

sausage

  chicken sausage, 242, 310

  meatless or turkey, 8, 24, 40, 58, 70, 102, 350

  Sausage, Egg 'n Cheese ChickGriddle, 58

Say Cheese! Egg Mug, 27

scallions, 80, 132, 140, 148, 206, 210, 212, 216,
  218, 222, 332, 388, 398, 404, 418, 424, 426

scallops, 324

seafood. *See* **clams; crab; fish; shrimp; tuna;
  tuna trios**

shredded chicken, 186, 191, 210, 212, 218, 310,
  318, 368, 386, 396, 444, 449

  *Better Off Shred: HG's EZ Guide to
    Shredded Chicken*, 211

shrimp, 131, 218, 242, 330

  Asian BBQ Shrimp Salad, 132

  Garlic Shrimp Tostada, 459

  HG's Caribbean Shrimp Surprise, 322

  Lean 'n Green Shrimp-chilada, 455

  Mexi-licious Shrimp & Corn Fandango
    Salad, 130

  Shrimpylicious Egg Rolls, 216

  Super-Delicious Shrimp Scampi with

Fettuccine, 226

Sweet Coconut Crunch Shrimp, 379

sides, 411

  Bean There, Yum That Salad, 428

  Cold Dog Slaw, 417

  Crazy-Delicious Caribbean Black Bean
    Broccoli Slaw, 430

  Creamy Dreamy Macaroni Salad, 414

  German-ish Potato-ish Salad, 424

  Insanely Irresistible Corn Pudding, 416

  Loaded Miracle Mashies, 412

  For the Love of Sweet Garlic Butternut
    Fries, 422

  Ranch-tastic Butternut Fries with Bacon, 418

  Sweet 'n Squashed Biscuits, 420

  Vegged-Out Potato Salad, 426

Simply Sweet Meatballs, 481

Skillet-Seared Scallops Fra Diavolo, 324

The Skinny Elvis, 294

sliced black olives, 136, 140, 158, 260, 268,
  312, 378

Sloppy Beans 'n Franks, 511

Sloppy Joe Stir-Fry Slaw, 474

Smokey Salmon Lettuce Wraps, 89

S'mores Oatmeal, 42

Snack-tastic Burger Wrap, 349

sodium tips, 26, 28, 219, 271, 278, 354, 384

  Salt-Slashing Swaps for Recipe Ingredients, 71

So-Good Grilled Veggie Panini, 280

So-Good Spinach Bites, 372

soups, 394

  Big Apple Butternut Squash Soup, 400

  canned, 156, 180, 397, 468, 523

  Chicken and Sausage Gumbo, 310

  Creamy Carrot Soup, 402

  Chicken Chili Surprise, 318

  Fully Loaded Baked Potato Soup, 398

  I'll Take Manhattan Clam Chowder, 397

  Mmm-mmm Minestrone, 407

  No-Buns-About-It Chili Dog Chili, 408

Not-Quite-Homemade Chicken Noodle
  Soup, 519

Ten-Alarm Southwestern Corn Chowder, 315

Very Veggie Bisque, 314

Very VERY Veggie Stew, 300

The Whole Enchilada Chicken Soup, 396

WOWOWOW! Wonton Soup, 404

Zazzled-Up Zuppa, 406

Southwest Stuffed Tomatoes, 386

soy burger patties. *See* **meatless
  hamburger-style patties**

soy chorizo, 79

soy crumbles, ground-beef-style, 7, 98, 252,
  270, 344, 346, 406, 456

  Crunchy Beefy Taco Egg Mug, 18

  Funkadelic Chili Mac, 184

  Gooey-Good Queso Dip 'n Chips, 392

  iHungry Spaghetti Tacos, 190

  Lasagna-Like Egg Mug, 29

  Super-Duper Spaghetti Pie Part Deux, 196

  Veggie-rific Noodle-Free Lasagna, 234

soymilk, 6

  light plain, 80, 98, 110, 180, 194, 314, 315,
    392, 398

  light vanilla, 50, 60, 68, 74, 76, 100, 106,
    114, 304, 420

Speedy Beany-rito, 453

Spicy Chicken Crunchtastic Supreme, 340

Spicy Mexican Sandwich, 276

spinach, 17, 19, 36, 129, 230, 238, 246, 296,
  326, 374, 399

  Classic Warm Asian Chicken Salad, 148

  So-Good Spinach Bites, 372

  Sweet Spinach Stir-Fry, 492

Splenda, 50, 96, 100, 106, 112, 116

squash, butternut, 156, 300, 344, 400, 418,
  420, 422, 431, 507, 520

  *Squash It! Hungry Girl's Guide to Mastering
    the Butternut Squash*, 431

squash, summer, 162, 166, 314

starters, 362

    Ab-Fab Artichoke Crab Dip, 376

    Baked Clam Halfsies, 384

    Cheesy Chicken Egg Rolls, 374

    The Crab Rangoonies, 388

    Crabby Patties, 362

    Crispy-licious Faux-Fried Frenzy, 390

    Gooey-Good Queso Dip 'n Chips, 392

    Grilly-Good Eggplant Bites, 364

    Hot Dog–Hot Potato Hotcakes, 377

    Mexi-licious Pot Stickers, 370

    Mini Nacho Dippers, 378

    Rockin' Roasted Corn Guac 'n Chips, 366

    Sassy 'n Steamy Artichoke, 380

    Sassy Wonton Tacos, 368

    So-Good Spinach Bites, 372

    Southwest Stuffed Tomatoes, 386

    Sweet Coconut Crunch Shrimp, 379

    United We Chew! Red, White & Blue Nachos, 382

Steamy Creamy Squash Packet, 162

stevia, 6, 51, 117

stir-frys & skillet meals, 320

    Breakfast for Dinner Skillet, 332

    Cheesy Bacon Noodle Skillet, 336

    Cheesy Burger Skillet, 328

    The Club Skillet, 326

    HG's Caribbean Shrimp Surprise, 322

    Rockin' Creamy Broc 'n Chicken, 334

    Skillet-Seared Scallops Fra Diavolo, 324

    Sweet Apple & Chicken Stir-Fry, 329

    Tempting Teriyaki Trifecta, 330

strawberries, 34, 52, 74, 86, 88, 91, 143

    Double-0-Strawberry Quickie Kiwi Smoothie, 87

    Super-Sized Berry-nana Oatmeal Parfait, 48

Strawberry Short Stack, 74

sugar snap peas, 132, 170

Sun-Dried Tomato Tuna Salad, 466

Super-Delicious Shrimp Scampi with Fettuccine, 226

Super-Duper Spaghetti Pie Part Deux, 196

Super-Sized Berry-nana Oatmeal Parfait, 48

Super-Speedy Chinese Stir-Fry, 448

Supremely Stuffed Pizza-fied Eggplant, 252

Surprise, It's Pumpkin! Enchiladas, 206

SW BBQ Chicken Quesadilla, 210

Sweet & Sour Chicken 1-2-3, 220

Sweet and Savory Breakfast Bread Pudding Bowl, 40

Sweet Apple & Chicken Stir-Fry, 329

Sweet Coconut Crunch Shrimp, 379

Sweet 'n Red Hot Apple Mash, 309

Sweet 'n Spicy Chicken Lettuce Cups, 441

Sweet 'n Squashed Biscuits, 420

Sweet Potato Apple Pack, 160

Sweet Spinach Stir-Fry, 492

Sweetness, Spice & 3-Things Nice Noodles, 516

T

Takes-the-Cake Ziti Bake, 230

Tempting Teriyaki Trifecta, 330

Ten-Alarm Southwestern Corn Chowder, 315

Thai Peanut Noodle Trio, 526

Thanksgiving in a Salad Bowl, 129

Thanksgiving Turkey Sandwich, 284

Three-Cheese Chicken Cannelloni, 236

Three-Step Pizza Burger, 495

tilapia, 152, 208

Tofu Shirataki noodle substitute, House Foods, 180, 190, 196, 200, 222, 226, 334, 336, 496, 516, 517, 518, 519, 520, 522, 523, 524, 525, 526, 527, 528

    Where in the World Is Tofu Shirataki?, 521

tomato paste, 154, 164, 168, 184, 198, 252, 300, 305, 316

tomato sauce, canned, 132, 254, 306

tomatoes, 15, 17, 19, 23, 36, 47, 98, 104, 128, 130, 136, 144, 146, 158, 168, 174, 208, 214, 226, 256, 268, 270, 277, 283, 286, 290, 296, 300, 315, 326, 328, 336, 340, 348, 352, 364, 386, 397, 408, 476

    canned crushed, 14, 29, 72, 120, 188, 190, 196, 230, 232, 234, 236, 238, 248, 252, 257, 258, 260, 264, 268, 292, 316, 324, 480, 481, 483, 494

    canned diced, 120, 154, 242, 252, 316, 324, 407

    canned stewed, 184, 408

    cherry or grape, 132, 366, 426, 509

    diced, with green chilies, 65, 310, 312

    green, 194

    sun-dried, packed in oil, 89, 138, 248, 278, 438, 466

Tomato-Infused Chicken Rollup, 438

Too-EZ Fish Taco Supreme, 152

tortillas

    corn, 25, 65, 70, 140, 152, 206, 208, 212, 214, 344, 366, 455

    high-fiber flour, 8, 46, 64, 72, 210, 264, 270, 340, 346, 348, 349, 350, 351, 452, 453, 454, 456, 457, 458, 459, 504

tortilla trios, 450

    Amazin' Onion Quesadilla, 457

    Easiest Thin-Crust Pizza Ever, 454

    EZ Cheesy Tostada, 456

    Fruity Quesadilla, 452

    Garlic Shrimp Tostada, 459

    Lean 'n Green Shrimp-chilada, 455

    Raw Apple Rollup, 458

    Speedy Beany-rito, 453

Totally Stacked Steak-Style HG Burger, 352

trios, 4. *See also* **chicken trios; ground meat trios; hot dogs, hot trios; meatless burger patty trios; noodle trios; tortilla trios; tuna trios**

Tropical AM Smoothie, 90

Tropical Wonder B-fast Bowl, 91

tuna

albacore, canned in water, 462, 463, 464, 465, 466, 467, 468, 469, 470, 471, 523

Hot Tuna Stuffed Tomatoes, 168

Lean 'n Green Fruity Tuna Bowl, 143

sodium and, 71

Tuna Noodle Casse-Bowl, 523

tuna trios, 460

Best-Ever Tuna Slaw, 471

Broc 'n Ginger Tuna Bowl, 462

Cheesy Tuna Muffin 'Wich, 465

Fancy-Pants Fast Tuna 'n Beans, 470

Hawaiian Tuna Salad, 464

Looney Tuna-Stuffed Pepper, 463

Salsa to the Tuna Salad!, 467

Salsa-fied Tuna Stacks, 469

Sun-Dried Tomato Tuna Salad, 466

Tuna Mushroom Cups, 468

turkey

BBQuick Saucy Turkey, 482

breast, 28, 129, 146, 274, 278, 326

chili, 351, 504

ground, 158, 188, 198, 308, 316, 370, 404, 474, 476, 477

Meat Prep 101, 167

Outside-In Turkey Tamale Pie, 312

Simply Sweet Meatballs, 481

Thanksgiving Turkey Sandwich, 284

Turkey Club B. Bowl, 47

Turkey Tetrazzini Bake, 180

Veggie-rific Meatloaf, 483

turkey bacon. *See* **bacon, turkey or center-cut**

turkey pepperoni, 7, 14, 257, 260, 264, 266

Pepperoni Pizza Pinwheels, 248

Pepperoni-Poppin' Veggie Calzones, 238

turkey sausage, 8, 24, 40, 58, 70, 102, 350

Twice-as-Nice *Guapo* Taco, 346

U

United We Chew! Red, White & Blue Nachos, 382

Unsweetened Vanilla Almond Breeze. *See* **Almond Breeze, Unsweetened Vanilla**

V

Vegged-Out Potato Salad, 426

Vegged-Up Ground Beef, 478

veggie burgers, 492. *See also* **meatless hamburger-style patties**

veggie chili, low-fat, 351, 504, 517

Veggie Eggs-plosion Mug, 23

Veggie-rific Meatloaf, 483

Veggie-rific Noodle-Free Lasagna, 234

Very Veggie Bisque, 314

Very Veggie-Eggy Explosion, 36

Very VERY Veggie Stew, 300

W

waffles, low-fat, 8, 78

Plate-Lickin'-Good Chicken 'n Waffles, 182

water chestnuts, can sliced, 170, 216, 224

Weight Watchers *PointsPlus*™, 5

The Whole Enchilada Chicken Soup, 396

Winner Winner Onion Chicken Dinner, 166

wonton wrappers, square, 188, 368, 370, 388, 404

Woohoo! Bayou Fish Pack, 164

World's Easiest Chicken Empanadas, 444

WOWOWOW! Kung Pao, 224

WOWOWOW! Wonton Soup, 404

"Wrap the Dog" Foil Pack, 502

Y

Yo! Chili Dog Wrap, 504

"*Yo Quiero* Taco Bowl" Noodles, 522

yogurt

fat-free fruit, 66, 86, 87, 88, 90

fat-free Greek, 7, 112, 366, 380, 467

fat-free plain, 66, 144, 200, 240, 430

fat-free vanilla, 44, 48

Z

Zazzled-Up Zuppa, 406

zucchini, 120, 138, 154, 254, 280, 314

Fluffy-Good Zucchini Nut Muffins, 96

Steamy Creamy Squash Packet, 162

Veggie-rific Noodle-Free Lasagna, 234

Very VERY Veggie Stew, 300